This book examines the outlooks of French academic historians and social scientists between about 1890 and 1920, which are in turn compared with views held on similar subjects by German academic humanists and social scientists at about the same time. The academic culture of the newly-reformed French university is conceived here as an "intellectual field," a constellation of explicit intellectual positions and of implicit assumptions perpetuated by the institutions and social relations of scholarly life.

Professor Ringer attributes the divergences between the academic cultures of France and Germany to crucial differences between the compositions of the two middle classes and the roles of the academic and intellectual elites in the two societies. Arguing that ideals of education have been more central to European middle-class ideologies than is commonly supposed, the author devotes two key chapters to the debates that took place in France (as in Germany) around the turn of the century over curricular alternatives in secondary and higher education.

Conflicting models of advanced general education were anchored in alternate models of textual interpretation. Through an analysis of these models or paradigms, the author also sheds new light upon notable divergences between the development of the historical and social sciences in France and Germany, and thus makes a major contribution to the historical sociology of knowledge.

FIELDS OF KNOWLEDGE

FIELDS OF KNOWLEDGE

French academic culture in comparative perspective,
1890–1920

FRITZ RINGER

Mellon Professor of History, University of Pittsburgh

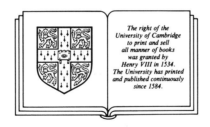

The right of the
University of Cambridge
to print and sell
all manner of books
was granted by
Henry VIII in 1534.
The University has printed
and published continuously
since 1584.

CAMBRIDGE UNIVERSITY PRESS

Cambridge   New York   Port Chester
Melbourne   Sydney

EDITIONS DE LA MAISON DES SCIENCES DE L'HOMME

Paris

Published by the Press Syndicate of the University of Cambridge
The Pitt Building, Trumpington Street, Cambridge CB2 1RP
40 West 20th Street, New York, NY 10011-4211, USA
10 Stamford Road, Oakleigh, Victoria 3166, Australia
and Editions de la Maison des Sciences de l'Homme
54 Boulevard Raspail, 75270 Paris Cedex 06

First published 1992

Printed in Great Britain at the University Press, Cambridge

British Library cataloguing in publication data
Ringer, Fritz
Fields of knowledge: French academic culture in
comparative perspective, 1890–1920.
1. French culture
I. Title   II. Maison des sciences de l'homme
044.081

Library of Congress cataloguing in publication data
Ringer, Fritz K., 1934–
Fields of knowledge: French academic culture in comparative
perspective, 1890–1920/Fritz Ringer.
p.   cm.
Includes bibliographical references and index.
1. France – Intellectual life – 19th century.   2. Germany –
Intellectual life – 19th century.   3. Learning and scholarship –
France – History – 19th century.   4. Knowledge, Sociology of.
I. Title
DC33.6.R55   1992
001–dc20   90-25944   CIP

ISBN 0 521 40118 6 hardback
ISBN 2 7351 0419 2 hardback (France only)

For Mary

Contents

ix

Tables

xi

Acknowledgments

My reading on French intellectuals, academics and ideologies began during a year in Paris in 1976–77, which was funded by a grant from the National Endowment for the Humanities; through the kindness of Clemens Heller, I was able to spend that time at the Maison des Sciences de l'Homme. On sabbatical from the strenuous life at Boston University in 1980–81, I enjoyed the hospitality of Martin Trow and Sheldon Rothblatt at the Center for the Study of Higher Education in sunny Berkeley. Arrived at the University of Pittsburgh in 1984, I was able to concentrate upon my topic and adequately to delimit it at last. Much of the writing was done in 1985–86, during a fellowship year at the Netherlands Institute of Advanced Studies in Wassenaar that was made possible through generous co-funding by the University of Pittsburgh and the National Science Foundation.

Parts of the introduction first appeared in a slightly different version in *Theory and Society*, vol. 19 (1990), pp. 269–294. Similarly, large portions of chapter 1 were originally published in an earlier form in Werner Conze and Jürgen Kocka, eds., *Bürgertum im 19. Jahrhundert*, part I: *Bildungssystem und Professionalisierung in internationalen Vergleichen* (Stuttgart: Klett-Cotta, 1985), pp. 109–146.

My thinking about the whole subject has been much affected by conversations with Sheldon Rothblatt, with Detlef Müller and his colleagues at the University of Bochum, and most especially with Pierre Bourdieu. In addition, I have learned much from readings of all or most of the text by Dana Polan of the University of Pittsburgh, by Christophe Charle of the Institut d'Histoire Moderne et Contemporaine in Paris, by Donald Fleming of Harvard University, and by my former students Paul Vogt of the State University of New York at Albany and John McCole, also of Harvard University. Hearty thanks to them all.

Last but not least, I am grateful to Mrs Amy Linn for the great care she has taken in the preparation of the manuscript.

The intellectual field, intellectual history, and the sociology of knowledge

This book is mainly about French ideas of education and of culture, of learning and of science. It is also about the social and political context of French secondary and higher education, about the role of intellectuals in modern France, and about what will be defined as French academic culture. The chronological focus is upon the period from around 1890 to about 1920, and especially upon the two decades surrounding the turn of the century. In France and Germany, this was a critical time for the academic and intellectual community.

The mention of Germany brings up the other main characteristic of the book, which is its comparative dimension. Despite the almost forbidding difficulties involved in comparing two such broad and complex entities as the academic cultures of France and Germany, the analytical device of comparison is to be applied to every topic taken up. A certain doggedness in this respect will be useful, I hope, even when it results in the raising of questions that cannot be answered in a fully satisfactory way. Indeed, this book is motivated almost entirely by the comparative issues that have concerned me ever since I completed *The Decline of the German Mandarins* in the late 1960s,[1] and a few paragraphs of explanation about this background may be helpful at the outset.

My treatment of the "German mandarins" made them a distinctive instance of a possibly more pervasive pattern. Because educational modernization came relatively early and industrialization came relatively late in Germany, I argued and still believe, an educated upper middle class of civil servants, Protestant pastors, lawyers, doctors, secondary teachers, and university professors achieved a particularly prominent position in nineteenth-century

1

German society. The "mandarins," members of the university-educated or "academic" professions, made up an educated stratum (*Bildungsschicht*) that was more a *status* elite than an economic *class* in Max Weber's terms. The social prestige of the educated, their style of life and their self-image were based more on their learning than on aristocratic birth, on the one hand, or on wealth and economic power, on the other. Their close ties to the monarchical civil service gave them a degree of political influence, at least during a transitional period in German history, and they claimed a broader cultural leadership as intellectual notables as well. Institutionally, it was the revitalization of the German universities during the late eighteenth and early nineteenth centuries that secured their position, together with the early emergence of a certified corps of university-educated secondary teachers, and of a highly developed scale of educational qualifications or entitlements (*Berechtigungen*). The preeminent place of the German university professors and the outstanding achievements of German university scholarship during the nineteenth century were built on these social foundations. The German academics were "mandarin intellectuals," partly because they were the most prominent representatives of the "mandarin" elite as a whole. But they also controlled the standards of access to that elite, and they were its natural spokesmen. They formulated and expressed its political and cultural aspirations, its "ideology."

The central element in "mandarin ideology," as I tried to show, was the immensely influential notion of "cultivation" (*Bildung*), the vision of learning as personal self-fulfillment through interpretive interaction with venerated texts. The ideal of cultivation in turn shaped the German meaning of "culture," along with the associated contrast between inward culture and external "civilization." The essentially interpretive model of *Bildung* inspired the dominant hermeneutic tradition in German philological and historical scholarship, as well as the German conception of the *Geisteswissenschaften*, the disciplines devoted to the objectifications of mind. The commitment to *Bildung* also fostered a profound distrust of instrumental or "utilitarian" forms of knowledge, which in turn colored the German tradition of academic freedom. The objective of *Bildung* implied personal and evaluative insight (*Weltanschauung*), rather than manipulative intervention in nature or in social processes. At a more immediately political level, the mandarin ideals of the "legal" and "cultural" state (*Rechtsstaat, Kulturstaat*) eventually gave rise to a revulsion against modern "interest" politics.

From the late nineteenth century on, the social position and cultural leadership of the German mandarin intellectuals came under pressure from changes within the educational system as well as in the larger environment. Industrialization, when it came, proceeded swiftly. It was accompanied by an unusually high degree of industrial concentration on the one hand, and by the rapid advance of working-class organization on the other. The growing power of money and of "the masses" confronted each other in an undisguised conflict of material interests. The high capitalist class society made traditional status conventions appear increasingly irrelevant, even as technical "civilization" threatened to overwhelm the inherited norms of humanist culture. In secondary and higher education, substantial enrollment increases and the rise of "realistic" or technical studies raised the spectre of "massification" and of "utilitarianism," while the advance of disciplinary specialization threatened to sever the tie between *Wissenschaft* and *Weltanschauung* in the idealist philosophy of *Bildung*. In response to these converging pressures, a creative and partly critical minority of academic "modernists" attempted to "translate" vital elements of the mandarin heritage in ways that might insure their continued relevance. But the large majority of "orthodox" mandarin intellectuals gravitated toward a more exclusively defensive position that ultimately took on escapist and purely irrational dimensions, under the impact of defeat, revolution, and inflation, during the Weimar period.

As even this simplified sketch makes clear, my argument about the German "mandarins" raises a whole series of comparative questions. From the outset, I suspected that elsewhere in Europe too, education was a more important element in middle-class status and middle-class outlooks than is commonly realized. Incongruities between class ranks and status attributions were certainly felt in England and France as well as in Germany; they provided some of the intimate drama of middle-class life in all of nineteenth-century Europe. We are too much accustomed, I felt and still feel, to identify "middle-class ideology" with an amalgam of economic individualism and utilitarianism that may indeed have characterized the entrepreneurial "bourgeoisie" of early nineteenth-century England. But at a minimum, the mandarin ideology of cultivation was an alternate form of middle-class individualism, quite as coherent as the entrepreneurial creed, and surely present, at least in variant forms, in modern France and England as well. In any case, I did not and do not see why a particular aspect of English social and intellectual history should serve as a norm for modern middle-class life in general and everywhere. My hunch was, rather, that historical circumstances favored a particularly pronounced development in Germany that had fainter analogues in other societies, just as the English entrepreneurial ideology of the early nineteenth century had fainter analogues on the continent, including in Germany.[2]

The difficulty was that I had no way of substantiating this hunch in the late 1960s, since I knew nothing about the relevant aspects of modern French and English history. Thus I could not say just what elements of the German pattern might be universal, or at least general for modern Europe, and what elements were specific to Germany, whether in degree or in kind. This was troubling, not only because I believed that *something* in the relationships I had been studying was probably central for the modern European experience generally, but also because my causal claims about the German academic elite could be adequately sustained only through comparison. To argue that aspects of the German intellectual tradition were largely (not wholly) shaped by aspects of German social history was to imply, after all, that divergent characteristics of modern French intellectual life, for example, could be traced to corresponding divergences between aspects of French and German social history. And just what aspects were relevant in this way, whether in France or in Germany? Only careful attention to cross-national similarities and differences could ever resolve these decisive questions even in principle, and thus I was committed to the classical starting point of the comparative method. My *Education and Society in Modern Europe* was a first reaction.[3] This book attempts a broader response, though it deals primarily with France and Germany, and only incidentally – and very tentatively – with England.

STUDYING INTELLECTUAL FIELDS

Before actually turning to my sources, however, I must address some methodological issues raised by the analysis I propose. My starting point is the concept of the intellectual field as defined by the French sociologist Pierre Bourdieu.[4] The intellectual field at a given time and place is made up of agents taking up various intellectual positions. Yet the field is not an aggregate of isolated elements; it is a configuration or a network of relationships. The elements in the field are not only related to each other in determinate ways; each also has a specific "weight" or authority, so that the field is a distribution of power as well. The agents in the field compete for the right to define what shall count as intellectually established and culturally legitimate. The field's constituents may be individuals; or they may be small groups, "schools," or even academic disciplines. Indeed, one can imagine field-like relationships within subfields that in turn occupy particular regions within the broader intellectual field. But the main point of Bourdieu's definitions lies in the emphasis given to the *positional* or *relational* attributes of ideas. The views expressed in a given setting are so thoroughly interdefined that they can be adequately characterized only in their complementary or oppositional relationships to each other. Indeed, opposed positions within an intellectual field tend to condition each other; their interaction is dialectical in the strictest sense of that term. The prevailing orthodoxies of a given context help to shape the heterodox reversals they call into being, and of course they determine the structure of the field as a whole. At the same time, heterodox ideas may well acquire a certain dominance in their own right.

The intellectual field is influenced by the concerns and conflicts of the larger society; but its logic is its own. Thus any influence upon the field from without is refracted by the structure of the field itself. The relationship which an intellectual has to a particular social class, for example, is mediated by the position he holds within the field. This is a way of conceiving the relative autonomy of the intellectual field, and it also applies to such subfields as academic disciplines and literary schools. Their autonomy is a matter of degree, and so, conversely, is their openness to outside influence. The emergence and maturation of an academic discipline is a process of autonomization, although even a mature discipline may traverse periods of epistemological *or social* crisis in which its receptivity to broader social and cultural influences may be increased. Thus the debate between "internalists" and "externalists" among historians of science and literary critics cannot be resolved on abstract principles or for all times. The relative legitimacy of the two approaches varies *empirically* with the subject of study. Intellectual fields themselves can change, of course; their structures are only relatively stable, whether in relation to external agencies or to individual positions within them.

The positional properties of theories in the intellectual field need not be traced to their authors' subjective intentions in stating them. On the contrary, the constellation of forces in the intellectual environment confronts individual theorists as objectively given. Even the public meaning of their own previous works tends to elude their control. When we ask about an author's "intention," moreover, we are seeking evidence, not about his or her state of mind while writing a particular work, but about certain objective characteristics of that work, and especially about its relationship to a given complex of other texts. We are asking questions, in short, about the positional characteristics of a text in its field.

An example brought forward by Quentin Skinner may help to make this clear. In *The Prince*, Machiavelli offered the advice that "princes must learn when not to be virtuous," and his interpreters have asked themselves what he meant.

> Here it cannot I think be doubted [Skinner writes] that the crucial question to ask, in order to answer this question, is what Machiavelli may have been doing in making this claim. One widely accepted answer . . . has been that Machiavelli was "consciously refuting his predecessors" within the highly conventionalized genre of advice-books to princes. Again it seems unquestionable that to ask and answer this question about the illocutionary force of Machiavelli's utterance is equivalent to asking about Machiavelli's intentions in writing this section of *The Prince*.[5]

Here is a striking example of the need to understand a great text positionally, by understanding its relationship to an intellectual field. Yet I believe it is not in fact Machiavelli's subjective intention that interests us in this connection. We do not expect or need additional evidence from his letters or private papers. Instead, we ask whether anything *in his text* can be interpreted as a response to the conventionalized genre of advice books to princes. To be sure, there are relationships both within texts and among texts that can be characterized as intentional. We may also find it convenient on occasion to describe the intention of *The Prince* as Machiavelli's intention. But what we are looking for in the case at hand, strictly speaking, is not Machiavelli's subjective project, but something about the relationship between *The Prince* and an existing *field of other texts*.

Historical and cross-cultural comparisons illustrate the degree to which the meanings of propositions or doctrines are defined by their place in an intellectual field. The comparative history of "positivism," which will concern us in later chapters, is a case in point. Among German academic humanists and social scientists between about 1890 and 1930, avowed positivists were rare indeed, though unconsciously positivist thought models probably affected certain types of empirical research, along with certain popular philosophies of science. At the same time, "positivism" was constantly discussed and decried. It was held to be a major threat to sound scholarship and philosophy in an age of excessive specialization, an obstacle in the path of a sorely needed revival of Idealism, and a potentially disastrous dissolver of wholistic concepts and of socially beneficial commitments.[6] In France around 1900, by contrast, many humanists and social scientists either accepted positivist doctrines; or they adhered to more broadly and vaguely positivist outlooks. Certainly "positivism" as seen by German academics had little to do with the quasi-official positivism of an Emile Durkheim in France – or with the positivism that is at issue in contemporary American debates about methods in the social sciences. We are tempted to regard the apparent affinities between certain doctrines in our own environment as timelessly psychological or even epistemological; but they only reflect the historically contingent "logic" of an intellectual field.

All sectors of an intellectual field or subfield are profoundly affected by the orthodoxy that is dominant within it. Even the most heterodox positions are partly shaped by their more or less deliberate orientation toward the orthodoxy they contest. More important, the relation of symbolic affinity and mutual reinforcement between an intellectual orthodoxy and the socio-political system in which it flourishes need not be either consciously intended or explicitly political in character. In my study of German academics between 1890 and 1930, as I reported earlier, I distinguished between an "orthodox" majority and a "modernist" minority.[7] Very broadly speaking, the orthodox were politically conservative or even reactionary, while the modernists were more progressive or "liberal." Yet the most important difference between the two groups was not political at all; it had to do, rather, with their divergent relationships to their tradition. The modernists shared many of the assumptions of their orthodox colleagues. Yet they did not merely repeat these common orientations; they described and analyzed them from a certain critical distance. They made it their overall project to free the German intellectual heritage from outdated and indefensible accretions, while "translating" its most vital elements for a new and broader audience. They accordingly took a selective and active stance toward a belief system that their orthodox colleagues merely perpetuated in a passive way. The real difference between the orthodox and the modernists, in other words, lay not on a political scale from right to left, but on a continuum from the uncritical reproduction to the self-conscious mastery of an intellectual tradition.

Indeed, I am convinced that original and coherent thought is a kind of *clarification*, an *emergence* toward clarity, a gaining of analytical distance from the tacit assumptions of a cultural world. I frankly find this model of clarification less mystifying, theoretically more useful and even humanly more compelling than the unreconstructed idealist's notion of the new idea as an uncaused cause. I believe that rapid social change tends to encourage the work of clarification, though this work may be favored by purely theoretical incongruities as well. In any case, as previously unstated cultural assumptions are made explicit, preconditions and occasions are created for a partial transcendence of these assumptions in intellectual innovation.

In order to account for the phenomenon of clarification or emergence, however, the intellectual historian must assume the existence of something like a cultural preconscious. There are precedents for such an assumption in the writings of Karl Mannheim, particularly in his emphasis on the common "pre-theoretical" grounding that accounts for the unity we detect in the world view of an age.[8] Even more helpful and explicit are Erwin Panofsky's reflections upon the structural homologies between gothic architecture and scholasticism.[9] Drawing upon Panofsky's work, Bourdieu has elaborated the thesis that the elements in an intellectual field also participate in a broader *cultural field* and in a *cultural unconscious*.[10] The "culture" Bourdieu here refers to includes not only stated theoretical positions (elements in the *intellectual* field) but also implicit assumptions that are part of a way of life. These assumptions function at a preconscious level; they are typically transmitted by institutions, practices, and social relations. Indeed, I somewhat prefer the term *preconscious* to the more emphatically psychonanalytical *unconscious*.

Bourdieu points up the common grounding of orthodox and heterodox positions in the realm of preconscious and implicit *doxa*. In a doxic relationship to the social world, he suggests, that world seems as inevitable as nature; questions about its legitimacy can stem only from criticism and conflict, which typically arise under conditions of objective crisis. In the struggles that take place, the doxa are "the propositions that the antagonists take for granted."

The open conflicts between tendencies and doctrines tend to mask from the participants themselves the underlying complicity which they presuppose and which strikes the observer from outside the system, that consensus within the dissensus which constitutes the objective unity of the intellectual field of a given period.[11]

At the same time, Bourdieu sees a special relationship between doxa and orthodoxy. Once "the self-evidence of doxa" has been undermined, he argues, those interested in the preservation of the socio-cultural status quo must protect orthodoxy as a "necessarily imperfect substitute."[12]

Following Panofsky, Bourdieu defines the *habitus* as the cultural preconscious in its active form. Panofsky wrote of the spreading of a "mental habit" and of a "habit-forming force." Bourdieu accepts the explicitly causal form of this model and spells out its implications. The *habitus* is a "structuring sturcture." It is *shaped* and transmitted by the social and institutional environment, as well as by the practices and traditions of a culture; it *acts* in its turn to give rise to recurrent patterns of thought. Though located at a preconscious or pre-theoretical level, it can generate conscious beliefs. More important, it can function as a cognitive disposition, a tendency to constitute the objects of knowledge in a certain way. As such it engenders particular schemes that appear and reappear in various realms of thought, including the academic disciplines of modern times. The *habitus* is one of those entities that are never observed directly. Yet we can usually circumscribe it reasonably well; for it is defined by the social relations and practices that sustain it, and it typically gives rise to such primary representations as theories of education, for example.[13]

It seems clear that in modern class societies, the *habitus* will be at least partly specific to socio-cultural milieus, and that it can be transmitted by a whole range of institutions, beginning with the family. Nevertheless, both Panofsky and Bourdieu particularly emphasize the role of "the school," meaning the several forms of institutionalized education that have arisen in Europe since the

Middle Ages. As a "habit-forming force," the educational system inculcates socially differentiated relationships to the dominant culture, including what Bourdieu calls the "cultivated *habitus*" of the highly educated. Just as "the school" actively generates the *habitus*, so the *habitus* in turn is genuinely *a cause* of cognitive dispositions and beliefs. That theories and practices of education can shape "schemes of thought" must of course be demonstrated empirically and in detail.

Now if any of what has been said so far is correct, then we must find a way to study the intellectual field. We must learn to understand a cluster of texts as a whole, or as a set of relationships, rather than as a sum of individual statements. One way to do this is to "sample" the literature produced in a certain environment over a specified period of time. In my study of German academics, for example, I worked primarily with a list of faculty at selected universities during my period. While this still did not enable me to write with authority about the work of any single individual, it gave me a somewhat anonymous sense of the major currents of thought and feeling in a certain intellectual environment. I did not find it difficult to identify the issues of greatest concern to German academics, along with major developments in key disciplines. Above all, my method directed my attention to certain structural properties of my sources: to the forms as well as the contents of arguments, to recurrent patterns or figures of thought, and to underlying assumptions that were widely shared but not often explicitly discussed. Instead of "sampling" the faculty of certain universities, I could have focused upon selected types of publications in a given subject area; or I could have canvassed the more frequent contributors to one or more scholarly or intellectual journals. Paul Vogt has shown how that can be done, and he has also explained the point of such procedures.[14] Disciplinary handbooks, anthologies and textbooks may be taken to represent specific portions of an intellectual field. Scholarly reviews will tend to reproduce the assumptions of a scholarly community. In what follows, I have focused upon academics and intellectuals who testified before a parliamentary commission. The sample this has given me is rather small and of course debatable. It has *not* enabled me to survey developments in major disciplines, as in my earlier book. In exchange, it has permitted fairly close readings of a few revealing texts. Too often in intellectual history, individuals or small groups are isolated for study on the grounds that they were either representative or influential; but only the most impressionistic evidence is offered in support of these claims. This flaw, at any rate, I have avoided.

Yet it is not only the case for a rigorous empiricism that persuades me in favor of "sampling" and related methods. I am also increasingly convinced that intellectual fields must be studied *as fields*. They are entities in their own right, and they must not be reduced to aggregates of individuals. To study them is at least initially to look away from the overt intentions of individual texts, so as to concentrate on shared intellectual habits and collective meanings. One wants to consider the sources from a deliberately impersonal perspective. In any case, one must avoid a false sense of identification or familiarity, which would prevent a full and self-conscious interpretation and analysis. Part of the aim, after all, is to penetrate below the surface of explicit thought, to the realm of the cultural preconscious, of tacit beliefs and cognitive dispositions.

To take the approach I have suggested is to break with certain practices typical of the "history of ideas." The most important of these is the tendency to treat coherent ideas as uncaused causes, and to invest them with the irresistible force of logic. As the implications of this conception are followed out, ideas are pictured as so many individual agents that "influence" subsequent thought and action in identifiable ways. Where the tracing of such discrete "influences" becomes difficult, or where broader and less articulate beliefs have to be accounted for, one imagines ideas being distorted and diluted as they "trickle down" from a surface of clearly stated propositions to a subsoil of incoherent but common opinion.

The weakness of this scheme lies partly in its extreme idealism or intellectualism. Ideas are never totally separable from their grounding in institutions, practices, and social relations. Their influence, moreover, is always selected or mediated by the intellectual field involved. One cannot chart the influence of Darwin or of Nietzsche, for example, without knowing and explaining a great deal about those who subsequently used or misused their works. But an even more serious weakness in the traditional view is a species of methodological individualism. This is the insistence that a belief system must be a sum of discrete and explicit propositions, and that each of these propositions can be traced through its various antecedents to a single aboriginal source. In reality, as we have said, belief systems are constellations of interrelated and partly implicit ideas – ideas which change with the field that surrounds them.

One of the practical lessons I would draw from this conviction is that we should radically alter our approach to intellectual biography. To study the thought of a given society and time, we tend to assume, one must begin by investigating an individual thinker or a small group. Only after a sufficient number of such specialized studies have been completed, we are tempted to believe, can an attempt be made to evolve generalizations about the period as a whole. We assume, in short, that the individual can be approached directly, but the period only through more specialized and usually biographical studies.[15] I believe, on the contrary, that biographies are more difficult to write than surveys of intellectual fields, and that they are likely to fail, unless they can draw upon prior investigations of their fields. This holds most clearly for biographies of outstanding thinkers, whose creativity makes them anything but "representative" of their world. To understand them at all, one has to grasp their peculiar relationship to that world. For on the one hand, they typically share in at least some of the assumptions and forms of thought that characterize their fields. On the other hand, they also make explicit what in most of their contemporaries remains implicit. They help to clarify the underlying assumptions of their field, even as they begin to transcend them in intellectual innovation.[16]

In fact, this changes their relationship to those of us who seek to understand their time. Whereas the thought of strictly representative authors is merely an object of study for us, the creative thinkers join us as senior colleagues and as guides to their world. Our own efforts, if successful, will incorporate, and perhaps somewhat extend, the clarification they have begun. We read their texts not only for their intrinsic interest, but also for their capacity to articulate what both we and their contemporaries knew dimly at best. There is no contradiction in the thesis that the surveying of intellectual fields and the study of the great clarifying texts must proceed interactively if intellectual history is to prosper.

ACADEMIC CULTURES, SOCIAL RELATIONS, AND THE INTELLECTUALS

The implicit meanings perpetuated by practices, institutions, and social relations assert an influence upon the explicit elements in the intellectual field. The historical sociology of knowledge attempts to trace out the relationships involved. Very often, sociologists of knowledge have concentrated upon the effects of social stratification, which are indeed important. Yet we have already touched upon another relevant realm, one in which practices and institutions decisively affect beliefs. This is the realm of what Panofsky calls "the school." The institutions of secondary and higher education do indeed transmit implicit as well as explicit aspects of the cultural heritage; they inculcate life styles and modes of conduct, along with forms of perception and cognition. Much of what they teach cannot be reduced to stated propositions. The contents and organization of the secondary curriculum, the articulation of the university faculties and disciplines, and the system of examinations and credentials: all these convey tacit knowledge that can help to shape a *habitus*. The same is obviously true of such important practices as the behaviors of teachers during the process of schooling. The way in which curricular materials are presented in secondary education, for example, may well establish cognitive dispositions that endure beyond the context of the classroom itself.

One way to think about these matters is to conceive of an *academic culture* as a particularly significant segment of the wider socio-cultural system. Defined in a narrower sense, an academic culture is an intellectual field or subfield, a network of interrelated and explicit beliefs about the academic practices of teaching, learning, and research, and about the social significance of these practices. Defined in a wider sense, an academic culture encompasses practices, institutions, and social relations, along with beliefs. I have been arguing, in effect, that an academic culture in the narrow sense of explicit beliefs cannot be fully understood apart from its more comprehensive sense. In the chapters that follow, I shall be concerned mainly with the explicit beliefs of French and German academics. Yet I propose to give some attention to institutions and social relations as well. Educational *practices* are harder to document; but one can sometimes infer a little about them from the controversies that surround them, particularly in periods of crisis. In any case, in so far as possible, I mean to study academic cultures in the comprehensive sense of beliefs, practices, institutions, and social relations.

The main point I have to add about social relations is that they are hierarchic and extremely complex. They must not be reduced to a unilinear scale of purely economic assets. Here again, Bourdieu has developed some helpful concepts. He distinguishes between economic, social, and cultural capital. Social capital consists of familial "connections" and the like. Cultural capital in one of its forms is cultural "background," a relationship to the dominant culture that is passed along by the family. Educational systems tend to "reproduce" or recreate the inherited distribution of cultural capital, rather than radically to alter it. In any case, educational credentials, or the amounts and types of schooling obtained, emerge as the institutionally encoded forms of cultural capital.[17] It is very important that the three species of capital may not be distributed in fully parallel ways within a society. While those poorest in economic capital are generally poor in social and cultural capital as well, there are groups who are *relatively* better endowed with cultural than with economic capital, and vice versa. Especially at the intermediate altitudes in the social hierarchy, the distribution of educational advantages may not be fully consistent with the distribution of wealth and economic power. The resulting incongruities may engender *comparative* advantages and disadvantages that can take on some of the characteristics and have some of the effects of absolute advantages and disadvantages. Bourdieu rightly insists that the social space too has to be understood as a system of relations, rather than as a scale of absolute magnitudes. Since he also recognizes the importance of social "trajectories," which arise from *changes* in one or more elements of a social position, his analytical concepts are far more discriminating than those we usually encounter in discussions of social structure and social mobility.

Another way to avoid a simplistic view of social stratification is to adopt Max Weber's distinction between class and status. A "class" position, for Weber, is an objective place in the system of production or in "the market"; it entails the ability to command goods and services, whether for consumption or for further production. "Status," by contrast, is the social prestige or honor associated with certain styles of life. It is an attributed quality, and yet the status order is objective in the sense that it cannot be altered by the individual. Weber saw class and status ranks as tending to converge, at least during periods of economic stability. On the other hand, he also recognized the possibility of incongruity between the hierarchies of class and status. Status conventions have a kind of inertia; they evolve only slowly. During periods of rapid economic change, Weber thought, the scales of class and of status may therefore come to diverge enough to make the "naked" class situation plainly visible.[18]

Weber's concept of status, in other words, is essentially historical. The status order is always in some sense an inheritance from the past. The most prestigious behavioral norms and life styles are typically associated with the ruling elites of former times. In late nineteenth-century Europe, these behavioral norms and life styles were transmitted primarily by the elite institutions of secondary and higher education. The distribution of status was therefore largely identical with the distribution of advanced schooling, or of cultural capital in Bourdieu's scheme. Indeed, there is only one reason to prefer Weber's concept of "status" to Bourdieu's "cultural capital," and that is the *historical* significance of "status." To understand the status system is to recognize the presence of the past: the role of historical residues that help to define and to legitimate the existing social hierarchy. Since these historical residues also serve to complicate that hierarchy, moreover, giving them adequate consideration is another way to avoid an overly simple analysis of social stratification.

The social group that most interests the historian of knowledge, of course, is the group or category of the intellectuals. If intellectual history is going to touch upon social environments at all, then surely it must try to chart the social role of the intellectuals. What needs to be said about this role at the outset is that it has differed greatly over time and from society to society. There is no single definition of the intellectual's condition that applies universally. Efforts to define "the intellectual" in the abstract have usually been problematic. Here, for example, is a formulation by Edward Shils.

In every society . . . there are some persons with an unusual sensitivity to the sacred, an uncommon reflectiveness about the nature of the universe and the rules which govern their society . . . a minority of persons who, more than the ordinary run of their fellow men, are inquiring and desirous of being in frequent communion with symbols which are more general than the immediate concrete situations of everyday life . . . This interior need to penetrate beyond the screen of immediate concrete experience marks the existence of the intellectual in every society . . . It is practically given by the nature of the intellectual's orientation that there should be some tension between the intellectuals and the value orientations embodied in the actual institutions of every society.[19]

What Shils offers here is not so much a definition as an idealization. The "true" intellectual is given qualities that can scarcely be ascribed to "the ordinary run" of professors and writers, for example. But even apart from that issue, one should not prejudge such empirical questions as the degree of tension between the intellectuals and the dominant groups in their society. Thus J. P. Nettl has argued in effect that only thorough-going dissent qualifies its authors as "intellectuals."[20] Like Shils, Nettl would presumably have to exclude orthodox thinkers from the socio-historical study of "the intellectuals"; but this would limit the field of investigation in a debilitating way. Something similar is true also of Florian Znaniecki's approach, which assumes a steady evolution of the intellectual from the practical "technologist" to the "sage," and then onward to the objective scholar and cultural philosopher.[21] It almost provokes the objection that intellectuals in fact have less and less in common with "sages," and more and more with practical "technologists."

In short, one has to insist upon the historical and changeable character of intellectual roles. As Shils himself acknowledges in another of his essays, "the intellectual classes differ from society to society in composition and structure . . . [as do] their beliefs about intellectual roles."[22] Thus the European intellectuals since the Middle Ages have in various degrees and proportions been clergymen, academics, publicists, and "free-lance" writers or artists. The material support for intellectual work has changed dramatically from the seventeenth to the twentieth centuries, and so have the audiences addressed. As Shils points out, moreover, there have been major transformations not only in the "composition and structure" of "the intellectual classes" but also in their "beliefs about intellectual roles." The importance of these beliefs can scarcely be exaggerated. For to conceive of the intellectual self at all is to opt for a certain vision of knowledge and of the mediating structures that intervene between intellectual work and its ultimate effect or import. Are intellectuals prophets and sages; or are they scientists, specialized researchers, or technical innovators? Are they critics of power or expert advisors to politicians, direct or indirect molders of public opinion? How do they imagine the "marketplace" of ideas, intellectual conflict, tradition, or "public opinion"? Positions on these questions, and on a host of related ones, are rarely held in full consciousness; they are implicit orientations that may be brought into discussion during periods of social or cognitive crisis. Yet, whether philosophically clarified or not, they form a permanent substratum of thought, a part of the cultural preconscious, a vital source of the cognitive dispositions at work in the intellectual field.

Shils writes of *beliefs* about social roles. He thus points up the remarkably two-sided character of social roles, the fact that they are partly objective and partly conceptual in character. The actually established institutions and practices of intellectual life will tend to suggest a certain range of role choices, while almost forbidding others. The objective place of the intellectuals in the social hierarchy will make some beliefs about intellectual roles more probable than others, and this is true also of relationships *within* the intellectual community, among such subgroups as academics and free-lance writers. Detectable *changes* in outward circumstances are particularly likely to affect role choices, since these choices often encompass projections for the future. On the other hand, no set of circumstances absolutely dictates a particular interpretation of the possibilities contained in it. Identical institutions and practices may be *perceived* in remarkably different ways, and it is perceptions, not realities as such, that enter into the constitution of roles. In a particular environment, perceptions may be decisively conditioned by inherited assumptions, including incompletely conscious ones.

Moreover, the role choice of a social group is a kind of self-definition, and a social self-definition in turn implies particular relationships to other groups. This is true, for example, of Shils' idealization of the intellectuals as a minority more desirous than "the ordinary run of their fellow men" of being "in frequent communion" with the most general symbols. But it is true also for more matter-of-fact self-definitions. A "technician" is bound to have a sense of his relationship to the "pure scientist" on the one hand, and to the technologically innovative entrepreneur on the other. Not surprisingly, social role definitions, including self-definitions, are often strenuously contested. Thus non-intellectuals are unlikely to accept Shils' summary characterization of them as "the ordinary run of . . . men." They are likely to see themselves in more complex and more flattering terms, and they will presumably seek public acceptance for their own classificatory schemes. In sum, social roles are partly shaped by objective conditions, but they are also conceptual schemes; they are typically inherited, partly preconscious and often contested.[23] It follows that the social historian must guard against suppressing the conceptual element in all social roles, including those listed in occupational censuses. The intellectual historian and the historical sociologist of knowledge, conversely, must not neglect the impact of objective social relations upon the role choices of intellectuals – and of other social groups.

REDUCTIONISM, RELATIVISM, AND THE SOCIOLOGY OF KNOWLEDGE

Obviously, I am aiming at an historical sociology of knowledge. But critics of that genre tend to suspect its practitioners of "reductionism," and this charge seems to break down into three more specific objections. First, critics doubt that sociologists of knowledge can give adequate attention to the *truth value* of the views they investigate. They may neglect the substantive merit of ideas in favor of certain kinds of explanations. Secondly, these explanations will tend to portray ideas as *mere effects* of social situations and preferences. Thirdly and finally, according to critics, sociologists of knowledge will tend to deemphasize the *originality of creative individuals*, confounding their thoughts with the common opinions of major social groups. I will try at least briefly to answer each of these critical questions in turn.

Before sociologists of knowledge can attempt any kind of explanation at all, of course, they must make sense of the historical record; they must achieve an interpretive understanding of the texts that are their subject matter. Such expert commentators on interpretation as Hans-Georg Gadamer and Paul Ricoeur nowadays stress that the texts and actions we interpret are objectively given, and that interpretation is a complex empirical and rational procedure, rather than a mysterious intuitive leap.[24] In trying to interpret a text, we proceed roughly as if we had to translate it from a foreign language into our own. Starting with a rudimentary knowledge of the relevant vocabulary, we actively posit *possible* translations, which we test by asking whether they yield results in our language that are both internally consistent, and coherent in their reference to realities outside the text. The method can be described as an *interaction* with the foreign text, since possible renditions of individual sentences are tested by being placed in a paragraph, which in turn is tested for its sense within a chapter, and so forth; there is a movement back and forth from text to translation that has the aspect of trial and error. The underlying aim is to maximize the rational coherence of subsections within the text in relation to each other and to the text as a whole.

In any case, the whole enterprise of interpretation can only proceed on the assumption of a partly shared *rationality* and a partly shared empirical world.[25] Our objective is to render what is to be interpreted in a version of our own language that is as free of obscurities as we can make it. Our strategy is to begin by assuming that the passage we interpret is internally consistent and free of error, or that the author reasons just as we would reason in a similar situation. We need this heuristic assumption of rationality to arrive at a "translation" at all. It is only where this assumption proves unworkable that we reach for supplementary hypotheses. This happens when we are unable to "match" a sequence of sentences in the text with a coherent sequence of clear sentences in our own language, or when an argument that seems to follow from its premises in one "language" does not similarly follow in the other. Perhaps some portion of the text is false; or it is based upon one of the many beliefs that are neither true nor false. Here for the first time we entertain the hypothesis that certain passages in the text need to be *explained,* and not merely interpreted. Possibly there are purely conventional differences between the two "languages," which must be taken into account. More probably, the explanation that is needed will refer to crucial differences not only in words, concepts, and beliefs, but also in practices, institutions, and social relations. Even in these circumstances, we hold fast to a background assumption of overall rationality. But in a selective way and as necessary, we now move beyond interpretation to certain kinds of environmental explanation. This is the method specific to the sociology of knowledge, and it must begin by confronting the *truth value* of the texts it addresses.

Another way to understand what I am driving at is to consider Imre Lakatos' account of "rational reconstruction" in the history of science.[26] Lakatos tries to specify the conditions under which a previously accepted scientific "research program" is superseded by a preferred successor. While the details are not pertinent here, his overall scheme portrays a history of science in which new theories are ultimately accepted because they are inherently sounder than what they replace. In Lakatos' rationally reconstructed history, in other words, the movement of history is dictated by the criteria of scientific rationality; for the substantive merit of a theory is a necessary and sufficient condition of its being preferred to less meritorious rivals. As Thomas Kuhn points out, however, the empirical historian of knowledge must deal with historically contingent relationships, not with rationally necessary ones. Of course the substantive merit of a theory *can be* a cause of its finding acceptance; but there are other possibilities as well. Indeed, the discussion between Lakatos and Kuhn is fascinating precisely because the *divergence* between a Kuhnian and a Lakatosian account of intellectual history defines a realm of contingency that is the domain of the sociology of knowledge and, more generally, of empirical history. And my main point about this realm is just that it can be defined only *as a deviation, in relation to* an independently charted world of rationally reconstructed intellectual history. Thus the more carefully and self-consciously sociologists of knowledge do their work, the more concerned they must be with the truth value of the beliefs they find in their texts.

As a matter of fact, much of what has been said can be restated in causal language. The philosopher Donald Davidson has argued that an agent's *reason* for performing a certain action may be the *cause* of that action. It is not too great an extension of that model to stipulate that someone's *reason* for holding a certain belief may be the *cause* of his holding it.[27] Thus good reasons are the usual causes of valid beliefs, beliefs that are grounded in sound observation and reflection. Such beliefs are almost always held consciously and rationally, and they are accessible to strictly rational interpretation. On the other hand, beliefs that are false, or that are neither true nor false, must be traced to causes other than good reasons. These rules hold in principle, rather than in practice; for the causes of belief are typically aggregates of good reasons, bad reasons, and causes other than reasons. Moreover, a belief may be overdetermined; it may be held for good reasons *and* from other causes as well.

Even so, there are three broad types of account in the study of texts, and the first of these is the *rational account*, or rational interpretation, of valid beliefs. Much of intellectual history consists of this type of reconstruction. It involves a reasoned movement from premises to conclusions; most of the propositions that figure in it follow from their predecessors in the sequence of argument, and there is no reference to causes other than good reasons. In the remaining types of account, by contrast, beliefs are traced to causes other than good reasons. Thus in the *traditional* account or explanation, the beliefs under analysis are held because they are inherited from the past. Even if they are valid beliefs, they are not independently verified or rethought. Rather, they are held *because* they were passed down, whether by known forebears or by impersonal cultural traditions. Strictly traditional beliefs are held irrationally, in a less than fully explicit way. Intellectual historians offer *causal explanations* for them, in that they identify the historical antecedents that gave rise to them and that sustain them. On the other hand, they do not leave the realm of beliefs to discuss institutions, practices, or social relations. The traditions or conventions involved are simply given; they cannot be further explained. In an *ideological* account or explanation, finally, beliefs are explained in terms of the institutions and social relations that surround them. Indeed an ideology may be *defined* as a belief system that can be explained at least partly in this way. The beliefs addressed in ideological accounts are almost never fully explicit. Rather, they are sustained at a tacit level by the nonverbal portions of a culture. To claim that the substantive contents of an academic discipline are partly shaped by the institutions in which it is housed, or that the political arguments of a certain group are partly conditioned by the group's social situation, is to advance an ideological account or explanation.

Needless to say, no belief system is ever wholly ideological. Indeed, the three accounts that have been discussed can rarely be offered in isolation from each other. Belief systems are typically complex aggregates of rational, traditional, and ideological elements. Their causes are mixtures of good reasons with inherited conventions, and with the orientations perpetuated by institutions, practices, and social relations. All these components of a culture tend to interact and to support each other. Each of the three accounts can therefore be applied to almost any belief system with at least partial success. There is no way of knowing in advance which of the three will prove most coherent in a particular case. Historians who use the techniques of the sociology of knowledge may emphasize ideological explanations, but never, if they know their business, to the total exclusion of rational and traditional accounts. Thus they never treat ideas as *mere effects* of social situations, as the critics of "reductionism" tend to claim.

Where sociologists of knowledge causally link ideas to institutions and social relations, moreover, their explanations are typically probabilistic, rather than invariant, in character. The generalizations upon which they are based do not hold invariably, but usually or for the most part, and other things being equal. Many of the generalizations advanced by historians are statistical or probabilistic in this way. They tend to apply to aggregates, rather than to individuals. A causal generalization that traces changes in the voting behavior of a group to changes in family income, for example, would hold not absolutely or for any particular individual, but with a degree of probability (other things being equal) and for the group as a whole.[28] Similarly, in the terms suggested earlier, the ideological explanations advanced by sociologists of knowledge apply less to individuals than to the intellectual field, less to explicit positions than to implicit assumptions, and less to clarified than to doxic beliefs. Thus competent sociologists of knowledge are not likely to confound the thought of the great clarifying thinkers with the opinions current in their intellectual fields; they are unlikely to deemphasize the *originality of creative individuals*.

Like other probabilistic causal relationships involving human beings, the influence of the social environment upon beliefs can be linked to a variety of particular interpretations. One can imagine a typical individual or social group being systematically misled by certain false appearances, and thus succumbing to a species of "false consciousness." Or one can speculate that, usually and other things being equal, people tend to believe what suits their interests. The notion of "interested thought" in turn can be further articulated in several ways. One can picture individuals consciously calculating what will maximize their immediate material advantages. Or one can suppose that they unconsciously or half consciously seek satisfying views of their relationships to other individuals and groups. The positing of such interpretations should not, of course, be *a priori* or automatic. There is no reason to think that a single model will suit all empirical cases. One just has to see what the evidence suggests.

Nevertheless, two more specific observations are in order. First, one must avoid the typically unacknowledged assumption that the "interests" of social groups must be economic ones. Particularly when dealing with intellectuals, one has to recognize that there are eminently "worldly" interests that are not specifically economic. Academics, for example, are interested in safeguarding the freedom of teaching, and in maximizing their collective influence upon the political system and upon the rest of society. The non-economic character of such concerns should *not* be taken to prove that intellectuals are "disinterested" by definition, but only that a narrowly economistic construal of "interested thought" is rarely warranted. Secondly, perhaps the most important link between the social environment and thought lies in the conscious and unconscious labor of social definition or classification. This has already been said, but I repeat it here because it is particularly important in the study of intellectual elites: The decisive hinge between their objective social situation and their thought lies in how they and others conceive their role. But this is a complex issue, not one that lends itself to broad and timeless generalizations. Coming back to the problem of "reductionism," we may say that the sociology of knowledge *need not* lead to anything like the dogma that ideas are "mere expressions" of economic interests, or to other abstract doctrines of that type.

This brings me at last to the problem of "relativism," and more particularly to Karl Mannheim's sociology of knowledge. The analytical starting point of Mannheim's *Ideology and Utopia* is the phenomenon of critical debunking, in which political opponents "unmask" each other's opinions by revealing the interests that lie behind them.[29] Broadening the implications of such unmasking, Mannheim arrived at a "total" conception of "ideology" as a socially conditioned distortion of thought. He argued that ideological bias affects not only the contents of particular propositions, engendering conscious or unconscious distortions, but also the "pretheoretical" fundaments and the whole "structure" of a mentality. In a further extension of his reasoning, he proposed that we accept the generality of the ideological phenomenon, regarding our own viewpoint as well as those of others as "situationally determined." He thus ultimately arrived at a theory of "relationism," in which the "absolutist" notion of an objective and universal truth was replaced with truth as the totality of possible perspectives, at least in the realm of socially relevant and "active" knowledge.

It is worth recalling that Mannheim used the term ideology in both a broader and a narrower sense. Indeed, it seems wise to follow him in this usage. An ideology in the wider sense is a network of more or less conscious beliefs that can be partly understood as the historical product of an institutional and social environment. To call beliefs "ideological" is to offer at least partly to explain them in this way. An ideology in the narrower sense is a "backward looking" perspective. The opposite of a Utopia, it may be further character- ized as serving to legitimate and to perpetuate an inherited social system and hierarchy. More generally, Mannheim's relationist sociology was a good deal richer than can be briefly indicated here. After all, we can in fact learn something substantive from a description guided by a perspective other than our own, as long as we can take the describer's "situation" into account. Nor is it impossible to construe the growth of knowledge as a progressive widening of our social understanding enforced by the need to subsume earlier or partial perspectives in a later and more compre- hensive synthesis. In any case, Mannheim cannot be faulted for holding that ideological analysis or criticism has joined the more traditional modes of intellectual assessment as a permanent element in modern social thought.

Yet the promise of Mannheim's sociology of knowledge was undercut when he posited the "free-floating" intellectuals as privi- leged agents of relationist "synthesis." Free from the compulsion of narrow commitments, he thought, a socially mixed intellectual elite was capable of bringing together the totality of possible perspectives. Modern intellectuals, he believed, were recruited from a particularly wide variety of social backgrounds. The experience of social mobility presumably lent them a certain detachment, and they were in any case less immediately involved in specifically economic interest conflicts than the major participants in capitalist production. They thus seemed suited to the task of understanding and integrating divergent viewpoints in a progressive "synthesis" that would sustain the idea of a Utopian alternative to capitalism. But while this view of the intellectuals is not simply unfounded, it almost certainly overesti- mates the diversity of social backgrounds among modern intellec- tuals. More important, it comes close to equating relative detach- ment from the economic interests of capitalists and of proletarians with freedom from *all forms* of interested thought and conduct. Misled by an inverted economism, Mannheim arrived at a plainly uncritical view of the intellectuals' situation. What apparently drove him to this position was the desperate need to find a sociological and "relationist" equivalent for the "absolutist" notion of objective truth.[30]

To me, the case of Mannheim strongly suggests that the historical sociology of knowledge must hold fast to the regulative ideal of

objectivity.[31] Imagined as a socio-historical condition, the achievement of a true and comprehensive understanding would be a
Utopia, an end of history. Regarded as an implied maxim of
scientific discourse, however, the norm of objectivity cannot be
dispensed with. Those who have abandoned it have tended to
replace it with inadequate socio-historical surrogates. Like Mannheim, they have dreamed of scientific or intellectual communities
that are factually, not just ideally, free of ideological entanglements.
But no "absolutism" could be as serious a danger to an empirical
intellectual history as the temptation to find Utopian conditions in
past or present realities.

CHAPTER I

Education, the middle classes, and the intellectuals: the social field in modern France and Germany

The comparative study of secondary and higher education is doubly crucial for social historians of knowledge. It provides access to aspects of general social history that particularly interest them. It focuses on the hierarchy of education, giving attention to what a narrowly economistic account of the modern social system would neglect. It is particularly fruitful in the light it throws on the internal articulation of the middle classes, and it also opens an approach to the whole issue of social meanings and classifications, to the way in which the dominant social groups have categorized themselves in relation to each other and to the rest of society.

At the same time, the study of modern systems of secondary and higher education serves as an introduction to the context of intellectual life. Modern intellectuals are increasingly academics, bound in one way or another to the institutions of higher education. Their factual roles as scientists, scholars and teachers are largely shaped by these institutional ties. Non-academic and even unaffiliated intellectuals continue to survive, of course; but even their role choices are deeply affected by the powerful presence of the academic context, without which highly specialized and increasingly capital-intensive research could scarcely be imagined. Thus neither the internal articulation of modern intellectual communities nor modern conceptions of intellectual roles could be adequately discussed without reference to the history of educational systems.

THE COMPARATIVE HISTORY OF EDUCATIONAL SYSTEMS

Modern European systems of secondary and higher education are best conceived as *systems* of interrelated institutions, curricula, and academic qualifications that cannot be understood in isolation from each other, or from the social process as a whole. Educational systems have played complex and relatively autonomous roles in their societies. They have not simply been functional extensions of economic or technological "needs." Their history has not been a steady progression toward greater "opportunity" or "democracy," but a discontinuous and crisis-ridden series of structural transformations that has nonetheless tended to reproduce relatively stable relationships of inequality among the major social groups. This will emerge from a brief and ideal typical sketch of modern European educational history that will also serve to introduce the more specialized discussions to follow later in the chapter and throughout the book.[1]

During the first two-thirds of the nineteenth century, the leading European secondary schools and universities prepared their graduates almost exclusively for the liberal professions, the higher civil service, the church, and secondary and university teaching. There was virtually no direct relationship between advanced education and the early industrial economy, and the social distribution of educational advantages was by no means congruent with the distribution of wealth and economic power. Two more or less distinct middle-class hierarchies rose above the broad base of a peasant and artisanal society: the economy-oriented hierarchy of early industrial capitalism, and an education-oriented hierarchy that encompassed the civil service and was closely linked to the state, especially in France and Germany. The rank order of education competed not only with the surviving hierarchy of birth, but also with the emerging commercial and industrial hierarchy. In fact, the status conventions and life styles transmitted by the leading educational institutions in England and France were quasi-aristocratic; the ideals of the educated gentleman and of the *honnête homme* were compromises, in an almost Freudian sense, between an inherited gentry and clerical culture on the one hand, and middle-class notions of advancement through learning on the other. In economically backward Prussia, the highly educated conceived of themselves as an intellectual and cultural elite, as distinct both from the burgher world from which they came and from the old aristocracy of birth. More generally, the outlook of the European educated classes was shaped more by ideals of education, of rational autonomy, and of state or professional service than by the entrepreneurial and market orientations usually associated with the rising industrial "bourgeoisie."

In France and especially in Prussia, it should be added, the educational systems of the early nineteenth century were socially rather open, or so it seems in retrospect. As Detlef Müller has argued, the Prussian *Gymnasium* of that time actually resembled a contemporary comprehensive secondary school in certain respects.[2] Along with pupils firmly intending to enter the learned professions, it took in substantial contingents of students from burgher and artisanal backgrounds, who could either leave school well before graduation to return to the social world from which they came, or be inducted upward into the hierarchy of education by an unusual taste for learning, with the encouragement of a teacher or clergyman, and perhaps with the support of a patron.[3] Apparently, a pervasive expectation of status persistence was not seriously threatened by the incidence of selective and even sponsored individual mobility. Perhaps the partial separation of the educational hierarchy from the main avenues to wealth and power helped to sustain these conditions, along with the humble circumstances of the clerical and teaching professions, the usual goals of students from modest backgrounds. There were periods during the late eighteenth century and again around 1830 when a relative excess of educated candidates for the learned professions raised anxieties of a socially conservative character. At least in Germany, short-term upswings in university enrollments per age group lay at the roots of these phenomena. Yet on the whole, the educational systems of the early and mid nineteenth century were characterized by generally stable enrollments and expectations.

Beginning about 1870, however, a whole series of structural changes thoroughly transformed the major European educational systems, creating institutional patterns that have endured in their outlines right up to the present. The rate of change was probably greatest during the 1880s and 1890s, a period shaken by acute social conflict in education, by furious public debates over the accreditation of competing secondary curricula and university-level institutions, and by renewed and more insistent complaints about a supposed excess of educated men. Major reorganizations of secondary education were undertaken in Germany and France between 1900 and 1902, while decisive rearrangements in higher education also took effect around the turn of the century. A thorough structural transformation of the two major educational systems on the European Continent was thus largely complete by 1910.

One way to describe the changes of this critical period is to point out that they brought secondary and higher education into closer interaction with the occupational system of the high industrial era. Primarily involved on the side of the educational system were certain younger and less prestigious institutions and curricula that were considered "modern," "technical," or "applied," and thus potentially fruitful contributors to economic and technological progress. Primarily affected on the side of the occupational system was a range of younger professions that came to be more educated than their early industrial precursors, yet arguably more relevant to commerce and industry than the older liberal and learned professions. The partial and sectoral convergence between the educational and the occupational systems that began in this way during the late nineteenth century has continued, through recurrent crises, ever since.

Economic functionalists have understandably been tempted to interpret this phenomenon of convergence as an adjustment of the educational system to the technological requirements of high industrial and late industrial economies. After all, contemporary societies do indeed have to equip large numbers of people with competences that early industrial societies could neglect. And "practical" reformers in education from the late nineteenth century on have certainly *believed* in the economic benefits of the innovations they have proposed. Nevertheless, one can acknowledge a loose and general relationship between technological change and educational change, without being convinced that any *particular* curriculum can be functionally linked to *particular* economic "needs." The case for a strict economic functionalism, in other words, has never been adequately specified. As we shall see, the "practical" reform proposals of the late nineteenth century were never exclusively economic in any case. They typically envisioned a certain structure of social roles and ranks that was as important in their overall conception as the supposed requirements of the economy. Even business leaders who pointed to the needs of industry often explicitly or implicitly directed their most "practical" advice to students from the middle and lower levels of the social hierarchy (who might be better off in an "honest trade"), while associating themselves, or their sons, with the more "elevated" objectives of the traditionally most prestigious institutions and curricula. As Müller has demonstrated, moreover, the elaborate hierarchy of educational qualifications that defined civil service ranks in late nineteenth-century Prussia almost certainly did more to shape the wider occupational system than the reverse. Thus the sectoral convergence between the educational and occupational systems was a genuinely *interactive* one. With little exaggeration, one can speak of an *educationalization* of the occupational system, rather than an industrialization of education. And that gives some meaning to the relative autonomy of the educational system within the larger society.

Another way to interpret the structural transformations of the late nineteenth century is to hypothesize that former expectations of status persistence were replaced by something like a rising demand for advanced education on the one hand, and by a conscious determination to limit social mobility through education on the other. The rising demand for certain forms of advanced education may have been due to the rapid development of primary schooling, to political and more broadly social pressures for "democratization" in education, and to the socially ameliorative or stabilizing intentions of educational reformers. Such ameliorative intentions, as we shall see, did not usually aim at more than sectorally limited forms of occupational mobility through education. They were also easily linked to the expectation that practically oriented studies would aid the economy, without seriously threatening the older forms of elite education.

These assumptions proved dangerous in practice, however, because a kind of generalist shift tended to transform "applied" or vocationally oriented curricula in a generalist and academic direction, primarily in response to the socio-cultural aspirations of teachers and parents. At the same time, larger proportions of pupils in the Prussian *Gymnasium*, for example, tended to advance into the higher grades, and thus to become candidates for full academic certification. Social conservatives responded with exclusionary strategies that became increasingly explicit during the conflicts of the 1880s and 1890s. The great depression that threatened the European economies from the mid 1870s to the mid 1890s gave rise to socially protectionist sentiments in any case. The anxieties publicly expressed about the prospect of an unemployable and discontented "academic proletariat" in Germany and France during this period probably owed as much to such protectionist sentiments and exclusionary strategies as to the substantial enrollment increases that did in fact occur.

But no matter how one assesses the conflicting motives and pressures that have been suggested, they jointly engendered a sequence of institutional changes that no one may have fully anticipated or intended. Müller has accurately described this sequence as a process of systematization, at least for Prussia. Of course educational systems have always been systems in the sense that their parts have been interrelated, and more or less fully defined and delimited in relation to each other. Yet the degree of such definition and delimitation certainly increased dramatically in the major European systems between about 1870 and 1910. The organization of individual school types and curricular programs was more and more rigorously specified, along with their entrance requirements and the prerogatives conferred by their leaving certificates. Stepwise and beginning at the apex of the educational hierarchy, fresh academic and social territories were in effect charted and colonized. Newly organized schools were at first defined negatively, in terms of the boundaries that separated them from their more highly accredited predecessors. But as even remoter lands were opened up, further academic and social distinctions were discovered or invented. Once created, the younger and less-favored institutions tended to assimilate upward, in imitation of the older and more prestigious ones, while the latter in turn defended their distinctiveness with increased vigor. Thus, as the intermediate positions in the educational hierarchy were filled in, each institution and curriculum was clearly set off from its neighbors above and below, and a more fully articulated scale of academic credentials was brought to bear upon the occupational system. In France and Germany, this process of codification displayed some of the characteristics of bureaucratic rationalization; yet the structures that emerged had striking analogues in England as well. Above all, systematization also meant stratification, and the process as a whole was more a conflict-ridden exercise in social demarcation than a bureaucratic search for order.

Further changes in the organization of European secondary and higher education between about 1920 and 1960 substantially modified, but did not fundamentally alter, the structures that had emerged by around 1910. One new element was the full accreditation of girls' secondary education, which allowed women to reach the universities in significant numbers from the 1920s on. A second cluster of reforms begun in France and Germany during the 1920s instituted common elementary schooling for future primary and secondary pupils, while also tending to lower the institutional and curricular barriers between the different forms of secondary education. At least in France, the reform movement extended into the 1940s and 1950s, with the partial assimilation of higher primary and full-time vocational schools into the secondary system. The compartmentalization and social stratification of the educational system was thus softened, though by no means removed, even while the systematization of the secondary hierarchy was continued downward into the primary realm. Above the secondary level too, university status was everywhere formally conferred upon existing networks of higher vocational, professional, and technical schools, which were thus integrated into more comprehensive and more fully articulated systems. Altogether, these institutional adjustments brought about a further degree of convergence and interaction between the educational and occupational systems of late industrial societies. Most affected, once again, were certain younger educated professions, whose status in the expanding white-collar hierarchy largely depended upon their "qualifications."

The further convergence between education and occupation was powerfully aided by markedly increased enrollments in European secondary and university-level education since about 1920. These in turn were due not only to the institutional adjustments that have been mentioned, but also to rapid and dramatic changes in the sizes of relevant age cohorts, and by short-term fluctuations in educational demand brought on by devastating wars and economic crises. Such dislocations have tended to disrupt established equilibria between the educational and occupational systems, and to weaken inherited conventions about what educational levels are appropriate for various socio-occupational groups. Socially conservative positions on these issues have continued to find expression in recurrent crises of academic "overpopulation," most notably around 1930, when an "academic proletariat" was supposed to threaten once again.

An obvious question about the whole development of European secondary and higher education since the early nineteenth century is whether it has significantly increased social mobility. The weight of the evidence is now against this optimistic expectation; but the issue is complicated enough to call for some preliminary clarification. One has to realize, for example, that even large enrollment increases may not alter the *relative* positions of various social groups within the educational system. This is true not only because a larger pie can be shared as unequally as a smaller one, but also because the new places made available to less-advantaged students have typically been located in the less-highly accredited sectors of the educational system. Such quantum changes as the admission of "modern" secondary students to the baccalaureate in France after 1890 may indeed have altered the social distribution of an important educational qualification. But one cannot simply assume such consequences; one has to look and see what the relative positions actually were.

Even when one knows the proportional distribution of all types of advanced schooling, moreover, one cannot easily assess the impact on social mobility. A "democratically" recruited secondary "technical" school may have the "undemocratic" effect of routing its graduates toward mediocre jobs. And even a substantially increased proportion of working-class students in an elite secondary program may not produce a corresponding improvement in working-class access to the highest social positions. After all, even the best educational credentials may not compete successfully with other *de facto* criteria of occupational selection, particularly if their "market value" has been reduced by their increased availability. This is the problem of educational "inflation" or "devaluation," an inevitable byproduct of educational expansion that has tended to cancel the effects of genuine "democratization" even near the apex of the educational hierarchy. One must never forget, finally, that the convergence between education and occupation since 1870 has made advanced schooling a necessary (though not sufficient) condition of occupational advancement, so that upward mobility *through* the educational system has to some degree reduced or replaced social ascent *outside* or *around* the educational system.

All this is not to say that the wider dissemination of education is a false path, or that efforts to equalize educational opportunities are pointless, for education is valuable in itself; it ought to be fairly shared, and its "devaluation" as a social currency may actually strengthen its broader purpose. Moreover, mobility may not be the best road to democracy even in principle, and social distances may be more important, both for social theory and for our everyday experience of society, than the rate of movement across them. The social historian, in any case, is less interested in individual social paths, or in absolute quantities of wealth and education, than in relative standings, in aggregate relationships among social groups, and more generally in relatively persistent structures that transcend the fate of individual agents.

Three summative statistical properties of educational systems are particularly important for comparative analysis. (1) An *inclusive* educational system is one that schools a comparatively large fraction of the population. Measures of inclusiveness are percentages of the relevant age groups. Absolute enrollment figures are largely meaningless, and even ratios of secondary enrollments per population, for example, cannot be made internationally comparable, since secondary programs differ in the number of grades or age years they encompass. (2) A *progressive* system is one that recruits a relatively high proportion of its students from lower-middle-class and lower-class backgrounds. Progressiveness in an educational system is a necessary but not a sufficient condition for upward social mobility through education. (3) A *segmented* system is one in which different programs of study at the same age level also differ in the social origins of their students.

Both progressiveness and segmentation can be measured in terms of *relative access chances* or of similar indicative ratios. If 2 percent of working-class youths and 20 percent of all youths in an age group reached secondary schools, for example, then the relative access chance for the working class with respect to these schools would be 2/20, or 0.1. Similarly, if 3 percent of students actually in these schools and 30 percent of the occupational census were identified as working-class, then one could specify an *opportunity ratio* for the working class in these schools of 3/30, or 0.1 again.[4] These technicalities are worth rehearsing because of the interpretive principle they imply: *In principle*, the sort of information typically available on the social origins of students in various types of institutions is meaningful only in relation to a norm, which can be found in the occupational census, in the corresponding data for the whole age group, or in the relevant indicators for *all* students in a given sector of the system.

The typical form of educational segmentation, of course, is *socially vertical*: that is, one of two major educational segments or "tracks" caters to a socially more "elevated" clientele than the other. There have been circumstances, however, in which segmentation has been *socially horizontal* to some degree; that is, groups ranked relatively low on the scale of purely economic advantages have nonetheless been *relatively* well represented in the more highly accredited of two major "tracks," and vice versa. Even mild forms of such socially horizontal segmentation are interesting, because they suggest the presence of a "horizontal" divide between economy-oriented and education-oriented social groups at the same social "altitude." Or, to put it another way, socially horizontal segmentation signals a more or less pronounced incongruity between the distribution of "economic capital" or of "class" advantages on the one hand, and the distribution of "cultural capital" or of "status" attributes on the other. Such incongruities rarely occur at the very top or in the lowest third of the social pyramid; they may therefore appear trivial in comparison with the brute facts of cumulative inequality. For the student of the European middle classes, of middle-class self-images and ideologies, however, these incongruities can be highly significant.

Curricular differentiation alone does not constitute segmentation; clear social differences must be involved as well. What matters is the *conjunction* of social and curricular differences; for it is this conjunction that allows curricular differences to take on social meanings. The process in which this happens is inescapably historical, since it can only take place over an extended period of time. Just as the social character of a school is defined by its former graduates, so educational programs tend gradually to acquire some of the characteristics of their ancient clients. Along with cognitive paradigms, secondary schools and universities transmit socio-cultural traditions that are partly unreflected meanings. Thus the inherited forms of nineteenth-century elite education were unconsciously held to confer qualities upon their students that echoed the idealized attributes of former cultural and governing elites. Because the life styles and status conventions thus perpetuated drew their symbolic force more from the past than from the present, they could occasionally come in conflict with the more rapidly changing realities of the industrial capitalist class hierarchy, which they more typically helped to reinforce and to legitimate. In sum, educational segmentation crucially affects what Hans Ulrich Wehler calls the "cultural patterns of interpretation" (*kulturelle Deutungsmuster*) that shape the way a society is experienced by its members; it literally gives meaning to social differences.[5]

Before moving on from these general considerations to the particulars of French secondary and higher education, I want briefly to outline those characteristics of German educational history that will serve as points of reference for comparative purposes. What I take to be peculiarities of the German pattern should *not* be assigned a special status; nineteenth-century German history was no more nor less "unique" than nineteenth-century French or English history. But of course there were differences between national paths that continue to be of interest for comparative and causal analysis. Thus economic historians have come to distinguish a universal history of industrial capitalism from distinctive national patterns of development that were partly shaped by the timing of each nation's entry into the broader dynamic of accumulation and technological innovation. National differences in industrial development, interestingly enough, have tended to fade with the passage of time, so that a convergence toward similar outcomes can be detected, as least in Western Europe. But much the same can be said about educationalization, the cross-national process outlined in the opening pages of this chapter. Treating it as a typical or normal course of events, one can begin to consider the causal significance of partly divergent national relations to it.

Indeed, the most obvious point to be made about the history of secondary and higher education in modern Germany is simply that key processes in it took place relatively early, both in comparison with similar processes in other countries and in relation to the German schedule of economic development. Well before the rapid industrialization of Germany after 1870, a kind of educational revolution occurred in the German universities of the late eighteenth and early nineteenth centuries that anticipated subsequent developments elsewhere. The German "philosophical" faculties broke through the institutional framework initially defined by the task of training and certifying secondary school teachers, and the modern research university was born.[6] The phenomenon had something in common with the proverbial "takeoff" into sustained economic growth. Once under way, it proved both cumulative and paradigmatic, and inquiries into its origins tend to focus on preconditions that were jointly but not separately sufficient to give rise to it. Among these preconditions, one has to count the survival and subsequent revitalization of the German territorial universities during the eighteenth and early nineteenth centuries, which were due in large measure to the intervention of princely governments.[7] The confessional history of the German territories, the presence of an educated Protestant pastorate and of influential theological faculties at the German universities, along with the efforts of the German states to control the clerical professions, all these mattered as well. But the most important precondition of the German educational revolution was the early emergence, in Prussia and in other German states, of professional bureaucracies recruited largely if not wholly on the basis of educational qualifications. This form of bureaucratic modernization gave great prominence to advanced education as a basis for middle-class aspirations in Germany, particularly since entrepreneurial capitalism long remained poorly developed as an alternate field of opportunity.

Thus during the late eighteenth and early nineteenth centuries, a social group emerged in Germany that had no full counterpart in France or in England. This was the *Bildungsbürgertum*, the educated middle class, my "mandarins." The term *Bildungsbürgertum* itself did not emerge until the twentieth century. Its ancestors were the "educated estates" (*gebildete Stände*) of the late eighteenth and early nineteenth centuries, and the "educated middle stratum" and "educated burgher class" (*gebildeter Mittelstand, gebildetes Bürgertum*) of the early and late nineteenth century, respectively. There is something fascinating in the fact that the group's contemporary name originated precisely at a time when the group itself experienced a sense of crisis and decline.[8]

The *Bildungsbürgertum* is probably best defined as encompassing all secondary school graduates, holders of the *Abitur* certificate, which became the sole prerequisite for university study. A more inclusive definition of the group could also include those who had at least six years of secondary schooling, and who thus became eligible for reduced military service as "one-year volunteers." Women of equivalent education did not earn formal credentials but should obviously be counted as well. Among the male members of the *Bildungsbürgertum*, some were university-educated members of the high civil service and of the liberal professions, who usually enjoyed fairly comfortable incomes as well. Yet, unlike the French *bourgeoisie* of the same period, the *Bildungsbürgertum* as a whole was characterized less by wealth and by political power than by a measure of advanced education. Particularly in the intermediate ranks of the civil service, in the Protestant pastorate, and in the teaching professions themselves, prospective entrants into the *Bildungsbürger-tum* found channels of social ascent and sources of self-esteem in which education was the primary measure of social and personal worth, and often the only operative one. In this context, the absence of competing sources of self-definition helped to shape an ethos that became characteristic of the *Bildungsbürgertum* as a whole. A modern concept of vocation (*Beruf*) evolved from earlier, largely religious conceptions, and the ideal of *Bildung* emerged as the most viable universalist alternative to the ascribed status of noble birth.[9] In sum, the German *Bildungsbürgertum* arose as a modern "merit" elite, an *intellectual* aristocracy as distinct from a hereditary one. But of course it also gradually separated itself from the artisanal world in which it originated, while the concept of *Bildung* came to echo some of the aristocratic qualities it was meant to replace.

Statistical social historians rightly try to "see through" the categories they find in their sources, to the realities that lie behind them. Yet they thereby run the risk of under-estimating the conceptual and historical elements inevitably present in social classifications. In nineteenth-century French statistical sources, for example, the amorphous category of *propriétaires* encompassed owners of landed and/or urban property and/or securities with a rather wide range of real incomes.[10] Obviously, historians want to assess as precisely as possible the amounts and forms of wealth involved. Yet one must not forget that the propensity to see a *propriétaire* where others at other times might have seen a landowner or a landlord, a *rentier* or a capitalist, was a historical reality in its own right. Thus the *propriétaire* was understood to be living on his income from property, and his social name focused on this clearly honorific feature of his overall situation. To explain why this was so, of course, one has to look into the prior history of the French bourgeoisie.

Two analogous examples from German statistical sources come to mind, and both underscore the enduring significance of the civil service and of higher education in nineteenth-century German patterns of social interpretation. Thus in the Wilhelmian period, certain higher grades of German clerical personnel were typically classified as "private officials" (*Privatbeamte*).[11] They would probably be termed higher-level "white-collar" employees in twentieth-century America, or "*cadres, secteur privé*" in twentieth-century France.

Each of these contemporary categories in turn has an interesting history, and a symbolic force that is far from socially "neutral."[12] In a similar way, the presence of "private officials" in Wilhelmian Germany signals a kind of symbolic induction; it marks the degree to which civil service classifications – and outlooks – were extended to structure the occupational system of the high capitalist era.

The other categories that are of interest in this connection are those typically used to identify the educated classes in German statistical sources of the late nineteenth and early twentieth centuries, which also figured in common usage. Thus the term "academic professions" (*akademische Berufe*) encompassed all occupations for which university-level qualifications were required in principle, and those exercising these professions were also called "academics" (*Akademiker*).[13] In surveys of students' social origins, moreover, distinctions among the various "academic professions," as well as among levels of education, were usually itemized with great care, while men without university credentials were long grouped more casually and less consistently, with a certain disregard for merely economic differences among them. Thus the *Bildungsbürgertum* of the early nineteenth century survived in the social categories of later eras. In any case, advanced education remained a particularly important and largely autonomous source of status in Germany even after the high industrial class structure had begun to assert itself as the dominant motor of social stratification, and even as the earlier differences between the major West European educational systems began to fade in a convergence toward similar outcomes.

This, indeed, is what struck such careful observers of Wilhelmian Germany as Friedrich Paulsen and Max Weber. Educational differences, Weber wrote, "are nowadays undoubtedly the most important specific source of *status group* differentiation, as contrasted with property and differentiation of economic function, the sources of *class* formation"; educational differences constitute "one of the very strongest purely psychological barriers in society. Especially in Germany, where almost all privileged positions inside and outside the civil service are tied to qualifications involving not only specialized knowledge but also "general *Bildung*."[14] These observations are plainly intended to apply "especially" *but not only* to Germany, and "the sources of class formation" are by no means ignored. Educational qualifications are considered central to the modern socio-occupational hierarchy generally, and yet there is a special emphasis on Germany, on the civil service, and on *Bildung*. Moreover, since status conventions are largely historical inheritances, in Weber's analysis, his sentences in fact imply the observable presence of a partly distinctive German past, and that is exactly my point.

At the top of the hierarchy of education in nineteenth-century Germany, of course, stood the university professors, my "mandarin intellectuals." Almost by definition, they were the most distinguished of the *Akademiker*, and the foremost representatives of *Bildung*. At the same time, they largely defined and filled the role of the intellectual in modern Germany.[15] Leisured amateurs and writers working directly for the literary market have contributed in important ways to modern German intellectual and cultural life; but they were clearly less numerous and probably less influential there, collectively, than they were in France and in England, at least until the end of the nineteenth century. In the pages that follow, I hope to show that this was so, and to begin asking what difference it made.

FRENCH SECONDARY AND HIGHER EDUCATION SINCE NAPOLEON

The French Revolution did not end by having a "democratic" effect on French secondary and higher education.[16] It swept away the ancient universities, along with the endowments of the clerical teaching orders that had run most of the secondary schools (*collèges*) of the old regime. The educational reform projects of the Convention had few enduring consequences, and so it was Napoleon who really established the basic framework of secondary and higher education for nineteenth-century France. Napoleon's main concern was with administrative rationalization and state control. The so-called University he created in 1806 was not an advanced institution of learning, but a hierarchically organized and centrally controlled corporation that encompassed all public secondary and higher education and its personnel. Napoleon's conception of higher education was narrowly practical. He saw a need for advanced instruction and state certification in law, medicine, and pharmacy, but the "faculties" or "schools" to which he assigned these functions were strictly professional institutions. As for the faculties of letters and of sciences, heirs of the old arts faculties, they had almost no regularly enrolled students until late in the nineteenth century. Their main task was the setting and grading of the *baccalauréat*, a secondary leaving examination and certificate similar to the German *Abitur*; but they also examined and certified teachers for the state secondary schools, and they usually offered public lectures of general interest to amateur audiences. In sum, for most of the nineteenth century, France had university-level faculties, but no universities.

The other institutions of higher education favored by Napoleon were the so-called "government schools" or *grandes écoles*. Some of these dated back to the eighteenth century; others had their origins in the revolutionary period. They were clearly designed to train specialists for the various branches of the government service, including the military. The very small groups of students they accepted on the basis of highly competitive entrance examinations were educated and boarded at the expense of the state, usually for a three-year term. The two most famous *grandes écoles* of the nineteenth century were the Ecole Polytechnique (1794) and the Ecole Normale Supérieure (1795, 1808). Officially a military school, the Ecole Polytechnique prepared civil as well as military engineers for government service.[17] Among its graduates, some went on to complete their training at such older "schools of application" as the artillery and naval schools, the School of Mines, and the School of Bridges and Roads; most ended up in the military, though a good number also went into the technical branches of the high civil service, and a few ultimately transferred to private industry. The Ecole Normale, by contrast, was a purely academic institution, preparing the elite of future teachers and adminstrators for the state secondary schools.[18]

The keystone of the Napoleonic educational system was the state *lycée*, which was patterned more on the old Jesuit *collèges* than on the so-called central schools of the revolutionary period. Established in 1802, the Napoleonic *lycées* offered an essentially classical curriculum, along with substantial training in mathematics. To put the new institutions on their feet financially, the Emperor established a cluster of state scholarships, which were also designed to aid pupils from the poorer classes, especially sons of loyal soldiers and functionaries. While these scholarships helped to lend the Napoleonic educational system an air of meritocratic opportunity, they fell short of matching the provision of free secondary education that had been funded from the endowments of the clerical teaching orders.[19] In 1808, the famous and all-important *baccalauréat* was instituted as a nationally standardized secondary leaving examination based on the curriculum of the *lycées*. It was a prerequisite for the more advanced teaching degrees in letters and sciences, and, from 1820 on, for access to the faculties of law and medicine as well.

The French *lycées* of the nineteenth century were financed directly by the central government and usually located in the larger cities. The more numerous public *collèges* were partly supported by the municipalities and typically found in the smaller towns. Their curriculum was largely that of the *lycées*, but many of them lacked the higher grades. In competition with the public secondary schools, private *collèges* attracted a substantial portion of the student population. During the early nineteenth century, a number of private secondary schools were run by laymen. Increasingly over the course of the century, however, private secondary schools were essentially Catholic schools. A few of the private *collèges* run by the Jesuits matched the most renowned Parisian *lycées* in academic standing, but there were also Catholic *collèges* that catered to a humble clientele in the countryside.[20]

Though they varied, the costs of secondary schooling were probably somewhat higher in France than in Germany during the nineteenth century. In addition to substantial tuitions, roughly half of French secondary pupils paid fees to board at public or private secondary schools. Scholarship funds declined from the First Empire to the Third Republic, and did not always go to the neediest students in any case. More generally, secondary education was as rigorously separated from primary schooling in France as in Germany. Many of the youngsters who reached the secondary classes of public secondary schools at around age eleven came from elementary classes attached to public or private secondary schools. In France as in Germany, moreover, primary teachers were trained at primary normal schools, not at the secondary schools and university faculties that prepared secondary teachers (*professeurs*).

Until the 1860s, the French secondary curriculum remained overwhelmingly classical. Small pre-vocational programs were attached to some municipal and private *collèges* during the early nineteenth century, but secondary schooling proper meant classical schooling. The first systematic alteration of this pattern was the curricular bifurcation of 1852, in which the four highest secondary grades were divided into a literary (classical) and a scientific (predominantly mathematical) branch. Even before this bifurcation was adopted, and again after it was dropped in 1864, students preparing to take entrance examinations for the scientific *grandes écoles* could in any case specialize in mathematics, while bypassing much of the classical program during the last three years of secondary study. Between 1863 and 1865, the introduction of the "special secondary" curriculum launched a whole series of further changes in French secondary schooling that will be taken up in the next chapter. The Ferry laws of 1881–82 not only made public primary schooling free and compulsory for ages six through thirteen; they also accelerated the development of free public higher primary and full-time vocational schooling. In 1891, the "special secondary" program officially became the "modern" stream within the French secondary system, with a duration one year short of the classical curriculum and a baccalaureate of its own.[21] Then, in 1902 a comprehensive decree established a framework for French secondary schooling that remained largely unchanged until after the Second World War. The full seven-year course of secondary studies that began with the Sixth at age eleven was divided into two cycles, four and three years in length. The second cycle encompassed curricular options labelled Latin–Greek, Latin–Sciences, Latin–(Modern) Languages and Sciences–(Modern) Languages. In theory, the decree recognized no differences of accreditation between the four streams. In practice, the strictly modern option suffered from a relative lack of prestige and from minor restrictions of access to higher education for some time to come.[22]

Obviously, the French secondary baccalaureate was the decisive criterion of membership in the educated upper middle class in nineteenth-century France. While the German *Abitur* examination was carried out separately at each school, the *baccalauréat* was nationally standardized. It was also notorious for its difficulty and for its impact on teachers and students in the higher secondary grades. Over half the candidates might fail all or part of the required tests, and some therefore repeated the concluding grades of the secondary curriculum. From 1820 on, the baccalaureate was a prerequisite for access to the faculties of law and medicine, and thus to the *licence* in law and the doctorate in medicine, the two professional degrees typically awarded by these faculties after three to five years of additional study. From its beginnings in 1808, the baccalaureate was also required of candidates for the three main advanced degrees offered by the faculties of letters and of sciences: the *licence*, the *agrégation*, and the state doctorate. Until late in the nineteenth century, all three were taken exclusively by future secondary and university faculty, and all three were rigidly tied to the secondary curriculum. The *licence* was just a slightly more elaborate version of the baccalaureate, required of all but the lowest ranks of secondary teachers. The more difficult *agrégation*, usually and most easily obtained after three years at the Ecole Normale, gave access to the highest positions in the state secondary system. It was awarded in the main secondary subjects, which were also the only ones represented by chairs in the nineteenth-century faculties of letters.[23] In fact, successful *lycée* teachers, usually *agrégés*, could advance from their secondary posts to positions in the faculties of letters and of sciences, most easily those in the provinces, during most of the nineteenth century. The state doctorate, formally required for professorships in the faculties, was awarded on the basis of two theses, one of them in Latin; but even the non-Latin dissertation evolved only gradually from a formality before 1850 to a serious research effort by the end of the century.

Several major *grandes écoles* did not formally require the baccalaureate of those taking their entrance examinations.[24] On the other hand, these very difficult examinations themselves were largely based on the secondary curriculum. To prepare for them, students took so-called preparatory courses for two to four years beyond the highest secondary grade. Expensive and typically found only at the most renowned Parisian *lycées*, these preparatory courses constituted a formidable barrier between secondary schooling and the *grandes écoles*.

Along with the Ecole Polytechnique and the Ecole Normale, the Military School of Saint-Cyr, several naval schools, and the Colonial School figured among the notable *grandes écoles* of the nineteenth century. The Ecole Centrale des Arts et Manufactures, privately founded in 1829 and taken over by the state in 1857, was designed to train engineers, managers, and entrepreneurs for French industry.[25] The Ecole Libre des Sciences Politiques remained a private school from its foundation in 1872 until after the Second World War. Its emphasis was on politics and international affairs, and it eventually acquired something close to a monopoly of access to certain departments of the higher civil service. Advanced theological education in France has generally taken place at higher seminaries (*grands séminaires*), rather than in university faculties of theology. The famous Ecole Pratique des Hautes Etudes was founded in 1868 to permit seminar-style ("practical") research training for small groups of advanced students in the arts and sciences. Among other purely scholarly or artistic institutions of higher education in Paris, one must count the Ecole des Chartes, which trains archivists and paleographers, the Ecole des Langues Orientales Vivantes, and the Ecole des Beaux-Arts. The ancient Collège de France is an institute of advanced study; its tenured faculty give public lectures but do not formally teach regular students.

At the side of these distinguished establishments, several clusters of younger institutions have sprung up since the late nineteenth century and especially since the First World War. Some have been oriented toward business administration; but the overwhelming majority have been specialized technical and engineering schools. Their ancestors are not so much the Ecole Polytechnique and the Ecole Centrale as the *écoles d'arts et métiers*, which did not attain university-level standing until the twentieth century.[26] The two oldest of these practically oriented schools of mechanical engineering were founded by Napoleon to train "noncommissioned officers" for French industry. The rapid development of higher primary and full-time vocational schooling from the 1880s on allowed the *écoles d'arts et métiers* to raise their standards, and they began to confer an engineering diploma in 1907. Further progress in vocational and "secondary technical" education, especially since 1945, has confirmed the now so-called *écoles nationales d'ingénieurs arts at métiers*, together with many younger engineering schools, in their role of university-level technical institutions.

While important structural changes took place in French secondary schooling and in French higher technical education during the late nineteenth century, at least equally significant transformations altered the university faculties, especially those of letters and of sciences.[27] Beginning in the 1860s, leading French academics and educational administrators began to call for reforms that would bring French higher education in the arts and sciences closer to the model of the German research university. The reform movement achieved its first practical success with the founding of the Ecole Pratique des Hautes Etudes (1868). Then, between 1877 and 1883, the faculties of letters and sciences themselves were affected by the stepwise establishment of 350 scholarships for students working toward the teaching *licence*, and another 200 for more advanced candidates seeking the *agrégation*. For the first time, the faculties of letters and sciences thus acquired a solid core of regular students, not merely examinees and amateur auditors. They accordingly began to replace the old public lectures with "closed courses" for regular students, and with small-group colloquia or seminars of a type first developed at the Ecole Normale. During the 1880s, a certain degree of specialization was instituted in the preparation for the *licences* in letters and in sciences. Beyond the level of the *licence*, the so-called diploma of higher studies was introduced to attest the capacity for independent research. It eventually became a normal step on the way to the *agrégation*. In 1893, medical students were required to begin their university work with a year of basic studies in the faculties of sciences. In 1895, a further reorganization of the *licence* in sciences established a flexible system of specialized certificates, any three of which could make up the *licence*. In 1897, the university faculties were empowered to institute so-called university diplomas of their own, on the basis of whatever requirements they chose to set.

In the meantime, a series of measures taken between 1885 and 1896 transformed the French faculties into something like modern universities. In 1885, the faculties were given limited powers to manage their own funds, especially private gifts and endowments, while interfaculty councils began to link the several faculties in each town. In 1893, the financial prerogatives of these councils were broadened, and in 1896, the existing faculties were grouped together to form sixteen universities in metropolitan France. While some of the new units were too small to be effective, and while none achieved the integration of their counterparts in England and Germany, one can reasonably date the creation of the modern French universities from 1896.

Even so, the real significance of the institutional changes that have been described lies in the partial loosening of the restraints that long bound especially the French faculties of letters to their teacher-training function, and thus to the major subject categories of the secondary curriculum. On the one hand, the "New Sorbonne" of the years around the turn of the century had acquired some of the autonomous character of a specialized research institution. On the other hand, a new flexibility in the system of accreditations, along with a measure of financial autonomy, enabled the stronger provincial faculties of science to seek local clients and financial support by offering applied scientific and technical courses of interest to local industries. By the beginning of the twentieth century, the French universities thus performed the full range of functions characteristic of the German universities, and perhaps some of those characteristic of the German technical institutes as well.

In France as in Germany, the period between the two World Wars brought a whole new wave of change, particularly in second-ary education. On both sides of the Rhine, leading reformers were inspired by the ideal of the common school (*école unique*), which was to reduce social barriers by starting all pupils off in the same schools, and by having curricular specializations branch off from a "common trunk" as late as possible. Progress toward this goal was slower in France than in Germany during the 1920s; but then the National Socialist regime slowed reform in Germany, while change acceler-ated in France during the 1930s and continued almost uninterrupted into the post-Second World War era.

During the 1920s, French reformers succeeded in reducing the curricular differences between elementary primary schooling and the elementary classes attached to secondary schools. In the higher secondary grades, the curricular option labelled Latin–Modern Languages was dropped, while common classes began to reduce the differences not only between the remaining secondary streams, but also between higher primary and secondary education. Then, in a stepwise sequence between 1928 and 1933, French public secondary education became free, except that students in the elementary classes of secondary schools continued to pay fees.[28] The Vichy regime temporarily reintroduced tuition for all secondary grades; but it upheld and continued a series of measures begun under the Popular Front that ultimately brought the former higher primary and full-time vocational schools into the secondary system. A further process of change in the French educational system was thus initiated that has extended nearly to our own day.

Table 1.1 describes the inclusiveness of French secondary and higher education at various levels from 1840 to 1950; that is, it reports enrollments in the several layers and parts of the French educational system as percentages of the relevant age groups. It should be noted that *total* secondary enrollments are related to the *overall* size of the appropriate number of age years in the population. The resulting percentage therefore represents declining enrollments in ascending grades as a kind of *average*; it understates enrollments in the lowest grades and correspondingly overstates enrollments in the highest grades. At the university level, total enrollment for both

Table 1.1 *The inclusiveness of French secondary and higher education, 1840–1950: degrees and enrollments as percentages of relevant age groups, with Prussian and German comparisons*

Enrollments and degrees as percentage of age group in:	1840–42	1854–56	1865–66	1875–76	1885–87	1910–11	1930–31	1950–51
Secondary enrollments	1.2	1.7	2.2	2.4	2.4	2.6	6.9	17.3
Baccalaureates	0.5	0.7	0.9	0.8	1.0	1.1	2.3	5.7
Law degrees		0.2	0.2	0.2	0.2			
Law students				0.2		0.7	0.8	1.5
Medical degrees			0.1	0.1	0.1			
Medical students				0.2	0.2	0.4	0.7	1.2
Letters and sciences – degrees		(0.02)	(0.03)	(0.04)	0.1			
Letters and sciences – students				(0.03)		0.5	1.3	2.4
All university students			0.5	0.5	0.6	1.7	2.9	5.4
Prussian/German comparisons								
Secondary enrollments			1.7	2.5	2.6	3.2	8.8	9.1
Abiturs			0.5	0.7	0.8	1.2	3.3	4.5
Law students			0.1	0.2	0.2	0.2	0.4	0.4
Medical students			0.1	0.1	0.2	0.3	0.4	0.4
Students in arts and sciences			0.2	0.2	0.3	0.6	1.1	1.6
All university students			0.5	0.6	0.8	1.2	2.1	2.5
Students at technical institutes					0.1	0.2	0.4	0.8

Sources: Ministère de l'Instruction Publique, *Rapport au Roi par ... (Villemain) ... sur l'instruction secondaire* (1843); *Bulletin Administratif de l'Instruction Publique,* 52 (April, 1854); *Statistique de l'enseignement secondaire en 1865* (1866); *... en 1876* (1878); *... en 1877* (1889); *Statistique de l'enseignement supérieur,* 4 vols. (1868–1900); Chambre des Députés, *Enquête sur l'enseignement secondaire* (1889); J. B. Piobetta, *Le baccalauréat* (Paris, 1937); *Annuaire statistique de la France,* vols. 42 (1926), 72 (1966); INSEE, *Population par sexe, age et état matrimonial de*

1851 a 1962 [Etudes et Documents, 10] (Paris, 1968); Wilhelm Lexis, ed., *Das Unterrichtswesen im Deutschen Reich*, vol. 2 (Berlin, 1904); *Statistische Mitteilungen über das höhere Unterrichtswesen im Königreich Preussen*, vol. 28 (1911); *Statistisches Handbuch/Jahrbuch für den Preussischen Staat*, vols. 2 (1893), 11 (1913); *Jahrbuch für das höhere Schulwesen im Deutschen Reich*, vol. 1 (1933); *Preussische Statistik*, vols. 204, 236; *Deutsche Hochschulstatistik*, vol. 7; *Statistisches Jahrbuch*, vols. 9, 34, 52, 54, and vol. for 1952; *Statistik der Bundesrepublik*, vol. 199. For details and annotation, see Ringer, *Education and Society*, pp. 272–279, 291–300, 316–329, 335–341.

For France, through 1885–87, total (male) enrollments in public and private secondary schools are related to the ten-year age group 8 through 17 (both sexes); thereafter, enrollments in the Sixth and higher grades (including girls in 1930–31 and 1950–51) are related to the seven-year age group eleven through seventeen. This may understate secondary access slightly through 1885–87, and overstate it slightly thereafter. The corresponding data for the baccalaureate are related to the four-year age group year seventeen. Beginning in 1875–76, enrollments in university faculties are related to the four-year age group nineteen through twenty-two. This may understate university access slightly for 1875–76, and overstate it slightly for 1930–31 and 1950–51. Insignificant numbers of theology students are included in the figures for letters and sciences; students in faculties or schools of pharmacy are not separately listed, but are included in the totals for all university students. Also included among university students are foreigners (7 percent in 1891, 13 percent in 1910–11, 22 percent in 1930–31, and 7 percent in 1950–51) and women (10 percent in 1910–11, 27 percent in 1936, and 40 percent in 1961). For years 1854–56, 1865–66, and 1875–76, medical doctorates, and *licences* awarded in law, and in letters and sciences, are related to age year twenty-two. Adding *agrégations* in letters and sciences, *capacités* in law, and *officiers de santé* in medicine would not have altered the rounded figures actually tabulated.

For Prussia (secondary enrollments and *Abiturs* through 1910–11) *and Germany* (all other figures), total secondary enrollments (including girls for 1930–31 and 1950–51) are related to the nine-year age group eleven through nineteen (both sexes), and corresponding figures for the *Abitur* are related to age year nineteen. University enrollments are related to the four-year age group nineteen through twenty-three, which probably understates university access slightly through 1875–76, and certainly overstates it somewhat for 1930–31 and 1950–51. (The sizes of relevant age groups for 1865–66 are estimated, not directly available.) Students in arts and sciences are those in faculties of "philosophy" or in subjects typically taught there (including pharmacy). Significant enrollments in faculties of theology (Catholic and Protestant) are not separately listed, but are included in the totals for all university students. Also included among university students are foreigners (7.5 percent at *Prussian* universities in 1900–3; 4 percent at German universities in 1931, and 7.5 percent at German universities in 1961) and women (2.5 percent at German universities in 1911; 21 percent and 16 percent at all German university-level institutions, respectively, in 1931 and 1951). The German technical institutes were not considered university-level institutions until 1899.

Not covered by the table are the French *grandes écoles* and related institutions (e.g. *écoles nationales d'arts et métiers*), French private or religious institutions of higher education (*grands séminaires*, Institut Catholique), and various German academies (relatively low enrollments and not considered university-level institutions until the interwar period, at the earliest).

France and Germany are similarly related to a four-year age group, although this procedure is only roughly justified by what is known about average durations of university study in the two countries at various times. If these limitations are kept in mind, however, the indicators in table 1.1 can safely be assigned an analytical signifi-cance that unrefined data would lack.

With respect to French secondary education, evidence not repro-duced in the table would clearly indicate that enrollments and baccalaureate awards as of 1840–42 were certainly no higher, and were probably somewhat lower, than they had been in 1831, in 1809, and even on the eve of the Revolution of 1789.[29] Thus, in a system that had been essentially stable for over half a century, the first notable increases in enrollments and baccalaureate awards took place during the 1850s and 1860s. The expansion of the 1850s was essentially confined to the private secondary schools, which bene-fited from the privileges granted them by the Falloux Law of 1850. The much more abrupt upswing of the 1860s occurred at the introduction of the "special" secondary program between 1863 and 1865. Thereafter, from the mid 1860s to the First World War and even into the 1920s, French secondary enrollments rose very little, in relation to the age group, although a gradually increasing propor-tion of the age group completed their secondary schooling and earned the baccalaureate. In fact, as more detailed breakdowns would show, what growth there was during this period took place exclusively in the "special" or "modern" secondary branch, which was simply superimposed, in effect, upon an unchanging classical mainstream.

The increase in French secondary enrollments and baccalaureates between 1910–11 and 1930–31 was due partly to further growth in the modern stream, and partly to the full accreditation of girls' secondary education during the 1920s. At the same time, a new set of structural changes began even before 1930 and accelerated during the 1930s and 1940s. In this further transformation, the barriers between classical and modern secondary schooling were somewhat reduced, and even formerly higher primary and full-time vocational schools were partially integrated into the secondary system. Much of the change was nominal, not real, since visible differences of academic and social standing continued to distinguish the traditio-nal forms of secondary education from their younger competitors. Nevertheless, a substantially increased share of the age group did earn baccalaureates of one sort or another by 1950–51, and a new set of relationships was thus established between the educational system and the white-collar hierarchy of the late industrial society.

The data on the French university faculties in table 1.1 indicate a striking stability in certificates and enrollments per age group from the 1850s to the 1880s. The faculties of letters and sciences awarded very few degrees before the 1870s, remaining narrowly confined to their function of examining baccalaureate candidates and certifying future secondary teachers. As a result, the numerically dominant faculties were the professional ones, particularly those of law and medicine. In the early industrial environment, in other words, French university education consisted almost exclusively of training and certifying institutions for the legal and medical professions. French legal and medical enrollments in fact grew substantially from the 1880s to the interwar period and through the Second World War. But the most dramatic change registered in table 1.1 is the explosive expansion of the French faculties of letters and of sciences from the late 1870s on. The *rate* of increase in enrollments was in fact greatest between 1876 and 1911, although growth continued at a more moderate pace to the end of the period covered in the table. What happened during the decades after 1876, obviously, amounted to a rapid and thorough transformation in the tasks performed by the non-professional faculties.[30]

Looking more closely at the relationships between French secondary enrollments, baccalaureates and university access percentages, one realizes that entrants to the secondary schools must always have been roughly twice as numerous as the "average" enrollments actually tabulated. Since up to half of all candidates typically failed the baccalaureate examination, much of the "weeding out" of pupils came rather late in their secondary career. In addition, the rate of early leaving was certainly significant as well, though apparently not as high as in the German secondary system. Until late in the nineteenth century, French baccalaureate awards were a good deal more frequent, in relation to the age group, than the rate of university certificates and enrollments. Thus the baccalaureate must have been held as a terminal degree by many students who chose not to go on to the professional faculties.[31]

The main purpose of table 1.1, of course, is to permit comparisons between the French and German (or Prussian) systems of secondary and higher education. And the first conclusion to be drawn from

such a comparison is that *in overall quantitative terms*, the two systems
were really rather similar.[32] Even the rhythms of change in education were not very different east and west of the Rhine. German
and Prussian data not reported in the table would demonstrate that
German university enrollments declined during the later eighteenth
century and reached a low point around 1801–5.[33] The recovery that
followed upon the Napoleonic wars and the civil service reforms in
Prussia reached a peak at 1830–31, a year that also saw particularly
high enrollments and *Abitur* awards in secondary schools. In fact,
recurrent concerns about the dangers arising from an over-production of educated men reached a crisis level in Germany during the
1830s and 1840s, just as similar anxieties were expressed, with less
obvious empirical grounds, in France.[34] In any case, German
university enrollments per population declined sharply during the
1830s, until they reached a plateau between 1840 and 1870 that is
adquately represented by the figures for 1865–66 in table 1.1.
German secondary enrollments and certificates per population also
declined during the 1830s, but then increased gradually from 1840
on. Nevertheless, it seems reasonable to interpret the plateau in
German university enrollments per population and age group
between 1840 and 1870 as a kind of early industrial equilibrium, and
to compare it to the relatively constant rate of French legal and
medical degree awards per age group during the decades around the
mid nineteenth century.

Secondary enrollments per age group increased somewhat more
vigorously in Prussia than in France from the mid 1860s to the
interwar period. But in Prussia as in France, these increases during
the high industrial period took place almost exclusively in the non-
classical sector of the system, while enrollments in the classical
Gymnasium stream remained essentially stable, in relation to the age
group, from the 1870s to the 1920s.[35] In Germany as in France,
public debates over the status of non-classical or partly classical
secondary programs during the late nineteenth century were accompanied by renewed anxieties over a supposed excess of educated men
and the danger of creating an "academic proletariat."[36] In Germany
as in France, finally, the interwar period witnessed the full accreditation of girls' secondary education, further substantial increases in
levels of inclusiveness, and another wave of concern over a supposed
overproduction of graduates during the 1930s.

One of the major differences between the French and German

indicators in table 1.1 reflects sharply divergent trends between about 1930 and 1950. In France, the educational reforms of the 1930s continued under the Vichy regime and into the postwar period. In Germany, the policies of the National Socialists and the impact of the Second World War retarded educational expansion. A postwar recovery had begun by 1950–51, but French levels of inclusiveness had not been reattained. As of 1950–51, moreover, the French secondary system had been enlarged in a partly nominal way by the integration of formerly higher primary and full-time vocational schools.

Secondary enrollments per age group were clearly higher in France than in Prussia around 1865, and what we know about earlier patterns in the two countries suggests that France in fact held a quantitative lead in secondary education throughout the first two-thirds of the nineteenth century. Even late in the century, the French secondary system produced more graduates, in relation to the age group, than its Prussian counterpart. The shape of the pyramid of secondary enrollments differed slightly in the two societies. Despite the high failure rate on the baccalaureate, a somewhat larger proportion of secondary students typically obtained the leaving certificate in France than in Germany during the nineteenth century. As a result, what advantage Prussia had over France in secondary schooling came after 1870, and was chiefly due to the continuous and vigorous expansion of the six-year *Realschulen* and of lower secondary education generally.

At the university level, the French system clearly produced more legally trained graduates than Germany until the 1870s, and again between 1910 and 1950. During much of the nineteenth century, this difference was undoubtedly due in part to the narrowness of the curriculum in the French faculties of letters and of sciences. Roughly half of French law students sought the *licence* in law as a kind of generalist degree, without intending to enter the legal professions.[37] From the late nineteenth century on, moreover, the French law faculties offered courses, as well as a doctorate, in economic, social, and political studies, so that the high enrollments per age group in the French law faculties of the early twentieth century were due in part to the expansion of the social sciences as a field of study within those faculties.

The most obvious differences between the French and German indicators in table 1.1, of course, reflect the fact that the French

faculties of letters and of sciences were little more than examining
boards for the secondary baccalaureate and for the teaching *licence*
and *agrégation* during the entire period from the creation of the
Napoleonic "University" to the late 1870s. This circumstance
certainly was of decisive significance, not only for the size and
character of the educated elites in nineteenth-century France, but
for the history of French science and scholarship as well. The
German "philosophical" faculties of the nineteenth century not only
fulfilled their institutionally primary function of educating future
secondary teachers in unique ways; they also transcended that
function relatively early in the century. Parallel developments in
France, by contrast, did not even begin until the late 1870s. One of
the consequences, obviously, was a crucial deficit in French university enrollments per age group, as compared to the corresponding
indices for Germany, that remained clearly visible until sometime
between 1890 and 1900.

Yet even this clear difference between the two systems should not
be overstated or misinterpreted. Thus the theory that German
industrialization was decisively aided by a strong system of secondary and higher education must be radically questioned, revised, or
even abandoned.[38] To sustain the theory at all, one would either
have to emphasize German lower secondary schooling toward the
end of the nineteenth century; or one would have to look more
closely at the graduates of the German faculties of "philosophy"
before about 1890. The German technical institutes were not nearly
as significant, from a quantitative and comparative perspective, as
has sometimes been thought. They are represented in table 1.1,
whereas the French *grandes écoles* and other non-university institutions of higher education were too diverse to be treated in a
summary table.[39] Yet it is clear that the German technical institutes
graduated a relatively small fraction of the age group before the
1890s. Both before and after that time, their output of graduates was
almost certainly matched or even overmatched by the Ecole Centrale, by the *écoles d'arts et métiers*, by any of a cluster of younger
technical schools created in France from the late nineteenth century
on, and as of about 1900, by the French faculties of sciences as well.
Moreover, even if it *were* possible to specify exactly when and where
Germany had significant educational advantages over France, it
would still be necessary to demonstrate that these advantages were
truly relevant to actual differences in the level, pace, or character of

economic growth in the two countries. It seems less and less likely that such a demonstration will succeed.

We thus return to a central thesis of this study. The development of secondary and higher education in France and Germany during the nineteenth century was not directly and functionally linked to economic growth. If anything, it was tied to the kind of bureaucratic modernization that received a new impetus, in France as in Prussia, at the beginning of the nineteenth century. It may also have been affected by state control of professional qualifications, especially in law and medicine. In any case, the educational systems of France and Germany developed in roughly parallel ways during our period, despite what differences there were in the levels and rates of industrialization in the two countries. In fact, if "the educated middle class" is defined to encompass all holders of secondary leaving certificates (the *Abitur* in Germany and the *baccalauréat* in France), then France and Germany had educated middle classes of approximately equivalent sizes from the early nineteenth century on.

Against this background of parallel developments and generally comparable magnitudes, a few statistical differences nonetheless stand out. Thus until late in the nineteenth century, France produced slightly more secondary graduates and substantially more university certificates in law, in relation to the age group, than its Prussian and German counterpart. Prussia and Germany, on the other hand, had a slight relative advantage in the six-year *Realschulen* of the late nineteenth century, and, above all, a highly developed system of university education and research in the arts and sciences that was not fully matched in France until around the turn of the twentieth century.

EDUCATIONAL SEGMENTATION AND THE FRENCH BOURGEOISIE

By far the best source of information on the social character of secondary education in nineteenth-century France is a survey conducted by the French Ministry of Education in 1864 that has been extracted from the archives by Patrick Harrigan, and that is briefly summarized in table 1.2. Within the limits of occasionally awkward categories, this valuable evidence gives us a glimpse of the French public secondary system as a whole, and of the early "special

Table 1.2 *Social origins and educational/occupational choices of French public secondary pupils about 1863 (Percentage by column)*

University level institutions and occupational groups	All secondary education		Special secondary only	
	IN	OUT	IN	OUT
Ecole Normale	—	1.5	—	0.5
Ecole Polytechnique	—	3.7	—	0.3
Mining (civil engineering)	—	1.7	—	0.1
Ecole Centrale	—	2.5	—	0.2
Arts and Métiers	—	1.9	—	6.4
Ecole Forestière	—	0.7	—	(—)
Officers/military schools	2.4	6.2	1.0	2.3
Law	6.4	12.3	0.6	1.6
Medicine	4.5	9.2	1.0	2.3
Other university-level education	—	1.7	—	1.6
Religion	0.3	2.0	—	—
Arts, writers	1.0	0.8	0.8	0.7
Subtotal	*14.6*	*44.2*	*3.4*	*16.0*
"Education"	2.3	1.7	0.4	0.2
Primary teachers	1.7	2.7	3.0	6.2
High(er) officials	1.6	0.1	—	—
Middle officials	1.0	0.3	2.0	0.7
Lower military	1.3	4.6	1.2	5.7
Subtotal	*8.9*	*9.4*	*6.6*	*12.8*
"Propertied"	17.0	2.8	13.5	3.4
Industrialists	2.9	0.7	—	—
Engineers	0.5	0.3	3.6	1.0
Large merchants	9.7	2.8	7.4	2.4
Subtotal	*30.1*	*6.6*	*24.5*	*6.8*
"Industry"	1.3	3.3	—	—
Railroads	0.1	0.3	1.2	4.2
"Commerce"	7.3	13.4	8.8	17.0
Shopkeepers	7.0	2.3	10.7	5.1
White collar	7.8	6.8	5.8	10.8
Subtotal	*23.6*	*26.1*	*26.5*	*37.1*
Clerks	1.7	4.4	2.8	8.5
Farmers	12.3	7.3	21.4	11.4
Artisans	6.1	2.0	12.5	6.9
Workers	1.9	0.4	2.4	0.8
Subtotal	*23.0*	*14.1*	*39.1*	*27.6*
Absolute Total known (100%)	12,603	6066	1548	1849

Source: From Patrick Harrigan with Victor Negila, *Lycéens et collègiens sous le Second Empire: Etude statistique sur les fonctions sociales de l'enseignement secondaire publique d'après*

secondary" stream as well. At the time of the survey, students leaving the small special program after at most four years of study typically went into "commerce" (17 percent) or agriculture (11 percent), or into various intermediate or lower-level white-collar positions (11 and 9 percent, respectively). The vast majority of students in the secondary system as a whole, of course, were enrolled in the classical stream. Among them, about 44 percent proposed to continue their studies, or actually continued them, beyond the baccalaureate, at the university faculties and *grandes écoles*, while 23 percent became large merchants, or entered "commerce" or other white-collar occupations.

Among the fathers of all secondary students, 17 percent were *propriétaires*, members of the upper and upper-middle classes, who, as we said, owned varying but substantial amounts of landed or urban property and/or securities. Since an additional 10 percent of fathers were large merchants, and 3 percent were industrialists, the older propertied and the currently active portions of the economic upper middle class jointly accounted for 30 percent of students. The liberal and educated professions, including fathers in "Education", were represented at 17 percent, or about equally with the *propriétaires* alone. Taken together, the economic and educated upper middle classes thus accounted for nearly half of all secondary students. The intermediate layers of the economic middle class were represented by a further 24 percent of the sample, while 13 percent of the fathers were farmers, 9 percent were artisans and clerks, and only 2 percent were workers.

l'enquête de Victor Duruy (1864–1865), (Paris, 1979), pp. 18–21, 27–30, and tables 1, 8, 9. The IN columns report the occupations of students' fathers; the OUT columns cover the educational or occupational plans of students as of 1864, as well as the educational institutions or occupations actually reached by students who left the secondary schools (most of them with the *baccalauréat*) from the late 1850s to 1863. Harrigan used a code of 96 basic educational/occupational *categories* to record both fathers' occupations and students' goals, along with a summary code of twenty eductional/occupational *groupings*. I have partly rearranged Harrigan's groupings to specify certain distinctions, insofar as Harrigan's (and the source's) basic categories themselves made this possible. The grouping "white collar" as used in this table covers a cluster of predominantly private white-collar employees of a middling or unspecified level, while the grouping 'clerks' represents the French *employés*.

The differences of social origin between the special secondary program and the secondary system as a whole provide a perfect example of socially *vertical* segmentation. The students in the special stream were recruited from a perceptibly lower portion of the social hierarchy than those in the classical stream, or those in the system as a whole. Dividing the tabulated percentages for the special curriculum by those for all secondary education, one can calculate a whole series of indicative ratios. Thus, among the parents of pupils in the special secondary stream, the liberal and educated professions were most markedly underrepresented, at ratios of 0.1 for law, and 0.2 for medicine, for "Education," and for the highly educated as a group. Less-pronounced underrepresentations or slight overrepresentations, with ratios between 0.8 and 1.1, characterized the middle and higher officials, the economic upper middle class, and the lower portions of the white-collar hierarchy. Notable overrepresentations can be calculated for "Commerce" (1.2), shopkeepers (1.5), farmers (1.7), primary teachers (1.8), and artisans (2.0). Obviously, the special secondary curriculum was markedly more progressive in its recruitment than the larger and more prestigious classical branch. Though quite small as of 1864, the non-classical sector of French secondary education clearly attracted a disproportionate share of students from lower middle-class families, who would probably have been prevented from entering the classical program by the practicalities and risks involved, and by a kind of social distance from the esoteric world of the traditional secondary schools.

Even so, the French secondary system of 1864 as a whole cannot be considered particularly progressive or "democratic."[40] In the French census of 1872, the liberal professions, magistrates, and secondary and university professors jointly made up around 1 percent of the working population, while all business owners and wholesale merchants accounted for 4.4 percent, and the propertied and *rentiers* for another 4.8 percent.[41] No matter how one interprets and "matches" the socio-economic categories of the census with those of the student survey, one has to come up with very large overrepresentations for the economic upper middle class, and with even larger ones for the educated and professional elite.

To be sure, the English "public schools" of the early nineteenth century were decidely more aristocratic than the French *lycées* and *collèges* of the 1860s.[42] But comparisons with Prussia provide a rather different perspective, and a more pertinent one. Thus among parents of about 1,600 pupils in selected but roughly representative Prussian secondary schools around 1800, according to K. E. Jeismann, some 40 percent were civil servants (all ranks) or members of the educated professions (including officers); another 33 percent were clergymen and secondary teachers; 2 percent were landowners; 6 percent were merchants and manufacturers, and 19 percent were noncommissioned officers and soldiers, primary teachers, artisans and workers, farmers and day laborers.[43] What stands out about these figures is the very low share of 6 percent for the propertied and entrepreneurial upper middle class, which accounted for 30 percent of fathers in the French survey of 1864. The place of this group was taken in Prussia by additional representatives of the *Bildungsbürgertum*, by Protestant clergymen, and by remarkably large contingents of secondary teachers and civil servants of all ranks.

A similar comparative conclusion seems warranted by a report on the social origins and career plans of the roughly 85,000 pupils who graduated from all Prussian secondary schools between 1875 and 1899.[44] Among these, fully *three-quarters* meant to enter the liberal and learned professions, including the high civil service, the church, secondary and university teaching, and the officer corps, whereas a mere *4 percent* clearly intended to take positions in industry and commerce. The comparable figures in the French survey of 1864 were *less than half*, and more than *25 percent*, respectively!

Among the fathers of Prussian secondary graduates, 22 percent were members of the educated middle class, including 6 percent who were Protestant clergymen; 8 percent were landowners and industrialists; and 21 percent were merchants, shopkeepers and innkeepers. Here the corresponding percentages in the French survey of 1864 were 17 percent for the educated middle class without clergymen; 30 percent for *propriétaires*, large merchants and industrialists, and 23 percent for "Industry," "Commerce," shopkeepers, and white-collar employees. On the other hand, at least 20 percent of the Prussian fathers were middle- and lower-ranking civil servants and primary teachers, a figure that cannot nearly be matched by any combination of corresponding categories in the French survey. Only the shares of farmers, artisans, and workers were of roughly equal size in the two samples, at some 18–20 percent in all. Thus altogether, secondary recruitment was almost certainly more progressive in Prussia than in France during much of the nineteenth century, although the two systems probably converged toward similar ratios after 1870. At the same time, the Prussian secondary schools appear to have had markedly less connection than the French *lycées* and *collèges* with an established economic upper middle class.

Interestingly enough, small portions of the Prussian graduates under discussion came from the non-classical *Oberrealschule* and the incompletely classical *Realgymnasium*, rather than from the numerically dominant classical *Gymnasium*. As in the French survey of 1864, one can therefore compare the social indicators to arrive at ratios of over and underrepresentation for various social groups. Some of what one discovers in this way can easily be described as socially *vertical* segmentation, in that groups higher on the social scale were predictably underrepresented in the *Realgymnasium* and especially in the *Oberrealschule*. At the same time, one can discern an element of what I call socially *horizontal* segmentation, in that "industrialists," for example, were actually overrepresented in the *Oberrealschule*, whereas the sons of primary teachers were underrepresented in this most "modern" of the three school types, although they would have to be ranked below the "industrialists" on a unilinear social scale.[45]

As has been suggested, this kind of horizontal segmentation reflects a difference between education-oriented and economy-oriented social groups at roughly comparable social "altitudes," or a horizontal articulation of society into sectors or strands that cut across the predominant pattern of vertically differentiated layers. In nineteenth-century France, the economically dominant elites held very strong positions in secondary education, which in turn sent graduates into the leading positions in industry and commerce, not only into the liberal and learned professions. In Prussia during much of the nineteenth century, by contrast, the traditional secondary schools were more rigorously separated from the economy, both in their recruitment and in the projected careers of their graduates. By the end of the century, moreover, the less prestigious "modern" schools in Prussia attracted disproportionately large representations from an emerging industrial middle class, and not merely from the lower regions of the social scale, as in France. The difference between the two patterns should not be exaggerated; for in France as in Prussia, it was the educated upper middle class, rather than the economic elite, which was most markedly overrepresented in the classical secondary program and in the secondary system as a whole.

Nevertheless, there was something like a divide between the educated and the propertied in Germany, whereas the French pattern can be *fairly* adequately described in terms of the vertical distance between the upper and the lower middle classes.

These impressions can be confirmed and further clarified by what data is available on the social origins of students at French university faculties and *grandes écoles*. Thus in the survey of 1864, secondary students who proposed to pursue university studies in law or medicine, or who had already begun such studies, came overwhelmingly from propertied as well as educated upper-middle-class families. Among prospective members of the legal professions, the indicative percentages were 37 percent for the liberal and educated professions, including "artistic professions" and military officers; 29 percent for the *propriétaires*; 10 percent for large or wholesale merchants and industrialists; and a round 75 percent for the upper middle classes generally. Among prospective physicians, the corresponding percentages were 37 percent (again) for the liberal and educated professions, 22 percent for the *propriétaires*, 11 percent for large merchants and industrialists, and a round 70 percent for the upper middle classes generally.[46] Considered in relation to the census, these are huge proportions.

Figures for the leading *grandes écoles* of the nineteenth century are equally drastic. At the Ecole Polytechnique, according to Terry Shinn, the transformation of "special" into "modern" secondary education after 1880 produced a substantial shift in a progressive direction. Comparing students who entered the school between 1848 and 1879 with those who entered between 1880 and 1914, one obtains the following percentages for the fathers' professions.[47]

	1848–79	1880–1914
Liberal professions and high officials	37	20
Propriétaires and entrepreneurs	52	38
Middle and lower officials	7	20
Shopkeepers and artisans	4	10
"Popular classes"	1	11

Before 1880, in other words, nearly 90 percent of students at the Ecole Polytechnique came from upper-middle-class backgrounds!

For the Ecole Centrale, John Weiss has summarized a more detailed account of students' social origins in the following broad categories and percentages.[48]

	1830–47	1881–1917
Upper *bourgeoisie*	68	57
Middle *bourgeoisie*	16	21
Employees and lower *cadres*	4	14
Popular classes	10	7

It was the same general pattern, although the Ecole Centrale ranked somewhat below the Ecole Polytechnique in academic and social distinction. There was a real change sometime after 1880; but before that time and to a more moderate degree afterwards, some of the leading *grandes écoles* were strongholds of the propertied and educated upper middle class.

Compared to the Ecole Polytechnique and the Ecole Centrale, the Ecole Normale was a socially unique institution. Its division for the natural sciences was a little more progressive in the origins of its students than the division of letters. Moreover, this school too experienced a shift in a progressive direction during the late nineteenth century. Looking beyond these distinctions, however, one can arrive at the following summary of Robert Smith's data on the fathers of students who entered the school between 1868 and 1909 (in percentages).[49]

Liberal professions	12
Higher officials and commissioned officers	8
Owners of capital and businessmen	13
Secondary and university professors and administrators	19
Primary and vocational school teachers and administrators	9
Middle and lower officials and white-collar employees	19
Artisans, shopkeepers, tradesmen	6
Lower classes	14

The unusual elements in this distribution are not only the substantial percentages for the lower-middle and lower classes, but also the very high representation of academics and teachers. Nearly 30 percent of students' fathers were professional educators, while only 3 percent belonged to the economic upper middle class. Indeed, the Ecole Normale was almost certainly the most purely "academic" institution in Europe, and that is what really set it off from its chief rival, the Ecole Polytechnique.

Much of what has been said about the *grandes écoles* can be put more precisely, though at the cost of a sharp change of chronological focus. During the late 1950s, French statisticians began to report on the fathers of university students in a well-articulated set of socio-occupational categories resembling those of the French census of 1954. In the early 1960s, a government report applied the new scheme to the *grandes écoles* as well. It thus became possible to construct a systematic survey of students' social origins for all of French higher education. The interest of such a survey is not overly reduced by changes in the social character of the French educational system between the late nineteenth and the mid twentieth century. The traditional *grandes écoles* in particular remained small elite institutions, even while the university faculties took in substantially increased fractions of the age group.

Of course there have been changes in the occupational census, and in certain key social classifications as well. The ubiquitous *propriétaires* of the nineteenth century have essentially disappeared, although a residual category of "*rentiers*, without profession" has continued to be used, in the distributions of students' fathers, if not in the census of the "active population." On the other hand, the so-called *cadres supérieurs* and *cadres moyens* have become very significant classifications, encompassing executive and middle-level white-collar workers and experts in the public as well as the private sector.

Table 1.3 summarizes some of the most significant distributions of fathers' occupations for all sectors of French higher education around 1961–63 in the new system of classifications. At the bottom of the table, the summed percentages for the liberal and learned professions are added to those for the industrialists and executive employees to yield indicative percentages for the educated and economic upper middle classes, taken together. Since the census percentages are listed at the left of the table, the opportunity ratios for all social groups and institutions can be quickly calculated or estimated. Looking at the university faculties alone, for example, one can see at a glance that the faculty of law ranked somewhat below the faculty of medicine by the early 1960s. At the same time, a more substantial social distance separated the two professional faculties from the faculty of letters. Though not covered in the table, the faculty of sciences resembled the faculty of letters, while the percentages for French university students generally fell between those for law and those for letters.[50]

Among non-university institutions of higher education, as the table indicates, the traditional *grandes écoles* stood well above the university faculties in the social origins of their students: The representation of the upper middle classes at these elite schools

Table 1.3 *Social origins of students at French university-level institutions, 1961–63 (Percentages by column)*

Fathers' occupations and (percentage of 1954 Census)	University faculties, 1963				Selected Grandes Ecoles, 1961–63						
	Law	Medicine	Letters	All Faculties	Normale	Poly-technique	Centrale	Instituts Politiques	Commerce	ENSI Chemistry	Arts and Métiers
1. Liberal professions (0.6)	11	20	7	10	7	16	7	15	8	7	3
2. High officials (0.4)	6	8	6	7	7	19	16	11	8	10	6
3. Professors (0.9)	3	4	4	4	33	8	4	3	1	3	2
1–3 Summary (1.9)	*20*	*32*	*16*	*20*	*47*	*43*	*27*	*29*	*17*	*20*	*11*
4. Teachers (2.0)	3	3	6	5	14	9	5	3	2	5	5
5. Middle officials (1.1)	7	6	7	7	5	3	6	7	6	7	6
6. Agriculture (26.8)	6	3	8	7	1	1	2	8	4	5	6
7. Industrialists (0.4)	5	3	2	3	2	5	3	8	12	5	4
8. High white collar (1.0)	7	6	5	6	4	14	20	15	17	10	8
9. Commerce (7.7)	8	9	10	9	5	6	7	8	17	10	6
10. Middle white collar (2.8)	6	4	7	6	7	3	7	3	6	7	8
11. Artisans (3.9)	3	3	5	4	2	2	2	3	3	4	9
12. Low white collar (10.9)	7	7	8	7	5	8	9	8	5	11	10
13. Workers (38.9)	5	4	11	9	3	2	2	3	5	8	19
14. *Rentiers* without profession (—)	8	7	10	8	4	1	6	3	5	5	5
15. Others (2.6)	16	3	6	7	1	3	4	2	1	3	3
16. Unknown (—)	1	10	—	2	—	—	—	—	—	—	—
1–3, 7–8 Summary (3.3)	*32*	*42*	*23*	*29*	*53*	*62*	*50*	*52*	*46*	*35*	*23*

ranged from 62 percent at the Ecole Polytechnique to some 50–53 percent at the Ecole Normale, the Ecole Centrale, and the former Ecole Libre des Sciences Politiques. The higher commercial schools followed with an upper middle-class percentage of 46, and with particularly high representations not only for industrialists and executive employees, but also for commerce and for middle-level white-collar employees. The higher commercial schools are now generally considered *grandes écoles* in a wider sense of that term, and so are such schools of engineering (ENSI) as those for electricity, aeronautics, and chemistry. The upper-middle-class representation at the ENSI for chemistry in 1961 was a good deal lower than it was at the higher commercial schools; but it still exceeded 29 percent, the comparable indicator for the university faculties. Only the now so-called Ecoles Nationales d'Ingénieurs Arts et Métiers ranked some-what below the university faculties in the social origins of their students. They should really be considered the apex of the French system of full-time vocational education, although they are now clearly university-level institutions.

The columns on the Ecole Polytechnique, the Ecole Centrale and the Instituts d'Etudes Politiques in table 1.3 typify what might be called the integrally *bourgeois* character of some of the traditional

Sources: Ministère de l'Education Nationale, *Informations statistiques*, vol. 69 (1965); *Les Conditions de développement, de recrutement, de fonctionnement et de localisation des grandes écoles en France* (La Documentation Française, 1964); INSEE, *Recensement général de la population de mai 1954: Résultats du sondage au 1/20ème, Population active, 1: Structure professionnelle.* "Professors" includes secondary teachers (along with "literary and scientific professions" *in the census*); "High white collar" covers engineers as well as administrative *cadres supérieurs* in the private sector, although the engineers are not separately mentioned in the survey of students; the same is true of "technicians" in relation to *cadres moyens*; "Low white collar" encompasses private commercial, as well as public and private office, clerks (*employés*); "Workers" includes small percentages of public employees and of servants (*personnel de service*); "Others" is further described *in the census* as encompassing artists, clergy, and the military and police. The faculties of pharmacy and of sciences are not separately treated in the table; the faculty of sciences resembled that of letters in the social origins of its students. The schools listed as *grandes écoles* (with the number of institutions surveyed in each case) are: Ecoles Normales Supérieures (two, including the one at Sèvres, which prepares teachers for girls' secondary schools), Ecole Polytechnique (one), Ecole Centrale des Arts et Manufactures (one), Instituts d'Etudes Politiques (five, including "Sciences-Po," the former Ecole Libre des Sciences Politiques), Ecoles Supérieures de Commerce (twelve), Ecoles Nationales Supérieures d'Ingénieurs (ENSI) for chemistry (fourteen), Ecoles Nationales d'Ingénieurs Arts et Métiers (six). For details, see Ringer, *Education and Society*, pp. 344–348.

grandes écoles. In modern French usage, the word *bourgeoisie* does not refer loosely to the entire "middle class," or to the intermediate social strata actually termed *classes moyennes*. It certainly does not have the specifically entrepreneurial connotation associated with the Anglo-American notion of a commercial and industrial "bourgeoisie." Instead, it describes the highest altitudes in the social hierarchy, the "upper class" or "upper middle class." It also typically implies a three-fold *conjunction* of social advantages that encompasses wealth and economic control, social influence and political power, as well as the high status or *distinction* associated with a quasi-aristocratic style of life.[51]

To see the reality behind this idea of a thrice-blessed *bourgeoisie*, one only has to look at the Ecole Polytechnique. The students of that academically and socially distinguished institution had already passed through the best secondary schools and the select and expensive preparatory courses before reaching the school. After graduating from it, they became not only elite military officers, but also high public administrators, technologists, and business leaders. Among the students' fathers, high officials and members of the liberal professions were hugely over-represented; but so were industrialists and executive employees. Thus the Ecole Polytechnique was not much more progressive and just as *integrally bourgeois* in its recruitment during the early 1960s as it had been during the late nineteenth century.

The former "Sciences-Po" and other Instituts d'Etudes Politiques typically prepared their students for the highest positions in the civil service.[52] Though not quite as exclusive as the Ecole Polytechnique, they were even more balanced in their recruitment from the several subgroups *within* the upper middle class. Similarly, the Ecole Centrale drew almost as large a share of its student body from the families of high officials (*cadres supérieurs*, public sector) as from those of executive-level business employees (*cadres supérieurs*, private sector). Here again, the notion of an *integrally bourgeois* pattern of recruitment seems appropriate.

In the early 1960s as during the late nineteenth century, the Ecole Normale was a kind of "academic" antithesis to the integrally bourgeois *grandes écoles*. This remarkable institution drew 47 percent of its students, more than the Ecole Polytechnique, from the liberal and learned professions. Its total for the upper middle class was 53 percent, the second highest in the table. Yet one could hardly describe the school as a bourgeois stronghold. After all, almost one-quarter of its students came from lower-middle-class backgrounds, and almost half had fathers who were university professors, secondary *professeurs*, and primary teachers. As during the late nineteenth century, the Ecole Normale thus stood out not so much for its progressive as for its overwhelmingly "academic" recruitment.

Among students at all university-level institutions in the German Federal Republic as of 1963, and among students of law, of the humanities, and of technological subjects at these institutions, the following percentages had fathers in selected socio-occupational groups.[53]

	All fields	Law only	Humanities	Technology
Medicine and other liberal professions	14	18	10	11
High officials	9	16	9	8
Secondary and university teachers	6	5	8	4
Learned and liberal professions	29	39	27	23
Big businessmen and executive employees	23	22	20	28
Workers	6	4	7	6

To compare these percentages with those in table 1.3 is obviously to run the risk of taking differences of categorization for genuine differences of recruitment. The German figures were not reported in the terminology of the German occupational census, so that they cannot easily be converted into opportunity ratios. The two societies differed somewhat in their occupational structures in any case. On the other hand, the quantitative differences between the French and German patterns were substantial, so that a few comparative generalizations may justifiably be attempted.

As of the early 1960s, it is probably safe to conclude, the German system of university-level education *as a whole* was somewhat less progressive in its recruitment than the French university faculties *considered alone*. We know that the French faculties were a good deal more inclusive than the German system at that time. We also know of at least two occasions when increases in the inclusiveness of French secondary and higher education probably engendered real gains in progressiveness as well. The first such change began during the 1880s, with the stepwise accreditation of "modern" secondary schooling and the explosive expansion of the faculties of letters and sciences. The second transformation occurred between the late 1930s and the late 1950s, with the integration of the former higher primary and full-time vocational schools into the French secondary system. Certainly this second wave of change had no full counterpart in Germany, where educational growth was checked by the policies of the National Socialists. Thus the German educational system, almost surely the most progressive in Europe during the early nineteenth century, had lost that rank by the 1960s.

To understand this reversal is to recognize, again, that the German universities of the early nineteenth century were extensively patronized by all sectors of the *Bildungsbürgertum*, including intermediate and lower-ranking officials and teachers, whereas the French professional faculties and *grandes écoles* of that time were largely, if not wholly, in the hands of the propertied and established bourgeoisie. In the expanding German universities of the late nineteenth and early twentieth century, the relative representation of the *Bildungsbürgertum* declined, but many of the new places were taken by the propertied and entrepreneurial upper middle class (*Besitzbürgertum*), which now entered the system in force. As a result, there was little net increase in the relative representation of the lower middle and working classes.[54] In fact, the high industrial convergence between the educational and the occupational hierarchies tended to move the German pattern of university recruitment closer to the French bourgeois model. In French higher education, and specifically in the rapidly growing faculties of letters and of sciences, on the other hand, the relative representation of the lower middle classes rose somewhat more markedly than it did in Germany, both after 1880 and after 1930, and the results are plainly visible in the comparative figures for the early 1960s.

In its internal articulation, the German system of the early 1960s was characterized by relatively mild and predictable differences between the pre-professional fields of study and the humanistic subjects. This part of the German pattern was closely paralleled in France. The French faculties of letters and of sciences once differed markedly from the faculties of law and medicine, but these differences had been much reduced by the mid twentieth century. Much more specifically characteristic of the German system, on the other hand, was the social distinction between university studies and the subjects typically taught at the technical institutes. Though itself no more than a muted echo of a formerly sharper division, this social distinction had no parallel in France. It should be noticed that the German economic upper middle class of the early 1960s was more strongly represented in "technology" than in law or in the humanities, whereas the learned and liberal professions were relatively underrepresented at the technical institutes. In a way, therefore, the distinctiveness of technology as a field of study entailed something like a socially horizontal segmentation in German higher education.

In France around 1960, by contrast, the Ecole Polytechnique stood at the very apex of the educational hierarchy. It was a partly technical school, but it drew its students from all sectors of the upper middle class. Even such younger technical schools as the ENSI for chemistry clearly outranked the university faculties of letters and of sciences in the social origins of their students. Thus the *grandes écoles* generally remained a socially elite sector of the French system, a bourgeois preserve that was not much affected by the "democratization" of the university faculties. The Ecoles Nationales d'Arts et Métiers, to be sure, were much more progressive in their recruitment than other sectors of French higher education. But even this instance of segmentation in the French system was almost totally vertical. It reflected the social distance between the upper middle classes on the one hand, and the lower middle and working classes on the other, whereas the social place of the German technical institutes faintly recalled a divide between the educated and the economic sectors *within* the middle and upper middle classes.

In sum, the German data cited throws into even sharper relief the three major traits of the French educational system that have held our attention. These are the sharp and socially vertical distinctions between most of the *grandes écoles* and the university faculties, particularly those of letters and of sciences, which largely undercut the "democratic" consequences of progressive recruitment in the faculties; the integrally bourgeois character of the Ecole Polytechnique and other traditional *grandes écoles*, which tended to absorb advanced education into the conjoined attributes of a thrice-blessed *bourgeoisie*; and the contrast between the Ecole Polytechnique and the Ecole Normale, which embodied an antithesis between the *bourgeois* and the *professeur* that took the place of a wider tension between property and education in modern France.

In table 1.4, these structural traits of the French educational and social system stand out in a further comparative perspective. The table describes large and random samples from two leading contemporary biographical dictionaries, one French and the other German. Entries considered are males born between 1800 and 1899, who are

Table 1.4 *University-level education of French and German elites, 1830–1930*

(a) French elite groups

Occupational categories	(percentages by Column)	University-level education: percent by row							
		No Uni-level	Type Unknown	Law, Letters	Medicine, Sciences	Polytech-nique	Normale	Other Grandes Ecoles	Religious, Military
Writers, arts, scholars	(23)	52	4	16	2	1	2	23	2
Academics	(16)	3	5	18	19	4	25	16	10
Clergy	(7)	14	2	4	—	—	1	2	78
Military, landowners	(19)	17	—	—	—	25	—	—	58
High officials	(5)	14	18	44	1	8	—	12	3
Politicians	(7)	51	3	32	3	3	2	3	3
Lawyers	(4)	—	22	96	—	1	—	1	—
Medicine and other Liberal professions	(6)	1	2	1	89	1	—	5	1
Entrepreneurs, Technical professions	(9)	25	5	5	8	28	3	25	1
Other, unknown	(3)	61	7	13	6	—	—	6	8
All Groups	(100)	25	4	16	10	9	5	12	19

(b) German elite groups
University-level education: percent by row

Occupational categories	(percentages by Column)	No Uni-level	Type Unknown	Law, Humanities, Theology	Medicine, Sciences	Technical Institutes	Professional Academies	Military Academies
Writers, arts, scholars	(13)	28	5	38	9	2	19	—
Academics	(45)	3	4	40	45	4	4	—
Clergy	(4)	31	2	66	2	—	—	—
Military, landowners	(3)	56	3	14	1	2	—	24
High officials	(8)	9	13	43	7	11	7	—
Politicians	(4)	28	8	60	2	1	1	—
Lawyers	(1)	—	13	88	—	—	—	—
Medicine and other Liberal professions	(3)	—	6	1	93	—	—	—
Entrepreneurs, Technical professions	(15)	42	8	7	19	15	8	—
Other, unknown	(3)	59	2	23	7	3	5	—
All Groups	(100)	18	5	35	29	6	7	1

classified in terms of their occupations and their university-level educations, if any. Of course, the criteria of eminence used by the editors of such encyclopedias are not really specified, and probably cannot be; the judgments made in the process of selection are partly

Note: The table reports on random samplesfrom the leading French and German biographical encyclopedias. In the case of the incomplete *Neue Deutsche Biographie*, vols. 1–4 (Berlin, 1953–1964), all entries for males born 1800–99 through Grasman (N: 2366) are considered. The *Dictionnaire de biographie française*, vols. 1–10 (Paris, 1933–61), also incomplete, treats more persons per letter more briefly than its German counterpart, so that coverage was restricted to entries at least twenty-five lines in length for males born 1800–99 through Dallière (N: 2953). "Writers, Arts, Scholars" includes all full-time writers outside the sciences, journalists, editors and publishers, along with the creative and performing arts, and a few private scholars or intellectually active "*rentiers*." "Academics" includes academic secondary school teachers, librarians, and archivists. "Military, landowners" are predominantly officers, though a few are owners, managers or lease-holders of large estates. "High officials" includes judges and diplomats. "Politicians" covers full-time elected politicians, whether national or local, along with leaders of political parties and labor unions. "Medical and other liberal professions" are owners, managers, and (rarely) executive exployees of large enterprises, along with somewhat smaller contingents of scientists, engineers, inventors, explorers, architects, and technicians who were not *explicitly* linked with business or the academic world. "Other" is made up chiefly of such "non-elite" occupations as farmers, shopkeepers, artisans, and lower-level civil servants. "No University-level education" means that no *attendance* was specified at institutions considered of university level around 1930, except that university-level education was assumed in the legal and medical professions in which it was required. "Type unknown" consists mostly of indivuduals who were said to have "finished their studies in Paris," or "studied at Heidelberg and Berlin."*In section a*, around four-fifths of cases under "Law, Letters" are law students, just as about four-fifths of those under "Medicine, Sciences" studied medicine or (in a few cases only) pharmacy. "Ecole Polytechnique" includes individuals who went on from that institution to various "schools of application." The category of "Other Grandes Ecoles" is dominated by the higher art and music schools (125 cases); but it also encompasses the Ecole des Chartes (55 cases), other high-level scholarly institutions in Paris (15 cases), "Sciences-Po" (11 cases), the Ecole Centrale (29 cases), and a cluster of less-distinguished technical, professional, and higher commercial schools (43 cases). "Religious, Military" covers the higher seminaries, theological faculties, and the Catholic Institute, together with the military schools, chiefly Saint-Cyr and the Ecole Navale. *In section b*, "Law, Humanities, Theology" includes the social sciences as well. "Medicine, Sciences" also includes pharmacy, dentistry, and mathematics, along with a handful of cases of university study of business. "Technical Institutes" covers the "polytechnical" ancestors of these institutions as well. "Professional Academies" encompasses art, music, and other professional and technical academies (mining, agriculture, forestry) other than the technical institutes. For details, see Fritz K. Ringer, "The Education of Elite in Modern Europe," *History of Education Quarterly*, vol. 18 (1978), pp. 159-172.

subjective. On the other hand, such judgments are neither gratuitous choices, nor are they based on merely individual opinions. In addition to the objective circumstances in which eminence was achieved, they reflect a partly collective sense of what constitutes eminence in a given social world. Thus, from a rather special perspective, the samples that will be described do tell us something about the role of education and of the educated in that world.

At the left of both sections of the table, the occupations of the eminent biographees appear as percentages by column. One is not surprised to find that entrepreneurs and members of the technical professions were more numerous in the German than in the French sample. These men would have been active between about 1830 and 1960, a period when industrial development based on advanced technology was probably more characteristic of Germany than of France. A notable feature of the French sample was a high proportion of lawyers and of parliamentary politicians, many of whom were in fact politically active lawyers. The disproportionate size of the law faculties and the prominence of parliamentary politics seem to account for this characteristic of the French elites. Much more surprising is the large number of military officers among eminent Frenchmen of this period. Many of them were members of landed and aristocratic families. Perhaps the visibility of colonial exploration and conquest during the late nineteenth century also contributed to this pattern. In Germany, despite the social importance of the officer corps as a whole, military men and landowners made up only 3 percent of the sample. Apparently then, there can be a difference between the visibility of eminent individuals and the recognized importance of an institution.

Particularly pertinent to the concerns of this study are the figures for academics and for the "unattached intelligentsia" of writers, artists and private scholars in the two samples. Among Germans who achieved eminence sometime between 1830 and 1960, no less than 45 percent, or almost half, were university professors. Writers, artists, and scholars added another 13 percent, to bring the total for German intellectuals other than clergymen to 58 percent. In the French sample, the total for the two groups of secular intellectuals came to less than 40 percent, and among these the academics were much less prominent, at 16 percent, than the unaffiliated writers, artists, and scholars. Here is a double contrast that sheds light on the role of higher education and on the structure of the educated elites in the two countries. While the universities and university professors played an extraordinarily prominent role in German society, the academic community as a whole long held a relatively unimportant position in France.

At the same time, the typically most eminent French intellectual of the nineteenth century was the free-lance writer or publicist, rather than the research scholar or scientist.[55] Indeed, as the table indicates, this French "man of letters" often had no university-level education at all, although he probably held the secondary bacca-laureate. Perhaps the literary market, especially the network of intellectual journals for general audiences, was more highly deve-loped in France than in Germany. Perhaps, too, some talents that would have been attracted to academic careers in Germany found less fully institutionalized intellectual roles in France, whether as private scholars dependent on family incomes, as politically active writers, or as more purely literary men of letters. In any case, some of the most interesting data in table 1.4 reflect profound differences in the organization of intellectual life in the two societies that must have deeply affected the predominant styles of thought as well.

The last line in each of the two sections of table 1.4 summarizes the role of higher education in the formation of prominent Frenchmen and Germans during our period. As might be expected, a somewhat larger proportion of the biographees terminated their formal school-ing before the university level in France than in Germany. More-over, only about one quarter of the French elites had attended the university faculties, almost always those of law and medicine, while an exactly equal proportion had received their advanced education at the Ecole Polytechnique, at the Ecole Normale, or at a few other non-university institutions of higher education, not including purely military schools, higher seminaries and other theological centers. The relevant percentages are really quite remarkable, since the traditional *grandes écoles* enrolled only minute fractions of the student population. Almost two-thirds of eminent Germans were educated at the universities, many of them at the "philosophical" faculties. In France, by contrast, the Ecole Polytechnique alone accounted for almost as many of the biographees as the university faculties of medicine and of sciences combined! Among eminent French aca-demics, some 41 percent were graduates of the Ecole Normale or of other non-university institutions, as against only 37 percent who had attended any of the university faculties. The contrast with the

German pattern would presumably have been even sharper if the nineteenth century alone had been considered. Some 85 percent of academics in the German sample, as might be expected, had been educated at the universities.

The data on the entrepreneurs and technical professionals in table 1.4 will provide a final indication of the important role played by the *grandes écoles* in French society. In the German sample, over 40 percent of entrepreneurs and technologists had no university-level education at all; this is another symptom of the divide between the educated and the economic and technical elites in nineteenth-century Germany. Just under 20 percent of the German entrepreneurs and technologists had engaged in scientific university studies, while another 23 percent came from the technical institutes and professional academies. Among eminent French entrepreneurs and technical professionals, a considerably smaller proportion (25 percent) were without university-level education, and only 8 percent had attended university faculties of science. Over half had been educated at the *grandes écoles*, and the Ecole Polytechnique alone accounted for 28 percent of the group! Since the Ecole Polytechnique also trained one quarter of the French military elite and 8 percent of eminent high officials, it must have been an unusually versatile and immensely influential school. One can scarcely imagine an institution more characteristic of the relationship between elite higher education and *bourgeois* predominance in nineteenth-century France.

BOURGEOIS CULTURE AND THE INTELLECTUALS IN MODERN FRANCE

We cannot here review the extensive secondary literature on the French bourgeoisie, its historical origins and development, its general characteristics, and its relationship to education in particular. Nor can we pursue these questions into primary sources that would reach back at least as far as the seventeenth century. Instead, we will briefly review a few particularly interesting approaches to the subject that may serve as background for the discussions to follow in later chapters.

Thus Régine Pernoud has written a social and cultural history of the French bourgeoisie that draws extensively on literary sources, as well as on memoirs, social commentaries and legal treatises.[56] As

Pernoud sees it, the French bourgeoisie of the seventeenth century was an elite of notables with close connections to state service, and especially to the legal system. There were bourgeois merchants, of course; but much of bourgeois wealth was derived from office-holding, and from involvement in the French monarchy's semi-public tax and fiscal system. The *financier* was not an entrepreneurial capitalist, but a fiscal agent, and thus not sharply distinguished from any of the various types of *officiers* who owed their income and status to the alienated royal offices they held. Members of the judicial bourgeoisie who acquired strategic positions in the royal *parlements*, of course, were ultimately to satisfy their aspirations to aristocracy in the emergence of the *noblesse de robe*.

Charting the upper echelons of the Third Estate, a jurist of the early seventeenth century began by listing the "men of letters" in the four faculties of theology, law, medicine, and arts. Next came the *financiers*, identified by Pernoud as holders of offices relevant to the royal finances. Third on the list stood judges and lawyers, along with other members of the legal profession (*notaires, greffiers, procureurs,* etc.). The "merchants" (*marchands*) ranked fourth and really lowest among those clearly distinguished. For the rest of the town population followed in an undifferentiated mass of "lowly persons" (*viles personnes*), who lacked instruction (hence *le sot peuple*), who therefore held no offices, and who worked with their hands in occupations considered "dishonorable" (*déshonnêtes et sordides*), chiefly the artisanal trades, the despised *arts mécaniques*.[57]

The obvious importance of advanced education in this hierarchical scheme was most directly visible in the functional role of the law faculties, which provided access not only to the legal professions themselves, but also to the wider network of quasi-public offices and "functions." Below this professional level, however, it was the secondary *collèges*, heirs of the old arts faculties, that truly shaped the French bourgeoisie and set it apart from the rest of the Third Estate. While the church was active in the education of the poor as well, the more distinguished full-length *collèges* of the seventeenth and eighteenth centuries were run by the Jesuits and other major teaching orders, and recruited their pupils in vastly disproportionate shares from the families of lawyers and doctors, large merchants, and *officiers* of various types.[58] The curriculum of the *collèges*, established by the Jesuits, was largely classical. The emphasis was less on philological reconstruction or on the historical sources themselves, than on selective emulation, Christian humanism, grammatical rigor, and formal clarity of thought. As Pernoud has pointed out, the classical ideal of ordered beauty was highly compatible with the Cartesian rationalism that became an almost proverbial attribute of the French bourgeoisie.

The educated bourgeois gentleman of the seventeenth century, as Pernoud has shown, was the *honnête homme*. In his occupation, needless to say, this idealized notable avoided the taint of *déshonnêteté*; but it was his education that really defined him. It made him not only more knowledgeable than "the people," at home in his cultural world and sustained by its values, but also more refined in his language and bearing, more dignified and "distinguished." His "outward" manner conveyed the "inner" balance of reason: prudence, moral self-restraint, and responsible moderation. These qualities also shaped his "manners," the forms of polite sociability that linked him with other men of high standing; for he conversed without shocking, with "civilized" control and ease.

In his brilliant history of modern Western manners and social types, Norbert Elias has contrasted the educated bourgeoisie of eighteenth-century France with the emerging educated middle class of eighteenth-century Germany.[59] In France, the *honnête homme* was also the *homme civilisé*. No great distance separated him from the social and cultural world of the French aristocracy. Whether as a man of letters or as a proponent of rational reform within the monarchical system, moreover, he could conceive the possibility of practical action for the public good. As a result, he adhered to an integral conception of progress that was embodied in the concept of *civilisation*. Introduced by the physiocrat Marquis de Mirabeau, *civilisation* came to stand for the totality of man's social and intellectual creations and arrangements. The word *culture* was used as well, but it had the narrower sense of *culture de l'esprit*, the development of the individual's intellectual faculties. *Civilisation* emerged as the more inclusive term, and it encompassed the softening or refinement of manners, the onward march of moral and intellectual enlightenment, as well as the improvement of social and political institutions.

In late eighteenth-century Germany, by contrast, a disjunction came to expression that had seriously troubled only Rousseau in France. The German poets, philosophers, and university scholars of that day were almost totally excluded from the aristocratic world of the small German courts, a world in which the brilliance of French classical *civilisation* was imitated but not equaled. At the same time, German middle-class intellectuals were effectively cut off from the prospect of practical social action. They accordingly developed a radical sense of the tension between outward civilization and "inner" culture. The realm of civilization, as they experienced it, was the realm of courtly conventions, of polite forms that were often superficial and sometimes in conflict with the more important qualities of the heart and mind. These qualities they came to associate with their own sphere of *Kultur*, of earnest moral reflection and serious art, of self-cultivation and inner growth, of education and scholarship. Thus *Kultur* came to signify the unfolding of man's intellectual, moral and artistic creativity, which seemed more important than outward *Zivilisation*, and unrelated or even opposed to it.

In 1784, Kant first explicitly distinguished between civilization and culture, identifying civilization with good manners and social niceties, culture with art, learning, and morality. He thought his age was civilized almost to excess, without being truly cultured. This underlying distinction between morality and manners was certainly informed by the social distance between the middle-class intellectuals and the aristocracy, or between university culture and courtly civilization. Yet as Elias has pointed out, this social distance also contained a national contrast in embryo. As the German intellectuals began to press their claim that the middle-class culture they had helped to create was German culture generally, the civilization of the German courts came to seem foreign, and its French origins took on a new significance. With the rise of German cultural nationalism, France thus ultimately came to stand for *Zivilisation*, as Germany was identified with the cause of *Kultur*. Indeed, much of Elias' work can be understood as an attempt to clarify an almost habitual set of associations that was much discussed and misused on both sides of the Rhine during and after the First World War. By that time, to be sure, the German usage of *Zivilisation* had been enlarged to include technology, another form of "outward" progress that was widely perceived as a threat to culture.

Returning to early nineteenth-century France, we catch a glimpse of French classical humanism and of its relationship to industry and technology in John Weiss' insightful history of the Ecole Centrale.[60] Following Napoleon's lead, the Restoration stripped the French secondary curriculum of most of the modern and scientific elements

that had characterized the revolutionary central schools. Mathematics retained a place in the higher grades; but the emphasis was
overwhelmingly on Greek and Latin, and even the methods were
those of the pre-revolutionary *collèges*. Indeed, the selective and
emulative approach to the classical sources, the attention to taste
and to formal perfection of expression, strongly recalled the social
and cultural type of the *honnête homme*. So firm was the belief in the
formative virtues of the classics for the dominant social groups that
more practically oriented studies, when considered at all, were
automatically associated with "intermediate" schooling for the
lower middle classes. Victor Cousin, the official philosopher of the
French University under the July Monarchy, charted the cultural
mission of the educated bourgeoisie under the headings of the True,
the Beautiful, and the Good.

There were those who objected to this program and to the
exclusive reign of the classics. During the 1830s and 1840s, such
scientists as Jean-Baptiste Dumas argued the case for a scientifically
oriented secondary curriculum.

The University knows that the study of letters can form the heart, exercise
the mind, and elevate the soul; it now must be convinced that the well-
directed study of the sciences has the same effects, and that it adds one more
advantage of its own, that of forming men ready to take their place in the
movement of progress and to contribute by their personal success to the
development of the wealth of France.[61]

The view that the sciences had a broadly educative value was based,
for Dumas and for other leading scientists of the day, on a commitment to scientific empiricism as a model of intellectual enlightenment. The emphasis on the social utility of science, moreover,
addressed the concerns of a wider constituency as well. Progressive
industrialists, entrepreneurial liberals and followers of Henri Saint-
Simon could all agree on the importance of science and technology
for industrial productivity. Indeed, this conviction made them
spokesmen for the emerging entrepreneurial wing of the upper
middle-class, or even for a more inclusively conceived society of
industrial "producers" (*industriels, producteurs*). The question was
whether their educational preferences could compete against the
deeply entrenched ideology that was beginning to express itself in
the contrast between mere practicality and "general culture" (*culture
générale*).

The answer to this question was contained in the history of the

Ecole Centrale itself. The classical secondary curriculum was not displaced or seriously modified until the end of the nineteenth century. Thus students seeking access to the scientific *grandes écoles* had to pass through all or most of the classical program before preparing for the scientific portions of the *grandes écoles'* entrance examinations, which emphasized mathematics at the expense of the experimental sciences, and which typically required one or two years of post-secondary studies in specially designed preparatory courses. This pattern was ultimately maintained even by the Ecole Centrale des Arts et Manufactures, although it had been privately founded for the express purpose of training industrial scientists and engineers. Thus, the sponsors of scientific secondary education failed to assert themselves against the heritage of the *honnête homme*. As classicists, the graduates of the Ecole Centrale escaped the taint of the *arts mécaniques*, and the school itself became a socially elite institution. In this respect, it far outstripped its closest counterparts in other European countries. But its success was not a victory for scientific empiricism or industrial utility. It was a rather one-sided compromise, for it tended to integrate the leadership of the entrepreneurial middle class into the social and cultural hierarchy of the traditional bourgeoisie.

The cultural critique of bourgeois life by nineteenth-century French men of letters is the subject of Cesar Graña's *Modernity and Its Discontents*.[62] Graña deals primarily with the writings and letters of Stendhal (Marie Henri Beyle), Gustave Flaubert, and Charles Baudelaire. While several of the texts he considers stem from the 1850s and 1860s, he assigns great historical importance to the 1830s and 1840s, and especially to the bourgeois regime of the July Monarchy. He notes that the industrial revolution reached France during this period. While factories were few, certainly fewer than in England, contemporaries were nevertheless struck by the advent of the machine, by substantial increases in coal and steel production, and by innovations in agriculture as well. They also observed the difficulties experienced by artisans, shopkeepers, and smallscale producers generally, and they were frightened by the emergence of an uprooted urban working class. They could not help but notice, finally, that the politics of the July Monarchy resembled those of a trading company, being designed to maximize the profits of its narrow electorate of *propriétaires*.

The intellectual life of the period was affected by the rapid growth of a commercial market for literature, which in France was highly centralized in Paris. Newspapers paid unprecedented sums to serialize the novels of popular authors. The importance of a large middle-class reading public had first become clear in England, and yet between 1830 and 1848, twice as many journals of ideas appeared in Paris as in all of the British Isles.[63] Some French journals, to be sure, were short-lived. Young men who came to Paris to study law or medicine typically found these professions overcrowded and expensive to enter; or they decided for more personal reasons to pursue the grander vocation of the intellectual publicist.

Literary periodicals, Alexandre Dumas *père* explained, had their genesis when a literary man without books met a doctor without patients and a lawyer without clients over a dinner to be paid with their last pennies. What to do? The answer was simple; start a journal. Paper and printing could be had on credit. Gall and *esprit* they already had.[64]

If this was an exaggerated account, it nonetheless captured the contrast between great expectations and radical insecurity in the literary life of the epoch. The writer had been liberated from aristocratic patronage, as well as from the norms of the classical tradition. He could see himself as a demigod, the unconstrained creator of a new intellectual world. But this vision also engendered anxieties; and above all, it contrasted sharply with the writer's market dependence upon the average tastes of an anonymous middle-class public.

In this context, as Graña points out, many intellectuals and artists from middle-class backgrounds turned against the class of their origins. Some found spiritual homes in radical reform movements, in social romanticism, and in other forms of identification with the people. But there was also another, more immediately personal and aesthetic revolt against middle-class outlooks, and this is the revolt that interests Graña. He writes about the ideological significance of "bohemian" life, about the idealization of the unintegrated gypsy, and about the "dandy" as a symbol of aesthetic discipline. Turning more particularly to Stendhal, Flaubert, and Baudelaire, he calls attention to an aristocratic ideal in their writings, an ideal of spiritual excellence that shaped the vocation of the French *homme de lettres*. Under the July Monarchy, the hierarchic order of the Old Regime was overtly replaced by the economic and political predominance of the bourgeoisie. At precisely the same time, a literary critique of modern society emerged that was directed less against capitalist exploitation than at the moral and cultural poverty of middle-class life, at the bourgeois as a philistine.

There was a two-fold irony in this conjunction. The literary critics of the middle class were its own sons, and their critique exposed much of what the middle class must have felt about itself. For especially in France, the established bourgeoisie tended to deny or to disguise its real origins.

The bourgeoisie had risen through its customary dedication to self-improvement and market efficiency. But while these virtues made it powerful, it did not make it self-assured. For, after reaching a certain eminence, it always turned to the cultural props of the aristocracy as a means of overcoming the homeliness and provinciality of outlook which tradition regarded as the taint of the middle-class soul. In spite of its triumphs, therefore, the bourgeoisie had not been able to produce a style of life capable of commanding universal admiration – that is to say, of setting the standards of cultural achievement and etiquette for the society as a whole ... The history of anti-bourgeois sentiment has been, in nearly all its forms, the history of defectors from the middle class, who in the struggle to live with the consequences of their secession, have worked to create a new order worthy of their approval.[65]

One of the main themes in the French literary critique of middle-class life is an allergic reaction to useful employment in pursuit of gain. Baudelaire claimed that only the priest, the warrior, and the poet were worthy of respect; the rest of mankind was "born for the stable, that is to say, to practice what they call professions." "To be a useful person," he wrote, "has always appeared to me to be something particularly horrible."[66] The desire to escape from the culture of capitalism here remains purely personal. There is no objection to the impoverishment of others, so long as they can be dismissed as "born for the stable."

Stendhal saw a connection between Calvinism and business acumen. "Love of money," he wrote, was "the great lesson of Calvinism." But he noticed that acquisitive skill did not beget any pleasurable use of the wealth it created ... Not only did the business spirit diminish the prospects of happiness. It undermined the proper basis of the social order. Businessmen did not distinguish between their rising material power and its legitimate function. They had, so to speak, "failed to keep their place."[67]

The emphasis on pleasure here is more universal in its implications than Baudelaire's perspective, and so is the objection to the confusion of means with ends.

Julien Sorel, Stendhal's protagonist in *The Red and the Black* is almost a stock character of the 1830s, part of "a whole class of young men who, born to an inferior position in society and, so to speak, oppressed by poverty, have had the luck to obtain a good education and the audacity to mingle with what the rich in their pride call society." The rich suspect "that Robespierre's return was made possible chiefly by young people from the lower classes who had been too well educated." Yet paradoxically, Julien is also a "natural" aristocrat, and not only because he has a fine mind. Stendhal describes him as a "proud and noble soul." He is brave, impetuous, and quick to defend his honor, but also sensitive and easily moved by inhumanity: "a fine plant . . . with age, he would have come into an easily touched benevolence." Even the provincials whose children he tutors cannot resist the force of his personality. When he stands up to leave a dinner, "everyone rose, in spite of decorum; such is the power of genius." The society in which he finds himself is not only oppressive and avaricious, but also hypocritical and incurably mean-spirited; its goals are trivial and ultimately pointless. Hoping to construct his life as a more significant narrative, Julien dreams of high adventure, of prowess and honor. And this, of course, is what leads to his ruin.[68]

None of the writers discussed by Graña placed much hope in politics, in social reform, or in the people. In this respect they differed from the utopian socialists and social romantics of the 1830s and 1840s. Flaubert saw no point in "the raising of the working class to the level of stupidity attained by the bourgeoisie." The prophets of social reform struck him as "philosophic-evangelical vermin."

They were a novel breed of pedestrian fanatics ("bookkeepers in delirium"), afire with the trivial vision of satisfying mass appetites and the fearful one of destroying "all individual initiative, all personality and all thought . . . A sacerdotal tyranny is at the bottom of these narrow hearts."[69]

On occasion, Flaubert recommended a purely aesthetic protest against his age, and in a rhetoric that smacks of the dandy.

Let us enlist ourselves in the cause of the ideal. Since we no longer have the means of dwelling in marble halls and covering ourselves with the purple, to rest upon divans stuffed with hummingbird feathers . . . or to read by emerald-encrusted lamps, let us cry against imitation silk, desk chairs, economy kitchens, fake materials, fake luxury, fake pride. Industrialism has developed the ugly to gigantic proportions.[70]

Yet in Flaubert's *Sentimental Education,* this yen for an ancient and distinguishing form of luxury too is submitted to a merciless scrutiny, along with a whole gallery of what are taken to be futile responses to the desolation of bourgeois society. The social revolutionary becomes a policeman for the reaction, of course, and kills the only uncorrupted worker we have been allowed to admire, who in turn is a good-hearted giant, deferential and almost impossibly naive. The prototypical young romantic continues to dream of an imagined self; but we are taught to see him as vacuous and self-indulgent, almost as incapable of real happiness as of undistorted perception, a contributor as well as a victim to the false appearances that surround him. The author's severity toward his protagonist suggests a strenuous exercise in self-criticism. And the only salvation that is implied lies in a discipline of aesthetic objectivity that may occasionally be rewarded by an experience of beauty.[71]

Obviously, there are limits to the sort of analysis offered by Graña, at least when it is applied to the work of a particular individual, and a highly reflective one. As an aggregate characterization of a social role, however, his account seems both plausible and empirically grounded. There is nothing surprising in the fact that a certain disenchanted view of bourgeois society drew much of its force from the sense that formerly existent human possibilities had been lost. One way to express that critical awareness was to contrast the self-expressive freedom of an idealized aristocrat with the narrowness of middle-class concerns. Another was to construct an asocial realm of pure experience in which absolute values were not denatured by the realities of the class society. In either case, the emphasis was not on the transformation of society, but on the preservation of the rare individual, and on the cultivation of spiritual excellence.

As portrayed by Graña, then, the French man of letters defined himself in antithesis to the *bourgeois.* Confirming instances are not hard to find, particularly for the early nineteenth century. Yet there certainly were other possibilities as well. Thus Jerrold Seigel has pointed to the ambivalence in the attitude of the intellectual "bohemian" toward the bourgeoisie.[72] Bohemian or not, the aspiring writer shared certain characteristic values and orientations with his supposed antipode. He was an individualist, and he believed in hard work and achievement. If the hardships he endured were ultimately compensated by success, a further assimilation to the emotional world of the bourgeois was a psychological possibility.

Certainly by the late nineteenth and early twentieth centuries, as we shall see, a certain type of established writer served as an unabashed spokesman for the *bourgeoisie*. His commitment was typically more to the cultural traditions than to the economic interests of the dominant class; but even that restriction was not absolute. I am thinking of someone like Ferdinand Brunetière, a thoroughly established essayist with connections to the more traditional literary journals, who became a leader of the anti-Dreyfusards and of conservative Catholicism around 1900. His case and others like it represent a role almost diametrically opposed to that observed by Graña for the early nineteenth century. This does not seem to me to undermine Granã's case; but it does tend to identify Graña's protesting bohemians as a chronologically specific and limited group within a social and intellectual field that encompassed other positions as well.

A more complete portrait of the French intellectual field – and of the French *bourgeois* elites of the late nineteenth century – may be found in two excellent recent studies by Christophe Charle. His main point about the *bourgeois* groups, specifically the business, the political, and the academic elites, is that they were more diverse in their social origins and more separated *from each other* by the turn of the century than they had been around 1860.[73] During the first three quarters of the century, an internally homogeneous and unified leading elite (*classe dirigeante*) of notables based its predominance on great wealth, and especially on landed property; it encompassed the aristocracy along with the upper ranks of the bourgeoisie. At the same time, this *classe dirigeante* dominated the intellectual and social life of the country, and it was thoroughly in control of the political system. This changed during the last quarter of the century in several respects. The elite groups in various sectors became somewhat more separated or autonomous in relation to each other. The Republic brought new social groups (*couches nouvelles*) into electoral politics, which took on a more professional character and became less dominated by notables. The intermediate layers of the middle class (*classes moyennes*), including currently active businessmen (as distinct from *propriétaires*), captured an increased share of the dominant positions; university faculty became professional researchers, and a generally greater emphasis on meritocratic recruitment greatly increased the importance of advanced educational qualifications.

What Charle writes about the *classe dirigeante* of the period before 1880 is entirely consistent with what I have tried to suggest about the "thrice-blessed bourgeoisie." Throughout most of the nineteenth century, it was as unique to France as the *Bildungsbürgertum* was to Germany. Its gradual replacement after 1880 coincided with the generally increased interaction between the educational and occupational systems in the major European countries, with the advent of the economic upper middle class in German secondary and higher education, and with the gradual convergence of the French and German educational systems toward each other. Charle's argument is also consistent with what we know about French student numbers and social origins. For secondary enrollments per age group increased steadily after 1850 and especially after 1860. The rise of "special" and modern secondary schooling really did produce a modest opening of the educational system to new social groups. Recruitment to some of the *grandes écoles* became mildly but noticeably more progressive sometime after 1880. At the same time, the faculties of letters and of sciences began their remarkable expansion during the late 1870s. There can be little doubt about the role of education, and of a partly meritocratic ideology, in this whole transformation.

Among the specific elite groups studied by Charle as of 1901, the 209 faculty members of the Parisian university faculties and other institutions of higher education are particularly interesting. What Charle finds noteworthy about the social origins of this elite is the relatively strong representation of the educated classes. Only 10 percent of the fathers were *propriétaires*, industrialists, large merchants, bankers, and the like; almost 27 percent were members of the educated and academic professions: doctors, secondary and university teachers, artists and writers, journalists, archivists and librarians; just over 13 percent were high officials and members of the legal professions; not quite 16 percent belonged to the intermediate ranks of the middle class (*bourgeoisie moyenne*); 10 percent were middle-level civil servants, and some 23 percent ranked with the lower middle and working classes.[74]

Although Charle's sample encompasses the professional faculties, there is a certain similarity of social recruitment between this academic elite of 1901 and the Ecole Normale of the nineteenth century. Indeed, this is not surprising. Until late in the century, the graduates of the Ecole Normale were in fact the elite of French secondary teachers, and of professors in the faculties of letters and of sciences as well. There was no sharp separation between the functions and career patterns of secondary teachers and those of their colleagues in the faculties of letters and of sciences. The highest positions in the more distinguished secondary schools were as prestigious as chairs in some of the faculties, particularly the provincial ones. A *lycée professeur* might jointly hold an appointment in a faculty, or he might be "promoted" to a faculty, where he would spend much of his time examining baccalaureate candidates. It was only after 1880 that holders of chairs in faculties of letters were routinely expected to engage in research – or that some of their students aspired to careers other than secondary teaching.

The German university professors of the nineteenth century were clearly set apart from German secondary teachers. Their great prestige was derived partly from their role as research scholars and scientists, and partly from their control of an examination system that gave access to positions of power outside as well as inside the academic world. Professors in French University faculties of letters and of sciences, by contrast, long remained advanced secondary teachers, or teachers of secondary teachers, even if they had attended the Ecole Normale and earned the *agrégation*. All this was changing during the late nineteenth century, but of course change was not instantaneous. Thus even during the late nineteenth century, both French Normaliens and French university faculty in letters and sciences were probably recruited somewhat lower on the social scale than their German colleagues, who typically came from the upper layers of the *Bildungsbürgertum*. In comparison with other French elite groups, however, French academics generally were rich in cultural capital and ever more plainly poor in economic capital. Thus a social divide opened between the academic and the other elites in France during the late nineteenth century that somewhat resembled the old contrast between the Ecole Normale and the Ecole Polytechnique.[75]

Changes in the social makeup and role of French intellectual groups were particularly rapid and socially visible during the 1890s. Secondary graduates reached the universities in growing numbers, while reforms and scholarship opportunities in the faculties of letters and of sciences helped to provoke fears of an "academic proletariat." Charle also charts large increases in the population of artists, writers, and publicists after 1870, which probably led to overcrowding and contributed to a new recessionary crisis in the literary market during the 1890s.[76] By that time, French "men of letters" rarely fit the model suggested by Graña. For on the one hand, the French literary field now encompassed an "establishment" of writers certified by the literary academies, a publicly accepted school of "psychological" novelists, and such fashionable literary critics and journals of opinion as Ferdinand Brunetière and the *Revue des Deux Mondes*. On the other hand, the rejection of politics by Flaubert and others during the Second Empire gave way by the 1890s to a new wave of social criticism and political engagement on the French intellectual left. Along with symbolism and literary modernism, vaguely "anarchist" sentiments attracted members of the literary avant garde, while socialist sympathies gained ground among university students and young scholars in the Latin Quarter, especially at the Ecole Normale. It was a perfect setting for some of the intellectual conflicts that will concern us in the chapters to come.

The defining role of education for the French bourgeoisie of the twentieth century, finally, is the central theme of Edmond Goblot's *La barrière et le niveau*, which has attained the status of a minor classic since its first publication in 1925.[77] As a *lycée professeur*, Goblot taught philosophy in the highest grades of French secondary schools during the decades before the First World War. He was not a trained historian or sociologist, and he may have taken certain appearances too much at face value. Yet he developed a kind of phenomenology of French social relations that seemed to echo Max Weber on education and status, and to anticipate Pierre Bourdieu on cultural capital.

The modern French bourgeoisie, Goblot argues, is a social "class," rather than a legal or hereditary caste. It is "open" in the sense that it encompasses a portion of new arrivals, the *parvenus*, even while it continually loses a few of its members, the *déclassés*, through downward social mobility. As a class, however, the bourgeoisie is a social reality, and this essentially by virtue of collective opinions, of unanalyzed, "prelogical" and even unconscious social judgments. Thus all the advantages of the bourgeoisie stem from the fact that it is unthinkingly *supposed* to be superior *as a class*; its dominance is due to an attributed quality, the all-important *considération*, a form of social status or prestige. At the same time, one becomes a bourgeois by adopting a bourgeois manner of life. For it is characteristic of the bourgeoisie that it keeps up appearances, along with the distances that separate it from the domestics, tradespeople, and shopkeepers who serve it. The bourgeois avoids work that is subservient, dirty, strenuous, repetitive, or merely manual. Like the Chinese mandarin, he signals his station in the conditions of his hands; his ideal is the life of the *rentier*. Or at least he works only to conceive and direct what others carry out. Perhaps he thus draws on traditions (*survivances*) from Antiquity and Christianity that elevate the intellectual and spiritual above the mechanical and material.

Goblot concedes that a minimum of wealth is necessary to sustain a bourgeois existence, but he believes that the socialists unduly stress this element in the equation. He distinguishes between an upper (*haute*), a middle (*moyenne*) and a petty (*petite*) bourgeoisie; but the gradations between these three subgroups strike him as downright elusive in comparison with the absolute divide between the bourgeoisie and the "popular classes" (*classes populaires*). In France, he points out, the term *classes moyennes* is typically used to encompass the lower portions of the bourgeois spectrum, along with the more well-to-do elements of the popular classes. The difficulty is that many a member of the petty bourgeoisie lives in greater economic need than many a prosperous artisan or peasant. Since the impoverished bourgeois nevertheless remains recognizably a member of his class, it cannot be money that sets him apart. At first glance, occupation seems a more likely source of class distinctions. The liberal professions, certainly, are quintessentially bourgeois, and no bourgeois would allow himself to stray too far in the directions of the "trades" (*métiers*). Still, a young man is clearly bourgeois before an occupation is chosen for him that will suit his social status and thus avoid the danger of *déclassement*. In short, Goblot insists, wealth and profession may rank a man, but they do not class him. They tend to place him on a continuous scale, rather than assigning him to a sharply delimited group. The bourgeoisie, however, depends upon an unmistakeable demarcation, a barrier that will visibly separate it from the popular classes.

This barrier, according to Goblot, is supplied by education, or more precisely by "the education that classes," as distinct from the education that simply develops personal capabilities. Along with a relatively short course of primary schooling for the popular classes, modern European educational systems offer a general and non-utilitarian form of secondary education as a prelude to more specialized university-level work. Those who complete the full course of secondary and higher studies cannot begin to earn a living until about age twenty-five. Their deferred wages and educational expenses represent a considerable investment, a kind of "human capital." Now the modern French bourgeoisie has always been "capitalist," Goblot argues, in its propensity to accumulate this form of capital. Even modest bourgeois families have gone to extraordinary lengths to send their sons to the *lycées*, and thus to insure their bourgeois status. And what they have sought is an education that classes, which is why the dominant model of secondary schooling as *culture générale* has always been based on Latin as an outward sign of social distinction.

As an educator, Goblot finds the so-called "question of Latin" easy to resolve in principle. Latin does indeed provide access to a fascinating and admirable civilization. As a language, it has educative value in that it differs sharply from our own. It thus permits us to attain an intellectually fruitful distance from our habitual patterns of thought and expression. More generally, a literary form of general education addresses moral questions and schools the imagination in a way that science does not. On the other hand, a scientific *culture générale* is certainly possible as well. For science need not be represented as a compendium of applicable rules. It can be taught as an active pursuit of new knowledge, an exercise in originality as well as in intellectual rigor. Indeed, Goblot sees no reason to doubt that *both* classical literature *and* modern science could be much more intensively studied by the ablest *lycée* students than has been assumed. If the "Latin question" were a purely pedagogical one, it could surely be put to rest in this way.

The point, of course, is that it is not a pedagogical question, but a social one. This accounts for its difficulty, and for the heat with which it is debated. Latin, for many of its vocal champions, is above all a mark of "class." It must therefore be taught, however mechanically, to the entire bourgeoisie, and to no one else. When thinking of his interests as an individual, the typical bourgeois may actually grumble at the uselessness of the traditional curriculum. When defending the interests of his class, however, he wants a pointedly esoteric education, a cultural "luxury" that will prevent even the ablest graduates of higher primary schools from gaining access to the bourgeois professions. At the same time, the bourgeoisie cannot permit the secondary curriculum to become too much of an intellectual challenge; for that would expose too many of its sons to the danger of failure and *déclassement*. What the bourgeoisie seeks, in sum, is not an education that ranks, but one that classes. It *needs* the miraculous divide between the lowest pass and the failure on the baccalaureate. For the factitious equality it creates among those who pass, the *niveau*, is almost as important, socially, as the *barrière* between the *bacheliers* and the rest of the population.

Like other good theorists, Goblot somewhat overemphasizes the relationships that chiefly interest him. Surely the French bourgeoisie of his time was characterized not only by the outward signs of high social status, but also by the underlying realities of great wealth and power. The alienation of public offices under the Old Regime, as Pernoud has pointed out, made possible a peculiar form of capital that helped to shape the outlook of its holders. Under the bourgeois governments of the early nineteenth century, too, a professional education in law could be considered a sound economic investment, a potential road to political influence in the parliamentary system, and to the rather obvious financial rewards of such influence as well. Thus from the seventeenth century on, higher education in France was an integral element in the investment strategies of a class that also had plenty of time to develop the quasi-aristocratic aspirations of the *propriétaire*. As Weiss has shown, the traditional secondary curriculum of the early nineteenth century played a key role in assimilating younger, entrepreneurial, and technical elements of the upper middle class into the culture of the established bourgeoisie. Much earlier and more clearly in France than in Germany, in other words, advanced education functioned as a further component and outward mark of a consolidated bourgeois class position, a species of "capital," in Goblot's own terminology.

Against this background, Goblot is understandably fascinated by the symbolic and classificatory role of education in the maintenance of a bourgeois "style of life." In a French opinion survey of the late 1940s, according to Natalie Rogoff, just under 8 percent of respondents answered an open-ended question about their class affiliation by ranking themselves as *bourgeois*, above the *classes moyennes*, at the apex of the social hierarchy. And 78 percent of these *bourgeois* cited "style of life" as the basis of their self-definition.[78] Goblot is right, too, in identifying advanced education as a crucial source of the vertical distance between the bourgeoisie and "popular classes." Characteristically, his attention is not directed at the faculties of letters and of sciences, but at the training grounds of the legal and medical professions, and of course at the baccalaureate itself.

Goblot admirably conveys his sense that educational systems transmit hierarchic social meanings, status attributions that are "prelogical" and collective, and that must not be confused with the psychologically accessible decisions of individuals. He rightly takes these attributions to be more persistent and categorical than income distributions and, above all, than the social paths of particular agents. To dramatize the force of the symbolic fields involved, he invokes the image of the "mandarin," who never gets his hands dirty in strenuous or subservient work, who is more a *rentier* than a tradesman, and who vaguely elevates the intellectual and spiritual above the mechanical and material.[79] We will want to seek out the models for this portrait in the French education debates of the late nineteenth and early twentieth centuries. For the moment, we can accept it as a preliminary account of the French bourgeois "education that classes."

As a critic of that education, Goblot clearly believes in a more universally valuable alternative to it. Indeed, he writes as if to expose a fraud. Deemphasizing the dependence of status on wealth and power, he treats the preeminence of the French bourgeoisie as something like a false opinion, a claim to superiority that can be challenged and eradicated like any other error. If genuine *individual* superiority and commitment to culture were substituted for their factitious collective surrogates, he implies, then the whole "class" system would simply collapse. Under the truly republican governments of the Third Republic, he argues, the French educational system has become increasingly progressive. At the same time, the pretentions of the bourgeoisie have come under mounting pressure from "the critical spirit." False social distinctions have been further weakened by the experiences of the First World War; they cannot resist the force of truth much longer. The time is ripe for an educational system that develops all genuine individual capabilities, and that "ranks" without "classing." This is the optimistic and unabashedly meritocratic language of socially progressive educational reform in interwar France. On the basis of a rigorous and purely intellectual "selection" of students, Goblot suggests, the secondary education of the future will create an "open elite" of personal talent to replace the spurious "class" superiority of the bourgeoisie.

In taking this position, Goblot also communicates the self-respect and good conscience of a *professeur*, whose work has been misused in a bad cause, and who therefore strongly feels the contrast between the true vocation of the intellectual and the factitious culture of the dominant class to which he partly belongs.

If the modern bourgeoisie were superior in intelligence and culture, then those who have been called intellectuals since [the Dreyfus Affair] would form a class superior to the bourgeoisie, or else a subclass occupying a superior rank within the bourgeoisie. But that's not how things are ... The intellectuals are bourgeois, and of a low social rank ... The respect one has for them is somewhat equivocal: one doesn't know whether these professions are humble or superior, envied or disdained ... One finds it remarkable that such enlightened men should impose so much work on themselves for so little profit ... Upon reflection, all the same, one respects their disinterestedness. For intellectual work is at least partly disinterested ... Every secondary and university teacher [*universitaire*] feels some pride in thinking that the salary on which he subsists does not adequately represent the value of his services. The magistrate, the soldier, the priest share the same sentiment. The modesty of their situation seems to them a guarantee that they are not selling science and scholarship, justice, the sacrifice of their lives, the salvation of souls.[80]

Pursuing this part of his theme, Goblot notes that Flaubert and other French writers of the nineteenth century caricatured the "bourgeois" as the philistine, the epitome of narrow-mindedness and mediocrity. Though properly speaking bourgeois themselves, they castigated the intellectual and moral poverty they found coupled with the appearance of virtue. The implied contrast was with their own unconventional, personal, and total commitment to art and to ideas. On its side, the bourgeoisie has typically felt an almost instinctive distrust of the intellectuals. It has avoided the original and personal in art and thought, as if banishing a danger, and it has consistently adhered to the traditional and securely accredited. Its relationship to high culture has never been truly "disinterested"; for it has always been a pursuit of social barriers and marks of distinction.

CHAPTER 2

The meanings of education, 1

Imagine a social world in which all differences of wealth and power are purely accidental and thus totally divorced from the personal qualities of individuals. The difference between that world and the real one, it seems to me, is due largely if not wholly to education. For education can transform apparently accidental into apparently essential differences among members of society. The quality of being educated cannot, like wealth, be conceptually separated from the remaining characteristics of those who have it; the educated seem to differ from the uneducated in their whole being, essentially and not accidentally. There have been various ways of describing the personal effects of education, or of distinguishing "true" education from such inadequate surrogates as "merely practical training"; but all of these exercises in definition have rotated around the central idea that education can enrich the student's *whole person.*

In the European cultures and probably elsewhere as well, this enrichment results from interpretive engagement with educative texts. Modern European and American theories of education have their roots in the tradition of classical humanism, in which the study of the ancients was the royal road to a fully developed humanity. From the later nineteenth century on, the Greek and Latin classics lost their formerly dominant place in the curriculum of European secondary schools, and classical philology too gave up its primacy among the humanistic disciplines. Texts other than those of classical antiquity have come to be major elements in modern curricula. On the other hand, this shift away from the classics has not displaced textual interpretation as the vital core of liberal education. The natural sciences, of course, cannot be ignored. Yet it is hard to imagine an advanced education that is *not* centrally concerned with the interpretation of texts, including those originating in cultures or ages different from our own. To recognize that is also to see that theories of secondary and of higher education are likely to include models of textual interpretation, along with explicit or tacit guidelines for the selection of the texts to be studied.

The other general point to be made about theories of education is that they have typically been "ideologies," at least in the broadest sense of that term: they have been systems of only partly explicit beliefs that cannot be fully described apart from the institutions, practices and social relations in their environment. Education would presumably be central even in a perfectly egalitarian society; conceptions of education are partly visions of human perfection. Yet, since the societies we know have been hierarchic, and since education has been unequally distributed, conceptions of education have also typically been "ideologies" in the narrower sense of that term: they have been more or less conscious eternalizations of past social inequalities, and they have deepened present social differences by giving them meaning and symbolic force.

In any case, ideologies of education in both the wider and the narrower sense have occupied a central place in the consciousness of the European middle classes, and in modern social thought generally. They have helped to shape modern European conceptions of knowledge, of the person, and of the relationship between the individual and his culture. The purpose of this and the following chapters is to analyze ideologies of education as they came to expression in French debates over the future of secondary and higher education during the period from about 1890 to 1920. Before turning to this main subject, however, I want to provide some framework for a comparative approach to it. I will therefore begin by briefly considering the concept of *Bildung* as used in German academic circles from about 1890 to 1930, and I will then just touch upon Matthew Arnold's idea of "culture" as well.

"BILDUNG" AND ITS IMPLICATIONS IN THE GERMAN TRADITION, 1890–1930

The word *Bildung* in the German tradition means education in the large sense of self-development or "cultivation." A standard encyclopedia of the Weimar period provided the following definition:

The fundamental concept of pedagogy since Pestalozzi, *Bildung* means forming the soul by means of the cultural environment. *Bildung* requires:

(a) an individuality which, as the unique starting point, is to be developed into a formed or value-saturated personality; (b) a certain universality, meaning richness of mind and person, which is attained through the understanding and experiencing (*Verstehen und Erleben*) of the objective cultural values; (c) totality, meaning inner unity and firmness of character.[1]

This is how the term *Bildung* was actually used by German university professors in the humanities and social sciences during the late nineteenth and early twentieth centuries.[2] Certain features of the concept, however, are more fully articulated in a 1911 essay by the sociologist and philosopher Georg Simmel, from which the following passage is taken.

Every kind of learning, virtuosity, refinement in a man cannot cause us to attribute true cultivation [*Kultiviertheit*] to him if these things function . . . only as superadditions that come to his personality from a normative realm external to it and ultimately remain external to it. In such a case, a man may have cultivated attributes, but he is not cultivated; cultivation comes about only if the contents absorbed out of the suprapersonal realm [of objectified cultural values] seem, as through a secret harmony, to unfold only that in the soul which exists within it as its own instinctual tendency and as the inner prefiguration of its subjective perfection.[3]

Both of the cited passages distinguish a process of *Bildung* from its starting point in the individual, and from its end effect, the state of being cultivated, which is also called *Bildung*. To look more closely at the formulations actually offered is in some sense to ask about their "implications," with the proviso that we are not seeking strictly logical implications in a universal language, but looser relationships of analogy and affinity within a historically generated conceptual field. What, in this sense, did the concept of *Bildung* imply?

Both passages describe the process of *Bildung* as a relationship between a learner and a set of texts. The texts are objectively given; they make up a "suprapersonal" realm of "objective cultural values." The learner "absorbs" the "contents" of the suprapersonal realm to become a "value-saturated" personality. Obviously, the "understanding" or "experiencing" involved is more than analytical or intellectual: for the learner's whole being is affected. *Bildung* transforms a unique "individuality" into a unified "totality." Particularly Simmel insists upon the "secret harmony" with which the cultural contents "unfold" only what already "exists" within the soul. He writes that this harmony *seems* to obtain between the end state of "subjective perfection" and its anterior "prefiguration." The cultivated individual is at once a unified totality and in harmony with his prior "instinctual tendency." The teleological image of personal development as an "unfolding" implies a narrative of the movement toward perfection that becomes fully coherent only when perfection has been reached, and when the soul's preexistent tendency can indeed be identified as a "prefiguration."

One way to "translate" these sentences and to reduce the air of mystery that surrounds them is to follow the lead provided by the words *Verstehen* and *Erleben*. For they point to an interpretive or "hermeneutic" relationship between reader and text. This relationship can be conceived as a dialectic interaction, in that the reader must actively posit *possible* interpretations, which the text then "shows" to be more or less effective in clarifying and integrating what at first appeared obscure or incoherent. The more one stresses this active role of the reader in a dialectic of "understanding" or *Verstehen*, the less mystery there is in the "secret harmony" between the soul's "instinctual tendency" and what it assimilates on the way to perfection. Yet particularly the encyclopedia definition strongly suggests a more passive account of the interpretive relationship as a repeated "experiencing" or *Erleben*. Here the reader empathetically identifies with the author and reproduces or "relives" the inner states that gave rise to the text. Because he identifies in this way, he can be "saturated" with the values embodied in what he reads. As Max Weber pointed out in a related context, the canonical sources of the tradition have charismatic or magical qualities that enrich and elevate those who "make them their own."[4]

If most German academics were more or less consciously committed to the concept of *Bildung* from the late eighteenth century on, then much is explained that would otherwise remain merely given. Thus the German research university of the nineteenth century drew much of its vitality from a neohumanist enthusiasm that was focused more upon Greece than upon Rome, and that also inspired a new vision of education. The birth of the research seminar and the subsequent expansion of the "philosophical" faculties were linked to the emergence of the philological and interpretive disciplines, which initially shaped the dominant paradigms of exact scholarship or *Wissenschaft*. The systematic study of antiquity in German *Altertumswissenschaft*, though grounded in critical philology, aimed at a full interpretive understanding of the classical texts and, through these texts, of classical culture in its concrete historical reality. In nineteenth-century German historiography, what may be called the *principle of empathy* demanded that historical epochs be understood "in their own terms," or that past-minded historians "put themselves in the place of" the historical agents they seek to comprehend. In philosophy, the post-Kantian Idealists were dedicated to the image of *Geist* or mind unfolding and comprehending itself in its creations. The word *Geisteswissenschaft* did not come into common use until the later nineteenth century, but the interpretive and philosophical tradition that really defined it was of course much older.[5]

The neo-idealist revival of the *Geisteswissenschaften* that began with the work of Wilhelm Dilthey in the 1880s was not so much a new departure as an effort to clarify a well-established pattern of interpretive practice. Georg Simmel was a major participant in this effort, and the main difficulty it encountered was precisely the one just raised. To what extent is interpretation based upon the "reliving" of the experiences "behind" the text, and thus upon the reproduction of inner states? Does the interpreter bridge the distance between himself and the text by intuitively identifying with the author, or is interpretation a less subjective but more complicated procedure? Support for the latter view can be found in Martin Heidegger, in the late works of Dilthey, and of course in the more recent elucidations of Hans-Georg Gadamer.[6] Yet the tendency to construe the hermeneutic relationship as an empathetic *Erleben* has survived almost into our own day.

Along with the principle of empathy and the hermeneutic tradition more generally, the two cited passages imply what may be called the *principle of individuality*. For *Bildung* is the self-development of a unique "individuality," the "unfolding" from within of a distinctive potentiality. Nothing "comes" to the learner from "outside"; his perfection is the actualization of a pre-existent "tendency." Obviously, this conception of education differs radically, not only from any "socialization" of the learner by an external agent, but also from any mere "superaddition" of information or of analytical skills. The cultivated individual, too, is a unique and unified "totality." Almost literally incomparable, he cannot be defined merely by being located on a single, universally applicable scale of rationality. The fullness or wholeness of his personality transcends any "abstract" or "reductive" characterization that would make him a predictable agent in the manner of the utilitarian rationalist or of "economic man."

To be committed to this concept of individuality, whether in full consciousness or not, is to be guided toward certain analogous schemes of thought about change, about the relationship of the particular to the general, and of the individual to the group. Thus change is likely to appear as the development of a unique whole "from within," the teleological unfolding of a potentiality, or the actualization of a preexistent essence, not a "mechanical" rearrangement of identical constituent units. On the analogy of a symphony, a grouping is likely to be conceived as a patterned whole, a configuration of unique elements in particular relationships to each other, a higher unity-in-diversity, with a "total" quality of its own, rather than a sum of similar parts or even an aggregate of dissimilar components.[7] Something like this *symphonic analogy* came into play, for example, when German academics of the decades after 1890 addressed the crucial relationship between the cultivated individual and his national culture. Merely aggregative views of that relationship could not seem adequate, especially since the creative genius was seen as a unique embodiment rather than an average representative of his culture. The *symphonic analogy* could also be used to criticize a merely additive view of knowledge as a sum of facts, or to point up the presence of *Gestalt* complexes in psychic processes, in opposition to more "atomistic" accounts of these matters. In social studies, the analogy favored an emphasis upon the interpretable individual, upon networks of interpersonal relationships, and upon unique "wholes," rather than upon statistical sets of rational agents. In the German historical tradition, nation states and epochs as well as persons could be conceived as unique individualities, rather than as products of timeless laws. This view was codified in the philosopher Wilhelm Windelband's 1894 distinction between "nomothetic" and "idiographic" disciplines. A nomothetic discipline approaches its evidence with a view to subsuming it under general laws or regularities, whereas idiographic description focuses upon the unique and particular. Since a given historical situation is a unique constellation of unique particulars, moreover, historical change cannot even remotely resemble the lawful transformations of mechanics.[8]

In a 1923 essay, the historian Ernst Troeltsch identified the

"concept of individuality" as the heart of the German Romantic
critique of "the whole mathematical-mechanistic West European
scientific spirit."

[An individuality is] a particular concretion of the divine spirit in unique
persons and in suprapersonal communal organizations. The basic constituents of reality are not similar material and social atoms and universal
laws...but differing unique personalities and individualizing formative
forces . . . The state and society are not created from the individual by way
of contract and utilitarian rationality, but from the suprapersonal spiritual
forces which emanate from the most important and creative individuals,
the spirit of the people or the religious idea . . . [Similarly, humanity is] not
the ultimate union of fundamentally equal human beings in a rationally
organized total humanity, but the fullness of contending national spirits . . .
All [cultures] together in mutual complementation represent the totality of
life.9

The passage makes quite clear how the idea of individuality was
connected with distinctive schemes of change and of groupings. Like
Simmel and others, Troeltsch meant to confront the uniform calculating agent of the French Enlightenment, or of the English utilitarians and classical economists, with a less "atomistic," fuller and more
qualitative model of the individual, and thus also to justify a form of
cultural individualism that could be reconciled with the individual's
obligation to his community. At the same time, he hoped to
recommend a German view of the relationships among nations that
seemed more supportive of cultural diversity than "Western" conceptions of democratic internationalism. That was the point of his
emphasis upon "the fullness of contending national spirits." *Bildung*
implied diversity and symphonic fullness.

The idea of self-cultivation profoundly affected the German
concept of *Wissenschaft*, which broadly encompassed all systematic
disciplines, including the interpretive ones, of course. There was a
common belief that productive involvement in research usually
would, and certainly should, have the effect of *Bildung*. The original
scholar was meant to emerge from his activity enriched in mind *and
person*. In the late nineteenth and early twentieth centuries, this
expectation was also expressed in the recurring proposition that
Wissenschaft should engender *Weltanschauung*, a comprehensive and
partly evaluative orientation toward the world.10 The pursuit of
truth was to lead to something like integral insight and moral
certainty, or personal knowledge, or wisdom. Of course, there is

much to be said for the *hope* that some kind of convergence between *Wissenschaft*, *Bildung*, and *Weltanschauung* might ultimately take place, if only in a distant and perfect future. As an immediate and conscious aim, or as an ordinary standard for distinguishing adequate from inadequate *Wissenschaft* here and now, however, such visionary aspirations can be problematic. In any case, the yen to derive *Bildung* and *Weltanschauung* from *Wissenschaft* put a considerable burden on the ordinary life of the German universities during the decades after 1890.

Similarly strenuous was a traditional insulation of *Wissenschaft* from practical concerns. Although mathematics had a place in classical secondary education in Germany as elsewhere, hermeneutic studies clearly ranked as the primary source of *Bildung*. To the extent that *Wissenschaft* was linked to the objective of *Bildung*, therefore, practical and experimental knowledge was at least *theoretically* undervalued, and rather difficult to conceptualize. Laboratory science depends upon controlled intervention in an environment. Yet German treatises on *Bildung* and *Wissenschaft* rarely included positive references to practical activity. On the contrary, they usually inveighed against instrumental or "utilitarian" conceptions of knowledge, and they tended almost automatically to identify "pure" *Wissenschaft* as impractical.[11] It was as if a symbolic hierarchy extended downward from abstract theory to experimental or causal analysis, and finally to merely "technical" or "applied" studies. Of course one may reasonably oppose premature demands for applicable research results, if only because they will tend to produce poor scholarship and bad science. But it is a long way from such a position to the methodological absurdity of a *Wissenschaft* insulated from all human interests, including practical ones. The German research universities of the nineteenth century certainly benefited from their principled commitment to academic freedom. Yet they were generally less explicit in their defense of thorough criticism, heterodoxy, and intellectual diversity than in their repudiation of "utilitarian" infringements upon the theoretical "purity" of *Wissenschaft*.[12]

I shall say little here about the origins of *Bildung* as a concept, and I am skeptical of precise intellectual ancestries in any case. Of course one can follow Troeltsch in attributing the idea of individuality to the German Romantics, if not to Leibniz before them. Or one can trace elements in Simmel's account of the hermeneutic relationship to the influence of the post-Kantian Idealists. But even at best, the pursuit of such intellectual influences leaves one with a scattering of discrete connections between particular writers and particular readers, when one really wants to understand a tradition, a network of partly implicit beliefs and practices. In other words, there was a certain unity in the currents of thought that converged in Germany during the late eighteenth and early nineteenth centuries, and I suggest that the organizing principle behind this unity was an emerging set of partly conscious beliefs about education, interpretation, and learning. If that is true, then there is nothing surprising in the fact that Protestant and particularly Pietist notions of self-development helped to shape their more secular successors, or that German Romanticism differed in characteristic ways from its French and English counterparts, or that Schleiermacher was as much a hermeneuticist and an Idealist as a Romantic. Wilhelm von Humboldt is generally and rightly considered the intellectual founding father of the modern German university. But his theory of *Bildung* and of *Wissenschaft* was affected not only by the formal doctrines of German neohumanism and Idealism, but also by the pedagogical debates of his day, and by the philological and interpretive *practices* that converted the neohumanist impulse into a paradigm of systematic scholarship.

Even in France and England, education was an important intellectual issue during the eighteenth century, along with economic individualism and political rationality. In Germany, education became the predominant concern of the new intellectual stratum, while economic individualism remained a comparatively minor theme. Much fruitful research has been done in recent years on the emergence of *Bildung* as a newly influential concept by around 1800.[13] I am not expert enough to form an independent opinion of these matters. Nevertheless, I am convinced that beliefs and practices in education decisively affected the wider German tradition that took shape during the late eighteenth and early nineteenth centuries. The concept of *Bildung*, as I have tried to show, engendered cognitive dispositions that played a structuring role far beyond the formative field of discourse on education itself.

My other main historical point is that there was a change in the meaning of *Bildung* sometime between 1800 and 1900, a change that is best described as a shift from a forward-looking or "utopian" emphasis to a defensive or "ideological" one. Around 1800, the idea of self-enhancement through *Bildung* was, among other things, a socially progressive and universalist challenge to permanent social distinctions based on birth. Advanced education was not in fact available to everyone, but it seemed universally accessible to talent *in principle*. The emerging educated middle class could in good conscience regard itself as an "open" or "merit" elite, a new aristocracy of intelligence and personal worth. To speak for education was in some sense to speak for all men against unjust and humanly irrelevant social barriers. By around 1900 or 1920, in sharp contrast, advanced education itself had taken on the character of a distinguishing social privilege. With the full institutionalization of secondary and higher education and of the credentials system, educational qualifications had become routinized sources of social status. An established educated upper middle class now sought to check the influx of new social groups into the universities, and thus to reduce competition for places in the "academic" professions.

A color will look different against a changed background, and so it was with the meaning of *Bildung*. As its social environment was transformed, it took on an "ideological" aspect almost of its own accord. This was possible, I believe, because it always contained an ideological potential that merely had to be activated. To see this, one has to notice that the traits of the cultivated man are in fact very poorly defined. He is characterized by "a certain universality, meaning richness of mind and person." But what his richness actually encompasses can only be specified if he is imagined passively "saturated" by an unbroken tradition that can be itemized as a set of canonical texts. The only other *clear* definition that can be offered is the utopian vision evoked in Simmel's reference to perfection, to the full unfolding of a "prefigured" self. But can we actually say what such perfection consists of, or whether all possibilities of human fulfillment have truly been realized? To ask such questions is to show that the Utopia of *Bildung* takes on a specific meaning only as an *antithesis* or a "negation" of imperfections that *are* known. Our ordinary awareness is of an incomplete relationship to a tradition that is itself no longer, or not yet, fully coherent. We can imagine ourselves moving toward a state in which mere "cultivated attributes" give way to the integration attained in "subjective perfection"; but we can scarcely imagine the achievement of that sense of "totality." The concept of *Bildung* here plays the role of an orienting ideal.

The situation changes completely, however, if we suppose that there actually *are* cultivated men, and we then proceed to ask, not what their specific characteristics are, but merely how they differ from the rest of mankind. In answer we are told that ordinary men may indeed have "every kind of learning, virtuosity, refinement," but that these "cultivated attributes" function in their case as "superadditions" that "ultimately remain external" to their person-alities. In the cultivated man, by contrast, a "secret harmony" obtains between the "contents absorbed out of the suprapersonal realm" and the soul's anterior "prefiguration." The "secret har-mony" has here become a deeply mysterious difference between a "cultivated" and an "uncultivated" relationship to tradition. The cultivated man alone truly "owns" his cultivated attributes; he *is* and always *was* what he knows. One is reminded of what Pierre Bourdieu calls "aristocratic essentialism." For what the aristocrat does (and knows) is the free expression of an essence that is "anterior and superior to its manifestations."[14] The doings and knowings of the non-aristocrat, by contrast, remain "external" to him, which is why they may be both denigrated and appropriated as "merely useful." This is the ideological aspect of *Bildung*; its capacity to confirm the social miracle that elevates the "truly" educated man above his fellows.

As the concept of *Bildung* took on a socially confirmative character during the course of the nineteenth century, some of its other implications changed as well. Thus there was an unmistakable shift in the relationship of the mandarin intellectuals to the state. In some of Humboldt's early writings, he had insisted that human improve-ment can come only from the development of free individualities in interaction with each other. This was the cultural individualism that so impressed John Stuart Mill. Even in Humboldt's projects for the reorganization of Prussian higher education in 1809–10, he saw the state as providing no more than a material environment for the autonomous life of *Wissenschaft*. Nevertheless, the institutional ar-rangements he ultimately conceded gave considerable scope to state intervention in university affairs. Indeed, to several of his contem-poraries, and to many German university professors of later eras, this did not seem troublesome; or it seemed less and less troublesome. For they tended to regard the existing state as an adequate embodiment of the "cultural state" (*Kulturstaat*), the disinterested supporter and earthly representative of their national culture. Especially as they began to see themselves as a threatened minority, German aca-

demics moved toward an ever firmer commitment to the bureaucratic monarchy, which sustained their institutions, protected their
social position, and accepted their claim to speak for the nation as a
whole.[15]

Bildung around 1800, moreover, had been invested with a collective and even transcendent significance that was gradually dissi-
pated in the century that followed. The early German neohumanists
had seriously looked to antiquity for universally and eternally valid
cultural norms. The Protestant antecedents of German Idealism,
too, had conferred an almost religious meaning upon the pursuit of
Bildung. Though that meaning was affected by the individualist
element in Protestantism, it still linked *Bildung* to a universal vision
of human salvation. In the metaphysical language of German
Idealism, the self-realization of mind was the transcendent aim of
human existence. As that spiritual connotation gradually faded,
however, it became ever more damaging that neither Humboldt nor
the great Idealists had taken a clear position on the material and
social preconditions of individual *Bildung*, or on its this-worldly
consequences for all members of a human community. Left in a kind
of spiritual and social vacuum, the cultivation of the isolated self
ultimately became a truly gratuitous and strictly private enterprise,
a higher form of selfishness.[16] The only counterweight to the radical
individualism that thus emerged was an unconditional commitment
to the bureaucratic state.

From around 1890 on, German university professors in the
humanities and social sciences expressed a sense of crisis that reached
its greatest intensity during the interwar period. Among the causes of
their concern, some were broad trends in the political and cultural
life of their time; others were changes in their more immediate
environment, in the situation of the universities and of *Wissenschaft*
itself. Included in this latter category were structural transformations in the educational system that were commonly perceived as
forms of modernization and of democratization. Thus from the late
1870s to the turn of the century, public controversies took place in
Germany as elsewhere over the accreditation of the so-called technical institutes (*technische Hochschulen*), and of the non-classical and
incompletely classical secondary schools that were sometimes collectively termed *Realschulen*. Whether rightly or not, contemporaries
tended to regard the rapid growth of these "realistic" and "technical" institutions as a kind of modernization, a functional adjustment

of the educational system to the requirements of a modern technological society. Even some of the opponents of the non-traditional programs considered them useful or even necessary; what they denied, at least until 1900, is that they ought to be accredited equally with the classical *Gymnasium* and with the universities themselves. Though the *Realschulen* and *technische Hochschulen* found a few energetic supporters among university professors, the prevailing sentiment in the "philosophical" faculties was against granting them full equality of standing. In this context, it proved remarkably easy and effective to use the language of *Bildung* in defense of the status quo. Pushed to conceptually precarious limits, the inherited animus against "utilitarian" conceptions of learning virtually dictated a hierarchic ranking of educational institutions according to their more or less exclusively "impractical" character. The traditional defense of "pure" learning thus served to justify a social divide between the gratuitously cultivated and those schooled at best for useful employments.[17]

During the late nineteenth century, and especially during the Weimar period, German academics also faced the questions raised by a substantial growth in secondary and university-level enrollments. We have reason to doubt that these increases in inclusiveness actually brought about a notable advance in the progressiveness of German higher education. Nevertheless, contemporaries tended to perceive the marked expansion of enrollments as a form of educational democratization. Particularly during the 1920s, modest government measures to widen access to secondary schooling, as well as to the *Abitur* and thus to the universities, suggested a deliberate movement toward greater equality of educational opportunity.[18] In these circumstances, the theory of *Bildung* was repeatedly brought forward to challenge the notion that school and university places might be distributed partly or wholly on the basis of tested academic aptitude. Since *Bildung* was a forming of the whole person and the fulfillment of a unique individual potentiality, statistical approaches to educability almost had to seem inappropriate. In 1917, the pedagogue and philosopher Eduard Spranger had this to say on that subject:

I see a . . . symptom of the connection between democracy and rationalism in the growth of technical methods by which the intellectual characteristics are to be tested, and in accordance with which the choice of schooling is to be organizationally regulated . . . For individuality is here ultimately looked upon as something measurable and numerically describable, not as a structural principle of the soul ... The human mind is not put together out of atoms of primitive acts, but [is] an organic unity ... Individuality can only be grasped through vital intuition.[19]

In a 1923 essay, the psychiatrist and philosopher Karl Jaspers distinguished four groups of requirements for university scholarship. The first encompassed the ability to learn, memory, and a variety of other functions we would associate with academic aptitude. While granting that these qualities might ultimately prove roughly measurable, Jaspers considered them far less important for scholarly work than "intelligence as such," "spirituality" (*Geistigkeit*) and "creativity, genius," which could never be statistically assessed. On these grounds, Jaspers held that the selection of university students should be left to unguided social processes. He was no ranting reactionary; yet he reminded his readers that "the masses" had always been known to have a low intelligence. A student's receptivity to learning would be low, he thought, unless he came from a "cultured family."[20] The classicist Ulrich von Wilamowitz-Moellendorf had taken a similar position even more firmly a few years earlier.[21]

Apparently, these views enjoyed wide influence within the German academic community. For in the late 1920s, the Corporation of German Universities passed and published several resolutions that put the case against a "lowering of standards" in the following terms.

[The Corporation] regards with grave concern the ever greater expansion of the circle of those admitted to the universities. [The universities are reached by students] whose preparation in general and whose language training in particular is insufficient ... This deterioration is caused as much by the whole orientation of our time as by certain pedagogical aims and methods ... Larger strata of the population [are entering secondary education.] Thus one often succeeds only through an artificial and wearisome process of forced breeding [*Höherzüchtung*] in making the cultural values [*Bildungsgüter*] of the secondary schools accessible to a kind of public which comes from its home environment without any sort of deeper intellectual needs.[22]

The critique of language training implied the primacy of hermeneutic knowledge and was directed mainly against the non-classical schools. The complaint at the "whole orientation of our time" condemned an excess of social ambition among the "larger strata." Those who were hard to teach were assumed to be identical with those from uncultivated backgrounds. And the overall presumption was that secondary education ought to be an almost undeliberate "making available" of "cultural values" to a public predisposed to absorb them.

THE POSITION OF MATTHEW ARNOLD

Matthew Arnold's *Culture and Anarchy*, published in 1869, contains what may well be the most influential definition of "culture" in the English language. The parallels between this definition and the German idea of *Bildung* are so striking, and even the differences so instructive, that I want briefly to consider them here. Arnold's initial formulation is as follows.

Culture [is] a pursuit of our total perfection by means of getting to know, on all matters which most concern us, the best which has been thought and said in the world; and through this knowledge, turning a stream of fresh and free thought upon our stock notions and habits, which we now follow staunchly but mechanically.[23]

The first half of this sentence, like *Bildung*, implies that the whole person is transformed by a relationship to sources that embody "the best which has been thought and said in the world." The utopian aim of this relationship is "total perfection," though Arnold deliberately identifies culture with the *pursuit* of perfection, rather than with perfection itself. He also avoids any hint of an empathetic identification, or of an absorbing of values. His emphasis is on cognition, on getting to *know* what has been *thought*. Indeed, the second half of his definition suggests the critical clarification of traditional beliefs and practices; for culture includes "turning a stream of fresh and free thought upon our stock notions and habits, which we now follow staunchly but mechanically." The clear intent is not only to change our thoughts, but also to transform our behavior, which at present is too much a mechanical following of stock habits.

Arnold was apparently on his guard against the socially classificatory uses of "culture." Thus he explicitly repudiated "a smattering of Greek and Latin... valued either out of sheer ignorance and vanity, or else as an engine of social and class distinction, separating its holder, like a badge or title, from other people who have not got it."[24] Yet Arnold himself occasionally used the language of "social and class distinction," particularly in his attacks on the wealthy "philistines."

The people who believe most that our greatness and welfare are proven by our being very rich ... are just the very people whom we call Philistines. Culture says: "Consider these people, then, their way of life, their habits, their manners, the very tones of their voice ...observe the literature they read, the things which give them pleasure, the words which come forth out of their mouths, the thoughts which make the furniture of their minds; would any amount of wealth be worth having with the condition that one was to become just like these people by having it?"[25]

This conventional portrait of "the vulgar" is surely an "engine" of social derogation. Elsewhere, Arnold chastises "the fashion of teaching a man to value himself not on what he *is*, not on his progress in sweetness and light, but on the number of railroads he has constructed, or the bigness of the tabernacle he has built."[26] This draws on the distinction between *being* and *doing*, the aristocratic essentialism that may well have been a universal theme in nineteenth-century models of the cultivated self. In Arnold's use of it, to be sure, being is identified with "*progress* in sweetness and light," not with an attained state of grace, and the critique of mere doing is directed against the overvaluing of railroads and tabernacles as self-justifying individual achievements.

There is no trace in Arnold's formulations of the German emphasis upon the uniqueness of personal cultivation, or upon individuality itself. On the contrary, Arnold insists upon the social significance of "perfection." He writes that we must "conceive of true human perfection as a *harmonious* perfection, developing all sides of our humanity, and as a *general* perfection, developing all parts of our society."

For if one member suffer, the other members must suffer with it; and *the fewer there are that follow the true way of salvation, the harder that way is to find.* Perfection, as culture conceives it, is not possible while the individual remains isolated. The individual is required, under pain of being stunted and enfeebled in his own development if he disobeys, to carry others along with him in his march towards perfection, to be continually doing all he can to enlarge and increase the volume of the human stream sweeping thitherward.[27]

Obviously, the religious foundations of Arnold's thought are very much intact, and scarcely affected by Protestant individualism. In any case, the humanity that must be harmoniously developed here is *our* (collective) humanity; the "true way of salvation" is a communal and universal path, and the individual is warned against isolation and contemplative inaction. He must "carry others along with him," not because *they* deserve to be helped, but "on pain of being stunted and enfeebled in *his own* development if he disobeys." This lends conviction to Arnold's famous paragraph on culture and equality.

Culture . . . does not try to teach down to the level of inferior classes . . . It seeks to do away with classes; to make the best that has been thought and known in the world current everywhere, to make all men live in an atmosphere of sweetness and light, where they may use ideas as it uses them itself, freely – nourished and not bound by them. This is the *social idea*; and the men of culture are the true apostles of equality.[28]

In the world we know, the idea of culture may never be quite disentangled from its hierarchic uses. But what Arnold claims is that the approach to perfection is also and necessarily a "doing all one can" to remove the "stunting" obstacles of class. Education, moreover, must not be a "teaching down," but a "making current" of the best thought that will enable all men to be "freely nourished" rather than "bound" by ideas.

In spite of this image of culture as liberation, however, Arnold comes very close to "orthodox mandarin" patterns of thought when he writes about "the best self" and the state. The "best self" in each of us, he argues, strives for a perfection that transcends the limitations of the "ordinary self," which are the limitations of self-interest and of class. He further supposes that "in each class there are born a certain number of natures with a curiosity about their best self, with a bent for seeing things as they are . . .for simply concerning themselves with reason and the will of God, and doing their best to make these prevail; – for the pursuit, in a word, of perfection."[29] These "aliens," as he calls them, rather resemble Karl Mannheim's "free-floating intellectuals." They somehow manage to elude the distorting effects of self-interest and of class, much as some German academics imagined themselves as rising "above" the politics of class conflict. Arnold's "aliens" do remain tied to the rest of mankind, since they merely extend the best self in each of us. Still, when Arnold goes on to define the state as an agent of the "best self," there is a disturbing note.

We want an authority, and we find nothing but jealous classes, checks, and a deadlock; culture suggests the idea of *the State*. We find no basis for a firm State-power in our ordinary selves; culture suggests one to us in our *best self*.[30]

This goes well beyond Humboldt asking an otherwise strictly limited state to give unconditional support to learning. It recalls Hegel's elevation of the state above the conflicts of civil society. Arnold, after all, was a government school inspector; like many German civil servants, he saw the rational state as a progressive force. Even so, the formulation remains striking; for culture and the best self here call upon a "firm state power" to subdue working-class protest. The context leaves no doubt that Arnold was reacting to "multitudinous processions in the streets of our crowded towns," which he promptly escalated into symptoms of "anarchy."

Our best self, or right reason, plainly enjoins us to encourage and uphold the occupants of the executive power, whoever they may be . . . It knows that it is establishing *the state*, or organ of our collective best self . . .on behalf of whatever great changes are needed, just as much as on behalf of order.[31]

Written by an orthodox German academic of the decades around 1900, this would certainly strike us as ominous. Arnold suggests that the state may act in behalf of "great changes," but his main concern is with order. He knows that the "occupants of the executive power" are just the presently most powerful among the "ordinary selves," but he confers upon them the authority of "our collective best self." This perfectly matches the foreshortened utopianism that led to the elevation of the ideal "whole" in the political rhetoric of mandarin orthodoxy.

In a fascinating analysis of nineteenth-century English social and political thought, Raymond Williams has placed Matthew Arnold's position into a wider framework.[32] From its origins in the early nineteenth century, Williams argues, the English concept of "culture" was defined in opposition to capitalist individualism; much of its meaning was drawn from this contrast. Writing as a socialist, Williams offers subtle and compelling readings, not only of prominent conservatives from Edmund Burke on, but also of such champions of culture as S. T. Coleridge and Arnold himself. Coleridge was inspired by German Idealism; he introduced the contrast between "culture" and "civilization" into the English context, in which "civilization" stood in part for the industrial capitalism of the early nineteenth century. His vision of a spiritually guiding "clerisy," too, had much in common with German "madarin" conceptions of the intellectuals' role. According to Williams, Coleridge and Arnold were remarkable precisely in their *heterodoxy*; they stood against the powerful tide of industrialism, utilitarianism, and *laisser faire* individualism in early nineteenth-century England. Indeed, that is just what Arnold thought about himself, as the following passage indicates.

But above all in our own country has culture a weighty part to perform, because here that mechanical character, which civilization tends to take everywhere, is shown in the most eminent degree. Indeed nearly all the characters of perfection, as culture teaches us to fix them, meet in this country with some powerful tendency which thwarts them and sets them at defiance.[33]

This is a historical and *positional* claim that could not have been advanced about the German states in Humboldt's day. But was it fully accurate even for England in 1869? Martin Wiener has argued that sometime after 1850, the English economic upper middle class assimilated quasi-aristocratic orientations that included a pronounced aversion to "trade."[34] So perhaps Arnold was not as isolated by 1869 as he – and Raymond Williams – apparently believed; perhaps his negative view of industrial civilization was no longer exceptional even in England?

Certainly there is much to be said for the hypothesis that educational segmentation helped to increase cultural distances in England as in Germany during the later nineteenth century. More generally, as has been suggested, substantial divergences among the major European educational systems before about 1860 were superseded after that time by a convergence toward similar outcomes. In England, the elite secondary schools and universities remained strongholds of the gentry and of the Anglican church long after their French and German counterparts had been opened to certain sectors of the middle and lower middle classes. The difference was due to the earlier and greater importance of an expert civil service on the Continent, particularly in Prussia, and to the relatively late and incomplete development in England of a network of certifying examinations and educational qualifications for office. Beginning in the 1850s, and especially between 1870 and 1920, however, a series of interconnected structural transformations brought the English education system into closer interaction with portions of the occupational hierarchy.[35] Thus in England as in France and Germany by the early twentieth century, a systematically articulated hierarchy of educational institutions came to define status positions within the middle-class spectrum. Advanced education became a more important element in the legitimation and reproduction of the social rank order. And the socially classificatory meanings that thus came to play an increased role were typically grounded in differences of life style and of "culture."

Indeed, the English "public" schools and universities proved particularly successful in transmitting inherited socio-cultural norms. Gradations of academic standing within English secondary and higher education were not quite as firmly linked as on the Continent to *curricular* differences. The less-distinguished English grammar schools of the late nineteenth and early twentieth centuries tended to imitate the curriculum of the ancient "public" schools, so that a form of general education was extended fairly far downward on the institutional and social scale. Similarly, the younger universities that came to compete with Oxford and Cambridge from the late nineteenth century on did not develop clearly distinctive programs of their own; instead, they followed the lead of the ancient universities, which acted as "defining institutions."[36] As a result, the culture of the ancient "public" schools and of "Oxbridge" was effectively and rapidly disseminated "downward." Once the professional middle-class began to patronize the ancient universities toward the end of the nineteenth century, the entrepreneurial bourgeoisie followed soon upon its heels. For Cambridge University, Sheldon Rothblatt has charted three relevant developments.[37] One of these was the emergence of a new and vital role for the university "don" as a committed and morally effective specialist in general education, more a personal mentor than a research scientist or scholar. The second was a renewed concern with practical ethics, as well as with ethical theory, in the thought of Arnold and others. The third was the creation of a professional ideal that emphasized "service," as against "commerical" motives and "market" relationships. Together, these three innovations allowed the ancient English universities to perpetuate a new ethos for a bourgeoisie that was no longer precisely "philistine" in Arnold's sense. Perhaps Arnold should be interpreted as a prophet of this new ethos, and not only as a critic of the old entrepreneurial individualism?

I put these questions without meaning to suggest that they are easy to answer. On the contrary, I am convinced that a fully adequate reading of Arnold would require a much more thorough (and preferably comparative) study of the English intellectual field than I can possibly offer here. I am frankly amazed at the ease with which some commentators are able to develop generalizations in intellectual history. Thus David Blackbourn has proposed that optimistic views of capitalism gave place to more somber perspectives after 1860 not only in Germany, but in all of Europe, and/or that the cultural pessimism that overcame the German *Bildungsbürgertum* after about 1890 was just another instance of a typically "bourgeois" capacity for self-criticism.[38] I believe that such conclusions cannot be sustained by a few selected quotations. (The need for *systematic* evidence is just as great in intellectual as in social and political history.) I therefore hope that my digression on Arnold will not be regarded as an attempt to understand English ideologies of education and of culture. It was written primarily as another way of bringing out the meaning of *Bildung* in the German tradition.

ROOTS AND DIMENSIONS OF THE FRENCH EDUCATION DEBATE OF 1890–1920

Nineteenth-century French conceptions of education were most fully aired – and contested – in a public debate that reached a high point during the decades around 1900. To understand that debate, however, we need to expand upon some aspects of the institutional history outlined in the last chapter. More specifically, we must follow the transformation of French secondary schooling that began between 1863 and 1865, when Victor Duruy, recently appointed Minister of Education under Napoleon III, introduced the so-called "special secondary" program.

Influenced by the example of the German *Realschulen* as well as by certain precedents within the French system, Duruy's *enseignement secondaire spécial* was designed to provide an alternative, at the secondary level and within the existing secondary schools, to the abstract and literary bent of the classical curriculum. A four-year course beginning at age eleven was to emphasize the applied sciences, along with French and a modern foreign language. In a frankly "practical" way, specific courses within the "special" stream were to be adjusted to the requirements of local industries. Four internally coherent one-year programs were to follow one another, so that early leavers would not take away a fragmentary education. Those who completed all four years were not to earn the baccalaureate; nor were they expected to continue their studies at a postsecondary level. Apparently, Duruy considered the new curriculum especially suited for less "gifted" pupils, who might be discouraged by the level of abstraction involved in the study of the ancient languages.[39]

Like his immediate predecessor in the Ministry of Education, Duruy had been much impressed with the International Expositions of 1856 and 1862. In justifying his curricular innovation, he repeatedly pointed to the need for economic productivity, and thus for trained manpower in industry, commerce, and agriculture. While housed in the existing secondary schools and considered secondary in status, the *enseignement spécial* was to be sharply distinguished from "general" secondary schooling. At the same time, Duruy clearly thought of his innovation as a socially progressive step, one that would offer educational opportunities to the intermediate layers of the economic middle class, whose specific occupational needs and social aspirations had hitherto been ignored by the French educational system. He saw the new program as bridging an educational and social "chasm" between the primary and secondary schools.

From the foundation provided by an enlarged and unified primary system, two parallel secondary programs will rise: One classical, for the so-called liberal professions; the other vocational, for careers in commerce, industry and agriculture. [These two] completely different [programs will be housed under the same roof; children] of different origins and destinations will thus live together . . . and this contact will profit both groups.[40]

One cannot miss the socially integrative intent in this formulation, but neither should one overlook the tacit assumption that most children's social origins would be their "destinations" as well. In the minds of many nineteenth-century educators, this underlying assumption of status persistence did not conflict with the expectation that a few exceptional youngsters from modest backgrounds would reach the "best" secondary schools, along with virtually all normal offspring of the more privileged social groups. In the same way, Duruy could genuinely believe *both* that his reform was in some sense "democratic" and that his new program would very rarely take students far from the social world from which they came. The son of a well-to-do artisan might enter the "special" stream to prepare for a foreman's position in a substantial machine shop, while the son of a small merchant might be trained to expand his father's business, using skills his father had not needed. In the meantime, if a very prosperous farmer had a very gifted son, an event assumed to be rare, he should presumably continue to enroll him in the classical secondary stream.

Yet whatever Duruy may have intended, the *enseignement spécial* eventually became a serious contender for equality of standing with the classical secondary curriculum. During the 1880s, a *generalist shift* gradually transformed the "special" program, partly in response to the aspirations of its teachers. In 1882, two successive cycles of three and two years were introduced. In 1886, with the addition of a sixth year, the program was given a baccalaureate of its own, though this at first remained incompletely accredited. In the meantime, the "practical" orientation that had originally been projected was gradually weakened, until the program differed from the classical curriculum only in its neglect of Latin and Greek, and in its greater emphasis upon the natural sciences, modern languages, and French literature. In 1891, under the Ministry of Léon Bourgeois, the *enseignement secondaire spécial* was officially reconstituted as a "general" but "modern" secondary stream, the *enseignement secondaire moderne*, with full access to a baccalaureate.

The most important supporters of the *enseignement spécial* in its stepwise "elevation" were the reforming politicians and officials who led the Ministry of Education and its section on secondary education from the late 1870s to the early 1890s, among them René Goblet and Léon Bourgeois, Octave Gréard, and Charles Zévort. Together with Louis Liard, the famous director of higher education, these men articulated and implemented the activist policies of the Radical Republic in secondary and higher education. Beginning in 1880, they had the support of an advisory Council on Education (Conseil Supérieur de l'Instruction Publique), which included representatives of various educational institutions, especially of the faculties of letters and of sciences.[41] Ultimately, of course, the series of educational reforms that began under Jules Ferry in 1880, along with the "laic" and "solidarist" ideologies in which they were framed, depended upon the electoral support of the broad middle and lower middle classes.

In any case, it is fascinating to observe how the Ministry of Education gradually transformed the public image of the *enseignement spécial* after 1880. Thus an official report of 1882 referred "on the one hand" to the need to preserve the "special" stream in "its own proper character and its normal direction, not forgetting what category of pupils it addresses, what needs it must serve, and what aptitudes it is designed to enhance." On the other hand, the writer continued, the *enseignement spécial* should fill in, to the extent possible, "the distance that separates it from the classical curriculum, and not only equip pupils with practical and immediately useful notions, but also give them a little of that disinterested and superior culture which is the purpose and honor of secondary education."[42] The idea of conveying "a little disinterested culture" implied, of course, that the "special" stream was a diluted version of the classical curriculum, rather than an alternative to it. In 1886, Zévort and Goblet extended this perspective in trying to impose the label *enseignement classique français*. They saw the younger of the two secondary curricula as both "general" and "classical," the latter in the sense of a formal "culture" or development of the mind and spirit. Zévort considered the new curriculum "scientific," a term quite different from the French *technique*, and he claimed that it was "literary" as well. He objected "in the light of experience" to an overly "practical" conception of the "special" program, stressing the need for the type of practice that is informed by "theoretical" knowledge of "scientific principles."[43]

All parties concerned were extraordinarily explicit about the status problems linked to these terminological issues. The ultimately successful opponents of the label *classique français* recalled that Duruy had initially used such words as "practical," "vocational" (*professionnel*) and "intermediate" to characterize the *enseignement spécial*. In objecting to the designation *classique français*, they said, they meant formally to reject "the idea of assimilating the program in question to the classical curriculum."[44] Nevertheless, the substantive innovations proposed by Zévort and Goblet were implemented, and by 1891, Léon Bourgeois could treat the transformation of the *enseignement spécial* in a generalist direction as an accomplished fact. Borrowing a tactic from the sharpest opponents of the "special" stream, he described Duruy's program of 1865 as self-contradictory: it could not at one and the same time be "specialized" or practical, and "general," theoretical and thus truly "secondary." Justice could not be done simultaneously to two sets of parents: those who "wanted to make their sons workers, foremen, men working directly with their hands," and those who wished their heirs to become "business owners, manufacturers, merchants, or substantial farmers." Since 1880, Bourgeois recalled, great strides had been made in the provision of free and public higher primary and vocational schooling. At the same time, "all the reforms instituted in the *enseignement secondaire spécial* since 1870" had tended to turn it into a "modern classical curriculum" (*enseignement classique moderne*).[45]

Bourgeois was arguing in effect that three types of post-elementary schooling corresponded to a presumably natural subdivision of the French middle class into three main strata. Once formed, the old *enseignement spécial* had more or less inevitably gravitated toward one of the two possible positions left open to it, while the new public higher primary schools had taken up the other. As a matter of fact, there was a grain of truth in this view. After the passage of the Ferry laws of 1881–82, two types of free public higher primary schooling were created in France, and a few of the new institutions eventually entered the field of full-time vocational education as well. Just as the *enseignement spécial* was undergoing the generalist shift of the 1880s, in other words, a group of new schools took up the position thus left vacant. Not surprisingly, this process occasioned competitive exercises in social demarcation. The roles assigned to the several segments of the educational system were defined in a systematic, interrelated and even interactive way. Indeed, the *enseignement spécial* almost *had* to move "upward" to avoid being ranked with the higher primary schools, and of course it became particularly threatening to the classical stream precisely during the 1880s, when it could no longer be "placed" in the securely subordinate station now occupied by a new set of post-elementary institutions.

From the 1870s to the end of the century, the running debate over the "special" or "modern" program was accompanied by an almost equally intensive discussion over the classical secondary curriculum. The basic question was to what extent the classical stream itself should be altered to accommodate such subjects as English and German, history and georgraphy, and the natural sciences above all. In 1872, this issue was raised by Jules Simon, another reform-minded Minister of Education, who proposed to have the study of Greek begin later than heretofore, to abandon Latin versification and translations into Latin, and to devote much of the time thus gained to the natural sciences. Simon's intent was to do justice to the "needs of the epoch," without overburdening pupils seriously enough to "tire their bodies, dull their minds, and weaken their wills."[46] As it happened, Simon was forced to resign before he could carry out his project, and his successors were unwilling to sacrifice any portions of the traditional curriculum. Yet even the most determined classicists of the 1870s succumbed to the universal sense that education had to be adjusted to the "exigencies of modern life," or however else the case was put. As a result, the discussions of the 1870s led to an odd compromise. In a curricular reform of 1880, the hours devoted to non-classical subjects were substantially increased, much as Simon had proposed. On the other hand, there was no proportional reduction in the time and effort traditionally committed to the ancient languages. The "modernization" of the curriculum was achieved, in effect, by simple addition.

This helps to account for the wave of public concern that swept France during the 1880s about the "overloading" of course schedules (*surcharge des programmes*) and the "overburdening" (*surmenage*) of pupils through overlong school days and excessive homework.[47] In a circular of 1882, the Ministry of Education acknowledged widespread complaints from the parents of overworked students. In 1886, an official described the "weight" of course work as "definitely too heavy." In the same year, the French Academy of Medicine warned of the danger to the health of adolescents given too little time for exercise and recreation. Indeed, physical fitness became something of a national passion in France at about this time. Several national sports associations were founded in the years 1887–89, at least partly in response to public anxiety over the health of secondary pupils. In any case, the two reorganizations of the classical curriculum that followed upon that of 1880 were clearly designed to alleviate the problem of "overburdening." In 1884–85 and again in 1890, the number of weekly class hours was reduced, and the reductions were achieved almost entirely at the expense of the "modern" subjects, so that the classical languages alone retained the full complement of hours assigned to them in 1880.

Yet one cannot interpret the reorganizations of 1884–85 and 1890 simply as traditionalist reactions. Léon Bourgeois, the Minister of Education who presided over the revision of the classical curriculum in 1890 was also responsible for the transformation of the *enseignement spécial* into the *enseignement moderne* in 1891. The official instructions issued in conjunction with the new classical course plan of 1890 provide an account of his position. One way to understand it is to recognize that curricular diversification is an obvious alternative to the encyclopedic temptation, as Octave Gréard had argued as early as 1884.[48] Given the steady increase in the quantity of knowledge that one generation must pass on to the next, "how can youth be prepared to sustain the weight of that heritage?" Gréard's question almost answers itself. There is no way of transmitting everything to everyone. Selection and concentration of subject matter is necessary and helpful, of course, but some degree of diversity is surely unavoidable in the long run. In making this point, Gréard meant to support the claim of the *enseignement spécial* to secondary status. He therefore rejected the idea of a polarity between "classical" and "utilitarian" education, noting that the classical curriculum had a "practical" side, while the "special" program was not without broadly educative value.

Even more interesting than Gréard's and Bourgeois' commitment to diversity is a subtle change in the position of certain traditionalists toward the end of the century. Thus by the late 1890s, the so-called Society for the Study of Questions of Secondary Education was ready to grant secondary status to a non-classical curriculum under certain conditions. In a circular of 1898, the Society belatedly announced that Duruy's *enseignement spécial* had been essentially sound, and should not have been abandoned or changed.

The Society . . . [recommends] the organization of a secondary curriculum that parallels the classical curriculum but that, far from seeking to imitate it, is clearly distinguished from it, and is plainly conceived to train farmers, merchants, manufacturers, and colonists, not actually to give them the technical knowledge they will only acquire in specialized schools or in the very practice of their professions, but rather, through general intellectual training [*une culture générale de l'intelligence*] and a well-directed education of the character and spirit, to develop in them the qualities useful in their occupational life, along with a taste for the exercise of their professions.[49]

The reference to colonists was not unusal; for colonization was regularly included among the "practical" endeavors in which France had to compete successfully with other nations. Equally widespread was the idea that a taste for the useful occupations required special nurture, and that many of those misled into attempting the classical curriculum ultimately became unsuccessful candidates for public office, or failures and alienated misfits (*ratés*, *déclassés*). The authors of the circular clearly meant to reduce competiton for the classical baccalaureate – and for access to the liberal professions – by channelling a certain class of students into the non-classical stream. To achieve this objective, they were prepared to grant "secondary" status to a "general" but non-classical curriculum, and even to flatter it with that magical formula about the *culture générale de l'intelligence*, as long as it was "plainly conceived to train farmers, merchants, manufacturers, and colonists." By the 1890s, in short, most participants in the French education debate acknowledged the need for curricular diversification. The crucial question, of course, was how much hierarchy was to remain associated with diversity.

There is yet a further way to understand Bourgeois' position of 1890, however, and it begins with another possible response to the encyclopedic temptation. Given more potential teaching material than can possibly be covered, one may emphasize the educative value of a selected curriculum, rather than the extent of the encompassed subject matter. Well before 1890, there were classicists who recommended the study of the ancient languages primarily as good intellectual training, and only secondarily as a means of access to an admirable body of literature. Such an emphasis upon the training value of Latin may have been somewhat stronger in France than in Germany even during the early nineteenth century, and it was probably on the rise everywhere toward the end of the century. In any case, it certainly became predominant in France from the 1880s on. In one of its variants, it pictured the learning of Latin as a kind of mental gymnastics. In another, it focused on the clarity and aesthetic appeal of classical literature, upon the "formal" perfection achieved by the authors of antiquity. Bourgeois and those who collaborated with him in preparing the official instructions of 1890 apparently had serious reservations about this "formalist" viewpoint, just as they disapproved of Latin versification and translation into Latin. Nevertheless, Bourgeois explicitly stipulated that the ideal materials for secondary education were those "most useful for their educative value and as intellectual discipline."[50]

The concern expressed by Bourgeois and by a number of his contemporaries with the educative potential of curricular options appears to have led to a new interest in specifically pedagogical questions during the late nineteenth century. The emergence of pedagogy as an academic discipline in France at about that time owed a good deal to the educational dilemmas of the 1880s and 1890s. Our main subject matter here, however, is the curricular debate itself. Like Ferry before him, Bourgeois urged teachers to give attention to substantive matters, to "things," as against mere verbal forms. In part, he meant that the interpretation of texts should focus on *what* was said, rather than on *how* it was said. In the famous *explication de texte*, he wanted pupils to discern arguments about the world, as against literary devices alone. While this preference pertained primarily to the interpretive disciplines, it offered points of contact with the natural sciences as well. On the other hand, a scientist could still insist that *no* textual interpretation was as instructive as the direct study of natural "things." After all, in what sense was Latin more educative than mathematics, or than the experimental sciences, or indeed than German or Chinese?

In a context of heated public debates on these questions, a parliamentary commission chaired by Alexandre Ribot was convened in 1899 to undertake a full-scale investigation of French secondary education. The Ribot Commission was established in part because enrollments in public secondary schools seemed to be declining or stagnating, while those in the Catholic private institutions appeared to be rising. Perhaps the Catholic secondary schools were benefiting from the known firmness of their commitment to the classical tradition, or from their interest in the moral and personal development of their pupils? The Commission was to look into these matters as well; but once it actually began its work, the conflict between the classical and the modern curriculum quickly moved to center stage. The Commission duly collected written responses to questionnaires from educational district adminstrators and advisory councils, as well as from chambers of commerce. In addition, in February and March of 1899, the Commission took substantial oral depositions from well-known publicists and spokesmen of agricultural societies and business interests, from directors of private secondary schools, from national school inspectors, and from public secondary school headmasters and teachers. Included among the oral depositions, finally, were the statements of seven former Ministers of Education, and of about fifty university professors, scholars, and members of academies, whose testimony will shortly be discussed in detail.

The French sociologist Viviane Isambert-Jamati has divided the positions taken by witnesses before the Ribot Commission on the future of the classical and modern curricula into five broad groups, along lines reproduced in table 2.1 One of the conclusions to be drawn from this table is that in France, at any rate, the economic upper middle classes of the late nineteenth century were not generally in favor of raising "modern" studies to equality of standing with the classical curriculum. Though they sometimes recommended *some*

Table 2.1 *Positions taken before the Ribot Commission of 1899 on classical and modern secondary educatıon (with percentages by row)*

Positions on this issue: taken by:	Classical incontestably superior	Reconvert "modern" into "special"	Divide non-classical options	Classical and modern streams equal	Modern incontestably superior	Total responses (+ on other issues)
Spokesmen, notables, publicists	5 (22%)	13 (57%)	3 (13%)	– (–)	2 (9%)	23 (14)
Chambers of Commerce (groups)	13 (19%)	25 (37%)	11 (16%)	16 (24%)	2 (3%)	67 (7)
Directors, private secondary schools	12 (48%)	7 (28%)	1 (4%)	5 (20%)	– (–)	25 (1)
Educational councils (groups)	12 (18%)	32 (48%)	5 (8%)	16 (24%)	1 (2%)	66 (14)
Inspectors, rectors, headmasters	8 (20%)	12 (29%)	13 (32%)	8 (20%)	– (–)	41 (7)
Lycée professors	6 (21%)	7 (25%)	4 (14%)	11 (39%)	– (–)	28 (5)
Former Ministers of Education	–	1	2	2	2	7
Professors, letters and sciences	3 (17%)	4 (22%)	2 (11%)	7 (39%)	2 (11%)	18 (1)
Professors, other faculties	8 (42%)	5 (26%)	– (–)	5 (26%)	1 (5%)	19 (–)
Academicians, professors Collège de France	5 (31%)	4 (25%)	2 (13%)	5 (31%)	– (–)	16 (2)
Total responses	72 (23%)	110 (36%)	43 (14%)	75 (24%)	10 (3%)	310 (51)

form of non-classical secondary schooling for the intermediate layers of the economic hierarchy, they insisted in their own behalf upon the socio-cultural distinction associated with the classical monopoly. So did the directors of the Catholic secondary schools. A sort of triple alliance between Catholicism, private secondary schooling, and the bourgeoisie was not just a myth invented by anti-clericals for their own political purposes; it was a social and ideological reality in France at that time. Within the academic community, the traditional curriculum found its strongest supporters in the professional faculties, the avenues to the liberal professions, which were strongholds of the established bourgeoisie. Moderate reformist sentiments prevailed among teachers and headmasters in public secondary schools, as well as among certain educational adminstrators. (The national school inspectors were decidedly more supportive of the modern curriculum than the headmasters and the rectors of educational districts.) Thus genuine enthusiasm for an upgrading of the modern curriculum was in fact specific to three groups that had been jointly sponsoring a whole cluster of educational changes since the late 1870s: the political leaders of the left center in the Chamber of Deputies, the republican educational administration, and a

From Viviane Isambert-Jamati, "Une réforme des lycées et collèges," *L'Année sociologique*, 3e série, vol. 20 (1969), pp. 9–60, especially pp. 13, 55. Figures in parentheses at the far right of the table are responses that address issues other than the curricular ones, often because respondents had in fact been asked to comment on other matters. "Spokesmen, notables, publicists" are invited representatives of agricultural associations and business groups, individual business leaders, and a few publicists who had become known for positions taken in public. Written responses from seventeen Rectors (*recteurs*) of educational districts (*académies*), which may also have reflected the views of their district School Inspectors, were included in this table with the oral depositions of fifteen national School Inspectors (*inspecteurs généraux*), and sixteen public secondary school administrators, most of them headmasters (*proviseurs*). From among some fifty-five depositions by public secondary school teachers (including about fifteen *répétiteurs*), Isambert-Jamati tabulated only those by thirty-three *professeurs de lycée*. The five broad positions taken may be further specified as follows: (1) the *classical* curriculum is *incontestably superior*, and there is no need for a non-classical secondary stream, (2) the classical curriculum should be maintained, and the *"modern"* stream should be *reconverted into* the *"special"* program as originally conceived by Duruy, (3) the classical curriculum should be maintained, and the *non-classical options divided* into two, one of them fully accredited, the other a reconstituted version of the "special" program as originally conceived by Duruy, (4) a *classical* and a *modern* stream should be *equal* in accreditation, and (5) the *modern* curriculum is *incontestably superior*, so that the classical program might almost be discarded.

substantial contingent of university professors in the expanding faculties of letters and of sciences.

The decree of May 1902, which grew out of the work of the Ribot Commission, was largely written by Ribot himself, though it was signed by the then Minister of Education, Georges Leygues. It duly reflected the views of the reform coalition, rather than the majority opinion of witnesses heard by the Commission. Public secondary schooling was broken into two successive cycles of four and three years in length. The choice between a modern and a classical option in the first cycle was followed by four alternatives in the second cycle: Latin–Greek, Latin–(Modern) Languages, Latin–Sciences, and Sciences–(Modern) Languages. Even the last of these, the purely non-classical sequence and the only one that could be reached from first-cycle modern studies, was accredited equally with all others, and the baccalaureate itself was divided into two stages and several versions of equivalent rank. Thus a degree of curricular diversity was encompassed by what was nevertheless conceived as an integrated system of secondary education. That system remained institutionally and socially separated from the higher primary schools, but it was intended as a continuation of public elementary schooling as well as of the pre-secondary courses that still prepared many students for entry into the secondary grades themselves.[51]

In the official instructions that accompanied the decree of 1902, and in public statements by its sponsors, a variety of stated intentions were somewhat uneasily conjoined. Thus statistics on French economic growth were offered as a prelude to the standard claim about "the exigencies of modern life." Secondary education was said to provide a form of "mental discipline" that was "as indispensable for the enlightened and liberal (professional) elite, for the aristocracy of mind, as for the general staff and officers of the army of labor." There was an explicitly utilitarian note; for the student was to be offered "the instruction most useful in view of his future career." But Louis Liard also came back to the diversity enforced by the growth of knowledge: curricular possibilities had to be selected and combined in different "mixtures" according to "their educative virtues and practical effects," so that families could choose what they wanted for their children, in the light of their "aptitudes, tastes, and (socio-occupational) destinations." Modern language instructors were not to interpret literature or train the mind, but to teach "the language of nannies and waiters." In the natural sciences, on the other hand, students were to learn how to "see, compare, generalize, and understand," while teachers of the classical languages were to make their charges "love the texts as they themselves love them."[52] This was indeed a "mixture" of almost all the educational objectives posited by reformers in the debates of the 1890s.

The settlement of 1902 remained the basic blueprint for French secondary schooling well into the interwar period. Nevertheless, a new initiative in behalf of educational "democratization" was launched during the First World War by "the Compagnons" and their program for a "new university." The Compagnons aimed at an internally differentiated "common school" (*école unique*) for all Frenchmen, much as the proponents of the integrated *Einheitsschule* did in Germany. Concretely, they meant to introduce fully common elementary education, and to reduce institutional and social barriers not only among the several secondary tracks, but also between the secondary and the higher primary schools. Departing from an extended "common trunk" of shared classes, students were to be guided toward divergent options as late as possible, and strictly on the basis of their aptitudes and inclinations. This also meant that secondary and pre-secondary education had to be made free of charge, as public elementary and higher primary schooling already was. Though their socially integrative intentions long met with determined resistance, not all of it due to the sheer tax cost of abolishing fees in public secondary schools, the Compagnons may be regarded as the intellectual precursors of a new wave of reform in French secondary education that began in the late 1920s and extended into the 1950s.[53]

In the meantime, even as the Compagnons' proposals were beginning to reach a wider audience, there were two further adjustments in the structure of the secondary system that emerged from the settlement of 1902. Under the conservative governments of the *bloc national* that came to power immediately after the First World War, the opponents of modern secondary studies found official support. In a "questionnaire" of 1921, Minister of Education Léon Bérard outlined a new scheme that was actually promulgated in 1923, though only for two years.[54] Among the four second-cycle options of 1902, only Latin–Greek and Latin–Sciences remained fully accredited secondary programs. Latin–(Modern) Languages had never become popular in any case. Sciences–(Modern) Languages, considered essentially higher primary in character, was demoted to non-baccalaureate status. The attempt to create a secondary program to prepare for "practical careers," according to Bérard, "violated any genuine conception of culture."

In 1925, under a government of the united left (Cartel des Gauches), however, a purely non-classical option was reinstituted in both the first and second cycles of secondary studies, so that Bérard's attack upon the modern stream had no permanent consequences. Nonetheless, as Isambert-Jamati has pointed out, the decrees of 1923 and 1925 actually had certain aims in common. Both assigned substantially increased class hours to the natural sciences even within the classical options; both specified that the curriculum of pre-secondary courses was to be identical with that of the public elementary schools, and both slightly reduced programmatic differences and institutional divides between higher primary and modern secondary schooling. The structural modifications of 1923 and 1925 thus concluded one phase in the history of French secondary education while opening another. They virtually ended the old debate between classicists and "modernists," and they helped to launch a new set of discussions, which were concerned primarily with the relationship between the secondary and the higher primary schools.

THE FRENCH IMAGE OF THE INTELLECTUAL PROLETARIAT

The next chapter will deal with major concepts in the French education debate of the late nineteenth century, and particularly with selected depositions before the Ribot Commission of 1899. Even before that Commission was convened, however, there was a public discussion, in France as in Germany, on the subject of the "intellectual proletariat." The uneasiness expressed in this slogan was presumably due in part to the growth of "modern" secondary studies, to increases in baccalaureate awards per age group, and to rising rates of access to the universities, especially to the faculties of letters and of sciences. The Ribot Commission heard about the "academic proletariat" in the invited testimony of Henry Bérenger, a publicist who had made something of a reputation as an expert on the subject. But Bérenger's pertinent essays, revised and collected in 1901, were clearly inspired by Maurice Barrès' *Les déracinés* of 1897, a polemical novel on "uprooted" students that probably originated and certainly popularized the idea of an "intellectual proletariat" in

France. Barrès' work in turn was dedicated to the "psychological" novelist Paul Bourget, whose 1889 *Le disciple* anticipated some of Barrès' concerns. Even a summary review of the literature on the "intellectual proletariat" in France around the turn of the century must therefore include a brief reference to Bourget's *Le disciple*, along with somewhat fuller discussions of Barrés' *Les déracinés* and of Bérenger's tracts.

Bourget's novel tells the story of Robert Greslou, a young *lycée* graduate who is misled by the doctrines of the materialist philosopher Adrian Sixte into committing a vile act. Employed as a tutor by an aristocratic family, he seduces the daughter of the house, though she is engaged to be married to a fellow officer in her brother's regiment. Robert Greslou and Mademoiselle de Jussat agree to commit suicide together after a night of love. But since he fails to kill himself after having dishonored her, she poisons herself alone. Awaiting trial for a murder of which he is technically innocent, Greslou writes an account of his aberrations for his philosophical master, who is thus confronted with his intellectual responsibility for a "disciple" he scarcely knew. As a person, the aging Sixte is unworldly in the extreme. He has severed all ties with his family and with society, so as to live for science alone. The only emotions he actually experiences are the passion for ideas and the vanity of the competitive intellectual. Greslou, by contrast, is divided against himself. He proves capable of ordinary human sentiments, of love, of moral awareness and of remorse; yet he allows himself to be ruled by the coldly analytical intelligence that responds to the teachings of his unwitting mentor.[55]

The doctrines developed by Sixte and lived by Greslou are explicitly associated with those of Hippolyte Taine, though Ernest Renan, Emile Littré, and Théodule Ribot (the psychologist, not the parliamentarian) are mentioned as well. Influenced by Kant's critical phenomenalism, by the English psychologists, and by evolutionary theory, Sixte holds that "the God-hypothesis" is but a necessary product of psycho-physical processes, and that all human sensibilities are manipulable effects of animal instincts and physiological transformations. Society may need a theory of Good and Evil, but the philosopher considers these concepts mere conventions; for he knows human volitions to be strictly determined by natural laws. A "positivist" and a "laic saint," Sixte utterly rejects "what Herbert Spencer calls the Unknowable" as a "metaphysical illusion." He is not interested in the "probable reconciliation of Science and Religion on the basis of the Unknowable." A "nihilist," a "great negator" and a fanatical atheist, he is quite untouched by the "modesty" of true science.[56]

In a preface to this cautionary tale, Bourget identified himself with the idealistic "young bourgeoisie" of the early 1870s, which had seen "its dearest beliefs proscribed in the name of liberty," which had been unable to "reestablish the traditional form of government" or to "resolve the formidable problems imposed upon us by the democratic error." He warned the young man of 1889 against "positivism," critical sophistry, intellectual "nihilism," and cynical "epicurea-nism," whether "intellectual and refined" or "brutal and scientific." In short, he wrote as a Catholic monarchist, in behalf of faith and free will, and against the dangers of a scientism too arrogant or dogmatic to acknowledge the claims of "the Unknowable."[57]

Along with this Catholic case against science, Bourget's novel also conveyed a secondary thesis, which was to be more fully stated by Maurice Barrès. This was the suggestion that a certain type of student was particularly vulnerable to the social and moral dangers of intellectualism. Bourget made Adrian Sixte the son of a modest watchmaker. He also described his early years as those of a single-minded and precocious pupil, who had almost no personal life apart from his studies. Singled out for encouragement by his teachers, Sixte evolved into a one-sidedly academic intellectual, a recluse isolated from all human association, a "laic saint." Given his manner of life, or his lack of genuine experience, Sixte was predisposed to misread philosophical propositions as if they were identical with the complex realities of human existence. He was therefore utterly incapable of meeting what Bourget took to be the responsibility of "the man of letters": he could not write to guide full human beings of flesh and blood. The idealized *homme de lettres* would presumably have suc-ceeded where the narrowly "academic" scientist was bound to fail. The tragic consequences might still have been avoided, if Sixte's "disciple" had been a normal individual. But Greslou in turn was only a slightly distorted copy of his unwitting mentor. Bourget described him as "the only son of an engineer who had died impoverished, and whom his mother had brought up at the cost of sacrifices." Though as one-sidedly studious as Sixte himself, he failed the entrance examination to the Ecole Normale. This deepened his emotional isolation, but it also increased his determination to pursue and actually to apply his master's scientific theories. In a pointed variation upon the ancient story of the talented student from a modest background, Bourget made him a tutor in an aristocratic house, an alien and unsavory force in a social world that was whole. He was not only a moral cripple, but also a prototypically arrogant intellectual and an enemy of society.[58]

In *The Uprooted* (*Les déracinés*, 1897), Maurice Barrès took up Bourget's thesis that pernicious doctrines could turn students into criminals, but he also tried to specify the social circumstances under which this was likely to happen. More explicitly than Bourget, he wrote to expose an *institutional* disorder, a structural flaw in the educational system of the Third Republic that was tending to pervert a portion of the nation's youth. He began his tale in 1879, in the highest or "philosophy" class of a *lycée* at Nancy, in the province of Lorraine. Focusing upon seven pupils in that class, he showed them profoundly affected by the Kantian philosophy of their teacher Paul Bouteiller, who was also an enthusiastic supporter of the Radical Republic and a political protégé of the "opportunist" parliamentary leader Leon Gambetta. In Barrès' critical portrait of him, Bouteiller perfectly represents the Republic's centralizing educational policies. His teaching combines a Kantian universalism with an abstract ethic of civic responsibility to the centralized Republic. His personal example even more powerfully conveys an arrogant indifference to the specific traits and practicalities of middle-class life in the provinces. Since his students are adolescent Frenchmen, according to Barrès, they are susceptible in any case to a one-sided passion for intellectual distinction. Upon graduating, therefore, they promptly abandon their chances for useful careers in their own region. "Uprooted" from Lorraine, they move to Paris, where in the mid 1880s they join the swelling ranks of a "proletariat of baccalaureate holders" (*bacheliers*).[59]

Only three of the seven young men from Lorraine emerge from their experiences in the capital with their moral health intact. One of them benefits from an encounter with Hippolyte Taine. Having been treated as a destructive force by Bourget, Taine's views serve in Barrès' novel as an antidote to Bouteiller's uprooting influence. What Taine has that Bouteiller lacks is a sound respect for the determining but also sustaining role of regional and social contexts. The four among Bouteiller's pupils who are most deprived of economic and moral support from home ultimately turn to immorality and crime in Paris. One becomes an unprincipled lawyer, another a venal journalist and informer for the corrupt political machine that proves the real goal of Bouteiller's own ambitions. The two others are driven into robbery and murder by the depth of their poverty and by the extremity of their dissociation.

Bouteiller's "Kantian" doctrine, in Barrès' somewhat elusive account of it, is a disorienting mixture of skepticism and abstraction.

Our mind perceives the world under the categories of space, of time, and of causality ... [But] we cannot verify whether these categories correspond to anything real ... The great issue for the preceding generations was the passage from the absolute to the relative; today it is a matter of passing from certitudes to negation, without thereby losing all moral values.[60]

Previous generations witnessed a conflict between materialists and spiritualists. Kant's critical philosophy, as taught by Bouteiller, undermines both of these dogmatic alternatives; but it also leaves students with "a sentiment of nothingness." The attempt to recover a grounding for ethics through "an appeal to the heart," or through Kant's categorical imperative, is a pedagogical failure; it makes no impression on adolescents. Moreover, it is far too abstract even in theory.

I must always act in such a manner that I can want my action to serve as a universal rule ... There is in this moral rule an element of stoicism, and also an element of great pride, for it amounts to saying that one can know the rule applicable to all men – and moreover a germ of fanatical intolerance, for to conceive a rule common to all men is to be strongly tempted to subject them to it for their own good; finally, there is a total misunderstanding of the rights of the individual, of all life knows in the way of variation, dissimilarity, and spontaneity.[61]

Bouteiller's Kantian universalism, in short, fails to do justice to the rich diversity of real human conditions. Worse, it smacks of intolerance, of intellectual pride, and of a will to homogenize and dominate.

Barrès objected on nationalist grounds to Bouteiller's preference for foreign and "exotic truths" that were "mixed with poison" for the French "temperament." While a few great minds in any age may attain a universal perspective, he argued, one should not try to turn a whole generation of students into "citizens of humanity" and "initiates of pure reason." Yet his harshest criticism was aimed not so much at Kant's philosophy as at French Republican educational practice, and at what he took to be its moral and social consequences. Bouteiller's main fault was that he ignored his pupils' specific "conditions of existence." Instead of "proportioning" his teaching to the "realities" by which they were severally "constituted," he disregarded even what they had in common as youths of Lorraine. He thus "broke their social ties"; he detached them from their "soil" and "milieu," from their "social groups" and "traditions." As a substitute for these restraining and nourishing "roots," he offered an abstract creed of civic duty to the state that was both pedagogically ineffective and politically dominative. For its real aim was to encourage young Frenchmen to submit to "a wise administration" that spoke to them through the mouth of Bouteiller.[62]

In a fierce attack on the Radical Republic, Barrès pictured it as a regime of parliamentary corruption under the ultimate control of German Jewish bankers. More pertinently, he saw a centralizing state adminstration, "the bureaus," as tending to misdirect and drain away the "national energy" of France. The country's "living forces," he thought, were concentrated in various "active groups" that unfortunately worked in opposition to each other. The resulting "dissociation" was aggravated by the fact that "natural" or spontaneous associations and enterprises were being gradually deprived of initiative by the ubiquitous "bureaus." Quite apart from the destructive work of internationalized capital, and from revolutionary doctrines inciting to "theft and pillage," France was moving toward a "collectivism" that meant decadence. And the whole of this fatal drift was aided by Bouteiller's doctrines.[63]

Taine, in Barrès' novel, is an intellectual counterweight to Kant and Bouteiller, and a spokesman for Barrès himself. Part of what he stands for is a diffuse causal determinism, in which human behaviors, institutions, and moral codes are "necessitated" variously by "epochs," "climates," and religious ideas, by regionally and occupationally specific conditions of life, and by social groupings and "milieus." In his *Origins of Contemporary France* (1875–93), Barrès reports, Taine has accordingly "condemned any attempt to reconstitute societies in the name of pure reason." He has also evolved a "Goethean" philosophy that is evoked in a lyrical passage about a tree as an organic system.

There was no need for a master to intervene from outside. The Planetree cheerfully ... extended its branches ... from year to year, until its perfection ... No predominance of its trunk over its branches, its leaves; it is a rustling federation. It is its own law, and it unfolds it. We do not see a symmetry in the French manner, but the logic of a living soul and its creations ... That powerful mass of green obeys a secret reason, the most sublime philosophy, which is the acceptance of the necessities of life. Without denying or abandoning itself, it has drawn the best, the most useful parts from the conditions furnished by reality.[64]

A teleological imagery is here superimposed upon a causal environmentalism. Though somewhat precarious, this juxtaposition allows Barrès to recommend an acceptance of social "necessities," even while championing the spontaneous vitality of regional and social "milieus" against the deracinating influence of the Republican adminstration. "Let us respect human dignity in others," Taine tells one of Bouteiller's pupils, "and let us understand that it varies to an important degree according to milieus, occupations, and circumstances." He further counsels the young people to form a group, and to cultivate the practice of "sociability."

Ideas are abstract ... They do not suffice for the heart ... The best school, the laboratory of society, is the group, the voluntary association.[65]

It is this associative and voluntarist theme in Barrès novel that is linked to teleological metaphors of organic growth. In its emphasis upon human diversity, it faintly recalls the German conception of *Bildung*. The analogy remains superficial, however, because the diversity Barrès refers to is the diversity of conditioning environments, not of self-defining individuals, and because the voluntarist element in his thought is ultimately overwhelmed by a tough doctrine of social determination.

Nowhere is this clearer than in his "sociology" of French secondary education. He begins by portraying impressionable adolescents isolated from the world in *lycées* that resemble military barracks or convents, and susceptible "like all groups to moral epidemics." A competitive pedagogical system based on class rankings "monstrously" develops their "vanity," their "capacity for being humiliated and envious," and their passion for "distinction." They do have a sense of honor and of comradeship, but it is chiefly directed against a disciplinary regime embarrassing even to those who must apply it. As a result, the school class becomes a "collectivity in revolt against its laws," a "solidarity of cunning and embattled serfs."[66]

To the pupils at Nancy, Bouteiller's exhortations to patriotic duty mean less than certain of his attitudes and actions. What these convey, along with a partisan commitment to the Radical Republic, is the dangerous maxim that individual superiority justifies disrespect for the established social hierarchy. The students can only think of becoming "great men"; they acquire a distaste for ordinary occupations. Both before and after their arrival in Paris, they have no contact with experienced older men, or with business leaders who might caution them against "overly professorial views." Some of the books made available to them, Rousseau for example, further "exalt them without furnishing them with social sentiments." They thus ultimately succumb to a peculiar mixture of "ambition" and "romantic melancholy." Since the days of Stendhal's Julien Sorel, Barrès argues, this sentiment has characterized "thousands" of young Frenchmen "for whom the conquests of the bourgeoisie have broken the social barriers, and opened up all possibilities."[67]

To demonstrate the importance of "roots," Barrès dwells at length upon the family backgrounds of Bouteiller's seven pupils. One comes from a Catholic family of landed *propriétaires* who have legitimately assumed an aristocratic name. Two others are the offspring of well-established middle-class families of moderate wealth. These three prove relatively immune against the demoralizing effects of their schooling and of their move to Paris. The opposite is true of the four students from less favorable backgrounds, who are more or less thoroughly corrupted. Two of them are scholarship holders (*boursiers*), and another is the grandson of a serf liberated at the Revolution. While the first-generation descendants of the former serf have accumulated a little capital by shady means, they have not "decently" managed and preserved it. They have also transmitted a propensity for violence and cunning to their latest heir, who is destined to commit murder. Arrived in Paris, the students with the lowest allowances from their families promptly gravitate toward an underworld of prostitutes and thieves that is portrayed as the natural milieu of the "proletariat of *bacheliers*." Of the two *boursiers*, one becomes the murderer's accomplice, the other a paid informer.[68]

The narrative suggests that the moral traits of fathers reappear in their sons, though nothing is said about how and why this happens. The explicit thesis is that students with inadequate budgets and non-vocational educations are almost forced to turn to crime. Barrès writes of the "gap" between university study and remunerative employment, which cannot be bridged without family capital. He sees a "contradiction" between an "intellectual development" that "requires leisure and expense," and the need to make a living without delay. Refusing to "submit to the conditions imposed upon them by circumstances," the less wealthy among Bouteiller's pupils pursue "vague illusions." Instead of preparing them for "agriculture, commerce, or industry," the "system of the humanities" has "turned them away" from modest but useful employments. The Republican "administration" has "prepared them only for itself," for the role of state officials. Worse, Bouteiller's doctrines and actions have stimulated their "vanity." They have lost "the good sense to renounce the dreams of domination" that have been "suggested" to them by "the University."[69]

In a simplified statistical passage, Barrès notes that there are vastly more candidates for teaching positions each year than there are openings for them. From the mid 1880s on, he reports, hundreds of secondary students annually have been awarded diplomas that appear to be "claims upon the state," though they ultimately prove worthless. And almost half of the unsuccessful aspirants for office have had the prior encouragement of public scholarships. While contradictory in itself, Barrès concludes, the educational policy of the Radical Republic has come to threaten the stability of bourgeois society. "Uprooting" *boursiers* and other lower-class students from their inherited places in a "natural order," it has precipitated them into "anarchy" and "immoral disorder." They have become "beasts without dens." The murderer among them is a "grandson of serfs hastily introduced . . . among young capitalists." All of them have "entered the bourgeois class by way of the *lycée*." But since this false position proves beyond their means, "the proletariat of *bacheliers*" is "not a democracy on the rise, but an aristocracy that is being degraded."[70]

This formulation reflects a widespread French conservative view of misguided students as potential "*déclassés*." Though the word evoked downward social movement, something like loss of caste, it was typically applied to those who tried to rise too fast, by means of a general and literary education, when they should have been content with a more modestly "practical" training. The underlying theory was that the accumulation of cultural capital should be left to families with adequate reserves of economic capital, or that upward mobility through education alone was dangerous even for those who attempted it, presumably from an excess of "vanity." Their failure to

achieve goals that were inherently unrealistic and vaguely "romantic," the traditionalists warned, was bound to make them personally
miserable and socially disaffected. The insufficiently wealthy students in Barrès' novel, after all, had never really been "an aristocracy." They had *tried* to become "a democracy on the rise," and he
wrote to show that their failure was inevitable. In short, *Les déracinés*
dramatized the conservative case against the progressive shift in
French secondary and higher education after 1880.

What was original and dramatic in Barrés novel, on the other
hand, was the lurid portrait of Paul Bouteiller as a destructive force.
In some of his traits, to be sure, Bouteillier recalled Bourget's Adrian
Sixte. The son of a worker from Lille, he early attracted the attention
of his teachers through his "precocious and studious intelligence."
With the support of public scholarships, he ultimately graduated
first in his class at the Ecole Normale. Taken out of his "natural
milieu" at an early age, he depended emotionally upon his teachers
alone. He became a "pedagogical product, a son of reason, a
stranger to our traditional, local, or family habits, wholly abstract,
and truly suspended in the void." At the same time, unlike Sixte,
Bouteiller was something more than an isolated individual with
dangerous views. Barrès made him "a perfect representative of a
psychological species and of a social group." He further described
him as a commissioned agent of the state and a "drill sergeant" in
the service of his Republican superiors. His teaching embodied the
"spirit of the new Ecole Normale," "Uprooted" in his own "superior
way," and "without family or fatherland" (*ce déraciné supérieur ... un
sans-famille et un sans-patrie*), he was an ideal tool for a parliamentary
clique that finally integrated him directly into its system of
corruption.[71]

Behind Bouteiller, of course, stood the political and social program of the Radical Republic. Affecting a "Kantian" universalism
and preaching a morality of civic duty that struck traditionalists as
partisan and dangerously "abstract," a new generation of parliamentary leaders seemed determined to undermine the prerogatives
of the established bourgeoisie. Particularly in education, they allied
themselves with a "psychological species and a social group" that
was epitomized by the Normalien and the *boursier*. Without substantial family backgrounds, and raised to respect none but "professorial" values, this new academic and quasi-political elite displayed an
arrogant indifference to the "natural order" of French society, and

to the traditional sources of vitality in it. Controlled directly by this group and indirectly by the leadership of the Radical Republic, the new "University" had spawned the "proletariat of *bacheliers*."

In January 1898, not long after the publication of *Les déracinés*, Henry Bérenger published an article on "the intellectual proletarians in France" that was subsequently included in an anthology of 1901. Since Bismarck first called attention to a "proletariat of *bacheliers*," he reported, people "everywhere" have come to refer to "the intellectual proletarians" as a problematic social group. While the "new French universities are proud of the ever growing number of their students," he wrote, they ought also to be aware of the many who are "elevated" by university study only to "fall into a greater wretchedness." He distinguished these new "intellectual proletarians" from the occasional "bohemians, dissidents and *déclassés*" who had arisen "at the margin of the bourgeoisie" from the eighteenth century on. Few in number and usually from bourgeois backgrounds, these "refractory" individuals of the past could always be reintegrated into the class of their origins by "luck, repentance, or a concession."

But there are men who are born poor, sons of peasants, workers, petty employees or impoverished high officials, men who are hard-working and steady, who have acquired considerable knowledge through work and privation, men who seek entry into the ranks of society with the benefit of their university degrees... aspirants to the bourgeoisie... who end by being candidates for hunger. These are the Intellectual Proletarians.[72]

Having thus set his theme, Bérenger proceeded to "statistics of the French intellectual proletariat," which loosely brought together assorted evidence on unemployment and insufficient incomes in the educated professions. After offering separate passages on "the proletariat of doctors," the "proletariat of lawyers and judges," and so forth, he arrived at the "proletariat of students." Of the approximately 27,000 university students in France, 14,000 of them "crowded together" in the Paris student quarter, he claimed, "a good two-thirds" had "no resources other than a *bourse* or a pension of 1,500 to 2,000 francs per year," whereas their minimal expenses could be estimated at 1,800 to 2,000 francs.

Badly housed, badly clothed, badly nourished, deprived of their families, uprooted from their provinces... devoured by ambition and by wretchedness... these poor students, the real embryo of the intellectual proletariat, make up a singular and disquieting legion within contemporary youth.[73]

The obligation to Barrès, acknowledged in a footnote, became even clearer as Bérenger moved on to "the consequences of the French intellectual proletariat," among them the "psychological," the "social," and the "moral" ones.

The souls of the intellectual proletarians are fatally inclined toward subservience or toward revolt... Psychological wretchedness creates a revolutionary and anarchist general staff; wretchedness itself creates criminality, prostitution and parasitism in all its forms.[74]

Unable to make a decent living in their professions, Bérenger supposed, impoverished "intellectuals" of lower-class origins were likely to "sell themselves" either to "the crowd" or to "the plutocracy." And the latter alternative apparently seemed to him more probable.

Turning to "the causes of the French intellectual proletariat," Bérenger emphasized that the French Revolution had instituted equality of access to the liberal professions and public offices, along with a system of selective examinations (*concours*). While this opened up new horizons for "poor young people," it also led to an expansion of the bureaucracy, to a fixation upon *concours*, credentials, and civil service careers, and thus ultimately to "academic overproduction" (*surproduction universitaire*). The latter had been seriously aggravated by a law of 1891, which had exempted the holders of university degrees from two out of three years of compulsory military service. To complete his case, Bérenger cited "the growing disproportion between salaries and the cost of living."[75] By way of remedy, he urged that university enrollments be decreased. He did not want to see the scholarship program cancelled, as some were recommending; for the *boursiers* seemed to him "the salt of the universities." Instead, he wrote, "the mass of the mediocre and the incompetent" ought to be "diminished and rejected without pity," and the military dispensation of 1891 ought to be promptly revoked. He admitted that it might prove difficult to moderate "the excessive love of the French for the bureaucracy."

While we lack industrialists, farmers, and colonists, posts in the public administration are furiously competed for. We are choking in a mandarinate of wretchedness.

The only concluding recommendation he offered was that the young be discouraged from trying to enter the liberal and educated professions; they ought to be warned that these were hopelessly overcrowded, and that salaries were unlikely to return to adequate levels.[76]

While conservative and populist motifs were uneasily joined in Bérenger's essays, he opened his testimony before the Ribot Commission on a more unambiguously egalitarian note. The growth of the intellectual proletariat and the "over-production of officials," he testified, were due "in large part to the way in which the liberally educated classes (*classes libérales*) conceive the education of their children . . . for by virtue of the law of imitation, the people conform to what is done above them." What the bourgeoisie wants is "rapidly to separate itself from the people, and to organize a caste education for itself." That is why it prefers boarding arrangements, and especially the Catholic schools. The latter "mold" children's minds in an illiberal way; but the passive learning they emphasize proves successful on the baccalaureate, which is itself a "caste examination." "If our primary education is good," Bérenger continued, "it is good for all French citizens." He therefore favored the outright disestablishment of the existing system of secondary education, the extension of tougher primary schooling, and the creation of "popular universities" that would prepare the most promising among the "youth of the people" for their future role as "intellectuals." He felt in any case that France "could only renew itself through a revolution," since "the present development of parliamentary institutions" was "powerless to effect anything profound and serious in national life."[77]

Conceding that he ought also to suggest something in the realm of "the possible," however, Bérenger went on to propose that the existing *lycées* be reduced to about sixty "regional" institutions. Given increased autonomy from "the bureaus," from the "omnipotent bureaucracy" in the Ministry of Education, these regional *lycées* were to be reorganized to encompass family-style units (*maison familiales*). They were to select their students strictly for their intellectual potential, rather than according to their parents' wealth and social position. Similarly, the classical secondary curriculum was to be offered only to a small and academically selected elite. The existing *collèges*, in anticipation of their future role as "popular universities," were to offer an augmented version of higher primary schooling.[78]

Particularly in his deposition before the Ribot Commission,

Bérenger took a self-consciously "democratic" stance. Like others in his own day and since, he took egalitarian policies in education to be largely identical with socially progressive recruitment, on what we would call "merit" principles. Yet he never specified how the rigorous academic selection he recommended was actually to be effected. Indeed, he referred to the centralized educational administration of France, and to the reputed French passion for examinations and state diplomas, in a consistently dismissive tone. He did not explain how a system of "merit" selection might operate without examinations, and without a degree of administrative centralization. In the actual circumstances, his hostility to "the bureaus" and to the educational policies of the parliamentary Republic were less consistent with his stated egaliterianism than with the ideological perspective developed by Barrès. This is true also of his proposal to diminish the "academic proletarians" by warning the public that the educated professions were overcrowded. The students most likely to be deterred by such a warning were those from unfavorable backgrounds, who had neither family capital nor social connections to supplement the weakening market value of their academic credentials. Though Bérenger apparently failed to realize it, Barrès opposed educational expansion as a consistent social conservative. The "academic proletarians" he most objected to were quite explicitly those without sufficient capital. Here again, Bérenger appears to have accepted a program that he did not fully penetrate. Perhaps this increased his effectiveness as a "neutral" expert on the public issue of "the academic proletariat" in France around 1900.

CHAPTER 3

The meanings of education, 2

We can now proceed to a closer look at the major positions and concepts in the French debate over the future of secondary education from the 1890s to the early 1920s. Our general objective will be to canvass a roughly representative "sample" of texts. We will try to understand and to chart a field of discourse, rather than to pursue the thought of any single individual. In the light of this aim, we will give particular attention to depositions before the Ribot Commission of 1899 by prominent university professors, scholars, and academicians, which may reasonably be taken to represent the larger universe of French academic opinion on the issues in question.[1]

THE DEFENSE OF "CULTURE GÉNÉRALE"

To begin, leaving the champions of reform to a later section of this chapter, we will consider the views of ten especially articulate defenders of the classical curriculum. All of them were members of the Académie Française, or of one of the other four sections of the Institut de France; two were professors at the Collège de France; two were professors (including a dean) at the Paris faculty of medicine; one was the director of the Ecole Normale; only two were professors (including a dean) at faculties of letters, and none were professors at faculties of sciences.[2] Thus as a group, these were established spokesmen for an older and more conservative wing of the French academic system, rather than for the reformist sentiments typical of the expanding faculties of letters and of sciences during the late nineteenth century. As a matter of fact, the three men from the faculties of letters and from the Ecole Normale were somewhat more flexible in their views than the other seven. Nevertheless, all ten agreed that the classical curriculum alone should be accredited as fully secondary, and that the "modern" option of 1891 should be reconverted into a short program of "practical" studies for the intermediate ranks of the economic middle class.

In their defense of classical studies, members of this group referred less often to substantive arguments or ideas in the ancient texts than to certain general sentiments and intellectual traits. Thus the philosopher Emile Boutroux saw Greek and Roman literature as exemplifying a perfect balance of the human spirit. He cited "reason" and "measure," an "upright and healthy nature," a "sense for the just and honorable [*honnête*]," along with "piety toward the dead, the fatherland, and the laws," and "harmony between the material and the spiritual, between idea and form." He believed that these qualities could be "made to penetrate the pupils' minds and souls," in what he and others conceived as a "slow impregnation."[3] The archeologist Georges Perrot, director of the Ecole Normale, considered ancient literature particularly accessible for the young. It expressed the "primordial sentiments of the human heart," such as patriotism, courage, and familial devotion, with "naive" sincerity, in an "elementary" and therefore "eternal" way. In being educated, he thought, "individuals ought to pass through the states of mind that have succeeded each other" in the evolution of humanity.[4]

This focus upon primordial sentiments, rather than distinctive ideas, was compatible with another perspective, which was expressed more widely and with greater enthusiasm. French educational traditionalists almost universally stressed the "latin" or "classical" character of French civilization, the lines of influence that ran from Greece to Rome, from Rome to France, and from there to the rest of the world. In a supportive comment on Bérard's project of 1923, the philosopher Henri Bergson did this at length.

I want to insist upon the special advantages that (classical studies) represent for the French mind, and also upon what they mean for the increase of our influence abroad . . . [Classical study] forms and develops the intelligence . . . in the same direction in which Greek thought formerly developed. Order, proportion, measure; exactitude and flexibility of form . . . these traits . . . characterize what I would call the spirit of precision . . . It is said that Eastern thought . . . remains imprecise unless it has come into contact with ours; and even in the West, the qualities of order and of composition . . . are generally called "latin" . . .

A France less penetrated by classicism . . . would be a France less admired and loved; and since considerations of practical utility are brought to bear against Greek and Latin studies, let us consider that a people has a

...vital interest in gaining the admiring sympathy of the rest of the world ... We also have an economic interest in remaining what we are. It is in the luxury industries that we excel, where elegance and taste are needed. More generally, our products are recognized for their precision and for their finished execution ... I know that our workers have not learned Greek and Latin. Nonetheless, they work in a society that has received a greco-latin imprint .. From the top downward to the less cultivated portion of the nation, the qualities, habits, and intellectual standards have always been transmitted that are summed up in the spirit of precision, or the classical spirit.[5]

The economist Paul Leroy-Beaulieu similarly argued that France would always be "an Athenian nation, drawing its superiority, even economically, from its qualities of elegance, finesse, distinction, and refinement." Like Bergson, he claimed that industrial producers, though not classically schooled, benefited from "living in a milieu" shaped by classical studies.[6]

The Hellenist Alfred Croiset, dean of the Paris faculty of letters, was both moderate in his opposition to the modern curriculum, and fairly receptive to the language of republican educational reform. Perhaps he was affected by the attitudes of colleagues in his own faculty. Nevertheless, he argued much as Boutroux, Perrot, and Bergson did, while giving particular attention to the practice of translation from the classical languages. He too seems worth quoting at length, if only to call attention to some of his characteristic terms and distinctions.

[Boys who will] spend most of their lives in intellectual work ... [need] the rigourous [*forte*] preparation of greco-latin studies ... [The object is] not to form polite lettered men, but robust intelligences, capable of producing a rich harvest of ideas and of actions, thanks to the profound cultivation [labour] they have received ...

Our literature, our philsophy, our private and public morality are permeated with classicism. We have antiquity, so to speak, in our blood ... Our ideal of the *honnête homme* is still approximately that of Socrates. Our civic morality [*morale civique*] comes to us .. from Athens and from Rome.

The translation of a text from a foreign language into French is an incomparable exercise for the development of the child's mind ... What is translation? It is a rethinking .. [The child] could not himself have invented the idea [he encounters], for it is a vigorous idea [*idée virile*], and he is only a child. But he makes it his own in comprehending it. The effort is serious but not excessive. And in this engagement [*lutte*] with thought that is more rigorous [*forte*] than his own, he imperceptibly gains strength, as in a flexibly graduated gymnastics [*gymnastique*] ... [Modern foreign texts] are too easy in some ways. Since the modern peoples have developed in a parallel manner and have borrowed from each other, there is in these several languages a . . . cosmopolitan portion, so to speak, which can be transcribed rather than translated. In other respects, these [modern] texts are too difficult, or at least too distant from our genius, since the non-cosmopolitan portion of the modern languages often reflects a particular turn of mind or of sentiment that lends itself poorly to a truly French translation . . . Latin for us is not a language like any other; it is a mother language in the full sense of the term . . .

The ancient literatures . . . are naturally simple, easily understood by the young, who are precisely at the stage of individual development that is represented, in the development of humanity, by the civilization of Greece and of Rome . . . These young literatures have the further merit of being naturally laic and civic in orientation . . . [They exemplify] love of the public good, devotion to the community, self-respect, submission to the laws, the higher sense of an unwritten justice, everything that is the soul of our democracies.

The purely literary qualities of the ancient works . . .[are educational primarily] in . . . their beautiful and simple order, in that luminous clarity . . . that fully satisfies and charms our reason . . . They conform to our inherited genius, to our deepest instincts. It is through them that our thought and our art have taken up the place they hold in the world.[7]

As the only scholar in our group of ten to suggest a hermeneutic model of translation as "rethinking," Croiset unearthed an interesting problem in his own position, and in that of French educational conservatives generally. Any coherent account of translation must in some way acknowledge and address the distance between the language of the original text and that of the translator. Yet this distance was consistently overlooked or minimized by the prevailing thesis that Latin was the "mother" of French. As this thesis was usually put, it implied not only genetic continuity but also similarity between the "civilizations" of Rome and of France. Croiset claimed that the modern foreign languages were too easy to translate, since they could be directly "transcribed." But he did not hesitate to dismiss them as too difficult as well, precisely because they embodied "particular turns of mind and of sentiment" that were "too distant from our genius."

From a comparative perspective, this emphasis upon the "Latin" character of the French spirit strikes one as distinctive and consequential. Among the German neo-humanists of the eighteenth and early nineteenth centuries, few would have been willing to consider Greek thought no more than an anticipatory element in the Latin heritage. Many revered Greece more than Rome, partly because they identified Greece with Germany and Rome with France. They idealized the ancient Greek authors; in a sense, they even identified with them. Yet they were nonetheless deeply aware of the distance between themselves and their models. The development of the German philological and hermeneutic disciplines surely required such an awareness. And if it did, then the French tendency to assimilate Rome to France may well have helped to impede the emergence of a comparably interpretive scholarly tradition in France.

There is also a contrast between Arnold's persistent focus upon what "has been thought," and the French educational conservatives' preoccupation with literary form. Bergson identified "the qualities of order and of composition" as particularly "latin." Croiset was clearly on guard against the dismissive reaction that this approach had begun to provoke in some circles; for he wanted greco-latin studies "*not* to form polite lettered men, but robust intelligences, capable of producing a rich harvest of ideas and of actions." Yet his own catalogue of the classical virtues in fact gave less attention to substantive ideas than to a certain range of sentiments and formal characteristics. He actually integrated Socrates into the French tradition of the *honnête homme*, and he went on to praise the "literary qualities of the ancient works" and their "luminous clarity." This typical elevation of formal perfection aided the claim that classical studies were universally educative; but it also tended to reduce learning to a pursuit of stylistic excellence, rather than an engagement with ideas.

A related characteristic of the French case for the classical curriculum was the almost universal recourse to the metaphor of mental gymnastics. No single definition of education acquired as much currency among French educational traditionalists, and indeed in reformist circles as well, as the notion of a "general cultivation of the mind" or of "the intelligence." Croiset dramatized this aspect of his argument by picturing the child gaining strength in a "contest" with thought more "vigorous" than his. But Croiset was certainly not alone in adhering to this muscular model of mental capacity, and to the agricultural metaphor of schooling as a "working" (*culture, labour*) of that capacity. French educationists of the late nineteenth and early twentieth centuries were virtually unanimous in defining academic secondary education as "general cultivation," or as a "general cultivation of the mind" (*culture générale de l'intelligence*). The "general" character of this education lay in its not being concentrated on particular subject matters, or mental functions, and in its not being guided by specific "practical" requirements. In these respects, *culture générale* was the French equivalent of the German concept of *allgemeine Bildung*. In other respects, however, there was a great difference between the French use of *culture* and the German use of *Bildung*, and that requires a comment.

If one looks up the words *culture* and *cultiver* in Emile Littré's scholarly French dictionary of 1875, or in various twentieth-century editions of the *Grand Larousse*, one invariably finds the list of variant definitions headed by the original, agricultural one.[8] *Culture* still primarily denotes the action of cultivating or working the soil. A first major variant refers to the "cultivation" of poetry, music, or the fine arts, the sciences and letters. The reflexive *se cultiver* is briefly noted; but it is defined as the cultivation of *one's faculties*, not of the self or of the whole person. The second "figurative" meaning of *culture* continues this emphasis; for it refers to the development of the faculties: the memory, the "intellectual faculties," or the mind or intelligence. The Larousse of 1929 observes that the word *culture* is "sometimes used, after the German *Kultur*, in the (broad) sense of *civilisation*, but chiefly in speaking of the Germanic peoples." Abandoning this tentative extension, the edition of 1960 instead captures some of the flavor of the French education debate, by associating the development of the faculties with "certain intellectual exercises," and by distinguishing between "*culture primaire, moderne, classique, technique,*" and "*gréco-latine.*" I called attention earlier to Elias' account of the divergence between the German conception of *Bildung* and of *Kultur* on the one hand, and the French tradition of the *honnête homme* and of *civilisation* on the other.[9] What I want to add here is only that *culture* in French usage by about 1890–1920 had come to mean the exercising of the intellectual faculties, or the "working" of the mind.

An even more striking difference between French *culture générale* and German *Bildung* lay in the fact that French theorists of education did not share the German commitment to individual uniqueness and diversity. On the contrary, prominent French educational conservatives fiercely opposed what they called "individualism." Thus Boutroux complained to the Ribot Commission that "the individual is less and less ... protected against his inexperience, his shortcomings, and his whims." Instead of making students conform to "the ideal type of humanity and the needs of the nation," educators are overly "preoccupied with serving the tastes and desires of individuals." The "principle of uniformity that is . . . a legacy of the Latin and classical spirit" has been abandoned in favor of "the principle of diversity." The "exaggeration of diversity in education" is a national danger; for it threatens to "loosen the social bond," which is based on common beliefs. But classical studies are particularly capable of "sustaining the soul of France." The "universal man" that was contemplated by our fathers in the works of antiquity must not be considered "abstract and unreal"; nor should educators be overly interested in "the specifically Greek, or Latin, or modern character of the monuments studied." Instead of seeking to "determine the relationship of these works to the moment in time and the point in space at which they appeared," teachers must focus upon "what has always been considered admirable and excellent" in them.[10]

Boutroux was objecting to the scholarly study of historical contexts. He thought that such misguided "erudition" might end by suggesting that the classical texts "would be impossible today." He called for the restoration of a single secondary program based on Latin and Greek, which was also to encompass a modern foreign language, along with elementary mathematics as a further "*gymnastique intellectuelle.*" The way to uphold the classical curriculum against potential rivals, he argued, was to have it do justice both to the "exigencies of modern life" and to "the preconditions of a complete education." The intrusion of false erudition was bound to overload the class schedule, and to prevent concentration upon the main aim of secondary schooling, which was the pursuit of "those general notions" that can "become the very substance of the mind, and assure its rectitude for a whole lifetime."

In a homily upon the words *éducation* and *instruction*, the conservative literary critic Ferdinand Brunetière argued that the two used to have similar meanings, though *éducation* referred more to the "forming" and "governing" of pupils and the "direction of manners," whereas *instruction* referred to "the *culture* . . . of the mind." The two concepts began to diverge, according to Brunetière, when the Encyclopedists wrongly defined the object of education as "the development of all powers of the human being . . . as if there were no radically evil ones" among them, and when "the most ill-bred of our great writers violently separated the two most inseparable things there ought to be in the world – the rights of the individual and those of society." But *éducation* necessarily entails the constraint of the individual "with a view to a social gain." For example, a "man of the world" is a man "formed" to constrain himself so as not to offend others.

To form a "citizen" or to form a "soldier" ... is to teach them the art of subordinating something of themselves and of their "natural rights" to the interests and rights of the community. Without that, no "army," no "fatherland," no "society" ...

Unfortunately, Brunetière continued, *instruction* as practiced by the state "in our days" no longer aims at "disinterested cultivation" (*culture désintéressée*), but only at "utility" for the individual. People learn in order to pass examinations and to get on in life, to make a fortune or to nourish their vanity.

And I say that anything that is done ... *for instruction* thus understood will be done *against éducation*. For what is thus primarily developed is the spirit of individualism ... The *instruction* that is given seems to have no goal but to insure the victory of the individual motivations over the social motivations.[11]

The French word *professionnel* was used to describe "vocational" as well as "professional" education. This allowed Brunetière to integrate a conventional distinction between professional and "general" schooling into his broader contrast between "individualism" and "social motivations."

Professional instruction will always have this against it: that it is essentially particular, and that in consequence, it is not general, or truly humane ... For it is only through general ideas that we are taken out of ourselves, that we separate from our professional specialty, that we raise ourselves above our present condition ... Our particular ideas divide us; our general ideas ... reunite us ... For our particular ideas are ... what is most individual and ... eccentric in us; but our general ideas are what is truly human in us, and therefore what in us is truly social.[12]

The identification of the "human" with the "social" reminds one of some of Emile Durkheim's sociological theories, just as the persistent image of *éducation* as a "forming" of the individual to suit "society" suggests Durkheim's account of education as socialization.

My main point at the moment, however, is only that *education, formation,* and *culture générale* in the French tradition differed sharply from German *Bildung* in their animus against individual uniqueness and diversity. The difference was partly semantic. As Steven Lukes has demonstrated, the word *individualisme* was almost always used pejoratively in France; it evoked egotism and therefore dissociation.[13] An orthodox German mandarin of the decades around 1900 might well have seconded many of Brunetière's substantive arguments, including the moralistic attack upon "utilitarianism" and the elevation of the "fatherland." But he would probably have used such terms as "egotism" and "materialism" where Brunetière used "individualism"; he would have contrasted these with "idealism," and he would have appealed to "the whole, the community," or "the state" where Brunetière championed "society."

Nevertheless, there was more than a nominal difference here. For as Lukes has pointed out as well, the theoretical commitment to "individuality" and to cultural diversity in the German tradition had no full counterpart in France. Certainly *individualisme* typically implied only egotistic calculation or asocial behavior. Brunetière's passage on the "man of the world" is interesting in that connection. Whether intentionally or not, it harks back to the "formation" of the *honnête homme* as the "civilizing" of a natural self that would offend others if left in its raw state. My inference is not that the concept of the *honnête homme* directly caused French ideas of education to be what they were; but only that this concept, together with its social preconditions, helped to shape the structure of the conceptual field that in turn at least partly caused men like Brunetière to write as they did, typically without being fully aware of their obligations. As a witness before the Ribot Commission, Brunetière praised the classical curriculum for its capacity to develop "the habit and the taste for general ideas." He hinted that the modern curriculum resembled the existing programs of higher primary and vocational schooling, which should not be encouraged to develop the "pretention of being in some way parallel and equal" with the classical secondary stream. And he pointed to the "egalitarian passion" to explain the "unfortunate tendency" of "the *petite bourgeoisie*" to send its children to "the highest form" of secondary education available.[14]

Paul Brouardel, dean of the Paris faculty of medicine, duly told the Commission that only two out of thirty-four members of his faculty had voted for the "assimilation" of the modern to the classical curriculum. He argued that "social necessities" required two distinct forms of secondary education. But he thought that pupils who "could not or did not desire" to pursue the classical program should be equipped with "a certain number of utilitarian and vocational notions" in a short course of studies that still allowed them to "enter into active life" or "into commerce and industry" at the age of fifteen or sixteen. To show that the conversion of Duruy's "special secondary" program into the "modern" stream had been a mistake, he cited the case of some modern foreign literature teachers, who "taught Goethe and Shakespeare as one would teach Virgil and Homer," with the result that their students did not learn German in the practical way that (by definition) was intended. Only the classical curriculum offered a truly rigorous "*gymnastique* of the mind," developing the "habits of reflection" and "precision" required for higher studies. Brouardel wanted the "old [classical] baccalaureate" restored, and to "exclude" from it "neither mathematics, nor the modern languages, nor history." Yet he was an opponent of "overloaded" programs, which he traced to the intrusion of materials that relied too heavily on memory, rather than "method." In a brief reference to the needs of practicing physicians, he argued that they would lose their "indispensable influence," unless their patients "found in them a superior culture."[15]

Georges Perrot, director of the Ecole Normale, was more moderate in his opposition to the non-classical curriculum. He proposed to let modern graduates enter the faculties on an experimental basis, while awaiting "results." He conceded that the "masterpieces of French literature" might indeed be suitably educative. He also anticipated that the classical program would benefit from being "relieved" of students who followed it reluctantly or out of "vanity." He thought "the majority of well-to-do-families" would continue to favor a classical "*culture générale.*" "For the others," who "want to devote themselves early to practical life," Perrot considered the higher primary schools more appropriate than the "so-called modern program," which he saw as a "counterfeit" of the classical curriculum.[16]

Alfred Croiset wanted all secondary schools to teach both Latin and Greek during the first five years of study. The dropping of Greek, he thought, would seriously "lower" the "*culture générale* of the mind." A "bifurcation" of the curriculum after the fifth year, however, was to permit the substitution of mathematics for Greek in a "sciences" branch. Teaching methods throughout were to be reconciled to "our scientific and realistic spirit" by the elimination of needless "erudition," and of an inappropriate emphasis upon literary "virtuosity." Croiset tried to show that a full-length modern secondary program was a "false conception," that ended by contradicting its original "idea," namely that "there are too many mandarins."

Everyone wants to enter the medical school or the faculty of law . . . it is a very great evil. A portion of the *bourgeoisie* must be brought back to active, practical careers, to commerce, to industry, to colonization.

A "mandarin" in this quite typical usage was simply a would-be state official or member of the liberal professions who shunned a "practical" career in business or in the colonies. Since many of those aiming at the liberal professions failed to reach them, Croiset argued, it was disastrous to create a modern program "leading to the same careers." For that was to steer young people precisely toward "the goal from which one wanted to dissuade them." Modern graduates did not have "the capacity to analyse and to understand the meaning of an abstract idea that one finds even in a mediocre pupil of the classical curriculum." To allow them to reach higher education would be a "fatal lowering" of standards.[17]

Many of those who complained that the modern program had been allowed to become a "counterfeit" of the classical curriculum conveyed a sense that both curricular elements and social groups had in some way been wrongly "placed." Paul Leroy-Beaulieu was particularly explicit on this subject.

There are exceptionally gifted persons, and there are those who are in a material position that permits them to take all the time necessary for a good education. It is for these two categories that classical studies are destined. Another category may be gifted in other respects, with respect to action, for example . . . These persons need a rapid course of instruction terminating at fifteen or sixteen years of age. Our modern program . . . should be only a more highly developed [form of] primary schooling.[18]

Again and again, French educational conservatives came back to the idea of two distinct and unequal forms of secondary schooling for what they considered the two main sectors of the French middle class. The economist Paul Levasseur, professor at the Collège de France, once more praised Duruy for having "instituted a mode of *gymnastique* inferior to the classical curriculum" but more "immediately practical" and "providing access to business more quickly- . . . for the many young people who have to earn their bread."

Duruy's program should have been called "industrial"; it should not have been housed in classical *lycées*, and of course it should not have been modified or extended. Addressing the Ribot Commission in his role as statistician, Levasseur estimated at 1.3 million the number of French males "working in the liberal professions, in the civil service, or belonging through their fortune or rank to what were formerly called the ruling classes" (*classes dirigeantes*). Within the remaining population, since "most workers have to content themselves with primary schooling," he then identified "about 5 million persons to whom it would be desirable to give a [form of] instruction that would lead them beyond primary schooling, without being the one that is appropriate for the 1.3 million persons constituting the social elite."

In explaining himself, Levasseur largely ignored curricular questions, while elaborately specifying the social implications of his categories. He reported that many business owners hesitated to employ a baccalaureate holder "because they suppose that he will have too high pretentions and will not go to work with a will, believing himself superior to the task he is assigned." Levasseur further argued that "a large merchant [*négotiant*] or an industrialist . . . at the head of an important enterprise" would be right to "have his son undertake classical studies," since the son "has his nest all prepared," and thus does not have to get an early start toward earning his living. The real difficulty with the modern curriculum, according to Levasseur, was that "it seems less appropriate than the classical for the formation of liberally cultivated intelligences, and it is too complicated to educate modest practitioners."[19]

Not everyone was equally blunt about the socially classificatory function of segmentation in secondary education. Yet as late as 1923, Henri Bergson described both the modern stream of 1891 and the settlement of 1902 as if they had confused crucial categories and distinctions. He called for the reinstitution of a single academic secondary curriculum based on the two ancient languages *and* on mathematics, and for a non-classical secondary stream that would not be housed in the same institutions, nor prepare for the universities, the *grandes écoles*, or the liberal professions. The role of this non-classical stream would be to provide "officers" for "industry, commerce, and agriculture." It would clearly signal this aim "from the beginning," so that its pupils would not end by feeling "*déclassés*" in business careers. Pursuing his theme of French national greatness,

Bergson stressed the need for a "division of labor," and for the "early recruitment of a double elite . . . of thought and of action." One of these elites was to develop "the productive powers of the country"; the other was to "obtain the greatest possible sum of pure scientific knowledge and disinterested research."[20]

There was an element of euphemism in Bergson's reference to a "double elite," since "thought" clearly outranked "action" in his scheme. His main point was precisely that there ought *not* to be different but equal forms of secondary schooling. Nevertheless, other French educational traditionalists were more specific than Bergson about the location of the boundary between the "generally" and the "practically" educated. What they intended was not a separation between an educated and a propertied wing within the upper middle class, but a divide between an integrated *bourgeoisie* on the one hand, and the "intermediate" layers of the occupational hierarchy on the other. Much more plainly and unabashedly than their German counterparts, they acknowledged the role of wealth in providing access to prolonged schooling. At the same time, they consistently grouped the highest commercial and industrial positions with what the Germans called the "academic" professions. This is particularly clear in the testimony of Charles Bouchard of the Paris faculty of medicine, which was submitted to the Ribot Commission in a written document full of lengthy enumerations and descriptions. Couched in what might be termed the declarative mode of social classification, Bouchard's text was meant at once to describe the French educational system, and to confirm its social mission.

Bouchard simply registered that the choice of schooling was determined by "the resources of the family," while simultaneously portraying each level and branch of the educational system as "giving the country" a specific set of occupational groups, and thus providing what "a society needs." In his longest list of "needed occupations," he grouped "the heads of all the great agricultural, industrial, and commercial enterprises," financiers, engineers, shipowners, and "promoters of colonial enterprises"; doctors, public adminstrators, civil servants of various branches, diplomats, legislators and justices, military officers, educators, and clergy; "men of science" and scholars, writers, poets, and artists ("ornaments of democracy"). Even "the young man who does nothing," he added, "finds his role in society if he is cultivated." All of these groups "used to be called the *classes dirigeantes.*" They owed their "guiding influence to their intelligence and personal worth." To retain this influence, they needed the "culture, intelligence, and morality" conferred by the humanities. Prior to their specialized university-level studies, they required a secondary education whose "character-istic quality" it was "not to be utilitarian, or to be so only incidentally."[21]

In a passage on the "abuse" of secondary education, Bouchard complained that many families enrolled their children in full-term secondary programs from "vanity" or "lack of foresight." They failed to consider the sacrifices necessary even beyond the baccalaureate to "obtain a remunerative profession." The only answer was to "reserve a long and costly preparation" for "the careers which require it," and to spare "those who need another preparation" a needless "loss of time and money." Bouchard therefore demanded that the "special secondary" program be "reconstituted," and that "there be directed toward it each year nearly fifteen thousand pupils who (now) to their own detriment crowd secondary education and ... lower its stan-dards." Five of these fifteen thousand did not absolutely "need" Latin. Hence the search for other means to "develop the intelligence and elevate the soul" of those who were "turned away from the ancient literatures by the nature of their minds."

Bouchard conceded that the sciences and the modern foreign languages had been found "educative." Until the modern stream was "given a dignity equal to that of the classical," however, he could not advise the admission of modern graduates to the medical profession, which "requires a high intellectual and moral culture." In the meantime, Bouchard did not think it "prudent" to talk about possible connections between higher primary and modern secondary schooling. Rather, the higher primary program should "find its natural development" in the "special secondary" stream, which should "prepare the children of well-to-do workers and *petits bour-geois*" for "intermediate positions" in society.

Let us leave to each curriculum its domain and its prerogatives, and far from facilitating the passage from one to the other, let us maintain the separations which are imposed by the nature of things.[22]

Bouchard's formulations strike us as both naive and transparent. Without any appearance of strain, and sometimes in a single sentence, he moved from the *de facto* segmentation of French secondary education to the "necessity" of the corresponding social distinctions, and on to the legitimating differences in the "nature" of students' minds. Few French educational conservatives quite equaled the untroubled ease with which he did this. Nevertheless, all of them actually shared some or all of his tacit assumptions, which they usually stated somewhat more fully. Particularly ambitious in this respect was the philosopher and social theorist Alfred Fouillée, whose systematic elaborations will round out our portrait of French educational traditionalism around 1890–1920.

Fouillée's specific recommendations to the Ribot Commission were relatively conventional and almost formulaic. He wanted the curriculum of the classical secondary stream enlarged to encompass the modern languages (taught for use) and more mathematics, the latter to replace Greek in a kind of bifurcation during the final years of the sequence. By dropping Greek as a requirement, and by somewhat reducing the class hours devoted to Latin, he thought it possible to accommodate the "needs of modern life" without premature recourse to "specialization." In the usual response to the problem of "overloading," he further proposed to "suppress philology, versification, the detailed history of literature, the pointless details of history, geographic nomenclatures, and the superfluous details of the physical and natural sciences." A more rigorous baccalaureate examination was to remain a prerequisite for entry into the university faculties, the *grandes écoles*, and the liberal professions. Fouillée was particularly interested, finally, in the course of philosophy that traditionally concluded the classical secondary program. Maintained and expanded, this course was to "furnish students with the moral and social principles we need more than ever in our epoch of religious dissolution."[23]

The Ribot Commission invited Fouillée's testimony because he had written several books on the future of French secondary education, and he actually continued to publish on this subject even after 1900. In a way, he became the leading social theoretician of French educational conservatism. His works are rather long and somewhat repetitive; but his main arguments can be extracted from just one of his books, for they embellished the well-established antitheses between "liberal" and "practical" education, "general" and "utilitarian" concerns, social cohesion and "individualism."

The majority of a people is made up of men who are preoccupied with present and personal interests, since they have neither enough material resources nor enough intellectual culture to act in the light of distant and general interests. For them, a certain utilitarianism is a necessity and almost a duty. On the other hand, there . . . [are men] who are enabled by their social situation and their intellectual culture, quite independently of any superior morality, to forget immediate interests in the light of a more distant goal... That the latter, in exchange for their advantages and their privileged position, should have the strict obligation to take in hand the interests of the entire people, that is quite obvious... An aristocracy of merit open to all is especially necessary in a [democratic] society... [In such a society] those who have some wealth [*aisance*] and leisure have the duty to counterbalance the influence of utilitarianism with the spirit of intellectual and moral disinterestedness... Any primarily practical education whose principal aim is to furnish, through the most rapid procedures, immediately applicable knowledge... is primary, no matter by what name it is decorated. Instruction detached from the cares of material life, instruction that cannot be improvised, nor acquired by mere effort of memory, which on the contrary must be like a slow impregnation of the soul: that is the only secondary instruction worthy of the name.[24]

Thus wealth was explicitly a prerequisite for membership in the guiding elite, as well as for access to "disinterested" education. That is why men only endowed with cultural capital could be identified as "intellectual proletarians." Secondary schooling was "impractical" in part by being long. Nonetheless, it automatically redefined those who could afford it as a natural aristocracy of mind.

The immediately following argument insured that "impractical" schooling would not prove utterly fruitless even for individuals.

It is... the duty of an enlightened government... to maintain the standards of the [liberal] professions... and to preserve them from the industrial or mercantile spirit, as well as from the narrowly individualistic spirit... In a democratic state, examinations... are the great means of selection and of natural hierarchy... It is essential that the liberal professions and the highest positions in industry and commerce be reserved, in so far as possible... to the true elite of the nation.[25]

Fouillée was not writing about academic testing. He simply wanted to exclude modern graduates from access to the baccalaureate and to the "true elites," which characteristically included the propertied upper middle class. Wealth and classical secondary education preserved even this portion of the integral *bourgeoisie* from the "mercantile spirit," and from the "individualism" that results from having to think about "material" things.

To show that "the magnificently disordered literatures of England and Germany" were pedagogically "unsuitable" for "young Frenchmen," Fouillée associated "the heroes of Shakespeare, of Byron and Goethe" with "unbridled individualism." He argued that France had to free itself from "intellectual, sentimental, moral, and economic anarchism," and to return to the "antique" sentiment of "civic solidarity." His denigration of the natural sciences was even more interesting.

A curriculum based on science will always be misdirected toward utilitarian ends, because the same sciences that could serve to educate the mind when cultivated for themselves can even better serve this or that profession ... Another fault of scientific education in its present form is that it favors the mechanical amassing [of information] and thereby the overburdening [of pupils]. The great means of selection at the entry of the scientific careers ends up being the *quantity* of information instead of the *quality* of the mind. The result is a sort of intellectual deformation.[26]

The deep-seated opposition between the "useful" and the "disinterested" was profoundly affected by the social symbolism at issue in the debates over secondary education. Fouillée's formulations let us see exactly why only pure mathematics was absolutely safe from the taint of the "useable." Certainly in France, the status inferiority of "applied" science infected the whole realm of merely empirical "information." In the pedagogy of mental "training," the "geometric spirit" might be valued as a complement to the literary "spirit of finesse"; but the natural sciences as traditionally taught were always in danger of being found too "utilitarian," or of being dismissed as a mere "overburdening" of the memory. As Fouillée also demonstrates, memorization almost had to be an attributed characteristic of non-elite schooling, which was explicitly *meant* to convey "a few useful notions" to an essentially passive audience. The associative reasoning involved was no less socially effective for being circular.

Fouillée persistently urged a greater emphasis within the classical secondary curriculum upon the concluding course in "philosophy," defined to include what he called "moral and social studies."

The ... need ... for social studies ... results in the first place from the advent of democracy, which makes indispensable ... a knowledge of political and economic questions. Furthermore, the weakening of religious beliefs necessitates, in compensation, a philosophical, moral, and sociological education. All those concerned with education deplore the spirit of intellectual egotism and moral individualism produced by the inroads of specialization; to conterbalance that spirit, philosophical studies are ... increasingly indispensable ... [The uneducated] scorn general ideas ... In reality, they accept ... those among the current ideas that best suit their individual prejudices ... Hence the ... theoretical anarchy ... that transforms itself inevitably into moral anarchy, the foretaste of social anarchy. Philosophy is the sole means of preventing a false dogmatism, and of recalling science to the modesty that Socrates used to counsel.[27]

Fouillée here faintly resembled an orthodox German university professor on the ravages of specialization and the need for *Weltanschauung*. There was the suggestion that the loss of tradition threatened modern society with "dissolution." The proposed cure was a renewal of "moral and social studies," which were clearly conceived as branches of a socially reintegrative philosophy, rather than as empirical disciplines. But while all this sounds vaguely familiar, there were significant deviations from the patterns of German mandarin orthodoxy as well. *Bildung* in the German tradition implied an integration of knowledge and evaluative insight *within the individual* that could plausibly be portrayed as endangered by specialization. Fouillée's account of specialization was almost perfunctory by comparison. It amounted to the bald assertion that specialization favored the diversification of unprincipled private beliefs among the uneducated. Indeed, specialization was not as central an issue even for traditionalists among French educational theoreticians as it was for most German academics. Men of Fouillée's conviction, in any case, saw "individualism" as the main enemy.

Like other French educational conservatives, Fouillée was remarkably frank about his strategies of social reproduction. While classical secondary education was "frequented primarily by the sons of the upper and middle *bourgeoisie*," he observed, modern secondary students came from "the humblest social classes." To offer them a *"culture générale"* was not to prepare them adequately for occupations that suited them, but "artificially" to make them "aspirants" for the liberal professions. "The public [primary] schools," Fouillée wrote, are not meant to "support the ambitions of fathers and mothers who want to shield their offspring from manual work." They may encourage a few exceptional pupils to "rise higher"; but their main aim must be to prepare men who will "honor even the humblest professions." In opposing educational policies responsible for "the demoralization due to the increase of the *déclassés*," Fouillée explained, he did not mean to deny instruction to "the people or the *petite bourgeoisie*."

Far from it; everyone should be instructed as much as possible, but not all in the same manner, nor by methods that finally produce a lack of adaptation in the child to his future condition.[28]

To "educate the *petite bourgeoisie*," in other words, was to adapt *petit bourgeois* children to *petit bourgeois* "conditions," since the social origins of students were to remain largely identical with their "destinations."

In the light of this perspective, the modern secondary program could be accused of having been "diverted" from its true mission, and of having created an "intellectual proletariat."

Let it be reduced to four years; let it orient itself exclusively and definitely towards industry, commerce, agriculture, and colonial needs: that is its only *raison d'être* ... Let us ... maintain the natural hierarchy, instead of pursuing a fictitious leveling ... The state undertakes ... [at great expense to offer] in its *lycées* the highest form of secondary education, but not to leave the public offices and the liberal professions open to egoistic mediocrities ... Democracy well understood does not consist in suppressing and leveling all differences ... of education ... The people would gain nothing by that; its greatest interest, on the contrary, is to have something above it to which it can aspire ... a sort of superior class that is not closed ... that owes its titles not to fortune alone, but to a higher form of education ... Instead of ridiculing classical studies, let us congratulate ourselves that something still has prestige with the people, something intellectual and artistic, something that is not money or power.[29]

What is new here is not only the moralistic mode, in which the "artificial aspirants" to the educated professions have become "egoistic mediocrities." Even more startling is the thinly veiled appeal to the legitimating role of educational segmentation. Fouillée has taught his reader that "utilitarian" preoccupations may be "a necessity and almost a duty" for the relatively disadvantaged, and that the choice of schooling is usually dictated by material circumstances. Yet he here invites the same reader to notice that higher education "still has prestige with the people," that it signifies an "open" elite, and that it is perceived as "something that is not money or power." Could he have been much more explicit without actually reversing the ideological thrust of his argument?

Compared with German professors of the same period, in sum, French educational conservatives were extraordinarily frank and specific about the social and political significance of what they proposed. They wrote as if more fully aware than their German counterparts that they were participating in a political confrontation, which was a species of class conflict as well. This was probably true in part because they had experienced the direct impact of changing parliamentary majorities upon educational policy. The political system in which they participated trained them, as well as their audiences, to see educational alternatives as political ones; they were almost forced to state their positions accordingly. It also made a difference that the existing segmentation of French secondary and higher education visibly divided an integrated *bourgeoisie* from the rest of the population. Neither the history nor the present configuration of the French educational system gave much support to other views of the divide between the highly educated and the "practically" schooled. Of course there were tensions *within* the elite sector of the system. Nevertheless, a man like Fouillée simply could not have explicated the supposed antithesis between a "disinterested" cultural elite and a "utilitarian" rank and file without having explicitly to place the business leadership on the side of *culture générale*, in opposition to "the industrial and mercantile spirit." Whether or not this weakened his arguments even in his own eyes, it certainly made them transparent for others. In a way, it almost *provoked* a set of plainly social and political counterarguments that we will now examine.

THE REFORMIST POSITION

Among the academics, academicians, and former Ministers of Education who testified before the Ribot Commission of 1899, or commented upon its work, twelve were particularly articulate spokesmen for what may be called the reformist position on French secondary education. Nine of these twelve were academics properly speaking, in that they held teaching and/or research positions in university-level institutions. One (Jules Lemaître) was a writer, a member of the Académie Française, and a former academic. Two were politicians, one of them (Léon Bourgeois) a former Minister of Education, the other (Jean Jaurès) a former academic. The nine current academics taught at the Ecole Normale (1), at the Paris and Lyon faculties of letters (5 + 1), at the Paris faculty of sciences (1, the dean), and at the Collège de France (1); two of them had been elected to the Académie des Sciences, and a third to the Académie Française. In addition, one of the nine academics (Marcelin Berthelot) was a former Minister of Education, and another (Ferdinand Buisson) had been a distinguished Director of Primary Schooling within the Ministry of Education.[30] Thus comparatively few of the individuals within this "sample" were academicians, and none were affiliated with the professional faculties of law and of medicine. In contrast to the defenders of the classical curriculum we have discussed, these twelve educational reformists were associated primarily with the expanding faculties of letters and of sciences, or of course with the Ministry of Education. They perfectly represented the alliance between a sector of the French academic community, a portion of the parliamentary leadership, and the educational administration of the Radical Republic that so thoroughly antagonized Barrès.

The main institutional recommendations of the reformists were conveniently summarized in the testimony of the historian Ernest Lavisse. With few exceptions, the rest of the group agreed with what he proposed, and even his terminology was typical of the reformist position. The "modern classical" curriculum, he said, should be accredited equally with the "greco-roman classical" one. He saw nothing wrong with a program based on French, on two modern foreign languages, on the natural sciences, and on history and geography. The French classical authors of the seventeenth and eighteenth centuries were widely held to embody educative virtues analogous to those of the ancient literatures. Lavisse insisted that the modern curriculum could "give pupils a true classical, intellectual and moral *culture*," and that arguments to the contrary were simply "prejudices." The availability of two different but equal forms of secondary schooling would "enrich the spirit of the nation." Once supplemented by a fully accredited modern alternative, the greco-latin curriculum could become "frankly classical, in the old sense of the term." Greek could be seriously studied again. "Greece, not Rome," Lavisse added, was "the great educator."[31]

The role of the old "special secondary" program, Lavisse suggested, was to be taken over by the higher primary schools, some of which would be renamed *collèges*. Within an enlarged system of three school types, transfers were to be possible until about age twelve. The teaching of Latin was not to begin before then, and the differences between elementary primary and pre-secondary schooling were to be reduced as well. The "vocations" of pupils cannot be discerned at the age of eight or nine, Lavisse observed, and should not "in a democratic country" be "determined solely by the wealth of parents." What he intended, in short, was an upgrading of the modern secondary curriculum, a partial integration of the higher primary sector, and a softening of the existing segmentation at the lower secondary level. This was the basic structure of the reformist position.

Like most of the reformists, and like some of the conservatives as well, Lavisse urged that national curricular guidelines be made more flexible, so that teachers and students could pursue their own interests to some degree. The "destruction of uniformity," he thought, would enhance the "autonomy" of the individual schools, particularly if their directors became something more than delegates of the educational bureaucracy. Advised by councils of teachers, headmasters were to set educational policies for their institutions, which were thus to take on distinctive aspirations of their own. Instead of merely presenting their specialties in the classroom, teachers were to participate more fully in the broader enterprise of *éducation*, and in the community life of the *lycées* or *collèges*. To make room for these innovations, the nationally standardized baccalaureate was to be replaced by "certificates of study." Juries composed of secondary teachers were to award these either on the basis of good academic records, or after short oral examinations. In its present form, Lavisse argued, the baccalaureate encouraged the "pursuit of an empty social distinction," along with the passion for civil service careers. Above all, it was "an obstacle to all reform and all initiative."[32]

Lavisse was convinced, finally, that future secondary teachers needed a professional preparation as educators, in addition to their scientific or scholarly training. In a final year at the university, he proposed, they should take courses in the philosophy of education, in the history of educational institutions, and in contemporary comparative education. The philosophy course would help to equip them for their role as "moral educators." In the history course, they would learn "why an education that suited one epoch no longer sufficed for another." In addition to attending lectures, they would do some supervised classroom teaching in a nearby *lycée*. A few educational traditionalists made similar recommendations; but the interest in pedagogy and in practice teaching was particularly great among the spokesmen for structural reform.[33]

Three of the eleven reformists in our "sample" were more guarded or more ambivalent than Lavisse in their support for non-classical secondary education: The mathematician Gaston Darboux, dean of the Paris faculty of sciences; Léon Bourgeois, the former Minister of Education, and the writer and academician Jules Lemaître. Darboux testified that his faculty almost unanimously favored the equal accreditation of the modern curriculum. The "encyclopedic" approach of adding ever more material to a single secondary program, he said, had overburdened students and caused them to lose the taste for study. The "principle of the division of labor" had to be applied to secondary schooling. He distrusted the conservative suggestion that the modern secondary program should be made shorter and more "practical." In the sciences, he observed, application must be joined to theory; the modern stream ought to encompass a full-length course with a strong scientific or mathematical component. At the same time, Darboux urgently called for the restoration of a "bifurcation" that would allow classical secondary students to opt for an upper-division specialization in mathematics. The reinstitution of this traditional option would provide for "a type of Latin scientific studies that would be very much in place in a country such as ours, and that exists, besides, in other countries." He apparently believed, and not without reason, that this curricular combination would be most likely to protect the natural sciences against the status inferiority that continued to threaten the modern secondary stream.[34]

Bourgeois' testimony paralleled that of Lavisse in many particulars, though with an occasional shift of emphasis. In addition to the classical and the modern curriculum, he envisaged a shorter program of "practical" studies that might be considered either primary or secondary. Primary and secondary education, he added, should not be separate "impenetrable circles." The pedagogical qualifications of future secondary teachers were to be insured by an internship (*stage*) of practice teaching, and by a supplementary professional examination. Bourgeois observed that German scholarly models had encouraged a "tendency toward encyclopedism and erudition" in the classroom. While certainly legitimate in its domain, he argued, scientific specialization ought not to encroach upon the true object of secondary education, which is the "formation of the mind." Like Lavisse and others, Bourgeois proposed the abolition of the baccalaureate. In its place, "certificates of study" were to be awarded by juries, and cumulative transcripts (*livrets scolaires*) were to be introduced for private as well as public secondary students. A certificate of modern secondary studies was to qualify its holder for university study, except that law faculties might require a makeup examination in Latin. Unlike Lavisse, Bourgeois further recommended qualifying examinations at the entry to the professions. Different certificates of prior study, he said, might at that point be assigned divergent weights in an overall score. While this sounded practical, it partly delegated the task of selection to the professional associations, who could be expected to favor the traditional curriculum.[35]

Bourgeois' general theme was the theme of "adaptation." He thought the current "crisis" of French secondary education ought not to be interpreted as a "decline." It could be observed in other European countries; it was a "transformation" that could be recognized as "organic . . . and therefore necessary." The "old framework of secondary education" was simply "no longer . . . adapted to the more complex conditions of modern societies." Reviewing some recent history; Bourgeois stressed the desires of "many families."

They said: "Greek and Latin are not indispensable for our children . . . Nevertheless, we would like them to be cultivated men [*honnêtes gens*] in the manner of the seventeenth century, that is to say instructed, well brought up, and [with] a general intellectual schooling [*une culture générale de l'esprit*]. One can be distinguished [*un homme distingué*] . . . without having mastered the literatures of Athens and of Rome.

Even while parents expressed this view, according to Bourgeois, teachers in the traditional secondary stream complained that "too many students without a taste for the ancient letters overcrowded their program," in which "the share of Greek and Latin" had been sharply reduced to make room "for the whole encyclopedia."[36]

In this situation, Bourgeois recalled, he and his collaborators created the "modern" option to meet "incontestable needs," knowing that "experience could reveal other necessities, and perhaps lead to other experiments later on."

In the infinite variety of a generation's needs and aptitudes, there is room for very divergent educational programs, ranging from the most elementary to the most advanced . . . oriented toward various bodies of knowledge, and suited to each [student's] quality of mind, level of intelligence, family background, vocation, and probable destination. It is by very different paths that, in a democracy, everyone can reach the summit.

Once fully accepted and given committed teachers of its own, the modern curriculum can be expected to equal the academic standards of the classical stream. Modern secondary students are less "brilliant" than their classical comrades, less "literary" and slower to develop ideas; but also more thorough, more capable of "reflection" and of "independent work."[37]

The classical curriculum, Bourgeois continued, is inevitably somewhat "verbal." The ideas it transmits in superb and striking formulations may not "always be in perfect accord with the world view to which twenty centuries of religious, philosophical and scientific revolution have brought humanity." Even so, it will surely survive.

The prestige of the ancient languages is far from disappearing; the literary culture they confer to the highest degree will always be prized in a country as enamored as ours of fine literature . . . There will . . . always be a certain kind of superiority, a refinement, an intellectual elegance that wealthy families will desire for their children . . . [Thus some will] continue to possess a profound and truly direct knowledge of the spirits of Greece and of Rome, from which our spirit has borrowed so much. The very high culture of an elite is indispensable, and to maintain it, we must preserve a classical education that is . . . ever purer and more thorough than that of our time. But in wanting to give it to the entire middle class [*toutes les classes moyennes*] one risks . . . offering it . . . in an incomplete and mediocre way to those not made for it.

The best way to "serve the cause of the ancient letters," Bourgeois concluded, was to reduce the number of pupils in the classical stream, and not to "stop the development of the modern curriculum, which meets the needs of the immense majority of our youth."[38]

Thus the "adaptation" Bourgeois recommended had very little to do with the economy. The supposed requirements of "commerce, industry, and agriculture" were much less often invoked by the educational reformists than by the traditionalists. In pointing to the "complex conditions of modern society," Bourgeois signaled the need for a more finely articulated hierarchy of *social* roles, and for a certain diversity in the "paths" that led "to the summit." A kind of curricular pluralism struck him as inescapable, not only because there was no other way to elude the twin dangers of "overburdening" and "encyclopedism," but also because a new set of family strategies could not, "in a democracy," be thwarted indefinitely. An experienced parliamentary politician and a virtuoso of gradualist reform, he responded empirically to socio-cultural expectations that seemed to be changing very slowly. With impressive skill, he undertook the partial revaluation required to fix the "traits" of divergent student groups as different but equal – or nearly equal. Despite the subtlety of his tactics, however, he remained attached to the traditional symbols of socio-cultural "distinction." He did not merely assert the plain right of committed classicists to pursue their ideals. Instead, he conflated the "tastes" and "aptitudes" of pupils with their family backgrounds and "probable destinations." The fine distinctions he offered thus collapsed into a rough divide between those "made" for the classical curriculum and those "not made for it." And the respect he expressed for "thoroughness" and "independent work" gave place to a rather conventional identification of classical learning with "refinement," with "intellectual elegance" – and with wealth.

The ambivalence at the heart of Bourgeois' position was even more clearly expressed by Jules Lemaître. Both before and during his appearance before the Ribot Commission, he took a self-consciously provocative stance. He found it "absurd" to teach to contemporary students from the middle and lower classes what had been taught "under the Old Regime, and under very different economic . . . conditions, to the sons of the nobility, of high magistrates, and of the rich bourgeoisie." It was pointless to argue the virtues of the classical languages, he added, since they were effectively communicated to only about one-tenth of the pupils currently enrolled in secondary schools. No one actually learned much Latin, not to mention Greek, so that the vaunted *culture générale* had become a "nullity" (*une culture nulle*). Praised for its "idealism," the traditional program was in fact "shamefully utilitarian," since it aimed only at the all-important diploma. The idea of a parallel but non-classical stream leading to commercial and industrial occupations was certainly sound in principle; but the "vanity" of parents was bound to defeat it in practice.

Those [parents] whose children have only average abilities or those who are not rich will [nonetheless] always make it a point of honor to demand . . . the education that they judge to be most distinguished [*noble*] and most aristocratic.[39]

The only way to escape from this dilemma, as Lemaître saw it, was to institute a common non-classical curriculum for the first four years of secondary schooling, which would resemble the existing higher primary and/or modern secondary streams. The French classics of the seventeenth and eighteenth centuries would convey "the moral substance of the classical literatures." The unified character of the program would stand as "a visible sign of the equality of the children of France." At the end of four years, some students would presumably leave to take jobs, or to transfer to higher commercial schools. The rest would prepare for the university faculties and *grandes écoles*, either by specializing in mathematics, or by quickly acquiring a thorough classical education. The baccalaureate would be replaced by university and career entry examinations. Though Lemaître spoke of the equivalence of "modern" and "classical" credentials under these circumstances, he explicitly intended future university students to pass through the classics or mathematics branches of an upper secondary division that was a concentrated version of the traditional curriculum. His proposal thus perpetuated the existing segmentation of the French secondary system at a higher level, even while it conceded an integrated lower secondary division. In his view of that lower division, moreover, he echoed the conservative thesis that "practical" training must somehow be imposed upon a certain class of parents, including those "not rich" but "vain." In short, his perspective was an essentially conservative one. He was certainly the most marginal of our eleven reformists, and also the only writer – academician among them.

The distinguished chemist Marcelin Berthelot, a former Minister of Education, stated the case for reform in a more forceful way. He too saw the classical curriculum as radically unsuited to modern conditions and destined to survive only as a kind of luxury. A minority of families, he thought, would continue to offer their children a "literary *culture*" that was more "delicate" and "esthetic" than that of the majority. But he insisted that this minority education was neither more "moral" than the majoritarian alternative, nor "higher from an intellectual point of view," since a "scientific *culture* is at least equal to a literary *culture* in that respect." One of the few reformists to refer to the economy at all, he claimed that the old literary education did not adequately prepare students for "industrial, agricultural, and commercial careers," and that it thus "pushed" too many pupils toward the public sector. He criticized the "modern" option of 1891 for failing to pursue its own legitimate vocation. Though its "general direction" should have been "chiefly scientific," it became an "inferior" copy of the classical curriculum, a "literary education" based on modern sources. Modern secondary pupils were taught to "admire the literary beauties of the German and English authors" just as aspiring classicists were taught to admire the authors of antiquity, partly because modern secondary teachers were trained almost exactly like their classical colleagues. Hampered by overloaded and overly specific curricular guidelines, moreover, secondary schooling failed in its principal task, which was to awaken intellectual curiosity and a taste for independent work. The "literary portion" of the modern curriculum should be based on French literature, Berthelot added less convincingly, since an emphasis on German and English texts might "distort our national culture."[40]

Berthelot too was an opponent of the baccalaureate, which he proposed to replace with certificates of study awarded by the secondary schools themselves. Modern certificates were to be considered equal with classical certificates, even though the modern stream was to remain one year shorter than the classical one. Such an arrangement could be expected to reduce enrollments in the classical program; but this did not trouble Berthelot. We are not concerned with "a consequence that interests only certain classes," he sternly observed, but with the broader issue of "social utility." One need not be a committed classicist to detect difficulties in this position. The identification of science with the occupationally useful is no more convincing for being common among educational "modernizers" of a certain type. Scientific knowledge, as Berthelot must have realized, may be as purely "theoretical" as the knowledge of the philologist. Experimentation does entail interventions in natural processes. But such interventions need not aim at "social utility," though both proponents and critics of scientific conceptualization seem occasionally to forget that. Berthelot's account of "a literary education" is even more problematic. Surely the interpretation of texts, including Greek and Latin texts, can and should be more than a means of esthetic refinement. And no adequate view of the hermeneutic relationship could justify the notion that "foreign" sources must be avoided for fear of "distorting" one's own culture. The most one can say in Berthelot's defense is that he was probably misled by some of his more "literary" colleagues.

In any case, as I have begun to suggest, most of our reformists did *not* conceive the modernization of French secondary education primarily as a functional adjustment to the "requirements" of the economy. While they often referred to changes in the occupational system, they were generally most interested in its growing "complexity." One could say that they saw educational modernization as a form of democratization; but their position was really more precise and more limited than that. In a way, they were realists. They mirrored their traditionalist opponents in the frankness and specificity of their *social* objectives. They meant to increase the inclusiveness of French secondary schooling, and thus to provide for an enlarged and more "complex" pattern of middle-class mobility through education. While this was no mean task in itself, they also thought of it, fairly enough, as a step toward greater "equality."

A good example of reformist realism – and firmness may be found in the testimony of Ferdinand Buisson, the former Director of Primary Schooling, who as of 1899 taught a course on education at the Paris faculty of letters. The question confronting the Ribot Commission, he said, is essentially a social question. Even the definition of secondary education can no longer be anything but social. It is "the education accessible to families...who can support their children up to a relatively advanced age" without having to make them earn their own living. The "general fact" to be reckoned with is "the continuous increase in the part of the population... especially of the *petite bourgeoisie*," that seeks schooling beyond the primary level. The *lycée* can no longer be considered a reserve for "a small group of the privileged," but must "increasingly be opened to all."

Whether or not it is in their true interest, all equally ought to have free access to secondary education, without the interposition of any artificial barrier. And that eliminates all those systems that lean more or less clearly toward the illusion of first constituting an elite of pupils to whom an elite education can [then] be reserved. That is no longer possible for us.[41]

The newly arrived clients of the secondary system, in other words, are still mainly middle-class groups, since they can defer potential earnings. Nevertheless, their arrival is and ought to be irrevocable; for there is a potentially universal right of access to education that is not subject to interpretation in terms of anyone's "true interest." The educational system presumably cannot eradicate all economic differences, or compensate for them; but it must not maintain "artificial barriers" of its own.

Buisson proceeded rigorously to the consequences of this position. The "immense majority" of students, he observed, can no longer afford the "ancient formula" that links liberal education to "the independence, the cultivated (*honnête*) and elegant leisure of the rich." They still want a "liberal education"; but they must also prepare for a remunerative occupation. One can no longer speak literally of a "distinterested education." Moreover, most parents know, "and want the University to know," that they may not be able to support their children to the very end of the secondary course. Nor can they risk investing in a curriculum that is profitable only if the course is completed. Indeed, they cannot know in advance whether their children will be good students. The real *déclassés* are not the unemployed *bacheliers*, but those who have aimed exclusively at the baccalaureate, and who then fail to pass it. In short, "the University" must offer a viable program even to pupils who cannot complete the full secondary sequence. It must "organize . . . a system of equivalences that will permit the child . . . to change his plans" during the course of study. It must test students, and possibly redirect them, well before the final year. And it must "open . . . divergent paths" to a "goal that may not be the baccalaureate."

Buisson called for qualifying examinations (*examens de passage*) to determine whether pupils ought to be promoted to the next higher grade, or advised of possible alternatives. He clearly intended a rigorous system of academic selection prior to the baccalaureate, which he proposed to retain as well. If modern secondary graduates are considered unqualified for entry into the legal and medical faculties, he said, then there are ways for them to make up the necessary work. He wanted "bridges" and "passages" to facilitate transfers among the several forms of secondary *and* of higher primary schooling. Despite the toughness of his meritocratic stance, he emphasized the "diversity" of aptitudes and educational possibilities.

Our classical secondary curriculum is too rigid a framework; it does not take into account the diversity in children's natures. We have to become accustomed to the idea of having not one but several secondary programs, just as there are . . . several types of intelligence and of character, and several . . . ways of being a man useful to his country, a man of worth . . . The ruling class of the future . . . cannot be composed of minds fashioned on the same pattern . . . [but must consist] of the best in all specialties . . . May they resemble each other in being superior men.[42]

Elsewhere, Buisson suggested that commercial and industrial positions could be as worthy as the liberal and public careers. Thus he recommended "diversity" mainly because he wanted secondary education to recruit more broadly, and to prepare for a wider (more "complex") range of specialized professions. He had little to say about the development of the individual. As a middle-class *social* reformer, he was frankly concerned with opportunity, with mobility, and with social utility.

All the same, the socialist leader Jean Jaurès offered institutional recommendations quite similar to those of Buisson, and he put an only slightly different construction upon them. He thought it "curious" that "the ruling classes" themselves should be abandoning the classical curriculum as a useless "overload." After all, it represented a "privilege of intellectual mastery," and "one more force" in their hands. But of course there was no point in reimposing Latin and Greek by "artificial measures." The classics might still be studied as upper-division electives by "an elite that would no longer be the elite of bourgeois wealth, but an elite of curiosity and intelligence." In the meantime, the modern curriculum could become the "fundament" of French secondary schooling. Indeed, it was now possible to bridge the "discontinuity" between primary, secondary, and higher education, and to create a "homogeneous" system "from base to summit." The "desertion of the old *bourgeoisie*" could thus be compensated by a "wider recruitment" of secondary pupils from the primary and higher primary schools.[43]

Jaurès commented with ironic detachment upon aspects of the ongoing debate. The baccalaureate was said to "uproot young people"; but surely the movement to Paris had deeper causes. If abolished, the baccalaureate was bound to reappear in other forms. It had actually encouraged French secondary teachers to keep in touch with the remarkable recent advances in "philosophical and historical studies." Particularly in the "philosophy" program of the final year, French secondary students were thus introduced to "German and English philosophy, positive philosophy," and "physiological psychology." Though he clearly felt a special attachment to the classics he had studied himself, Jaurès offered a remarkably comprehensive perspective on curricular questions.

I have never thought that the Latin and Greek literatures [alone were educative] ... The human mind, which has produced all things, can find itself in all things: having created the sciences and literatures of all orders, it can easily find its own image [in them]. For the human mind finding itself in its works, that is general education [*culture générale*].

This is just what a German neo-idealist might have said in an ecumenical mood. It certainly breaks away from the narrow identification of the French spirit with the "Latin" heritage. Jaurès went on to suggest that "the method of historical and evolutionary interpretation" could be used even in the teaching of mathematics; for students could retrace the paths taken by "the great creative minds" toward new theoretical discoveries.[44]

All of the reformists believed, of course, that the modern curriculum could be made as educative as the classical one. While some were content to defend this position in general terms, well over half actually proceeded to recommend particular teaching materials and methods. Thus both Darboux and Berthelot understandably proposed an emphasis upon the natural sciences. As we have seen, Berthelot expressly warned against a second "literary" program, in which students learned to "admire the beauties" of modern texts. He also suggested that a scientific education would in some sense be "useful"; but he did not fully explicate this one-sided thesis. It was thus left to the philosopher Alexis Bertrand to state the case for the sciences in a systematic way. Recent changes in the secondary syllabus, Bertrand told the Commission, had created a confusing and contradictory situation. The piecemeal introduction of scientific studies had fragmented a "system prepared exclusively for the teaching of letters." It was time to accept and to channel this "invasion," by "putting the sciences resolutely at the center" of the secondary curriculum. The way to do that was to adopt "Auguste Comet's classification" of the sciences, which recapitulated their "order of historical development." Bertrand was convinced that the intellectual growth of the individual paralleled that of "humanity." He therefore recommended a four-year secondary course that would focus successively upon mathematics, physics and chemistry, biology, and "sociology and ethics." In addition, students would choose two languages other than French, and Bertrand hoped that Latin would be one of these. Greek would have to be sacrificed; but that would scarcely change its current status. If the scheme were adopted, perhaps as an experiment, secondary schooling would not begin until age fourteen, when students already knew "many things," including arithmetic, though not yet "the reason for things."[45]

Primary schooling, according to Bertrand, was essentially "empiric" (*empirique*) in character; secondary education was "theoretical", and higher "professional" studies were "utilitarian and practical." One of the virtues of his plan, he said, was that it provided for a natural transition from (higher) primary to secondary education. While pedagogically sound, this was also desirable "from a democratic viewpoint." It made for a selection of secondary pupils that was "exactly coextensive with universal suffrage," whereas the present regime allowed "what we are pleased to call the elite" to be "designated" by financial circumstances.

And not only would primary [schooling] be "joined" to secondary [eduction]; but . . . the crying discordance . . . between the school and life would be largely extenuated. In sum, it is science, it is positive knowledge [*connaissances positives*] that we need above all. If I stipulate that this positive knowledge must have a clearly theoretical character, I am thinking in the first instance about the schooling of the mind [*la culture de l'esprit*] but [I am also suggesting] that theory is the best guide to practice, to utilitarianism well understood.[46]

The passage establishes a significant contrast between "positive knowledge" and the merely "empiric." In primary school, one learns "many things" in a strictly "empiric" way; but one gains "positive knowledge" only as one comes to understand "the reason for things." *Connaissances positives* may be constrasted with "a priori" knowledge, or even more tellingly, with the "formal" perfections pursued by a certain type of "literary" schooling. Secondary education is not to aim at elegance of expression, or at the "unfolding" of the individual, or at professional preparation; but at *connaissances positives* that are more-than-empiric, or theory-laden. "The sciences," which lie at the heart of secondary education, convey a "theoretical" understanding of the world. Because they have practical implications as well, they bring "the school" into contact with "life"; or they do so more effectively than the study of Latin. Like Berthelot, Bertrand makes us wonder whether the interpretation of texts *must* be a purely "formal" exercise – and thus irrelevant to "life." Like Berthelot again, he associates "the sciences" with "utility." Yet he answers at least some of the questions raised by this position by stipulating that "theory is the best guide to practice," and that "utilitarianism" must be "well understood."

Even while thus celebrating "the sciences," moreover, Bertrand was particularly interested in what he called "sociology and ethics." Anticipating certain characteristic reactions, he insisted that the word "sociology" was "synonymous neither with positivism nor with socialism." Along with "indispensable complements of history and economics," it encompassed studies well known "to the primary teacher under the name of civic education; to the *professeur de philosophie*, under the name of social ethics" (*la morale sociale*). Though a "young discipline" devoted to "the analysis of social institutions," it had an ancient lineage and a clear pedagogical mission. Indeed, it continued the work of the great French educators of the seventeenth century. A "very French science," it nonetheless met with obstinate "detractors" only in France. It was "the most necessary of studies." Thus the secondary education recommended by Bertrand, like Comte's classification itself, treated the scientific study of nature as a prelude to a rational understanding of contemporary social and moral problems.[47]

The reformists generally agreed, of course, that the modern secondary curriculum should extend beyond the natural sciences, to encompass the modern languages and literatures, along with history and related subjects. It was in commenting upon these further elements in the syllabus, in fact, that several of the reformists developed particularly interesting views. Thus Alphonse Aulard addressed the Ribot Commission as a politically engaged historian of contemporary France. To teach his subject in a "philosophical" spirit, he suggested, was to present it from a frankly "republican" and "democratic" point of view. Its highlights were the "rational principles of the Revolution," the conflict "between the principle of authority and the principle of reason, between science and faith, between the rights of the secular state (*l'Etat laique*) and the pretensions of the Catholic church." The education offered by the Catholic private schools seemed to Aulard "entirely formal" and "superficial," based on digests rather than original texts, and on "formulas learned by heart."[48] While few of the reformists stated this "laic" perspective quite as bluntly, it was of course quite common among republican academics.

What is interesting about it is that it could be taken to imply a set of pedagogical principles as well. Aulard claimed that French secondary education was not in decline, as some observers believed. While little Greek was learned, and while Latin verses and themes had rightly been dropped, there was a general improvement in teaching methods and results. This was true even in Latin, but more particularly in French literature and composition, as well as in history. The key to this improvement, according to Aulard, was that texts were now "explained in a more critical fashion." Students were "taught to reason," to consider "the how and the why." They were no longer invited to "admire" the works of celebrated authors in an unquestioning way, but really to think for themselves. The authority of tradition was no longer simply accepted; there was an increased "appeal to reason." French secondary education had become more "reasonable," Aulard said, and he clearly considered this "reasonableness" a republican virtue.[49]

Charles Andler, a young assistant professor (*maître de conférences*) at the Ecole Normale, was an expert in German literature and philosophy, an international socialist and a friend of Jaurès. In his testimony before the Ribot Commission, he urged that French secondary education generally be based on modern studies, and particularly on the modern languages and literatures. Latin and Greek might be retained as electives at a few *lycées*, he thought; but only three years in the upper division were needed to teach students more than they learned at present. This made it possible to create a continuous system of public elementary, higher primary, and secondary schooling. Like other reformists, Andler believed that pupils presently enrolled in the modern program were negatively selected, since parents and teachers tended to steer youngsters who appeared academically promising toward the classical stream. This pattern could be expected to change with the full accreditation of the modern curriculum. Even under present conditions, moreover, Andler found "no profound intellectual difference" between modern and classical secondary students. The modern students typically came from modest backgrounds, and their ambitions were usually modest as well. At least initially, they had some difficulty in "purely literary" courses; for they were not "refined" (*des délicats*). Nevertheless, their minds were no less "keen" than those of their classical colleagues. Thus gradually over several years, modern secondary classes evolved what they lacked to begin with: a "top" of students whose "intelligences" had "opened."[50]

Andler thus repudiated the view that modern secondary pupils were endowed at best with the "practical" abilities that suited their "destinations." Even some reformists inclined to this view; for it was easily reconciled with their emphasis upon the "diversity" of aptitudes, of educational paths, and of socially useful occupations. Even when put in a "positive" tone, of course, a classificatory judgment of this sort can be debilitating for students and teachers alike. It excludes the possibility that pupils from "uncultivated" backgrounds, who do not at first *appear* academically promising, might nonetheless *learn* to understand complex texts and arguments. In a way, the judgment anticipates and rationalizes a pedagogical failure. It also narrows the horizons of education to the reproduction of established social types, as if all human potentialities were exhausted by them. While conceding that students should learn to *speak* the modern foreign languages, Andler rejected the conventionally "practical" emphasis upon "ordinary conversation." Taking a resolutely "academic" view of modern secondary schooling, he insisted upon "the explication of classic texts." These should be chosen "judiciously," he said, to respond to "different needs"; they might be "very literary," but also "very scientific." German and English sources should not be translated, but explicated as much as possible in their own language. To show that a "modernized" curriculum could be pedagogically effective, he too cited the "philosophy" class of the final year. Here young minds were introduced to "the modern humanities," to the "principal notions" of the "exact sciences," to modern psychology, and to contemporary history. The course is "alive," he said, and "passionately followed." But it would be even more successful if students learned something about the "civilization" of the authors they read.[51]

To complete his case, Andler consolidated well-established perceptions of the classical curriculum into a sharply critical perspective. Created to train priests, he argued, it left its graduates to face the modern world with ideas taken from the seventeenth century, at the latest. The best of them were equipped to become *professeurs* in "rhetoric" classes; most acquired no more than the "exterior sign by which a certain bourgeois aristocracy recognizes itself." Instead of "talking so much about the mediocrity of the modern program," he added, "one ought to insist a little upon the mediocrity of the classical program." He cited "the old verbiage of the Latin theme," the "habits of verbal virtuosity" that destroyed the students' capacity for "direct thought and expression." He saw no point in "touching phrases" about the "ennobling of the soul," the "moral culture," and the "artistic taste" conveyed by the Latin authors, since even "elementary Latin" was not effectively learned. Andler was a particularly blunt critic of the inherited curriculum; but he was not alone in his conviction that what classical education had become in France by the end of the nineteenth century was not worth preserving.

THREE HISTORICAL PERSPECTIVES

Three of the reformists in our group of twelve, Alphonse Aulard, Ernest Lavisse, and Charles Seignobos, were historians. In addition, Charles Andler and Jean Jaurès were clearly sympathetic to historical perspectives in the analysis of cultures, and Gustave Lanson, as we shall see, saw the study of French literature as an essentially historical enterprise. This prominence of the historians among the reformists had both institutional and intellectual causes. Institutionally, the historians had held a modest but secure place in the traditional secondary system. They were an established presence in the faculties of letters, and they were clearly going to benefit from the reorganization of secondary programs that would accompany the decline of the classical languages. Intellectually, the historians had two important contributions to make to the reformist cause. First, they were equipped to develop historicist arguments for change. They could associate the classical curriculum with the political and cultural conditions of former times, while supporting the need to adjust education to new circumstances. Secondly, they could offer their own perspective as the obvious alternative to the mode of textual interpretation that had come to characterize the study of antiquity. Against the eternalizing approach to the ancient authors as timeless models, they could urge the need for contextual and historical readings. If they succeeded in making their case, then history would have to be recognized as the true mother of the interpretive disciplines.

Typical of the historians' stance on these questions was a 1903 lecture by Ernest Lavisse, in which he recalled his own years as a secondary pupil and as a Normalien. Few of his memories, as he described them, were particularly fond ones. The great texts of Periclean Athens, of Augustan Rome, and of seventeenth-century France, he reported, had conveyed to him "the permanent foundations of human wisdom" in a "slow penetration." Yet ten years of this experience had left him with "no precise notion of anything."

Why was I never told that the spirit of a people is expressed by (its language) ... and that its manner of thinking determines its way of acting ... its particular vocation in the [history of humanity] ... A misuse was made to our detriment of the superficial and incomplete truth that man is the same in all times and places. We were not helped or invited in any way to imagine the persons and things of former times ... Even less ... were the civilizations explained to us, of which the works of art are representative monuments.[52]

In history courses, "assorted facts" were presented; but there was no sense of "the transformations in the way of life, nor of the stages in the march of humanity toward us."

The main critical standard here, obviously, is historical, and it is applied without the slightest misgiving. There is a strong awareness of the *distance* that separates us from the sources of antiquity. Precisely this distance was usually minimized by conservative defenders of the classical curriculum, who tended to assimilate the Greco-Roman heritage to the "latinity" of the French spirit, while also stressing the "primordial" character of the sentiments embodied in the classical texts. In response, Lavisse points to the historical difference between the ancient "civilizations" and that of modern France. He does not construe this difference as a hermeneutic distance or a specifically philological one; for his emphasis is not upon the separation between the classical author and the contemporary reader *as individuals*, nor upon the differences of *language* between them. Instead, he moves immediately to the divergence between the two relevant ways of thinking *and of acting*, and to the historical "transformations" that have altered whole *civilizations*. He asserts not only that texts must be rescued from the false immediacy of the "eternal", but also that they become truly instructive and exciting only as "representative monuments" of a "way of life." He wants students to imagine the "words *and things*" of the past; his emphasis is on patterns of practice and on something like mentalities, rather than on the individual. At the same time, he unabashedly conceives the "march of humanity" as proceeding "toward us," and this is consistent with his sense that we must aim at an *historical* understanding *of ourselves*.

Continuing his recollections, Lavisse identified himself, and scholarly history, with the ethos of "science." Science students (*les scientifiques*), he recalled, were "relegated to an inferior status" in the "schoolboy hierarchy" of his youth. Teachers gave no attention to "method"; there was no suggestion that scientific procedures (*la science*) might be relevant "to history or to life." The work of the upper secondary grades rotated around the teaching and practice of rhetoric. Students gained the impression that "not the knowing, but the saying" was what mattered. Even at the Ecole Normale in those days, future historians were not introduced to research methods, and "no historical text of any kind" was ever critically examined in detail. Louis Pasteur, who was on the faculty of the Ecole and could have taught students much about "the critical spirit," was ignored by those in the letters division (*les littéraires*), because he was a *scientifique*. This was the "absurdity of a regime that mutilated our intelligences."[53]

Lavisse's scientism was undoubtedly reinforced by a "laic" animus against the known classicism and traditionalism of the Catholic *collèges*. To underscore the inadequacies of the old literary and "rhetorical" education, he portrayed it as embedded in a specific social and political environment. The educational ideal of the seventeenth century, he wrote, "was simple and could be." The future subject of Louis XIV had his existence "regulated in advance; he was not in charge of himself; the Church thought for him, and the king willed for him." The educated men of those days needed only "the humanities" as then understood. "The esthetic and moral study of the great writers" was intended to "form the *honnête homme*, which more or less meant the well-bred man" (*l'homme comme il faut*). It was time to recognize that this type of schooling could not be "eternal," and that "new needs" had to be met. Instead of fighting against "the evidence," educators must find a new "guiding idea," and a "new definition of the humanities." Since man lives in a specific relationship to nature and to history, Lavisse wrote, "the humanities are the study of man in nature and in time." Without commenting further on the importance of the natural sciences, he took this definition to imply an essentially historical perspective. Teachers of literature and of history were to make students "understand the evolution of humanity," and the way in which men's souls are ceaselessly "modified by history." Without losing themselves in detail, educators were to convey "the general conditions of life at the classical epochs," and to "guide" the student "toward himself," toward "his moment" in the history of humanity.[54]

The "new needs" Lavisse had in mind were clearly social and political, rather than economic. The "simple" education appropriate for a subject of Louis XIV seemed to him unsuited for citizens of a society that was both more "complex" and more "democratic." The hallmarks of modern man, he suggested in effect, are rational autonomy and active citizenship. This allowed him to link the political significance of the educational ideal he proposed to a new scholarly ethos. Every student, he conceded without hesitation, must be "a specialist"; but a common spirit must nevertheless unite all forms of education and research. This unifying bond is "the spirit of the University, which is the scientific spirit"; for "the principles of scientific work are everywhere the same." In the secondary schools and particularly in the university faculties, the regime of "passivity" must end, a regime in which students are mere auditors and readers of manuals. Instead, the student of the future must learn "to practice a method, to discover a fact, a concept, an idea." He must be "invited, excited, constrained" to do independent work. The objective is "the liberation of his mind," and the awakening of "the critical spirit." Even while thus championing an education that seemed to him "more positive and more direct," moreover, Lavisse saw a need for interdisciplinary lectures at the unversities on "resolutely contemporary" topics. In his testimony before the Ribot Commission, he also envisaged teacher-preparatory courses that would convey to future educators a high sense of their "mission." Though they would be speaking as laymen, he said, they should be able to address their pupils as "men and citizens," to appeal to their "consciences" and to their sense of "duty." The historical and "scientific" elements in Lavisse's educational ideal were thus smoothly joined to a republican morality of civic obligation.[55]

Charles Seignobos, somewhat younger than Lavisse, was probably the most determined educational reformist among French historians. Indeed, he was to help in preparing the new teaching programs of 1902. Along with a predominantly modern secondary curriculum, he proposed a highly flexible system of study certificates. The several types of certificates were to be equivalent, with supplementary courses and examinations available to fill gaps in students' records. While this approach would facilitate transfers from higher primary to secondary schools, it would also permit teaching programs to be adjusted to individual interests and aptitudes. The academic heads of particular institutions were to be elected by the *professeurs*, who were also to participate in the setting of educational policies for their schools. Secondary courses on French history were to give more emphasis to the modern and contemporary era.[56]

In a 1903 lecture, Seignobos fully stated the historical argument against the traditional curriculum that was also suggested by Lavisse. Offering a brief social history of the French educational system, he proposed to distinguish its "living" from its "dead portions," its modern features from "survivals (*survivances*) of the old regime." His presentation was couched in descriptive and narrative terms; yet he explicitly intended to "arrive by an impersonal procedure" at a "practical conclusion." In the Middle Ages, he wrote, the educational system trained priests, and "clerks," and the teaching personnel too was "clerical." Latin was taught in a "vocational" spirit, because it was genuinely needed in the clerical professions. Students and teachers were recruited primarily from among the poor; but the educated "proletariat" thus created was not truly "democratic," since its members sought only to rise above their "condition." Thus schools were factories for the production of *déclassés*. At the same time, there was a sharp divide between two quite unrelated educational systems or paths. On the one hand, the vast majority of the population prepared for practical vocations by means of an apprenticeship; they learned, so to speak, by hand. On the other hand, an education in language, by means of books (*la culture par le livre*) was confined until late in the Middle Ages to be the clerical, legal, and medical professions, which jointly formed "a special class, at the margin" of society.[57]

The patterns thus established were altered not so much by the advent of humanism or of the Reformation, but by a "change in the manners of society" that took place between the sixteenth and eighteenth centuries. The sons of the rich, of aristocrats and of wealthy *bourgeois*, began to enter the higher schools and universities as pensioners, and the result was a transformation in the character of language instruction. As Latin was taught to future "men of the world," the emphasis shifted from a practical and vocational to a literary and formal perspective; Latin verses and orations (*discours*) made their appearance, and the study of Latin came to seem a salutary intellectual exercise. Seignobos clearly considered this a fateful shift; for he abandoned his "impersonal" narrative to offer a series of "practical" judgments.

The idea of creating an education without a practical aim, solely to serve as an intellectual gymnastics, has never guided any real innovation ... It is with pedagogical practices as it is with religious rites. When one ceases to believe in the real efficacy of a rite, one begins to regard it as a symbol. In the same way, when an old teaching procedure has ceased to serve a practical need, one explains it – and justifies it – as a gymnastic exercise.

The secondary and higher education of the Middle Ages had been "verbal, monastic, and clerical." Without altering these traits, the social changes of the early modern period had superimposed an "aristocratic character" as well. Secondary education became "the mark that one belonged to the upper class." "Future clerks and future gentlemen" were taught in the same establishments and by the same methods. But "the contradiction between these two conceptions" gave the educational system "an indelible character of incoherence."[58]

In education as in other fields, Seignobos continued, Napoleon "restored the Old Regime," and the "liberal *bourgeoisie* that governed France during the nineteenth century" hardly altered Napoleon's system. Two significant reforms were introduced toward the end of the Second Empire: Duruy's "special secondary" program, and the *Ecole Practique des Hautes Etudes*. "Inspired by the spirit of the Revolution," these new institutions were intended to "found secondary education upon the study of contemporary reality and higher education upon the practice of science." But "the profoundest reforms of our educational system," Seignobos continued, "have been the work of the Republic, and have been carried out during the last twenty years (since 1880)." Primary education has been made universal and free of charge, which is to say "democratic"; its character has become "laic, that is to say rational." The modern secondary curriculum has been fully accredited, and the faculties of letters and of sciences have been thoroughly transformed. All of these reforms have been carried out "in the spirit of the Revolution, or in the scientific spirit of the nineteenth century, to respond to the needs of a democratic and rationalist society."[59]

Like other determined reformists, Seignobos believed in a kind of natural alliance between the militant Republic (or the spirit of the Revolution), scientific rationalism (or laicism, or "science" broadly defined), and socially progressive educational recruitment (or "democracy"). Without explicitly examining the affinities he thus implied, he allowed them to structure his historical narrative, along with the practical conclusions it seemed to dictate. Once we have understood the history of our educational system, he argued in effect, we can distinguish between "what was conceived for a clerical and aristocratic society that wanted to form priests and gentlemen, and what has been reformed or added with a view to a democratic society, to form citizens and workers." Particularly our secondary schools still tend to perpetuate the Old Regime. They are "founded upon a commercial, hence aristocratic principle," in that they are "open only to the children of the *bourgeoisie* who can pay." The instruction they offer continues to be more "verbal" than substantive in character, and they still pursue a "monastic" insulation from the realities of the contemporary world. They thus rob their pupils of the capacity for "physical activity and spontaneous initiative," leaving them "sedentary, passive, bookworms or functionaries." As further industrialization eradicated the remnants of the apprenticeship system, Seignobos speculated, France would ultimately be forced to adopt a more balanced educational regime, one in which "a theroretical education in science" was coupled with "an apprenticeship in real life."[60]

Apart from an occasional reference to industrialization, Seignobos had little to say about economic or technological change. He challenged the traditional identification of *culture générale* with "disinterested" or "gratuitous" learning. While it produced an imbalance between theoretical reflection and practical activity within the individual, he charged, it was also unsuited to a democratic society. Yet he proposed no increase in vocational or technical schooling. As a champion of "science," too, he was less interested in technological progress than in "the scientific spirit" as a cognitive ideal and a cultural force. His overall argument was certainly based on functionalist assumptions, assumptions that allowed him to move with ease from his descriptive narrative to his practical conclusions. But his functionalism was broadly social or even cultural, rather than specifically economic in character. He tacitly equated education with socialization, rather than with individual development on the one hand, or with strictly occupational preparation on the other. As a result, his historical analysis suggested reformist policies almost automatically, as if by definition. For an educational system designed to form clerics and aristocrats must surely be cleansed of disfunctional "survivals" before it can serve to socialize future "workers and citizens" in a democratic society.

Another rigorous reformist, the literary historian Gustave Lanson, did not actually testify before the Ribot Commission of 1899. But he commented upon the subsequent course of reform in a series of articles between December 1900 and June 1901; he contributed to the official instructions that accompanied the settlement of 1902, and he came to be widely regarded as one of the foremost champions of the new regime in French secondary and higher education. His articles of 1900–01, collected and published in 1902, summarized the reformist position as systematically as Fouillée stated the traditionalist case.[61] Citing the requirements of "democracy" and of a complex "division of social labor," Lanson envisaged a modern secondary stream suited to "the urban and rural petty bourgeoisie." Instead of trying to produce "poets, critics and savants" – and of actually producing failures, the modern program was to equip pupils for "the agricultural, industrial and commercial occupations." In the characteristic idiom of social realism, Lanson wrote of training youths "to manufacture cloth, to sell hardware, and to harvest beets," of preparing "earnest, solid men . . . with practical knowledge," capable of "methodical work." "Our democratic sentiments" are offended by "barriers" that exclude many people from the liberal professions and from public administration. Lanson therefore welcomed the proposal to provide "bridges" and "easy passages" between the classical and the modern stream, both at the beginning of the secondary course and at its end, when secondary modern graduates were to have access to the baccalaureate. At the same time, he insisted that most secondary modern students should aim at "practical" vocations, and that they should typically leave school before the age of 18 or 19.[62]

The curriculum of the modern secondary stream, according to Lanson, was to be "resolutely scientific." The emphasis was to be "practical"; the natural sciences were to be taught with a view to their applications. Yet the study of the sciences was also to provide a form of intellectual discipline; students were expected to assimilate something of "the scientific spirit."

The *culture générale* needed for the occupations in which success depends on the account taken of facts is that which habituates the mind to extract exact knowledge from the confusion of the real; it is the *culture générale* provided by science.

Lanson clearly used the word science in a very broad sense. Indeed, he repeatedly drew upon an even broader antithesis between a "scientific" and a "literary" education, in which "science" encompassed everything we would call knowledge, while "literature" stood for the purely formal or "rhetorical."[63]

What the "humanities" meant to some of their defenders, Lanson thought, was just "the old literary method, the sole cultivation of taste and of eloquence, the exclusive study of form and of rhetoric." The classical secondary program seemed to him "more bad than good" for all but future "vaudeville writers, novelists, poets, critics . . . journalists, or simply men of the world." After the "bold exertion of the Renaissance," he argued, the Church had taken over the cultivation of "the humanities," but not without stripping them of their critical force. What was left was "the exquisite expression of received ideas," the ability to give "an agreeable or persuasive turn to what ... faith in authority exempted from verification ... an art of speaking well without thinking."

From the eighteenth century on, it was clear that this education was insufficient ... All the more absurd is it today to let the schooling of the mind consist in the *humanities*, that is to say in rhetoric. The source of ideas is no longer there. The ... natural sciences and the historical sciences have entirely revised our conception of the universe, of society and of man.

Even the teaching of literature, Lanson insisted, could and should be guided by the "scientific spirit"; for only science was "methodical," and only science developed "the taste for truth." Thus the "modern humanities" were in fact the sciences, including the "historical sciences."[64]

In a brief passage on "moral education," Lanson wrote of "an ideal and a faith" based on science that was presumably as firm but more tolerant than Catholicism.

Our ideal and our faith are not tyrannical, because they do not decide upon the cause of the universe and upon the metaphysical problems. They leave to everyone his faith ... They only define the *conditions* of moral and social activity, leaving to everyone the choice of ends. These conditions are the following. Thought must be free ... of the exterior constraint of authority and fear, and free as well of the interior servitude of ignorance and prejudice. Thus intellectual liberty prepares the ground for moral liberty. Thought must be upright, reaching the good by way of the true. The will must be strong ... [rising above] fear ... interest ... and even the affections ... [ready to] sacrifice everything to the truth that one knows and to the duty that commands.[65]

The position on metaphysical issues here is pure positivism, and the tolerance it represented was probably not as great as Lanson suggested. The doctrine of the will, on the other hand, was partly neo-Kantian, typically "laic," and firmly linked to a rigorous ethic of civic "duty."

Lanson did not hesitate, in fact, to portray the choice between the "literary" and the "scientific" method as a moral one.

Literary education ... principally cultivates the imaginative and sentimental faculties; aiming at the discernment of the beautiful, it accustoms the individual to exalt what pleases him; striving to awaken creative powers in everyone, it... easily kindles the passion to excel and to shine... Scientific education... values verification more highly than invention and, above all, than the presentation of ideas; it develops the faculties of reasoning and observation; it accustoms [the student] to research, to methodical and patient verification, and to not believing that things are as they are because it is agreeable or useful to us... It prepares the individual not to conjecture poetically what can be known exactly, to take the work and the invention of other men into account... and to coordinate his activity with theirs.

Literary education is excellent for producing, along with many failures, a few superior individuals who will dazzle the world with their original and egoistic fancy. Scientific education alone can improve the whole youth of a nation and give it the spirit of precision, of method and of discipline necessary for collective works.

The defect of [our] nation... stems from the fact that most minds are without rule and method, prepared to worship brilliant fancy and oratorical virtuosity, indifferent to truth, and incapable of choosing the means that permit truth to be attained more or less completely, given over without defense to the impulses and convulsions of the imagination and of sentiment.[66]

Three quite different antitheses are here brought into association to evoke the moral and social shortcomings of the old learning. First, there is the contrast between imaginative fancy and methodical observation. Literary education not only privileges esthetic form, rather than substantive knowledge; it is also impulsive, moved by irrational urges, occasionally "dazzling" but permanently unreliable, and fundamentally indifferent to truth. Scientific research, by contrast, is based on reasoning and patient verification; methodical and precise in the quest for what truth can be attained and, above all, reliable, communicable and thus progressive. At the same time, the literary man is self-indulgent to the point of egoism; his cultivation of oratorical virtuosity borders on sophistry, and his fundamental motive is the passion to "shine." Not so the man of scientific education, who exercises an almost ascetic restraint, and who has the discipline to recognize the truth even when it does not suit or flatter him. The faults of the literary method, finally, are the much-lamented vices of the French individualist, who risks everything to strive for individual superiority, whereas the true scientist participates in the inherently cooperative research of the scientific community. Scientific education aims at secure advances for the collectivity and for its average members; in that sense, it is more democratic than the old literary education as well.

In a remarkable conclusion, Lanson explained how the classical curriculum itself could be renewed to reflect a modern conception of "the humanities" and of "the scientific spirit." Latin and Greek would continue to be taught, and only "rhetoric" would be abandoned, along with the "unfortunate habit of not examining the truth of things under the pretext of analysing or admiring their beauty." The ancient languages would no longer serve to mark the *honnête homme*, or to provide access to desirable positions. They were said to serve as "intellectual gymnastics"; but that was true only if there was "a firm and sincere intention to acquire the science in which one exercises." The only point of knowing Latin and Greek, in short, was "to be able to read the Latin and Greek authors, and to read them well."

The efficacious work that forms the minds consists of showing the pupils the paths by which one arrives at the true meaning [of a text], by a meticulous study of the sense of the words and of . . . [their] relationships to the phrases, and by a judicious use of grammatical, historical and literary knowledge; having [students] personally engage in [such] research, one leads them to notice . . . [by what methods one progresses] from the confused sketch of the first reading to the nuanced clarity of the definitive translation.[67]

In further amplification of his position, Lanson proposed that Latin orations be dropped, along with Latin versification and other forms of "literary art." Though a historian of literature himself, he wanted literary history and "philological curiosities" excluded from the classroom at the secondary level. His whole emphasis was on interpretation, on "translation and oral explication," or on "the contents of texts," as distinct from their "forms." "Moral commentary," he thought, must take precedence over "esthetic commentary."

Let us discard . . . what used to be called bringing out the beauties of a . . . text. Let us slowly prepare a knowledge of . . . the ancients, from which in due time will spring . . . the sincere and spontaneous sentiment of the beauty of antiquity. In trying to hasten that . . . one would obtain nothing but falsehood and idle talk.[68]

Along with "esthetic commentary," Lanson sharply repudiated unhistorical readings of the ancient sources. He joined Lavisse in stressing the *historical distance* between modern times and the classical texts. Again and again, he challenged the view of the classics as timeless. The masterpieces of antiquity cannot be regarded as "absolute models," he argued, since they can be fully "clarified only in their relation to their time and milieu." The "ideas of the ancients" are not "absolute and eternal truths."

In reality, literary commentary, moral commentary, and every elucidation of the contents of a text must take the form of historical explication. And even while insisting that the *texts themselves* could be understood only historically, Lanson also treated them as sources of evidence for such historical entities outside themselves as "the personality of a writer, the genius of a nation, and the character of an epoch."[69] Like Lavisse, Lanson thus made the interpretation of texts an integral element in the comprehensive study of historical "civilizations" or ways of life.

No longer concerned to transmit the "immutable precepts of good taste," we shall strive to have our pupils advance to an understanding of the life of antiquity; there they will surely find the sense and the love of the literature and the art that ... the civilizations of the Greeks and Romans have created in order to express themselves. In the moral, political and social ideas of the ancients too we can only show our pupils ideas relative to certain states of mind and to certain conditions of existence.[70]

The understanding aimed at is both of "ideas" and of the "civilizations," the "states of mind and conditions of existence," that "create" these ideas and are "expressed" by them.

If all textual commentary is a form of historical instruction, Lanson went on to ask, what benefit does it yield for the present-day "general education of the mind?"

That of knowing man, and the life of humanity, and how we have become what we are ... The young people will be informed of the great problems that pose themselves to every mind and to every society ... They will realize that other conditions, in other times, compel [humanity] to pose and resolve the same problems in different ways ... They will understand that human solutions are always provisional, that each century modifies the old solutions according to its lights and needs ... The historian's study of literary works will convey to them the profound and salutary sense of the relativity of things ... of the effort always necessary in a world that is always changing.[71]

A distinctive form of historicism here emerges at the theoretical grounding for the new and "scientific" approach to be taken in literary studies. Like Seignobos, Lanson used historicist arguments to prove that educational practices must be adjusted to suit modern conditions. Like Lavisse, he drew upon the historicist framework to make what we would call intellectual history the dominant form of all textual interpretation, and thus a key element in all branches of French secondary education. While he wanted literary history in the narrow sense to be kept out of the secondary classroom, his theses could also be taken to legitimate new departures in the historical study of "civilizations."

It is particularly fascinating that neither Lanson, nor Lavisse, nor Seignobos was even mildly troubled by the relativist aspects of the historicist position. On the contrary, Lanson wrote of the "salutary (*bienfaisant*) sense of relativity." What he found beneficent, presumably, was the historicist antidote to "absolute" or eternalizing readings, including what he called "esthetic commentary." Like Lavisse, moreover, he joined a historicist vision to a confident view of his own age. Thus he saw historical studies as revealing "how we have become what we are." He left no doubt that the views of the classical authors had been superseded in some subject areas, especially in the natural sciences. In historical research as well, one suspects, he considered the critical methods of his day superior to their antecedents, as indeed they were. Thus altogether, he saw no conflict between a form of historicism and an unabashed reliance upon the rational standards of his time. Like other French educational reformists, he was an optimist and a champion of scientific and scholarly progress.

TOWARD MERITOCRACY

In 1917, among the young men assigned to French army headquarters at Compiègne, there were seven young peace-time secondary teachers and aspiring academics, among them Albert Girard, Jean-Marie Carré and Edmond Vermeil. Meeting in their spare time, these young people began to formulate and to set down their ideas for a thorough reform of the French educational system. In February 1918, they issued a first manifesto in the weekly *L'Opinion*, and they signed it "Les Compagnons de l'université nouvelle," the associated artisans or journeymen of the new university. Somewhat later in 1918, the group published a two-volume work on their proposals. In April 1919, together with thirty-eight new recruits to their cause, they made their names public and formally constituted themselves an association. In the years that followed, the Compagnons became the foremost spokesmen for the ideal of the "common school" (*l'école unique*) and for the principle of meritocratic selection in French secondary education.[72] Their thought is interesting for us here because it completed certain lines of argument begun by the French reformists of the years around 1900, even while extending them downward into the realm of elementary and higher primary education.

One of the most important institutional changes recommended by the Compagnons was the introduction of common primary schooling to age twelve. The elementary classes attached to secondary schools were to be tolerated a while longer; but they were to be taught by regular primary teachers and to offer the program of the elementary primary schools. With the help of periodic examinations, rigorous academic selection was to route the ablest primary pupils toward the secondary schools at age twelve, regardless of their wealth and social background. This meant that public secondary education, like public primary schooling, was to be entirely free of charge. To the extent that this was not possible immediately, scholarships were to be made available in unlimited numbers to all qualified but needy pupils. Indeed, to ensure that private secondary education would not become an exclusive preserve of the wealthy, the state was to provide partial subsidies for private secondary schooling as well. The Compagnons dismissed the old conflict between the public and the Catholic schools as a socially destructive relic of more dogmatic times.[73] In this respect, their position differed radically from that of earlier reformers, who knew that innovations in the state schools might cause parents to transfer their children to the private sector.

At age twelve, the school system proposed by the Compagnons began to branch out. Some pupils were to remain in the primary schools until the new school leaving age of fourteen, unless they belatedly demonstrated academic talent, in which case they were to be transferred to the secondary system after all. The graduates of the primary schools were to be given part-time vocational and civic instruction during a period of apprenticeship extending to age eighteen.[74] For those leaving the primary system at age twelve, two forms of secondary education were to be offered. One branch was to be essentially vocational-technical; some of its graduates would presumably reach certain higher technical schools. The other branch was to emphasize "the humanities"; it would offer a "disinterested" *culture générale* to an elite of students, who would prepare for the baccalaureate and proceed to one of the traditional institutions of higher education. The curriculum of the humanistic secondary schools was to be based primarily upon French, mathematics and the natural sciences; but Latin was to be a requirement, and so were courses in French history, geography and the modern foreign languages. The Compagnons defended Latin as good "intellectual gymnastics"; they wanted to inculcate "rigorous intellectual and moral habits." Much of what they wrote about the academic secondary stream was quite conventional. Yet they were apparently willing to abandon Greek, and to supplement instruction in Latin with an increased emphasis upon the "modern" subjects. Beyond that, they persistently emphasized the need to train the body and the will as well as the mind.[75]

In matters of organization and administration, the Compagnons strongly urged decentralization; they believed that an excess of bureaucratic direction in education had provoked a countervailing spirit of "anarchy," of alienation and rebellion among totally isolated individuals. In the face of these deeply entrenched structures and habits, they hoped to institutionalize a measure of cooperation, initiative and diversity. They meant to form a national association (*corporation*) of teachers in all layers of the system, and in both public and private institutions. A mutual aid society as well as a professional organization, the association was to seek cooperative relations with other business and professional associations, as well as with parents' committees, especially at the local and regional levels. The old University, the Compagnons claimed, had been a "hierarchy of mandarins," a series of "closed castes." It was time to establish a more open and active network of institutions.[76]

The transition from secondary to higher education was to be made easier in several ways. The baccalaureate would no longer be required for access to the universities. It would continue to be given, but the single line between those who passed and those who failed would be replaced by more detailed grades that could be considered at the point of entry into the professions. General introductory courses given in the faculties of letters and of sciences during the first and second years were to help students to make their way into more advanced work. Consistent with the new spirit of openness, university faculties were to give up their critically detached stance as "intellectuals," and to become more actively involved in the life of the nation. They should accept their responsibility not only for research, but also for the popularization of knowledge and for the schooling of practitioners. Above all, they should give more thought to the pedagogical and professional preparation of future secondary teachers. Indeed, they themselves should be neither collectors of notecards nor wordsmiths, but true mentors (*maîtres*). German academics and teachers had begun to make plans for educational reform even while the war continued. They were not disdained as "intellectuals"; nor did they fail to support their men of action. While the French should not imitate the narrow nationalism of the Germans, of course, they could learn something from them. The English and the Americans too offered useful examples of "healthy realism" and "confidence in life."[77]

In justifying their recommendations, the Compagnons came back again and again to the theme of efficiency or utility. France had expended much of its wealth and lost many of its best men during the war, they argued; she urgently needed to concentrate her remaining material and intellectual resources. She could not hope to hold her own in the "peaceful battles of tomorrow," unless strenuous efforts were made to increase productivity. Here again, the Compagnons differed markedly from the reformers of the years around 1900. They aimed at a major expansion of higher primary, vocational and secondary schooling, and they went much further than their predecessors in linking educational change to the requirements of the economy. They saw improved schooling as necessary to ensure the optimal exploitation of the country's human resources; their objective was to "draw the best yield" from every individual. "All must produce," and "the best must govern." In this context, the standard of utility was applied even to the "humanistic" branch of the secondary system. The education provided by that branch to an elite of students, according to the Compagnons, could not be "purely utilitarian"; its character had to be "aristocratic" in some sense.

An elite must . . . master its domain, and it cannot accomplish that without raising itself to a certain generality of education . . . The fact is that for a future member of the elite, the care given to his *culture générale* has a vocational value. This apparent luxury is at bottom a necessity . . . The outreach of his action depends upon the quality of his general education. And that is a very utilitarian concern.

There was little left in these formulations of the old rhetoric of "disinterestedness," not to mention the broader human purposes of education.[78]

Even more dominant in the writings of the Compagnons than the theme of utility, however, was the emphasis upon a strictly meritocratic distribution of access to advanced education. The most dramatic of the reforms they proposed, after all, was the introduction of free secondary schooling. While they envisaged a continued hierarchy of academic secondary, vocational-technical secondary, and post-primary schooling, they meant totally to remove the economic and institutional obstacles to equality of educational opportunity. That is what they meant by "democracy in education." They undoubtedly saw common primary schooling as socially ameliorative in itself; but their main objective was to create equal conditions of competition for places in "humanistic" secondary and higher education. They were passionately interested in "selection," in locating and supporting "the gifted," in "drawing the best out of the crowd." They wanted "room for talent." Repeating an old republican doctrine, they argued that a democracy needs an elite, but that the only hierarchy it can tolerate is "the hierarchy of merit and utility."

The *école unique* simultaneously resolves two questions: it is democracy in education, and it is selection according to merit . . . The fathers stood watch in the same trenches; wherever possible the sons can sit in the same benches.[79]

Social utility, democracy in the form of opportunity, selection on strictly academic grounds, and a reduction of experienced social distances: these were the guiding ideas of the Compagnons.

These ideas were only slowly turned into practice. The rivalry between the public and the Catholic schools revived, as conservative Catholics led the opposition to the *école unique*. Fiscal problems and determined obstruction from the political right delayed the abolition of fees in public secondary education. On the other hand, the principles of the *école unique* also attracted strong political support, from Edouard Herriot and the Radicals, from Ferdinand Buisson and the Ligue de l'Enseignement, from Ludovic Zoretti and the syndicalist movement among secondary and university teachers, and from Léon Blum and the Socialists. Thus very gradually from the mid 1920s on, modest progress was made in the direction broadly defined by the ideal of the "common school." The elementary secondary classes were assimilated to the primary schools. Common courses in common subjects tended to reduce the institutional barriers not only among the secondary streams, but between the secondary and the primary schools as well. Then, in a series of steps between 1928 and 1933, tuition was abolished in public secondary education, except that fees continued to be paid in the elementary secondary classes until 1945. Jean Zay, Minister of Education in the Popular Front government of 1936, built on these foundations in completing most of the projects initially outlined by the Compagnons.[80]

The ideas behind the *école unique* were not really new, of course, even when the Compagnons published their first manifesto in 1918. On the contrary, meritocratic principles had been implied in the educational reform programs of the late nineteenth century as well. In a way, the Compagnons merely extended and completed a movement toward meritocracy that had characterized French educational reformism at least since the days of the Ribot Commission. Yet the interwar period certainly witnessed a high point in the enthusiasm for meritocracy among educational and political progressives.

In a previous chapter, we discussed Edmond Goblot's 1925 *La barrière et le niveau*, a commentary on the significance of education for the French bourgeoisie that has become a minor classic.[81] I recall it here because it was perhaps an even more perfect expression of the meritocratic perspective than the work of the Compagnons. Goblot saw classical secondary schooling, particularly the *baccalauréat*, as the true basis of bourgeois status. Conflicts over alternatives in education, he argued, were social struggles, rather than pedagogical disagreements; for the bourgeoisie was committed to maintaining an "education that classes," rather than one that merely "ranks" individual pupils. He wrote as if the "opinion" that maintained bourgeois supremacy was something like an intellectual error, a fraud that could be unmasked. If students were selected and advanced strictly according to their abilities, he implied, the whole class system would simply collapse. He praised the reforms of the Third Republic for the progress that had been made toward equality of educational opportunity. Writing in the mid 1920s, he saw bourgeois pretensions as coming under increasing pressure from "the critical spirit." Echoing the Compagnons, he argued that the experience of the First World War had further weakened the old social divisions. The time was ripe, he thought, for an educational system that would develop all individual capacities, and that would "rank" without "classing." By means of a rigorous and purely intellectual "selection" of pupils, the educational system of the future would create an "open elite" of talent to replace the spurious "class" superiority of the bourgeoisie.

Goblot, like the Compagnons, apparently felt that a purely meritocratic social hierarchy was in some sense "democratic" and in any case unobjectionable. His total commitment to this vision strikes us as remarkable, precisely because we no longer fully share it. We still favor meritocratic standards in academic selection, at least in principle – and in preference to other ways of regulating access to schooling. Yet we have come to distrust our measures of academic potential, along with the old distinction between "aptitude" and "achievement" tests. Much of what our examinations register, we suspect, is the cultural capital associated with family background. Our best approach in practice might be to adjust our meritocratic norms in some degree to compensate for cultural disadvantages. Yet difficult theoretical questions remain. Perhaps there really is no singular and even partly asocial quality that could be called "intelligence"? And would great educational inequalities be tolerable even if schooling could be distributed according to fully clarified criteria? Are we not equally concerned to make sound educations more widely available across the whole social and academic spectrum? To ask such questions is merely to indicate that we have moved away from the views expressed by Goblot and the Compagnons. And that is why we can begin to see them as specific to a particular moment in the history of modern educational thought.

CHAPTER 4

The new French university

My objectives in the remaining two chapters are to describe at least some of the characteristics of the French intellectual field during the decades around 1900, to analyze the controversy between spokesmen and critics of the reformed French universities of that period, and to relate the terms of this controversy to major positions in the French debate on secondary education. Before addressing these topics, however, I want once again to look at comparable phenomena in Germany, and thus to prepare the ground for a comparative perspective.

THE CRISIS OF GERMAN ACADEMIC CULTURE

In chapter 2, we discussed the mounting sense of crisis that prevailed within the German universities from about the 1890s to the 1920s. Particularly the orthodox majority of German academics feared and opposed what they took to be a trend toward modernization and democratization in German secondary and higher education. What most deeply troubled humanists and social scientists from all sectors of the German academic community, however, was the problem of scientific and scholarly specialization, or rather, a whole cluster of issues they associated with specialization. They faced a peculiar dilemma; for most of them were deeply involved in specialized research. They enjoyed the unprecedented material prosperity of their research institutions, along with the just national and international renown of German specialized scholarship and scientific research. Yet they could not shake the sense that something vital to them was being undermined, and that their practice was becoming incongruous with their ideals. The branching out of existing disciplines into increasingly autonomous subfields, and the decreasing topical breadth of the average product of scientific and scholarly work: these seemed to portend a kind of intellectual atomization, in which researchers would lose sight of the interrelationships among their several findings and hypotheses. Going even beyond this cognitive disconnectedness, however, specialization was widely held to threaten the theoretical unity of knowledge, or the relationship between empirical *Wissenschaft* and fundamental philosophy. Interpreted in the light of the German tradition, incoherence in specialized science and scholarship stemmed from the loss of the integrative framework that had once been provided by the Idealist systems.[1]

This helps to account for the almost automatic association of specialization with "positivism." The latter in turn was rarely described in detail. One has to remember that intellectual disciples of Auguste Comte or *self-confessed* "positivists" of any other kind were virtually unknown among German university faculty between 1890 and 1930. The label "positivist" was almost always used in a derogatory sense, and those charged with "positivism" were typically thought guilty of *unacknowledged* fallacies. Chief among the errors ascribed to positivists was the possibly implicit belief that the concepts of the natural sciences can be extended to the humanities and social studies, or that the search for lawlike regularities is the main task of the interpretive and historical disciplines as well. Indeed, even unreflected research *practices* could be viewed as positivist, if they were guided by a naive objectivism (envisaging a theory-free adding up of "basic facts"), or by a strong causalist program. Obviously, all forms of determinism, "materialism," or doctrinaire Marxism were considered positivist in inspiration or tendency, as were mechanical, "atomistic" or otherwise reductive analyses of organic processes, complex mental states, cultural meanings, or social wholes.

According to a generally accepted historical thesis, the decline of Idealist philosophy set the stage for an era of positivism that extended from the 1840s into the 1880s. The positivism of the intervening decades was less a set of stated theories than a cluster of vaguely scientistic attitudes, tacit assumptions, and research practices. This was of course a period of very high achievement for the German research university; but it also looked in retrospect like an unphilosophical epoch. An attack upon its assumptions was launched during the 1880s by a "critical" and empiricist strand of neo-Kantianism that was eventually superseded by the more "constructive" rationalism of the Baden neo-Kantians and allied schools. In a brief history of German philosophy, Wilhelm Windelband described the difference between the "critical" neo-Kantians and his own later and more "doctrinal" position in the following terms.

This agnostic neo-Kantianism of the eighth and ninth decade of the nineteenth century had a decided bias toward positivism, because it neglected the rational element in [Kant's] critical philosophy. The empiricist epistemology that was read into Kant tended to replace philsophical criticism with a psychological and causal analysis [of experience]. And because it confused Kantian a priority with psychic priority, it ended by leaning again toward David Hume on the one hand and toward Auguste Comte on the other. But the consequence of this empiricism . . . was the complete reduction of philosophy to epistemology. This had never been truly intended by Kant: He always saw his "critical task" . . . as a prelude to "doctrinal" work. The epistemology that partly identified itself with his name, however, was at bottom the deliberate abandonment of all *Weltanschauung* based on *Wissenschaft*. And in this abdication, in this empiricism, a certain naive materialism probably also played a confused and unconscious role.[2]

The passage is not an unsophisticated polemic; it could easily be further elaborated and even partly defended. Yet it also shows quite plainly how broad the charge of positivism actually was, how thoroughly it was linked to an even broader case against untutored empirical research itself, and how the critique of naive empiricism in turn was informed by a determination to revive aspects of Kantian and post-Kantian Idealism. In sum, the widespread concern over the problematic consequences of excessive specialization that actually deepened from the 1890s to the 1920s reflected a sense that the eminent successes of the German research university during the nineteenth century were accompanied by a loss of philosophical coherence. Scientific and scholarly practice had lost touch with its theoretical foundations in German Idealism. To overcome the problems raised by specialization and positivism alike, it was commonly believed, there was an urgent need for a revitalization of philosophical Idealism that would also reinstate *Wissenschaft* as a ground for an integral and partly normative *Weltanschauung*.

"Positivism," in other words, occupied a definite place in the German intellectual field of that period. Much discussed and almost unanimously decried by German academic humanists and social scientists from the 1880s to the 1920s, "positivism" was a theoretical and practical failing that had to be "overcome" as soon as possible.

This view prevailed across all disciplines and sectors of the political spectrum. The anti-"positivist" position was linked to the animus against "utilitarian" or instrumental rationality that was present in the German academic tradition from the early nineteenth century on; it was a reservation about the common-sense and practical forms of empiricism. After 1890, in any case, "positivism" was perceived as a major threat to sound scholarship and philosophy in an age of excessive specialization, and as an obstacle in the path of a sorely needed renewal of Idealism. To the orthodox, it was a kind of intellectual acid, a potentially disastrous dissolvent of wholistic concepts, traditional beliefs, and socially integrative certainties. To some, it was a Western intellectual vice, an ally of Marxism, and chiefly responsible for the apparent loss of a national sense of community.

In a 1929 manifesto, the members of the Vienna Circle, originators of what we know as neo-positivism, belatedly enacted and thus actually ratified the "radical" role assigned to positivism in the German intellectual tradition. Writing in the tone of exasperated outsiders, they proposed to combat the "growth of metaphysical and theologizing tendencies" in the philosophy of the German academic establishment. While conveying their sense that most supposedly philosophical problems could be analyzed out of existence, they also expressed their sympathy with the progressive social and political movements of their time. They noted a "curious unanimity" among themselves in an area of concern that had not, after all, brought them together. Why should agreement in philosophy be accompanied by political consensus? Rudolf Carnap suspected that "those who hold on to the past in the social field also cultivate . . . (outdated) positions in metaphysics and theology."[3] I need scarcely point out how little Carnap's conception of positivism has in common with the positivism that has sometimes been disapproved by radical critics of the social sciences in the United States. It has even less to do, as we shall shortly observe, with the forms of positivism current in France during the decades around 1900. We are easily tempted to assume that "positivism" and similar orientations must have specific social and political implications. We tend to trace the "curious unanimity" mentioned by Carnap to timeless psychological affinities, or even to epistemological relationships. In fact what we are dealing with in such cases is the historically contingent "logic" of an intellectual field.

Even disciplinary specialization itself aroused more anxiety in the German academic community between about 1890 and 1930 than it did in other contexts. Other scholars at other times have certainly experienced an uneasy tension between their cognitive and educational ideals on the one hand, and their actual practices on the other. But the sense of loss among Germans was particularly deep, in part because their tradition perpetuated a particularly sanguine view of the problematic relationship between knowledge and wisdom. Thus, as their accounts of specialization reveal, they feared not only intellectual fragmentation or cognitive incoherence, but also the collapse of personal, evaluative, and integral knowledge. They firmly *expected Wissenschaft* to yield *Bildung* and *Weltanschauung*, and they were accordingly disappointed that this was often or even normally *not* the case. A further expectation they inherited from their tradition was that the universities and *Wissenschaft* would have considerable authority and influence within the larger society. They had always conceived this influence as a direct and unmediated flow of spiritual authority. They saw themselves as sages, not as specialists. At the conceptual level, their vision of spiritual power linked *Wissenschaft* to *Weltanschauung*, rather than to instrumentalism and to practice. In social and political life before 1918, it linked the German universities to the higher echelons within the Prussian bureaucracy, via a reformist paternalism, rather than, more indirectly, via public opinion and the electorate of a liberal polity.[4]

It must be remembered, too, that in nineteenth-century Germany, the role of the intellectual fell almost exclusively to the university professors. Unaffiliated writers were relatively less numerous in Germany than in France, and Golo Mann argued that they were less esteemed as well. They achieved a slightly increased prominence during the late nineteenth century and again during the Weimar period, but that only helped to confirm their bad reputation as "journalists," or *Zivilisationsliteraten*, overly politicized allies of mass civilization. There was a literary and artistic *avant-garde*, and there were a few socially and politically radical journals; but these never competed effectively with the centrally placed academic elite.[5] Accustomed to great authority, the German mandarin intellectuals were acutely sensitive to the apparent decline in their influence after 1890 and again after 1918.

In any case, a sense of lost authority, and even of impotence, was a recurrent theme in German academic literature between about 1890 and 1930. One way to understand this theme is to return once more to Simmel's passage on "cultivation," which in fact occurred in one of several essays he wrote between 1900 and 1910 on the concept and the "tragedy" of culture.[6] In all of these essays, Simmel drew on the key definitions of neo-Idealist cultural philosophy. In his use of a common terminology, "personal culture" was identical with "cultivation"; "subjective mind" stood for the experience and thought of the individual knower and, by extension, of mankind in general; "objective" mind or culture encompassed the external expressions of subjective mind, the social and material forms in which it is fixed and transmitted. Simmel emphasized that subjective and objective mind can only develop in dialectical interaction; a purely subjective life can never attain any degree of complexity or coherence. On the other hand, the inescapable need for objectification leads to consequences that have a tragic aspect. The fullness and elasticity of subjective culture give rise to the diversity and rigidity of objective mind. As the latter grows ever more extensive, there is an increasing "incommensurability" between the subjective and objective poles in the dialectic of cultural development and of individual *Bildung*. An estrangement occurs as well; for the reified elements of the objective culture acquire a necessity of their own. Man is oppressed by the artifacts, institutions, and theories he has invented; he does not recognize them as his creatures; they confront him as alien forces. The division of labor and intellectual specialization are the two great exemplars of the disjunction between subjective and objective mind. The subjective mind of the producer is drained into machines and commodities that impoverish and enslave him. Harmonious individual cultivation becomes ever more difficult; means overwhelm ends, and sensitive individuals acquire something close to a hatred of the objective culture that threatens to engulf them.

Though influenced by Marx, Simmel made no serious effort to distinguish between the timeless paradoxes of objectification and their historical embodiments in a particular place and time, or between their unavoidable and their malignant or curable forms. The neo-Idealist framework also obscured the need for a separation of causes from effects, or of the social from the intellectual dimensions of alienation. But I cannot here attempt a fuller discussion of Simmel's texts, or of their intellectual ancestry. All I mean to suggest is that his vivid portrait of modern dilemmas drew much of its force from the perceived tension between scientific specialization and personal *Bildung*. Simmel was certainly not alone in observing this tension. He merely articulated more completely what many of his colleagues also felt and feared: that objective and subdivided *Wissenschaft* was losing its former relevance to *Bildung*, to personal knowledge or wisdom. Thus the inherited distinction between inward "culture" and outward "civilization" was revived in the decades after 1890, and the word "civilization" now took on a broader meaning as well. It no longer referred only to superficial good manners, or to mere "virtuosity and refinement" in Simmel's terms; but also to merely external progress, to urbanization and technology, to scientific specialization and social rationalization, or to all those aspects of the modern environment that seemed inimical to man's inner development. Indeed, the perceived threat to personal culture sometimes gave rise to fearful and all-encompassing visions of "civilization" as decadence and decline.[7]

Simmel's reflections on the "tragedy of culture" convey the image of the sorcerer's apprentice who has raised spirits that now elude his control. This is one variation upon the theme of lost authority, which was often sounded when German university professors wrote about their social and political environment after 1890. It seemed to many of them that their world was increasingly dominated by blind economic processes, by the power of money, and by the weight of numbers. "Mind" appeared to have lost its influence in public life; for ideas and principles played a shrinking role in the organized confrontations among economic organizations and political machines. Before 1918, most German academics liked to think, against strong evidence to the contrary, that the bureaucratic monarchy could "rise above" class conflict and reverse the disaffection of "the masses" by pursuing a paternalist program of "social policy." Economic individualism and unrestrained capitalism found few supporters in the German academic community; the mandarin intellectuals were not "bourgeois thinkers" in that sense of the term. Yet many of them identified with the conservative and national forces in Wilhelmian politics, distrusted potentially democratic alternatives, and directed their deepest hostility against Social Democracy and the "materialism" of "the masses."[8]

During the Weimar period, the "orthodox" majority of German university professors supported the "national" opposition to the new regime. Unable to perceive democratic liberalism as a genuine political principle, and unwilling seriously to address the distributive questions that strained the Republic's parliamentary system, the orthodox mandarins became addicted to moralistic attacks upon modern "interest" politics. Striking a characteristically "apolitical" pose, they preached the primacy of "the whole" or of the "national community" over its parts, or the need for an "idealistic" alternative to economic class conflict. Some dreamed of an "intellectual revolution" that would restore the empire of "mind" in public affairs, and of course such "apolitical" or "idealistic" prophecies had very material political consequences.[9]

In both the Wilhelmian and Weimar periods, to be sure, a substantial minority of German university faculty in the humanities and social sciences took less one-sided positions on the political issues of their time. They were more critical than their colleagues of the Wilhelmian political and social system, and they partly or wholly resisted the annexationist hysteria that infected the German academic community during the First World War. After 1918, they supported the genuinely republican parties. In this they were guided less by a genuine enthusiasm for democracy, not to mention socialism, than by a sense of realism, and by the hope that the Republic might be encouraged to pursue moderate policies. Among the members of this relatively progressive minority, some were determined cultural individualists and therefore "liberals" in some sense of that term; others more closely resembled the type of the enlightened or reformist "conservative"; only a handful directed truly radical criticisms at the political assumptions prevailing among their colleagues. In short, the republicans among German academics of the Weimar period took a wide range of specific positions. Yet I chose to call them all "modernists" or "radical modernists," because they held one important belief in common. This was that the German intellectual heritage had to be systematically reexamined in the light of modern conditions, that patently outmoded or socially indefensible accretions had to be stripped away, so that the vital core of the tradition could be preserved and transmitted to a wider audience in an inescapably more democratic age.[10]

The modernists asked themselves, for example, how the ideal of self-cultivation might be relevant to the experience of a factory worker, or to a much enlarged system of secondary schooling, or to sources of *Bildung* other than those of classical antiquity. In pursuit of the modernist program, such scholars as Troeltsch and Simmel in fact became critical "translators" of German Idealism and Roman-

ticism, of the hermeneutic method, or of the "principle of individuality." In almost every discipline, and especially in the social
sciences, some of the most prominent innovators were modernists,
and this is not surprising. For the modernists were open to the
creative experience of intellectual incongruity. While the orthodox
almost unconsciously perpetuated the ideology of *Bildung* in its
socially confirmative form, the modernists had to raise the ideology
to critical consciousness. Thus my distinction between "orthodoxy"
and "modernism" is meant to capture something more than the
divide between the right and the center left in a political spectrum.
It is also intended to point up the crucial difference between the
unreflected transmission and the conscious clarification of a
tradition.

As a matter of fact, it is possible to locate the German academic
modernists of the Weimar period on a scale of increasing critical
distance from mandarin orthodoxy. From the near-orthodox
reformism of Friedrich Meinecke, the scale extended to such typical
modernists as Georg Simmel, Ernst Troeltsch, and Max and Alfred
Weber, and further on from there to the radical modernism of the
early Karl Mannheim and the left Hegelianism of the Frankfurt
School. Varying degrees of heterodoxy were not only individual
responses to unusual or distancing experiences of all kinds, from
contacts outside the academic world to an encounter with anti-
Semitism or a close reading of Hobbes; they were also immediate
consequences of intellectual crisis and incongruity, especially for the
most perceptive and intellectually rigorous participants in the
debates that took place. Once dislodged from the position of naive
adherence, the critics of orthodoxy were precipitated into a characteristic chain of reversals that nonetheless reflected the tradition they
challenged. Thus German Idealism provoked self-conscious anti-
idealisms that are hard to imagine in other intellectual fields.

I am thinking less of Marx or of Freud in this connection than of
several more immediately pertinent examples. Thus Ernst von Aster,
a radical critic of mandarin orthodoxy, once complained of the
"merciless moralizing" that often took the place of political analysis
in the German academic debates of the 1920s. Pushed to an extreme,
the "idealist" language of "unpolitical" politics, the recurrent calls
for a "rising above" individual and class interests, for a submission to
eternal values and to the "whole" of the national community,
virtually forced dissenters into a debunking stance. They had the

choice of unmasking the non-spiritual interests actually served by such rhetoric, of rudely reducing the good of the whole to the interests of its members, or of countering elevated laments about lower-class "materialism" in Bertolt Brecht's language: "Erst kommt das Fressen, dann kommt die Moral!" (First eats, then morals).[11] This, surely, is a perfect example of a *positional* truth.

The early work of the Frankfurt School may be understood as a more complex variation upon the same theme. In rejoining Marx to Hegel, Horkheimer, Adorno and their colleagues also recovered the perspective of the young Hegelians. They could insist that human self-development and self-expression had to entail an active transformation of his total environment, including his material and social conditions of life. They could also reactivate the element of this-worldly, sensual liberation that Feuerbach, for example, had associated with the return from alienation. Reversing the purely contemplative and ascetic thrust of orthodox Idealism, they were able at the same time to perpetuate other components of the Idealist heritage. This helps to account for certain similarities of tone and emphasis between their critique of twentieth-century "mass culture" and the more orthodox variants of mandarin anti-modernity. Particularly after their emigration to America, they occasionally responded to their new environment as "mandarins," though of course as mandarins of the left. Indeed, in their critique of the Enlightenment, Horkheimer and Adorno fell back upon the deep distrust of instrumental reason that had been a principal theme of the German mandarin tradition from the beginning. Deprived of their earlier confidence in the proletariat as an agent of human liberation, they ultimately recovered even some of the purely Utopian and quasi-religious significance that had been attached to the ideal of *Bildung* by the great neohumanists and Idealists of the German classical age.[12]

By the 1920s, German academics wrote and spoke of an existing "crisis of *Wissenschaft*." In describing this crisis, they usually repeated the well-established view that excessive specialization posed a threat not only to the coherence of knowledge, but also to the interconnections between *Wissenschaft*, *Bildung*, and *Weltanschauung*. Max Weber and a few other scholars defended specialization as an inescapable precondition of advanced research; but this was a minority position. Moreover, the divide between the orthodox and the modernists, which deepened greatly after 1918, now came to affect methodological positions to an unprecedented degree. Thus the recurrent demand for "synthesis," though initially expressed by some modernists as well, became ever more clearly an orthodox device. Indeed, "synthesis" itself was more and more broadly conceived. At first, it meant no more than cognitive integration, the attempt to interrelate research hypotheses and results; but it ultimately acquired much wider connotations as well. Thus the neo-Idealist revival of the *Geisteswissenschaften* since the 1880s was reinterpreted to signify a more integral and spiritually profitable engagement with the values embedded in great texts. The rhetoric of *Erleben* was used to suggest an intuitive *identification*, just as "phenomenological" methods were taken to authorize a direct "viewing" of "essential" meanings (*Wesenschau*). "Synthesis" seemed to offer a cure for "positivism," which occasionally came to stand for the analytical "dissolution" (*Zersetzung*) of inherited convictions and moral certainties.[13]

The identificationist construal of historical interpretation probably aggravated a further dilemma that was intensively discussed during the 1920s, though it originated a good deal earlier than that. This was the "problem of historicism" (*Historismus*), which was carefully analyzed by Ernst Troeltsch between 1918 and 1922. In Troeltsch's account of it, the problem arose because historical study revealed all values and convictions to be expressions of particular historical contexts, so that no unconditional certainties could be rescued from the limitations of historicity.[14] This is not the issue usually referred to in Anglo-American discussions of "historical relativism," which has to do with the difficulty of attaining objective *knowledge* of the historical past, not with the precariousness of present-day *value judgments*.

I suspect, in fact, that the problem of *Historismus* was largely specific to Germany, and to the Wilhelmian and Weimar periods. We will find little trace of it among some of the leading French historians of the decades around 1900, although they certainly were "historicists" in some sense of that term. Certainly *Historismus* is rarely debated in the United States – or in Germany – today. It was closely linked to the "idiographic" scheme and to the principle of individuality. In the German historical tradition, the concern with the unique and the individual probably encouraged an emphasis upon the creative role of "great men." Indirectly, it may also have helped to sustain the predominant interest in diplomatic and military history, the commitment to the "primacy of foreign policy" that retarded the emergence of social history in Germany. The idiographic approach was applicable not only to individual persons and particular events, but to aggregates as well. Whole epochs and cultures were treated as unique totalities that could be understood only in their own terms. But if this methodological commitment is taken seriously, it begins to suggest that the historian's own standpoint too is inseparable from a particular historical situation. There are no objective certainties or reliable standards to preserve the historian's own judgments from the fatal entanglement in the flux of history. That is the "problem of *Historismus*," and it is surely aggravated by the identificationist approach to historical intepretation. That approach in effect suppresses the rational standpoint of the present-day interpreter as an autonomous element in the dialectic of interpretation. It makes the interpreter abandon himself in order to reproduce the experience behind the historical text. But the entanglement in historical change becomes ever more inescapable as understanding becomes "reliving." Thus to the extent that the ideal of *Bildung* was converted into an ideology of identification, a wanting to reproduce and to internalize the values of the classical heritage, to that extent the "problem of *Historismus*" was likely to become as troublesome as it apparently did during the crisis of *Wissenschaft*.

SCIENCE AND POLITICS: ASPECTS OF THE FRENCH INTELLECTUAL FIELD DURING THE LATE NINETEENTH CENTURY

Some form of positivism was to the French intellectual field of the late nineteenth century what philosophical Idealism was to the German academic tradition of the same period. It was a cluster of incompletely articulated cognitive preferences, rather than a precisely formulated position. It can be traced partly, though by no means wholly, to the way in which Auguste Comte's doctrines were perpetuated beyond 1870, primarily by Emile Littré.[15] A careful student and almost a disciple of Comte, Littré stressed the master's scientific phenomenalism. According to Comte, each science passes through a "theological" and a "metaphysical" stage, before it reaches the "positive" stage. What chiefly characterizes "positive" science is that it abandons "the vain search after absolute notions, the origin and destination of the universe, and the causes of phenomena, and applies itself to the study of their laws – that is, their invariable relations of succession and resemblance."[16] Comte held that scientific laws are simply "general facts"; yet he insisted that reasoning as well as observation plays a role in scientific discovery, and he strongly disapproved merely empiric approaches. He ordered the sciences in a "hierarchy" of increasing complexity and decreasing generality. But while he believed that the more complex sciences depended upon the simpler ones, he was in no sense a reductionist. Physiology differs from physics and chemistry, he argued, in that it studies "organized" bodies and "vital" phenomena. Similarly, "social physics," the highest of the sciences, cannot be deduced from physiology, since "the social conditions which modify the action of the physiological laws are here the most essential consideration."[17] Nevertheless, Comte saw no great difference of method between the natural and the human sciences, both of which must seek to discover objective and invariant laws. In politics, he disapproved of "revolutionary doctrine," against which he cited the "law of continuous human development."

Tenets of this general type certainly reappeared in the works of French thinkers of the late nineteenth century; yet Comte's influence may not be solely responsible. Littré himself was rather selective in his appreciation of Comte, and others gave even less attention to his specific teachings. Ernest Renan and Hippolyte Taine have been numbered among Comte's successors; yet what they transmitted was not Auguste Comte's Positivism (with a capital P), but a viewpoint more vaguely scientistic or "positivistic" (with a small p).[18] Or to put it more generally, the scientistic climate of opinion in late nineteenth-century France probably owed less to the direct influence of Comte than to other, more general causes. One such general cause was the overall prestige of the natural sciences, which was certainly greater in France around 1900 than in Germany a century earlier. Another was the relationship of mutual reinforcement between French republicanism and a broadly positivist philosophy of science. John Scott has described the intellectual fundaments of republicanism from the 1870s to the First World War, and he too has assigned a major role to Littré.[19] What Littré perpetuated, Scott suggests, was just a firm sense of scientific method and a strictly secular approach to philosophical problems. Scott rightly regards these preferences as decisive, however, in that they helped to sustain the "laic" position. For nothing was as central to all shades of French republicanism from the late 1870s on than the laic creed. Laicism was not only the latest incarnation of the ancient conflict between the principles of the Revolution and the Catholic church; it also reflected a profound sense of the need to develop a secular replacement for the moral authority of the Catholic world view. Science, including positivist social science, might be expected to yield this replacement.[20]

Along with Littré, as Scott points out, the neo-Kantian Charles Renouvier greatly influenced the French republicans of the late nineteenth century.[21] Renouvier accepted the idea of a natural world governed by deterministic causality; but his Kantian "criticism" allowed him simultaneously to see man as standing outside the world of natural phenomena, choosing his actions in moral freedom. The idea that the realm of human action could be analytically separated from the world of natural causes made it possible for Renouvier's "philosophical criticism" to coexist with the positivism of Littré. It also mattered that Protestants found neo-Kantian principles more congenial than Catholic theology, since Protestants were disproportionately numerous among "laic" republicans. In their political views, Littré and Renouvier somewhat resembled the liberal republicans known as "opportunists." Led by Léon Gambetta, they were the dominant party in the Chamber of Deputies from the late 1870s to the turn of the century. Scott also calls them "neo-Girondists," and he distinguishes them from the "dynastic" (royalist and Bonapartist) bourgeoisie that mainly governed France from the Restoration to the 1870s. The neo-Girondists believed that the entire bourgeoisie, not only its upper echelons, should govern France, and that it should do so through republican institutions and universal suffrage. They also held that the workers should seek to improve their lot only through such reformist means as mutual aid societies and trade unions. As a matter of fact, they took universal suffrage to be no more than a framework in which an elite of talent would actually rule. The need for an "elite" – or for "elites" – was emphasized across the whole spectrum of republican opinion.

During the 1880s and 1890s, a political grouping gradually gained in strength that stood immediately to the left of the opportunists. This was the "Radical" caucus, led for a time by Georges Clemenceau. It emerged as the dominant group within the Chamber of Deputies by the turn of the century, and it became the Radical and Radical–Socialist Republican Party in 1901. Scott thinks of the Radicals as "neo-Jacobins," but one can consider them left liberals as well. They had much in common with the neo-Girondists, including intellectual obligations to positivist and neo-Kantian theories. On the other hand, they advocated a politics of social reform that was not acceptable to most of the opportunists. A key element in their thought was the theory of "solidarity" or "solidarism," which can be traced back to Renouvier, to Henri Marion's 1880 *Treatise on Moral Solidarity*, and to some of the early work of Alfred Fouillée, the social theorist whom we have encountered as an outspoken educational conservative as of 1899. Solidarism gained in coherence and prominence as the radicals grew in strength toward the end of the century. Scott reports that a number of former neo-Girondists converted to neo-Jacobinism and to Solidarism during this period. Léon Bourgeois, a leading Radical politician, one-time Minister of Education and witness before the Ribot Commission, published his book on *Solidarity* in 1897. Three years later, in connection with the Universal Exposition of 1900, an International Congress of Social Education met in Paris to discuss solidarist principles. Bourgeois presided, while Ferdinand Buisson, Emile Durkheim and Charles Seignobos were among the speakers. Solidarism by this time was something like the official ideology of the Radical Republic. It obviously functioned as a progressive bourgeois alternative to revolutionary socialism.[22]

The political virtue of solidarist theory was that it reconciled *laisser faire* liberalism with a rationalization for state action in behalf of moderate social reform. At first, for Renouvier and for Marion, the solidarity among members of society was a feeling of moral commitment and of brotherhood. For the later solidarists, however, the existence of a "quasi-contract" guaranteed to all members of society a reasonable return for their contributions to the general good. To the extent that an adequate balance between services and benefits was prevented by an abnormal concentration of property in the hands of the few, the state could act in a redistributive way to ensure a minimum of social security and welfare for all. And above all, the solidarists of the 1890s believed that their doctrine rested upon the scientifically demonstrable fact of social interdependence under the division of labor. Durkheim's *The Division of Social Labor*, published in 1893, may serve as an example of positivist social science sustaining solidarist principles.

The contrast between the French and the German meanings of *positivism* could not have been much greater than it was. For German university professors of the 1890s and 1920s, positivism was almost invariably a regrettable deficiency in the nation's intellectual life, a failing to be overcome as soon and as thoroughly as possible. Among French republican intellectuals and Radical politicians around the turn of the century, by contrast, positivist assumptions or theories were almost automatic. In Germany, "positivism" was perceived as an analytical threat to wholistic certainties. In France, it was an orthodox philosophy of science and the methodological underpinning of republican social and political doctrines. Its dominance during the 1880s and 1890s was not absolute. The old eclectic "spiritualism" still retained a measure of influence within the University. More important, Emile Boutroux and others challenged major assumptions of scientism from the 1870s on, and Henri Bergson's first major work appeared before the turn of the century. But these critical interjections did not undermine the role of positivism as an orthodoxy, and as an ally of the Radical Republic.

As a matter of fact, certain forms of positivism or of scientism appeared even on the political right in late nineteenth-century France. Claude Digeon has cogently analyzed the way in which this happened. Both Renan and Taine, Digeon reports, were considered intellectual opponents of the Second Empire. Not that the two writers directly criticized the politics of the regime. What made them heterodox, rather, was their dissent from Catholicism, and from the eclectic "spiritualism" that dominated the French University for decades before 1870 and that was not without influence even in the 1880s and 1890s. Renan and Taine were prophets of science and explicit critics of religious beliefs. Renan had left the Catholic church, while Taine was known for an environmental and psychological determinism. Traditional conservatives would not have been willing to learn from either of them.[23] With the collapse of the Second Empire and the stablization of the liberal Republic after 1877, however, it became possible to perceive Renan and especially Taine as conservative in relation to the new regime. Renan was in fact a critic of democracy, while Taine wrote his six-volume *Origins of Contemporary France* (1875–93) as an indictment of the Revolution. The Commune of 1871 had clearly increased his suspicion of democracy. Nevertheless, what changed after 1870 was not so much Taine's thought as his public image, and that is Digeon's point. He observes that an important ideological reversal took place in France sometime between the Commune of 1871 and the Dreyfus Affair of 1897–99, probably during the Boulanger crisis of the late 1880s. A warlike nationalism, which until 1871 was typically a position of the left, came to be associated by the 1890s with a new popular right, while the socialist and non-socialist left moved toward internationalist views. Maurice Barrès was one of the earliest literary representatives of this new right; Charles Maurras emerged as its most prominent theoretician after the turn of the century.

The leading spokesmen of this new right showed a marked preference for a scientistic rhetoric. From their perspective, French Romanticism, epitomized by Jean-Jacques Rousseau, Victor Hugo and Georges Sand, was preeminently a doctrine of the democratic left. For a right-wing critic like Pierre Lasserre, it was also irrational, self-indulgent, and "individualistic."[24] But we have already encountered a more specific example of the new rhetoric in Barrès' *The Uprooted* of 1897.[25] Taine makes an appearance in this novel as an intellectual savior. His wisdom consists in giving adequate attention to the conditioning influence of the geographical and social environment. Indeed, Barrès appears to be following Taine's lead in arguing a rigid social determinism; for his "sociology" shows that "uprooted" students from unfavorable backgrounds must turn into dangerous "intellectual proletarians." Barrès thus identifies both Taine and himself with a socially conservative positivism. Taine's role as a model in *The Uprooted* contrasts sharply with Bourget's portrait of him as Adrian Sixte in *The Disciple* (1889).[26] For in *The Disciple*, Taine appears as an agent of intellectual destabilization. His "cold" scientific reasoning leads him to psychological determinism, to "positivism" and to atheism. This transformation of Taine from the threatening atheist of *The Disciple* to the wise environmentalist of *The Uprooted* is a perfect example of positional change in an intellectual field.

But we must turn back to the broader subject of republican opinion. For we have a major interest in the French middle-class liberals of the late nineteenth century, who sponsored a series of crucial reforms in education. Some of them were moderate republicans; but most were Radicals, "neo-Jacobins" rather than "neo-Girondists" in Scott's terminology. They typically adhered to "laic" principles, and many of them also believed in "solidarism." In methodological questions, they were more or less explicitly positivists. Educational reform was a central element in their political program. For moderate republicans, the extension of state education took precedence over other reforms; the schools were to wean the people away from the Church on the one hand, and from socialism on the other. For the Radicals, education was to insure improved opportunities for the lower middle class, and to disseminate a progressive and socially integrative ideology based on laic and solidarist principles.

It is worth noting that the three main sectors of the educational system were assigned divergent tasks in the overall scheme. In primary schooling, the emphasis was mainly on reaching the whole population, on social integration and on the encouragement of patriotism. In secondary education, access to elite positions was the major issue. Educational reformists and conservatives alike explained again and again that France was no longer a caste society, and that it could only be led by an "aristocracy of merit." Educational conservatives were particularly insistent that a democracy needed "an elite" to manage its affairs. Since they were satisfied that the traditional structure of secondary education adequately selected this elite, their meritocratic rhetoric served primarily to confirm the existing social hierarchy. The reformists took a more genuinely meritocratic stance. Though they did not propose to remove the economic obstacles to equal educational access, they did insist on lowering some of the non-economic barriers in the system. That is why they challenged the classical monopoly. They meant to recruit a somewhat increased proportion of students from the lower middle class and thus to create an enlarged network or plurality of partly distinctive "elites." This was significant politically as well; for it secured a widened constituency for the Republic – and for the Radicals.

In higher education, republican politicians and educational administrators pursued a reform program that has been briefly described in chapter 1.[27] Their overall objective was to raise the status of the university faculties, and thus to invest the Republic and the laic program with the cultural authority of science. In this they were supported by a substantial contingent of republican academics, who were professionally and ideologically committed to converting the existing faculties into research universities. From 1878 on, these academics were organized in the Higher Education Society, whose Secretary General was Ernest Lavisse.[28] From 1877 to 1883, the introduction of scholarships and of "closed courses" gave the faculties of letters and of sciences some regular students, along with specialized lectures and colloquia. Then, from the 1880s to 1893, several measures permitted a greater degree of specialization in the preparation for the higher degrees. Betwen 1885 and 1896, finally, the existing faculties were given a somewhat increased measure of budgetary autonomy, and they were loosely grouped together into "universities." In the meantime, the number of faculty positions was gradually but significantly increased.

An interesting sequel to the reforms in French higher education involved a change in the status of the Ecole Normale. That prestigious institution had been too closely identified with the old regime in French secondary schooling, and its elite character conflicted with the "democratic" spirit of the reform movement. In any case, the school was officially "reunited" with the reformed Sorbonne in 1903. Henceforth, Normaliens took most of their courses at the Sorbonne, where they had always taken their advanced examinations and degrees. The most important course still offered by the Ecole Normale was a required course in the science of pedagogy for all future secondary teachers, including those preparing exclusively at the Sorbonne. The new requirement reflected the enthusiasm for theoretical pedagogy among such reformers as Ernest Lavisse. Indeed, Lavisse replaced Georges Perrot as the Director of the Ecole Normale in 1903. At the same time, all faculty appointments at the Ecole were transferred to the "New Sorbonne" or to the Collège de France. The only exception was the prominent conservative Ferdinand Brunetière, who had been on leave from his teaching assignment since 1894, and who was in effect deprived of his position. In theory, the Ecole Normale now became a pedagogical institute within the University of Paris. In reality, a variety of specialized seminars and colloquia continued to meet in the buildings of the Ecole at the Rue d'Ulm, and the school ultimately retained its distinctive identity.[29]

French university reformers were inspired by the example of the German research universities. They did not mean to copy German models exactly or passively. Few of them knew the German system in exact detail, and many of them had reservations about some of its characteristics.[30] But they did intend to encourage serious research, to consolidate the existing faculties into a number of regional institutions, and ultimately to equal the German universities in scientific eminence. Of course French academics had an immediate professional interest in citing the German model; as Lavisse said about the German universities, "they are rich, they are free, they are powerful, they are honored."[31] Concretely, the German example implied increased faculty salaries and a higher status for the academic profession. But it also suggested a degree of statutory autonomy for the French universities, and it identified specialized research, rather than the support of secondary schooling, as the main responsibility of the university professor. The historian Gabriel Monod looked forward to a time when "the faculties, discharged from the care of state examinations and devoting themselves exclusively to scientific work, find themselves elevated to a great height above the other sectors of education, at the same time acquiring direct influence and powerful effect over them. They will grow infinitely in importance and dignity."[32] It was precisely by separating from the primary and secondary sectors that the reformed universities were expected to acquire a guiding influence upon them. As envisaged in the "laic" program, the whole enterprise of national education was to be informed and strengthened by the rational authority of science.

The ideas associated with the reforms of the French universities during the late nineteenth century are well known, at least in general terms.[33] The single most important principle stressed by the reformers was that the universities must actively engage in the pursuit of science. The word *science* was used in a very broad sense. It did not, like the German *Wissenschaft*, refer equally to the natural sciences and to humanistic scholarship; the French *science* could be used in contrast to *lettres*, to distinguish the natural sciences from the humanities, as in the naming of faculties and secondary programs.[34] In Ernest Lavisse's recollections of his secondary school days, the *scientifiques*, meaning science students, were assigned an inferior status as compared with students in letters.[35] Indeed, precisely because it retained this specific meaning, the term *science* had a certain force when applied to disciplines outside the natural sciences, and it was very often so applied during the period we are considering. To recommend the example of *science* to specialists in letters, as Lavisse did, was to urge them to break with a purely "literary" approach in their work. This might mean that texts should be studied in a philologically critical way, or in their historical contexts, or substantively, for the ideas contained in them, and not merely in their more or less pleasing "form."

Associated with the appeal to science was an emphasis upon systematic methods of empirical research that could be communicated to anyone, and that would produce reliable results, even if slowly. This was the point of the recurrent call for *connaissances positives*, meaning objective, testable, or even just factual knowledge, as distinct not only from a priori speculation, but also from more or less brilliant but essentially personal insight. We have encountered at least one case in which "positive" knowledge was more than merely empirical, in that it encompassed an understanding of presumably lawlike connections.[36] Alexis Bertrand, the proponent of that definition, was an announced follower of Comte. But the evidence suggests that the typical reference to "positive" knowledge among French reformist academics of the late nineteenth century was meant to call up something a good deal broader than Comte's philosophy. Not that the positivist current was unimportant. There may have been French natural scientists who either ignored it or at least keep it out of their substantive work.[37] Among the French humanists and social scientists we have been discussing, however, at least a loose sort of positivism was a significant methodological preference, and one which encouraged the application of "scientific" models to the human and social studies.

From the commitments that have been outlined there follows a belief in the unity of "science." Indeed, when in 1896 the various French faculties were drawn together to form universities, the institutional consolidation had a symbolic significance as well. Science was perceived as one, and so was the work of research and intellectual innovation. George Weisz describes the situation very well.

By 1880, republican ideology was suffused with the belief that an essential unity lay beneath the diversity of knowledge and that it could be perceived only if existing intellectual divisions were overcome. In the words of Lavisse, "all subjects today are interdependent and all obey the discipline of that one science which penetrates them all. Today everything is in everything." This belief [Weisz continues] was a basic principle of positivism *as well as a reflection of actual developments in science; disciplinary boundaries were being broken down by increasing specialization and interdependence* [my emphasis].[38]

I have italicized the last portion of this convincing passage because it shows just how deeply French academics believed in the unity of science. Their belief was profound enough, it seems, to infect one of their foremost historians. For although Weisz is generally on his guard against academic ideology, he here accepts as inevitable a view that was in fact specific to the field he describes.

Having read many German academic humanists and social scientists of the period between 1890 and 1930, I have not encountered *one* who believed that disciplinary boundaries were being broken down by increasing specialization. Instead, all without exception lamented – or at least observed – a fragmentation of *Wissenschaft* that seemed to be a dangerous and possibly inevitable byproduct of cognitive progress. In pursuing specialization, to put it plainly, French reformist academics sought precisely what many of their German colleagues feared or hoped to "overcome." In reality, of course, intellectual advances can cause previously separated realms of inquiry to *converge* into a new unity; but they can also create two *divergent* specialties where previously there was one. The long-term net effect, considered institutionally, has been one of divergence. But the only point I wish to make here is that Weisz has taken on some of the intellectual characteristics of his subjects. He echoes their conviction that specialization must confirm the unity of science, which was as deep-seated as their German colleagues' fear of intellectual fragmentation. Perhaps the Germans were thinking primarily of the personal effects of intellectual progress, of its impact on *Bildung*. But in any case, there is no single or inevitable position on issues of this sort; they are resolved by the beliefs, relations and practices that make up an academic culture.

One other assumption of French academic culture must be stressed, and that is the conviction that the progress of "science" was closely linked with the advance of "democracy." Not surprisingly, this belief drew a good deal of nourishment from the actual history of the French universities since the late 1870s. The reforms that ultimately brought French academics significant increases of income and status were the work, after all, of a left liberal regime that came much closer to democracy than its predecessors. Just as the Prussian universities of the early nineteenth century identified with the Prussian state of the reform period – and the German universities of the Wilhelmine period supported the bureaucratic monarchy that then sustained them, so the French universities of the 1880s and 1890s were committed to the democratic Republic. French reformist academics firmly believed, moreover, that this commitment was grounded in good reasons. They typically associated authoritarian politics with the predominant influence of religion; unquestioning obedience to the traditional authorities must surely be based on faith. Democracy, by contrast, can only be founded upon rational choice, and thus ultimately upon science. Indeed, the reformers expected science to provide reasoned alternatives for the irrational fundaments of pre-democratic social and political life. "Solidarism" is the obvious example.

If French university reform was partly an intellectual movement, it was also a significant social change. Parisian university professors of letters and of sciences around the turn of the century were typically "academic" in their social origins. They came dispropor-tionately often from the families of secondary and university teachers, doctors, men of letters, and members of other intellectual professions, whereas descendants of *propriétaires* and entrepreneurs were not particularly numerous among them. Indeed, the academic character of their social origins became substantially more pro-nounced between 1860 and 1901, while the university reforms were gradually implemented, and while the number of faculty positions increased.[39] In Pierre Bourdieu's terms, they were unusually rich in cultural capital, but relatively deprived of economic capital.[40] This relative deprivation helps to account for their critical distance from the social and political conservatism of the *grande bourgoisie*. Typi-cally, they were convinced republicans and at least moderate liberals. Many of the most prominent and vocal among them were Radicals, neo-Jacobins rather than neo-Girondins in Scott's termi-nology, and a few among them sympathized with reformist socia-lism. As the Radical Republic became firmly entrenched during the early twentieth century, their alliance with the reigning political powers took on some of the characteristics of a dominant orthodoxy.

This takes on additional significance from the prior history of the French university faculties. As Christophe Charle has argued, French university professors of letters under the July Monarchy exerted a certain public influence as individual notables. In fact, they were integrated into a network of notables, so that they did not develop a collective sense of distance from the established regime. Then, during the Second Empire, the French University passed through a period of government control and outright repression. During the late nineteenth century, by contrast, French academics came to enjoy a degree of autonomy and of freedom; but they no longer held the status of notables or the influence *as individuals* that they had had before 1848.[41] As Robert Smith has shown, a good number of Normalien *graduates* entered parliamentary politics after 1870.[42] Yet on the whole, the *academics* of the Third Republic could influence the political system only "from the outside," as *intellectuals*, through such means of collective action as the formation of pressure groups, the circulation of group petitions, and the like.

All of this may serve as background to the Dreyfus Affair, which agitated the politcal and intellectual life of France for about a year and a half beginning in the fall of 1897, and which thus partly coincided with the hearings of the Ribot Commission during the first three months of 1899. Captain Alfred Dreyfus, a Jew, had been unjustly condemned for espionage in late 1894. Significant evidence tending to exonerate him while implicating the army leadership was found in 1896, and a public campaign demanding a revision of the judgment against him began in late 1897. Emile Zola's open letter ("*J'accuse*") was published on January 13, 1898, and two collective protestations followed promptly on January 14. The signatures affixed to these two parallel protestations were accompanied by the academic degrees, ranks or intellectual functions of the signers; partly for that reason, they came to be known as "the manifesto of the intellectuals." In an *ad hominem* attack upon this proclamation, Maurice Barrès suggested that many of its supporters were obscure graduates (*licenciés*), who simply followed the lead of their professors. This linked the cause of the revisionists or Dreyfusards with the image of the "intellectual proletariat" that Barrès had helped to create. By way of contrast, the anti-Dreyfusard Ligue de la Patrie Française subsequently published a list of its adherents under a set of institutional categories designed to show that every leading social group, beginning with the Académie Française, sided with the army and the judiciary against the revisionists. The whole Affair thus became a confrontation between the bourgeois elites and "the intellectuals."[43]

Indeed, the Dreyfus Affair has been of particular interest to sociologists, because the very term "intellectual" came into common use in France during this public debate. The noun first appeared during the 1880s; it was initially used in a negative sense to characterize self-consciously esoteric groups within the literary avant-garde. It then occurred in Bourget's *Le disciple* (1889) and, more decisively, in Barrès' *Les déracinés* (1897). Its connotation remained largely negative; this did not change until the Dreyfusards in effect accepted the label in their own behalf. On the other hand, Bourget and particularly Barrès wrote in a broad and almost sociological sense about a distinctive social group, with common experiences, life chances and attitudes. As Christophe Charle has pointed out, the historical context favored the emergence of a new social role, especially during the 1890s. A crisis in the literary market and rapid increases in university access raised the spectre of a disaffected "intellectual proletariat." A new sense of social and political engagement spread among students, young scholars and writers, while "anarchism" and reformist socialism gained converts in the Latin Quarter. In 1889, a protest was organized against official censorship and the legal persecution of a politically radical author. There was a growing tension between a party of "order" and what ultimately became the "party of the intellectuals." The Dreyfus Affair simply brought these developments to a climax.[44]

In any case, the writings of Bourget and Barrès created an extraordinarily vivid critical portrait of "the intellectual" as a social type. Bourget's misguided student and Barrès' "intellectual proletarians" were totally shaped by their teachers, because they came from unfavorable social backgrounds. Their exclusive dependence upon the school gave them their bookish quality, along with an uncontrollable penchant for abstraction. They were uprooted and alienated, strangers to real life. Barrès directly linked this characteristic of theirs to the truculent egalitarianism and the fatal Kantian universalism of the teacher Bouteiller. In other words, the French "intellectual" was born with the salient traits and the universalist commitments of the "intellectual proletarian." To conservatives, he was a frightening cross between an anarchist and a pedant; to more sympathetic eyes, including his own, he was a principled champion of truth and of justice. The German university professor of the nineteenth century was integrated into his society as a leader of the educated upper middle class; he could exert his influence as an individual notable, or by directly advising his close colleagues in the monarchical civil service. The French Dreyfusard intellectual, by contrast, challenged the established order from the position of a critical outsider; he could best assert himself politically through the "mass" tactic of collective protests designed to move the democratic electorate.[45]

Of course there were anti-Dreyfusard intellectuals as well; indeed, they were roughly as numerous as their opponents. In publicly announcing their adhesion of the Ligue de la Patrie Française, they partly imitated the tactics of the revisionists; but of course they necessarily emphasized the authority of the established elites, rather than the distinctive mission of the intellectuals themselves. Charle has carefully charted the distribution of French writers, academics, and students between the two camps. Within the literary field, the more prestigious schools and individuals stood almost solidly in the anti-Dreyfusard faction; this was true of almost all those consecrated by the Académie Française, of Brunetière and other literary critics for the more fashionable journals, of most of the established "psychological" novelists, including Bourget, Barrès, and Lemaître, of all but one of the "Parnassians," and of two "idealist" writers. At the opposite pole, the less-established writers of the avant-garde and of the "little reviews" were overwhelmingly Dreyfusards; this was true of the "symbolists" and of the writers for the *Revue blanche*, among others. They called for a revision of the judgment against Dreyfus in the name of justice, much as they spoke for "pure literature" against "the market." Only the high-volume literary producers, the naturalists, neorealists, and writers of popular fiction, were distributed over both camps, though a number of naturalists followed Zola into the Dreyfusard front.[46]

At the universities, the revisionists were particularly strong in the most purely "academic" institutions at the Parisian center of the system: among professors and students at the Ecole Normale and at the Sorbonne, especially in the reformed Paris faculty of letters. More moderate levels of Dreyfusard sentiment characterized the Paris faculty of sciences, the Ecole des Chartes and the Ecole Pratique des Hautes Etudes. The anti-Dreyfusards, in compensation, were particularly well represented in the professional faculties, the faculty of law above all, and in some of the bourgeois *grandes écoles* as well. In academe as in the literary world, the younger generations were more often revisionists than their elders. Among the major academic disciplines, history and philosophy stood out as disproportionately Dreyfusard, while classical literature and especially law were weighted in the opposite direction. More generally, Dreyfusard commitments were liveliest in the academic fields most thoroughly transformed by the new research imperative.[47] While fascinating in itself, this circumstance also helps to explain an initially even more puzzling phenomenon. Contemporaries apparently identified the Dreyfusard intellectuals almost exclusively with the academic community, especially with the reformed Sorbonne. Thus leading anti-Dreyfusards virtually ignored the novelists and writers among their opponents, concentrating their wrath upon the scholars, and particularly upon the research specialists. They were apparently accustomed to the presence of anti-bourgeois sentiments in avant-garde literary circles; but the prospect of radical disaffection within the University struck them as unprecedented and deeply shocking.

This perspective informed a famous March 1898 essay by Ferdinand Brunetière, which attacked the "manifesto of the intellectuals" in terms initially suggested by Barrès. In the concluding portions of his polemic, Brunetière wrote about "some intellectuals, as they call themselves." He professed himself unable to accept the "superiority" claimed by mere specialists in paleography, chemistry, Chinese, and the like. They were dangerous, he thought, because they supposed that their narrow expertise "communicated itself to all they think." In reality, they were "talking nonsense with authority about things beyond their competence." Their understanding was limited by their specialty; they were "narrowed and shrunk" by it. "Learning and science," unfortunately, could coexist with a "mediocre intelligence," and of course knowledge could not take the place of such non-intellectual virtues as "firmness of character" and "energy of will."[48] The academic intellectuals tended to stress the "scientific" character of their methods; but such specialties as paleography and ethnography were not sciences at all, since they could not predict. And even if physics and chemistry did have a "sure method, who has decided that they would be applicable to the most sensitive questions involving morality, the life of nations, and the interests of society?"

Scientific method, aristocracy of intelligence, respect for truth, all these big words only serve to cover the pretensions of *Individualism*, and *Individualism* is the great malady of the present.

The intellectuals appear to identify with "Nietzsche's superman" or with "the enemy of the laws." But "when intellectualism and individualism arrive at that degree of self-infatuation," they plainly amount to *"anarchy."*[49]

In a democracy, Brunetière concluded, "intellectual aristocracy is the most unacceptable of all forms of aristocracy, because it is the most difficult of all to demonstrate."

While I understand well enough what superiority of birth and of fortune are, I do not see how a professor of Tibetan has the qualifications to govern his fellows, nor how knowledge of the properties of quinine . . . confers rights to the obedience and respect of other men.[50]

The claims of wealth and of birth are here acknowledged, once again, with remarkable frankness. They appear more understandable than the claims of intelligence, which are made to seem questionable when isolated from more substantive assets. In Germany around 1900, an attack upon left-wing intellectuals would have been directed against "journalists" or "literati"; the authority of the university professors could not have been challenged; nor could they have been plausibly relegated to the role of mere specialists. Like Bourget before him, Brunetière apparently felt that academics were less eligible than writers to offer integral advice.[51] In any case, since the Dreyfusard intellectuals were by no means all university faculty, his focus upon specialized science and scholarship was highly selective. He was reacting as a conservative "man of letters," not only to the Dreyfus Affair itself, but also to the new intellectual roles that had emerged with the reforms in the French universities.

This was acknowledged by the sociologist Emile Durkheim in a sharp response to Brunetière.[52] Durkheim's main point had to do with Brunetière's charge of individualism. Those who have levelled this charge against the intellectuals, Durkheim observed, have falsely identified individualism with "the utilitarian egoism of Spencer and the economists," which is indeed "anarchical." But modern individualism properly speaking, the doctrine of Kant and of Rousseau, is almost the opposite of utilitarianism and requires a profound commitment to the norms of the community. Thus Kant insisted upon the supraindividual character of ethics, while Rousseau elevated the "general will" above particular wills.

Individualism thus extended is the glorification not of the self but of the individual in general. It springs not from egoism but from sympathy for all that is human, a broader pity for all suffering . . . a greater thirst for justice. Is there not herein what is needed to place all men of good will in communion?[53]

This philosophical individualism, Durkheim argued, has become a kind of religion for modern man, the only religion that can continue to hold his allegiance. For "everything converges in the belief that the religion of humanity, of which the individualist ethic is the rational expression, is the only one possible." Thus the defender of individual rights also defends "the vital interests of the society, for he prevents the criminal impoverishment of that last reserve of collective ideas and feelings which is the very soul of the nation."[54]

In raising these considerations, Durkheim was writing very much as a sociologist. Along with an almost Comtean religion of humanity, he evoked a key element in his analysis of modern society. In his concluding paragraphs, however, he also commented more particularly upon Brunetière's portrait of "the intellectuals." The cult of humanity, he argued, implies "the autonomy of reason" and the "doctrine of free inquiry." This has encouraged "the adversaries of reason" to suggest that "liberalism" must lead to "intellectual and moral anarchy." But in fact intellectual freedom has had no such consequences; for it does not prevent us from respecting rationally grounded authority, or from following more competent opinions in matters beyond our knowledge. The artists and scholars who questioned the legality of the judgment against Dreyfus did not speak as specialized experts; nor did they mean to arrogate a "special privilege" or "right of control" in judicial matters. Rather:

being men, they intend to exercise all their human rights and retain before them a matter which is amenable to reason alone. It is true that they have shown themselves to be more jealous of that right than the rest of society; but it is simply because in consequence of their professional practices they take it more to heart. Since they are accustomed by the practice of the scientific method to reserve their judgment as long as they do not feel themselves enlightened, it is natural that they should yield less easily to the sway of the masses and the prestige of authority.[55]

This rejoinder is of course double-edged. It identifies the Dreyfusard intellectuals as ordinary citizens, rather than experts; but it simultaneously claims for them a professionally heightened capacity to resist prejudice and unjust authority in the name of eternal reason.

Without meaning to question the sincerity of "our adversaries," Durkheim continued, "we cannot fail to sense to what extent their conviction is impoverished."

They are neither apostles who let their anger or their enthusiasm overflow nor scholars who bring us the product of their research and reflections; they are men of letters seduced by an interesting theme. It would therefore seem impossible that these dilettantes' games could long succeed in holding back the masses if we know how to act.[56]

Here is the real thrust of Durkheim's counterattack upon Brunetière. The specialized *scholar* may contribute the results of his research and reflection, Durkheim suggests, and he may also properly speak as a citizen with a particularly firm commitment to human rights. The conservative *man of letters*, on the other hand, does not deserve the respect due to serious thought or scholarship, or to profound moral conviction. His approach to public issues is "literary" in the worst sense of that term; a "dilettante," he is all too easily "seduced by an interesting theme." Fortunately, as Durkheim boldly proclaims, "the masses," if properly led, will be found on the side of human rights – and of serious scholarship. As we shall see, this view was widely held among the spokesmen for the "New Sorbonne" around the turn of the century.

THE IDEOLOGY OF THE NEW SORBONNE, 1900–1904

The opening years of the twentieth century were eventful ones for the reformed University of Paris. The "people's universities" (*universités populaires*) movement, which had been launched in the wake of the Dreyfus Affair to put university teachers in touch with the working class, reached its peak about 1904.[57] The reform of secondary education that grew out of the work of the Ribot Commission was completed in 1902. The sociologist Emile Durkheim gave a course in pedagogy at the Sorbonne for the first time in 1902–3. Following a 1902 vote by the Chamber of Deputies, the Ecole Normale was "reunited" with the Sorbonne in 1903. It appears to have been at about this time that the term New Sorbonne came to be used to describe the reformed faculties of letters and of sciences of the University of Paris.[58]

The views of some of the leading academic reformists at this time are conveniently available to us. In the winters of 1902–3 and 1903–4 at the privately founded Ecole des Hautes Etudes Sociales, prominent faculty from the Sorbonne offered lectures on the recent educational reforms and on their social and political significance. Among those who spoke on secondary and higher education were four academics already known to us. They were Gustave Lanson, the literary historian; Alfred Croiset, Professor of Greek eloquence and Dean of the Paris faculty of letters; Ernest Lavisse, the historian and soon to be Director of the Ecole Normale, and Charles Seignobos, another historian.[59] In addition, about three years earlier, Emile Durkheim addressed a major solidarist convention, the Congrès international de l'éducation sociale, on "the Role of Universities in the Social Education of the Country." It seems appropriate to include his lecture with the others that have been listed; together they will convey a vivid sense of what, in the broad sense of the term, may be called the "ideology" of the New Sorbonne.

Gustave Lanson was probably the most militant of the five

academics in this group. As we noted earlier, he was an important commentator upon the secondary reform of 1902, which he really helped to define. This made him particularly aware of the *social* significance of advanced education. He described the traditional forms of secondary schooling as a "class education" (*culture de classe*) designed to assure the "glorification and preservation" of the (upper) bourgeoisie.[60] If the new system of secondary education differed radically from its predecessor, he observed, this was due in large measure to the change in the social origins of pupils. Important portions of the upper middle class had abandoned the state *lycées* in favor of the Catholic private schools. Partly in compensation, sharply increased numbers of students from lower-middle-class backgrounds now entered the public secondary system. There was a significant reduction in the distance between primary and secondary schooling. Lanson saw the ongoing educational reforms as a search for "democracy," for equality and social justice. Thus the new secondary schooling was to benefit not only "the elite," but "the whole mass of the nation."[61]

The pedagogical tasks of the old secondary system, according to Lanson, had been simple. Religion had long established the norms of conduct, and when the authority of religion began to decline, family or class traditions or prejudices guided behavior. So the teacher of letters could confine himself to providing a certain mental polish and the ability to shine in the world. The class character of the system was given partly in the contrast between "memorization and docility" in the primary school and "originality stimulated" in the secondary school. Whereas the primary pupil often had difficulty talking about what he knew, the secondary pupil was sometimes "skilled at talking about what he didn't know." The model of the secondary graduate, of course, was the *honnête homme* of the old regime. The education he received was purely "formal," "oratorical," "brilliant and superficial"; it encouraged "hollow verbalism," preparing pupils primarily for "the rhetoric of the salon and of the tribune."[62] The reformed system of secondary courses, by contrast, had to offer a substantive education, and a total one. Religion and family background were less pertinent than formerly, and the new egalitarianism demanded that all pupils be educated, not only the best of them. In place of the old rhetorical training, the schools were to emphasize scientific methods and a "capacity to discern the true." They were to focus upon "positive knowledge," to "habituate minds to value the precision of exact knowledge, to prefer observed facts and confirmed statistics to hypothetical general ideas and to brilliant intellectual constructions." To replace the catechism, moreover, they were to provide a rational morality. What democracy demanded from education, according to Lanson, was the forming of a "sense of truth, a sense of justice and of solidarity, and a civic orientation."

Education in a democracy that wants to guide itself must form men capable of guiding themselves. Hence [we need] free minds, with a passionate love of the truth, knowing how to search for it with rational methods... Further, [we need] free consciences, free of inner as well as outer servitudes, incapable of finding the good outside the true, and able to act in the name of justice, of love, and of solidarity.[63]

The formulations here may owe something to the Dreyfus Affair; but the insistence on positive knowledge and on scientific method was generally characteristic of the reformist academics.

One of Lanson's main subjects was the teaching of French and French literature, which was to be the mainstay of the modern secondary curriculum. He wanted French composition to be an "intellectually and morally healthy" exercise; students were to treat only limited questions on which they were fully informed, and their style of exposition was to be clear and precise. A business report seemed to Lanson a better model than an academic address or a literary essay. What he termed "French explication" or "explications of texts" was to be a form of guided close reading, in which the "question of truth" was to be posed "in all its forms." The authenticity of the text was to be examined without entering into philological niceties. Truth of form and articulation in relation to the ideas was to be considered next, along with sincerity, naturalness, and simplicity of expression. Finally, pupils were to learn something about the truth of the text's ideas "in relation" to the author's biographical circumstances and his time: the prevailing "state of knowledge, of beliefs, and of civilization." For Lanson insisted that literature was most interesting and instructive for the pupil when he learned to "observe the human life inscribed in the literary forms," when he could see the individual work as "an aspect of humanity, a moment in civilization."[64]

Lanson was clearly aiming at a substantive and historical explication of literature, the latter broadly defined to encompass works by Descartes and Montesquieu, for example.

All the great moral and social problems are registered in our literary texts . . . simplified, clarified, reduced to [their] essential elements. Each of these problems, raised in its historical form, as a historical question, can be defined, without polemics, without fanaticism, without wanting in scholarly neutrality.[65]

Part of the objective here was to find a tactful way of putting the laic and republican viewpoint. The historical approach permitted a kind of indirection. At the same time, the reading proposed to the student was intended to bridge the gap between the past of the text and the present of the reader.

We are forming a man of today. It is not enough to make him understand what was true at a given time: he must understand what is . . .true at present. Hence incongruity or accord of the idea with the present state of science and of society. Continual and profound transformations of the truths that are called eternal: their perpetual rebirth and renewal, their adaptations to each form of civilization. Moral and social equivalence of divergent ideas.[66]

This was plainly a historicist position. In place of the old "literary" approach to the classical texts, Lanson proposed a contextual form of intellectual history. He actually wrote of the "reduction of literature to history";[67] yet he safely avoided the bedevilment of *Historismus*, of historical relativism in the German vein. For he tacitly accepted the primacy of the present, or of the reader's own standpoint, in the enterprise of historical interpretation. A robust confidence in the progressive character of science and of "civilization" immunized this form of historicism against the excesses of skepticism.

If Lanson was an especially determined reformer, Alfred Croiset was a particularly conservative one. He continued to argue that the non-classical secondary program should be reduced in length and given a strictly "practical" orientation, and he recommended a single, essentially classical secondary curriculum. He wrote in traditional terms about secondary schooling as "intellectual gymnastics" and about the grave perils of "utilitarianism." He disliked the caricature of the traditional literary education as "formal" or "oratorical"; the only cure for empty verbalism, he wrote, is a sound training in rhetoric. His defense of classical studies has already been considered.[68] Yet, despite his essential conservatism, Croiset expressed many of the general principles that structured the reformist position. Thus he saw "general eduction" as forming "the man and the citizen in the professional," preparing him to "fill the role in the state that is assigned to him by the society of which he is a member." Though Croiset thus conceived education as socialization, his subsequent emphasis was not on shared beliefs but on freedom.

The free citizen of a ... 20th-century democracy certainly needs factual knowledge [*notions positives*] and qualities of mind and character ... [that were unnecessary for] a man of the Middle Ages or for a subject of Louis XIV ... [or for] those in our own time who are governed more or less despotically.

The intellectual education of democracy must be "essentially scientific" in the broad sense that "the spirit and the methods of science must penetrate it wholly."

The only moral force before which we feel obliged to bow is the force of evidence. And it seems to us more and more that this evidence has to derive from a free and methodical search. In other words, we believe only in science.

To be sure, science cannot explain everything; it has its limits; yet it remains a common fundament for "all the other forms of knowing." Moreover, no one can know all of science; the specialists themselves are laymen outside their fields. What most citizens need is the ability to judge the solutions proposed by the specialists.[69]

Above all, education must communicate good intellectual habits, along with a few general conclusions of scientific study. Among these general conclusions Croiset included an injunction against revolution.

All educated minds are nowadays persuaded that human things, like those of nature, evolve slowly, through the unceasing progress of thought. Abrupt revolutions, which would resemble miracles, are impossible. Since progress can come only from knowledge, moreover, there is a primary social need for absolute freedom of thought and discussion.[70]

The intellectual habits to be fostered, according to Croiset, included a "firm and clear good sense" that would "see the ideas behind the words, and the things behind the ideas."

Really to know is not to fashion beautiful logical or verbal constructions: it is to penetrate straight to the real, and to model one's ideas upon the real.[71]

One must submit to reality, respect the facts and be "objective." One must proceed patiently and with method in one's study of things.

We... readily believe that good sense... is a very French quality... Our great classical literature of the 17th and 18th centuries... really is above all a literature of good sense... Let us not be deceived, however; our good sense has formidable enemies.[72]

Croiset here proceeded to standard formulations about the intellectual vices of the French: they are too fond of "general ideas"; they quickly convert facts into systems, which they strive to make "harmonious" and "elegant." Moreover, individualism "badly understood" inclines them toward "intellectual fencing," and "biting polemics." Even for Croiset, it seems, the antithesis of the "scientific" was something like the merely "rhetorical."

In the field of moral education, according to Croiset, democracy needs the "good old virtues," taught by all the great religions and philosophies, along with the "civic virtues" that will bring free and vigorous individuals into harmonious collective action. Recommending a form of "individualism well understood," Croiset distinguished it from "egoism and indiscipline," from any "cult of the self" or of the "superman." Sound individualism, he wrote, is the strength to resist impulses, to pursue noble goals regardless of difficulties, and to stand by the right, when necessary, in defiance of the crowd and of one's party. But of course the individual energies must be brought together to work in concert, and that required "solidarity."

The idea of the solidarity necessary among citizens of the same country is not only an abstract idea that imposes itself upon reason; it is also the source of a sentiment of mutual love... Education must strive to develop this sentiment.[73]

In fact, since ideas and sentiments do not alone guide the individual, education must seek to instill good habits, including the habit of sociability.

Coming to some of the delicate tactical problems of French public education, Croiset asked what position the schools should take on the nature of the true and the good. He was clearly on guard against the missionary zeal often associated with the "laic" creed.

Let us dare once and for all, three centuries after Descartes, to believe in intellectual freedom, and in the moral wholesomeness of an independent science. Let us cease putting our confidence in dead formulas and credos without virtue. That whole laic theology is only a strange survival of... scholasticism.[74]

Yet Croiset cautioned against letting philosophies in the classroom confront each other in "anarchic liberty"; for that would leave the crucial decisions in the hands of children. He further rejected "neutrality," or "systematic abstention with regard to all the essential problems." For if education was to be more than "purely formal," then it had to "rest upon something positive and substantial." The way to offer a republican education without attacking religion, according to Croiset, was to found it upon "love and respect for scientifically established truth." He emphasized that a commitment to science could be emotionally nourishing.

The almost religious love for scientific truth lifts otherwise quite ordinary souls above themselves . . . This scientific faith, moreover, is essentially republican and democratic . . . since the republic and democracy must be conceived as a social state in which the progress of all is assured by the free play of thought . . . And why not add that this republican faith founded on science cannot but be tolerant and pacific.[75]

To show more concretely how republican education could be tolerant, Croiset urged a "scientific" and overwhelmingly "historical" approach to the texts taken up in the higher secondary grades. In teaching Bossuet and Pascal, for example, it was only necessary to "apply the scientific method to literature, that is, to substitute the historical and explicative for the dogmatic and polemical point of view." The object, after all, was "to understand," not "to praise or to blame in the name of an absolute doctrine." Dogmatic theology, of course, could not be taught; for it drew upon "extra-rational principles" that the teacher should disregard, while leaving everyone free to believe that "there are things knowable outside of what is accessible to reason."[76] In touching upon controversial historical topics, the teacher was to understand and not to judge. If he was a convinced republican, he should avoid "grand theories," while presenting democracy as "a fact," and while analyzing the profound historical reasons that " have made the Republic possible and necessary." In the highest class on philosophy too, the examination of metaphysical and ethical systems was to be "scientific, rather than polemical or oratorical." The teacher might present his own conclusions with all due "reserve"; but again the "scientific" approach was essentially a recourse to the historical method – and to the indirection it entailed.[77] For to read and to understand *historically* was in some degree to suspend judgment upon the doctrines examined, and this suspension of judgment was socially desirable in Croiset's view.

Quite apart from the study of ethical systems in the philosophy class, finally, the principles of morality were to be taught "over the entire course of studies," and again the approach was to be "purely scientific." Croiset argued that all historical societies "derived from their conditions of existence a set of rules of conduct" that formed their "moral ideals." These ideals have progressively entered into the "collective consciousness [*conscience*] of civilized humanity." Today, they "form the substance of our moral life"; we need only become aware of them and let them guide our actions. The ideal of solidarity, of course, has a special place among them.

All agree in recognizing a law of fraternal and republican solidarity as the essential rule of all private and social morality. Each religion, each philosophy establishes its fundaments in its own way... That is enough for us. Public education should not enter into doctrinal quarrels... Civic morality can be taught... without arbitrary speculation, without polemics, in a positive and scientific spirit... [Democracy and the Republic], by merely existing, imply a number of rules of conduct, virtues that are indispensable for the good functioning of our societies. Let us explain what these virtues are. Let us show why they are necessary... The more the ideal emerges from the facts, the more positive the education will be, and the more we can be sure that the teacher's task is well done.[78]

In these paragraphs, Croiset not only brought together solidarism, republicanism and positivism; he also outlined a positivist science of moral and civic education. In this he was probably inspired by Durkheim, but his moral science also fit perfectly into the rest of his thought on public education.

Another important contribution to the lecture series of 1902–3 was an essay by the historian Ernest Lavisse that has already been discussed in another context.[79] It was important because it insisted that texts read in secondary schools ought to be conceived as "representative monuments" of historical "civilizations." Lamenting the lack of such historical readings in his own schooling, Lavisse also clearly identified scholarly history with the ethos of "science." At the old Ecole Normale, he complained, there was no suggestion that science might be relevant "to history or to life." Future historians were not trained in research methods; no one ever actually looked at a historical document, and all this despite the fact that Louis Pasteur could have taught students a great deal about "the critical spirit." Lavisse explicitly postulated that "the principles of scientific work are everywhere the same," which also guaranteed the underlying unity of the research university.

Charles Seignobos, another historian, contributed to both the lecture series of 1902–3 and to its sequel of 1903–4. The first of his presentations has already been considered.[80] It was a historical sketch of French secondary schooling from the Middle Ages to the present. Seignobos was able to draw a rich fund of practical conclusions from his narrative; for he distinguished between the "living" and the "dead" portions of the existing system. In his contribution to the second group of lectures, he developed a somewhat similar approach to the history of French higher education, except that his emphasis in this case was on the promise of the recent reforms.[81] Starting from the same medieval foundations, Seignobos explained, the French and German arts faculties developed in divergent directions. In France, primarily because of Napoleon's preferences, research was separated from teaching. But beginning in the 1860s and increasingly after the War of 1870, the model of the German faculties of philosophy was adopted in France. Because the reforms remained unsystematic, there continued to be some functional overlap between the various higher schools. But a certain amount of institutional competition was probably useful, according to Seignobos, and the faculties of letters were now well established in their fields.

The inherited name "faculty of letters" was misleading, Seignobos continued; for it suggested an institution in which one learned "the vocation of the *littérateur*, the art of making speeches or verse." In reality, the subject matter of the faculties of letters and related institutions was "the sum of the psychological and historical sciences." Thus literature and the study of philosophical doctrines "have become historical sciences," and "the rest of philosophy belongs to the psychological sciences." If economic history and the history of law were transferred from the faculty of law to that of letters, the latter would "extend over the whole territory of the sciences of man, the psychological and social sciences."[82] While supporting Lanson's "reduction of literature to history," Seignobos thus also dissolved philosophy into history and psychology. Presumably including history among the social sciences, he further consolidated the psychological and social sciences into the "sciences of man." Obviously, this was not just a terminological recommendation; it was an attempt to define a broad new territory for the old faculties of letters. While the sciences of man do not have material applications, according to Seignobos, they make it possible to understand "man, his sentiments, his motives, his actions," and thus also society. An education in the human sciences is thus the natural preparation for various positions of leadership: for professors, lawyers and judges, civil servants, archivists and librarians. The faculties of letters should be organized to provide the common higher education of future lawyers, secondary teachers, and archivists, who should then go on to such specialized professional schools (*écoles d'application*) as the law schools, the Ecole Normale and the Ecole des Chartes.[83]

In a democratic society, Seignobos argued, many need a complete schooling in the human sciences, and all need a partial schooling, because a liberal, democratic, and rationalist society is the complex product of an advanced civilization. Such a society is constantly under threat from man's "natural inclinations" towards authoritarianism and superstition, and it is only by educating himself that he can guard against the dangers that lie in his own passions – and in those of others.

It was an advance in the sciences of man, in empirical psychology and history, that prepared the French Revolution and the establishment of freedom of thought. The science of man has remained the practical means to combat tendencies towards privilege and towards political and religious absolutism. It accustoms us to carry the rational method even into the study of sentiments, and it thus raises scientific truth above respect for tradition and shelters thought from the old religious authorities. It makes us aware of the instinctual passions and thereby permits us clearly to perceive the abstract justice that is equity, and to maintain it against all the egoisms, of the individual, the family, the classes and the nation. It is the guarantee of truth and justice against the natural enemies of science. Thus the science of man is united to democracy by shared interests.[84]

Here again, one senses the presence of the Dreyfus Affair in the background; yet the sense of a natural alliance between science and democracy was common among the spokesmen for the New Sorbonne.

Seignobos in fact saw it as a very recent alliance. During much of the nineteenth century, he said, learning was considered an aristocratic luxury, incompatible with republicanism. It was only toward the end of the century that democracy and science joined together against their common enemies, in a "union of intellectual and manual workers." The universities now had a vital interest in maintaining this union, and one way to do that was to adhere to strictly "democratic" principles of selection according to talent and achievement. The professors in higher education were indeed chosen for the quality of their research work, as in Germany. The procedures involved might be improved in some respects; but the principles were sound and compatible with democracy.[85] At a lower level, Seignobos disapproved of the entrance examinations to the *grandes écoles* and of the special post-secondary courses that prepared for them; he saw these as means of sustaining a privileged elite. His own preference was for a baccalaureate awarded by the secondary school teachers alone, and for immediate entry into the university faculties on the basis of the baccalaureate. At the faculties of letters, a two-year common introductory education was to encompass "practical" exercises as well as general courses. These early years would then be followed by a further selection of students for advanced studies in the faculties, or in such specialized schools as the Ecole Normale and the Ecole des Chartes. Women were to be admitted to the universities on the basis of their own secondary certificates; this was a way of counteracting the influence exerted upon them by "the enemies of democracy." The whole system was to be organized with the clear understanding that in a democracy, "the mass of students – and the most serious ones" – are "intellectual proletarians" who need to prepare for a profession and to earn a living.[86]

Thus Seignobos' lecture on the future of the faculties of letters can also be read as a contribution to the ongoing debate about "the intellectuals." Seignobos clearly had more in common with Lanson than with Croiset. He was not interested in improving relations between the republican educational system and the moderate or conservative middle classes. He spoke in militant terms about the alliance between "intellectual and manual workers." Above all, he insisted upon "merit" principles of academic selection, from which he clearly expected a "democratic" recruitment of faculty and students. So certain was he about this that he adapted a conservative stereotype to his own uses. Thinking particularly about future secondary teachers, archivists and librarians, he approvingly described students of letters as "academic proletarians," which was to say: universalist intellectuals and militant republicans.

Emile Durkheim approached the relationship between the universities and the Republic from another direction. In his 1900 lecture to the International Congress on Social Education, he assigned the universities the task of completing the moral education of their students.

It is untrue to say that the university has neither the right nor the means to exercise a specifically moral influence. To be sure, it is not the university's role to form the moral character of those whom it admits, but there is something which it alone can contribute to the task of moral education. Only the universities can make the habits ... [acquired in the schools] as fully self-conscious as the present state of science allows.

By the time the student reaches the university, Durkheim continued, he has already formed attachments to others that "make him a moral being." But there is the danger that he will fall prey to "moral skepticism." The bonds that link him to others, which are created by custom, may appear to him "simple products of artifice and convention." He must now be rationally convinced that "the sense of solidarity is the foundation of morality."

It is necessary to show young persons how man, far from being self-sufficient, is only part of a whole from which he cannot be isolated except by abstraction; how society lives and acts within him, how it is the best part of his nature.[87]

Durkheim here portrayed the university as providing a form of rational clarification that could reinforce inherited commitments and thus help to ensure the viability of the republican regime. He called for courses and chairs in sociology at all the universities, and he hoped that his ideas would affect the teaching of pedagogy to primary teachers as well. He further suggested that university students be encouraged to form voluntary associations in line with their academic and avocational interests; for this would offer them practical experience of group cooperation. He gave special attention, finally, to the people's universities, urging university faculty to play a larger – and more dominant – role in these institutions. The *universités populaires*, as they were called, were primarily designed to reach the working class. Durkheim accordingly called for emphasis upon such practical subjects as "the past and present history of industrial organization, the state of industrial law, and the main ideas of political economy."[88] He too apparently envisaged a kind of alliance between intellectual and manual workers.

In the reform of the universities since the 1870s, Durkheim argued, the emphasis had properly been upon the rigorous scientific training of regular students, not upon the public lectures that used to be given before fashionable audiences. The universities had justifiably turned inwards, in other words; but the time had come for them to extend their outward influence once again. "It is precisely democratic societies which . . . have the greatest need for a higher scientific culture"; but this culture must of course be genuinely useful to society as a whole.

> However essential the scientific and scholarly work of universities, they must never lose sight of the fact that they are also, and above all, educational institutions. They have therefore to play a role in the moral life of the country . . . Just as the universities of Germany contributed to the formation of German unity, the universities of France must strive to form French moral beliefs [*conscience*]. Thus, they must not remain estranged from any current of public opinion . . . This is also the best way to demonstrate clearly their utility to the mass of the population. For if the ordinary people have constant dealings with universities, they will not even dream of asking themselves what purpose they serve and whether they are not a sort of luxury with which, if necessary, it is possible to dispense.[89]

Durkheim apparently accepted the widely held view that the German universities were partly responsible for the German patriotism and vitality that contributed to the defeat of France in 1870. Worth noting also is the uneasiness conveyed in the image of the people asking themselves whether universities are luxuries. The fact that this issue could arise at all may help to explain the emphasis upon the affinity between science and democracy that was so central a theme in the ideology of the New Sorbonne.

THE LITERARY OPPOSITION

Between July and December 1910, the journal *L'Opinion* published a series of articles in which the "New Sorbonne" was sharply criticized. The authors wrote under the pen name "Agathon"; they were Henri Massis, a student of letters, and Alfred de Tarde, a young lawyer with literary inclinations. Their essays launched a public debate, in which several members of the Paris faculty of letters participated. Both the original essays by "Agathon" and a number of responses were later brought together in a substantial volume published in 1911. It is this volume that concerns us here.[90]

Massis and de Tarde portrayed themselves as students in revolt against their professors. They levelled a whole cluster of charges against the Sorbonne. Some of its leading members, they argued with good grounds, had been instrumental in bringing about the defeat of classical secondary education in the settlement of 1902. Prominent faculty had used their influence with the republican parties to advance the cause of the modern secondary program; they were probably preparing to open the universities to primary school graduates as well. They had totally transformed the *licence* in letters by dropping the requirements of a Latin and a French dissertation. The introduction of the specialized *diplômes d'études supérieures* had completed the destruction of broadly literary and cultural studies at the New Sorbonne, which had been transformed into a factory for narrow specialists and outright pedants. Determined to remove potential rivals for intellectual leadership, the Sorbonne had in effect annexed and subordinated the Ecole Normale in 1903. One of the consequences of these several innovations, according to Agathon, was the "crisis of French." Teachers and examiners, especially those reporting on the *agrégations*, testified that the ability to write good French was generally in decline. A misguided preoccupation with Germanic "erudition" had been allowed to overrun the traditional strengths of French thought: its "order, clarity and taste."[91]

Massis and de Tarde directed their criticisms against the entire Paris faculty of letters; but they also stressed the influence of a few individuals. They mentioned Alphonse Aulard; but they more particularly focused upon Gustave Lanson, Charles Seignobos and Emile Durkheim. These men, they claimed, were "revered and feared" within the faculty. Durkheim's authority was especially great. He taught the required course in pedagogy for future second-ary teachers, which made him almost a "prefect of studies." Of course all four of the men singled out in this way were determined reformists in education, good republicans and Dreyfusards in poli-tics. Massis and de Tarde clearly positioned themselves in the conservative camp. Their views on secondary education were almost wholly predictable. In destroying the traditional secondary curricu-lum, they charged, the leaders of the New Sorbonne were guided by utilitarian considerations and by a misguided sense of democracy. They had opened the universities to the social clientele of the primary schools, and some of them were actually beginning to think about the abolition of fees in secondary schools. The teaching level in the secondary schools had been adjusted to suit the mediocre. In the process, the words "humanities" and "rhetoric" had become terms of abuse. But according to Agathon, the traditional barrier between the two "orders" of primary and secondary education had to be restored. For primary schooling had always been directed at the "needs of the lesser occupations," whereas secondary education was a general schooling of the mind in preparation for "intellectual careers." The inherited form of secondary education preserved the "turn of mind" of the French lineage (*race*). The settlement of 1902 was a victory for "the primary spirit"; it robbed the secondary program of its "traditional idealism."[92]

In higher education, according to Massis and de Tarde, the Sorbonne had imposed mindless specialization. Narrow erudition was pursued for its own sake, and the division of labor had become an obsession. In literature and in history, there was an exclusive emphasis upon ancillary skills, upon philology and textual criticism, bibliography, chronology, and the tracing of literary influences. Students were directed to perform routine and almost menial research tasks; for that was held to be a requirement of "scientific" method. Totally neglected, in consequence, was what a higher education used to entail and ought to entail: the nurturing of the student's innate "gifts," the broad schooling of the intelligence, the fostering of general ideas and of a capacity for "synthesis," the development of a penchant for form and finesse. Young minds were deprived of the chance to evolve an inner life of their own, a personal interpretation of the great literary works, along with a degree of originality, imagination and invention. A liberal, general, and philosophical *culture*, Agathon wrote, is not an assemblage of information, but a state of suppleness and maturity of the intelligence.[93]

Massis and de Tarde were particularly contemptuous of their professors' tendency to imitate the terminology and the methods of the natural sciences. There was too much talk, they felt, about "laboratories" of French philology, about "teams" of scientific workers doing "practical" work and thus placing a stone in the growing edifice of science. They complained of "positivism" and "scientific materialism." One of the things they disliked about it was that it led to a distrust of originality and intuition. The research of the historian, they insisted, was not similar to that of the physicist; for history deals with ideas, beliefs, and passions, with phenomena that elude quantitative measures and require qualitative judgments, along with insight and finesse. One cannot expect to find historical laws comparable to those of the physical sciences. And above all, there is no progress even in the natural sciences without imagination, intuition, and the creative formulation of hypotheses.[94]

The influence of German "erudition" and of scientistic ideology, according to Agathon, tended to reduce all of the humanistic disciplines to a certain narrow brand of history. Thus philosophy proper was no longer taught at all. It was replaced by a physiological psychology, by Durkheim's triumphant sociology, and most particularly by the *history* of the main philosophic doctrines, which were no longer regarded as more than historically interesting. Much the same was true in the study of literature. In Lanson's conception of it, there was no room for "personal" interpretation, for judging literary works in relation to one's own ideas and taste. There was no sense that works of literature could be appropriated to gain new ideas and to enrich one's inner life. Instead, there was an oppressive insistence that all explication of literary texts must be historical, designed to locate them in their original milieu, to "fix" their historical physiognomy. The exclusive commitment to historical methods in fact came down to textual criticism and "erudition" for its own sake. Thus Lanson's 1909 edition of Voltaire's *Philosophic Letters* was an elaborate treatise on everything Voltaire read or might have read, and that presumably exerted an influence on some of his formulations. The accumulation of such "glosses" was bound to end by robbing great literature of its interior force and educative character.[95]

While philosophy and literature became history, Agathon claimed, history in turn lost its former life. Aulard and Seignobos were clearly at war with such great historians of France as Hippolyte Taine and Fustel de Coulanges. They feared and rejected any connection between history and literature. Seignobos tried to reduce history to a set of mechanical research procedures. But surely intellect and tact were needed to choose among the many documents available to the historian. No historical account could ever be better than its writer, and no merely documentary work could ever replace the intellectual effort of interpretation. If talent and intuition were eliminated from historical work, then history could only decline to an unsorted assemblage of little facts.[96]

Durkheim's pedagogy and sociology struck Massis and de Tarde as particularly ominous. They were indignant that his course on the history of education had been singled out as the only one required for the *agrégation*. They found his manner "dogmatic and authoritarian." In its content, they wrote, his obligatory course was a history of pedagogical doctrines devised to demonstrate the superiority of the new methods in French education and of their positivist inspiration. As for Durkheim's sociology proper, it was based on nothing more than minutely detailed observations of the manners of savages; yet it aspired to primacy among the sciences of man. It also reflected Durkheim's peculiar horror of anything psychological or individual. If anything of value *was* found in the individual, then Durkheim traced it to the influence of the group. A social fact, as Durkheim saw it, was mysteriously something more than a product of individual actions. Society itself was a real being, outside of individuals and superior to them. Such "pseudo-scientific mysticism" sustained Durkheim's "authoritarian fanaticism," his quest for domination not only in sociology, but in pedagogy, ethics, and politics as well.[97] His *Division of Labor in Society*, moreover, reflected the cult of specialization that characterized the New Sorbonne. On typically utilitarian grounds, he rejected the aspiration to become a complete human being and insisted that the individual must specialize in order to perform a useful task in society. He characterized the traditional *honnête homme* as a dilettante. He preached the vanity of the inner life, of all culture and of any moral ideal. He thus prepared the ground for the final defeat of all individual superiority, and for the tyranny of the group. He held that our intimate self-observations merely mislead us about the real causes of our actions. Surely such perversions of logic were "inhuman in the true sense of the word." In Durkheim's world, a "somber determinism" obscured social life, rather than explaining it. A theory of increasing specialization and intellectual fragmentation was based upon the worship of the great "social Being," which was "vague, monstrous, tyrannical, incomprehensible and fierce, like the god of the Jews."[98]

Agathon's darkest suspicion was that the New Sorbonne actively cultivated mediocrity and despised individual "talent." Its emphasis was explicitly upon educating the great number. The natural clients of the primary schools (*les primaires*) had been allowed to reach higher education and would presumably reach it in ever greater numbers. Thus the Sorbonne "assures the domination of numbers and prepares the elevation of the mediocre." Teaching methods reflected this bias; for they assimilated intellectual work to manual labor. The mind played almost no role in the pursuit of erudition. Creativity was discounted, along with the enthusiasm that would be aroused by a direct and personal relationship to literary texts. The dominant approach sacrificed "the elite to the mass"; it levelled all individual superiority; for nothing was more suspect at the New Sorbonne than "talent and genius." Education and natural ability were considered exorbitant privileges, and the barely formed mind of a primary school pupil was thought capable of the same work as an intelligence slowly and profoundly enriched by classical education.[99]

Against the democratic orientation of the New Sorbonne, Massis and de Tarde invoked the claims of "talent" and the charisma of "genius." They warned that scholarly methods could not replace refined intelligence or "innate gifts" (*le don*).

Perhaps talent is indeed a privilege and a natural one, which makes it even more execrable [in the eyes of the Sorbonne]. But is it not also one of the primary conditions of all progress? The world can only renew itself by means of quick, free and audacious minds, not by means of the average and the mediocre.

As Agathon saw it, society needed an elite of disinterested researchers, who would work for glory and not for profit. Even in economic terms, the worth of a nation depended upon the "beneficent influence of a small phalanx of superior men." It was the elite that produced profitable inventions, along with the masterworks of art and literature.[100]

Some of what Agathon wrote could have appeared in Germany, in an orthodox academic's defense of the classical *Gymnasium*, or in a broader discussion of the "crisis of learning." This is certainly true of the pejorative contrast between the low "utilitarianism" of the modern secondary program and the high "idealism" of the classical stream. The deep distrust of scholarly specialization, too, was widespread among German university professors of various sociopolitical orientations. Many of them felt that the growth of science and schorlarship coincided with a decline in the personal significance of learning. "Positivism," of course, was much more widely repudiated in Germany than in France. Indeed, the arguments of German philosophers and social scientists about these matters were much more developed and sophisticated than Agathon's superficial reactions. Such comparisons can be utterly misleading, however, unless they are carefully related to the structures of the relevant social and intellectual fields. Thus Massis and de Tarde wrote as consumers of the education they disliked. They were young literary lights, or would-be lights, not academics. They also represented a limited *and declining* sector of French academic opinion. They presumably spoke for many classically educated secondary teachers, for at least a few university professors of Greek and Latin literature, and more generally for the generalist emphasis of the old faculties of letters. Yet as they fully realized, that emphasis was being superseded by the research ethos of the New Sorbonne. Thus the ascendant and increasingly dominant groups in the reformed French universities were aligned in diametric opposition to them. In Germany, by contrast, views like those of Agathon characterized the whole orthodox camp within the academic community, along with portions of the modernist spectrum, especially on the issues of specialization and of "positivism."

If Massis and de Tarde most directly represented the conservative wing of the French literary intelligentsia, they also clearly spoke for the thrice-blessed bourgeoisie, or for those privileged culturally as well as economically and socially. They expressed resentment at seeing their educational advantages diluted by the reformist policies of the Radical Republic. The cultural capital they could bring to their education from their family backgrounds took the form of "talent" or even of "genius" in their eyes. The education they approved was a discovering and nurturing of pre-existent, presumably biological "gifts," not a communication of information and of analytical skills. They were defending something like the socially confirmative version of *Bildung* against a more impersonal view of learning. Education as they conceived it could never reverse the "mediocrity" of pupils from less-favored backgrounds. The two young men were furious at being assigned "menial" tasks, as if learning were merely practice. A central theme in their attack upon the New Sorbonne was their outrage at their teachers' apparent willingness to sacrifice "the elite to the mass," and to assure the "domination of numbers."

At the same time, Massis and de Tarde championed the cause of the free-lance writers against the newly emerging scientific and scholarly elite; they wrote as aspiring "men of letters." This is clear in their repeated emphasis upon the qualities that presumably characterize the successful writer: originality, imagination, invention, and some combination of clarity and "finesse." They felt particularly threatened by an approach to literature that did *not* aim at a "personal" interpretation, in the light of one's "taste." The literary history sponsored by Gustave Lanson was the professional scholar's usurpation of an intellectual realm that had hitherto been reserved for the highly "personal" judgments of prominent literary critics, generalist impresarios of the literary world. History itself had always been literature as much as systematic reconstruction; it had drawn upon the "tact" of the great writer. As a matter of fact, Massis and de Tarde wrote more particularly for the "psychological" novelists and essayists, a genre of "psychological" writing central to the French literary tradition. Agathon plainly favored the meticulous observation and interpretation of inner states that characterized this genre. Here was another reason for the two writers' violent reaction against Durkheim and his polemical indifference to psychology.

Equally interesting, finally, is what Massis and de Tarde had to say about the relationship of the universal literary man and of the specialized researcher to the educated public. The theme they thus took up had first been stated in Paul Bourget's *Le Disciple*.[101] Bourget there described the problematic elderly philosopher as so totally absorbed in his outlandish theories and so utterly estranged from ordinary life that he could not meet the responsibility of truly educating his wayward disciple. He could not guide a full human being, as the generalist writer–intellectual presumably could. Ferdinand Brunetière continued this theme in his attack upon the specialists who forgot their limitations and presumed to speak to the general public about such broad issues as those involved in the Dreyfus Affair.[102] It was thus only a further step in the same direction when Agathon contrasted the universal audience addressed by Voltaire's *Philosophical Letters* with the much smaller number of individuals who could be expected to take an interest in Lanson's scholarly edition of that work.[103] Massis and de Tarde had no conception of the way in which a position established through specialized scholarship can ultimately, if indirectly, equal or exceed the "weight" of more popular works. Here was another contrast between the world of the literati and that of the New Sorbonne.

Part of the interest of Agathon's essays lies in the fact that they attracted a great deal of attention. Indeed, they elicited a number of responses that were included in the volume published a year later. It may be worth reviewing at least the reactions of individuals already known to us. Thus Maurice Barrès sent a brief personal note that was friendly in tone but less than fully supportive in substance. He said he preferred the exactitude of Agathon's teachers to the overly "oratori-cal" style of his own. Ernest Lavisse wrote two substantial commen-taries to defend the Paris faculty of letters. He suggested that the two young critics were really asking for an extension of the secondary grades in rhetoric, rather than for a higher education. But the Sorbonne rightly sought to train them to do independent scholarly work. Lavisse thought it better for students to write badly about a subject they had seriously explored than to express themselves well about nothing at all. Nevertheless, he admitted that questions of style might now be receiving too little attention, and he called for inter-disciplinary lectures on current philosophical issues. He thus partly recognized the legitimacy of Agathon's complaints, even while emphasizing the advantages of the new scholarly orientation.[104]

Dean Alfred Croiset gave Massis and de Tarde a certain public recognition when he discussed their attacks in an address to mark the reopening of classes. Talk of a "crisis of French," he declared, was simply exaggerated. Pupils leaving secondary education might write with less elegance than formerly, but they wrote with more precision and judgment. Like Lavisse, Croiset suspected that Massis and de Tarde were dreaming of the Sorbonne of a hundred years ago, which was indeed a prolongation of secondary schooling. He saw nothing wrong with erudition, with notecards, bibliography, and textual criticism. He particularly expressed his support for the new histori-cism. Literary texts, he wrote, were not only works of beauty to be enjoyed in the present, but also documents about the life of past generations. To learn more about the realities of the past was surely not to abandon literary culture. Of course there were scholars who lost themselves in historical details; but even they helped to prepare the ground for the syntheses of the more gifted. It was not the task of the Sorbonne to form charming dilettantes; for France needed workers. Modern societies held their place in the world through intellectual productivity. Moreover, the sciences created a culture that had its own virtues. The scientist learned carefully to verify his own affirmations and those of others, to deflate overblown phrases and vain sophisms. Thus a kind of moral education through science instilled a commitment to conscientious work, a need for sincerity and a just distrust of precipitate judgments.[105]

The philosopher Emile Boutroux was asked by an associate of Agathon to comment upon the state of his discipline. He obliged by insisting that philosophy must not be confused with the specialized disciplines; it is their source and goal. The task of philosophy, he wrote, is to make us understand our place in the world, and to assess the value of things. Philosophy gives us wisdom, which the empirical disciplines cannot do. Experimentation pushed to its limits still cannot satisfy the intelligence; for the realm of the sciences is narrower than the realm of reason. We have many adroit specialists, Boutroux wrote, who have too much pride and too little wisdom. Yet philosophy will survive; it will once again produce a genius who will penetrate beyond current knowledge to distill the wisdom of the age. In the meantime, the faculties must not be allowed to become pedagogical institutions. They must remain real centers of learning, at which youth can be put in touch with the general movement of ideas.[106] Altogether, Boutroux wrote remarkably like a German philosopher recommending the pursuit of *Weltanschauung*. His negative remarks about the pride of specialists and about pedagogy at the universities could also be read specifically as an attack upon Durkheim.

A year after the publication of Agathon's essays, the monarchist writer Pierre Lasserre published some lectures that he had initially delivered at the royalist Institute of the Action Française in 1908–9, and that probably influenced Massis and de Tarde. In any case, the published version included most of the charges levelled against the New Sorbonne by the two young writers. In fact, Lasserre was a good deal more violent than Agathon in his attack. He argued that the Paris faculty of letters had succumbed to a left-wing conspiracy, that those engaged in this conspiracy were mostly Protestants and Jews, that its aims were anti-patriotic and deliberately divisive. Like Agathon, Lasserre focused upon Durkheim, Lanson and Seignobos. His attacks upon these men were highly personal and almost scurrilous, but they did not add much substance to the criticisms expressed by Massis and de Tarde.[107]

Still, Lasserre's book should remind us that to some degree at least, the French intellectual field was further transformed after the turn of the century, especially between 1905 and 1914. Part of the change may be described as a reaction against scientism and positivism. In 1904, Henri Bergson began lecturing to growing audiences at the Collège de France. From 1906 on, Charles Péguy attacked the scholarly pretensions of the French academic establishment, along with the political exploitation of republican and Dreyfusard doctrines. At about the same time, the monarchist right extended its influence within the Latin Quarter. There were student disturbances at the Paris faculties of law and of medicine, although they did not greatly affect the faculties of letters and of sciences. At a deeper level, Eugen Weber has pointed to a revival of nationalism in France that began in 1905 and extended well beyond the circles usually reached by the radical right. Rising international tensions certainly nourished the new nationalism, but a defensive reaction against socialist internationalism probably played a role as well.[108]

In a chronologically extended narrative of French intellectual life, all these new currents would have to be more fully considered. But the present study is intended less as a descriptive account of change over time than as a predominantly synchronic and comparative analysis of configurations within an intellectual field. The relationships that have been emphasized are those involved in the debate over educational reform and in the conflict between the specialized researcher and the generalist man of letters. Of course the ideology of the New Sorbonne continued to meet opposition long after Agathon's specific formulations were forgotten. In important respects, nevertheless, the research ethos that moved French reformist scholars during the decades around 1900 has remained a permanent ingredient in the academic culture of twentieth-century France.

CHAPTER 5

Perspectives upon selected disciplines

We can now ask how some particular disciplines were affected by the reforms in French secondary and higher education and by the ideological conflicts that accompanied them. One of the most interesting cases is that of history, including that of Gustave Lanson's history of literature; the other obvious instance is that of Emile Durkheim's sociology. Before turning to these two subjects, however, I want briefly to touch upon the situation of philosophy, which has been analyzed by Jean-Louis Fabiani.[1]

PHILOSOPHY AND THE SCIENCES OF MAN

From the beginning of the nineteenth century on, an eight-hour course in philosophy held a special place in the highest or "philosophy" grade of the French classical secondary curriculum. Philosophy teachers enjoyed a special status among their colleagues; they habitually described their course as the "crown" of the classical secondary program. The share of *agrégés* among them was particularly high. Like their colleagues, they could move upward to positions in the faculties of letters or in the educational administration; but they could also achieve something close to fame within the secondary system, particularly if they taught in one of the elite Parisian *lycées*. The contents of the philosophy course proved remarkably stable over time; Victor Cousin's eclectic "spiritualism" remained influential until late in the century. Only obligations to society and related topics were given increased attention from 1880 on, being assigned to the province of ethics (*morale*).

The reforms in French higher education after 1870, the professionalization of the professoriate and the new emphasis upon original research affected philosophers along with other disciplinary groups within the faculties of letters. While such non-academics as Comte and Renouvier still figured among prominent philosophers earlier in the century, the philosophers of the 1880s and later decades were all university faculty formally trained in their discipline. They now also became *creators* of philosophy, rather than transmitters only. Partly for that reason, the period between 1880 and 1914 was subsequently regarded as a "golden age" of philosophy. The liberalization of intellectual life under the Third Republic probably contributed to this aura; but the decisive factors were the university reforms and the rise in the status of the academic profession. The sense of an alliance between the non-professional faculties, the republican educational administration and the political parties of the left center encouraged a spirit of optimism in academic circles. In a 1908 survey of philosophers by Alfred Binet, the respondents also had a lively sense of their intellectual and personal influence upon their students.

Nevertheless, French philosophers of the late nineteenth and early twentieth centuries repeatedly expressed the view that there was a crisis in their discipline, and the question is how this sense of crisis could have arisen. Fabiani rightly excludes the possibility of a malaise as deep as the German "crisis of culture" and "of learning" between 1890 and 1930. German philosophers of those decades contrasted their own time with a golden age of German philosophy during the decades around 1800. They were concerned about the widening separation between systematic philosophy and the specialized empirical disciplines. But the anxiety aroused by this disjunction was greatly aggravated by a broader sense of social and cultural decline. In France, these broader grounds for pessimism were absent. The social status and cultural influence of the academic community were on the increase; there was no bygone golden age to regret, and specialized research was welcome to many as an element in the new professionalism. The "crisis" in French philosophy therefore had to stem from narrower and more specific causes.

The close identification of philosophy with the classical secondary curriculum was one such specific cause. As modern and scientific secondary subjects gained in strength, philosophy lost ground to mathematics in the program of the highest secondary grades. This may help to explain why the majority of philosophers testifying before the Ribot Commission, including Emile Boutroux and Alfred Fouillée, favored the maintenance of the classical monopoly. In any case, philosophy was no longer securely established as the "crown" of secondary education; it remained a requirement in only two of the four options created by the settlement of 1902. The university reforms of the late nineteenth century raised the status of *higher* education to such a degree, moreover, that a discipline identified primarily with the secondary system ultimately found itself at a comparative disadvantage. The public reputation of philosophy, meantime, was ambiguous. There was something like a renewed Catholic interest in its heritage of "spiritualism." Yet Barrès' portrait of the Kantian philosophy teacher as a deracinating universalist also suggests a conservative revulsion against the critical potential of the discipline.

A second specific cause of the sense of crisis in French philosophy had more in common with German trends and attitudes. In France as in Germany, the growth of specialized research in the empirical disciplines struck some philosophers as problematic. The progress of the "positive" sciences was most threatening, of course, when it encroached upon territory traditionally occupied by philosophy, as in the cases of psychology and of history. From the 1830s on, both psychology and the history of philosophy figured as subtopics within the secondary course of the final year. But when Jaurès defended that course before the Ribot Commission, naming German and English philosophy, "positive philosophy" and "psysiological psychology" as subjects of particular interest to contemporary students, he sounded almost as if he were recommending autonomous specialities, rather than subtopics within philosophy.[2] One of Agathon's main complaints about the New Sorbonne was that it reduced philosophy to the history of philosophical doctrines, or else to sociology.[3] Responding to one of Agathon's colleagues, Emile Boutroux warned that philosophy must not be confused with the empirical disciplines; for it is their source and goal. It lets us understand our place in the world and the value of things. While rebuking the inordinate pride of certain specialists, Boutroux predicted that philosophy would survive nonetheless. Once again it would produce a genius to redirect the intellectual life of the age.

While Boutroux thus took a cautiously optimistic view of the future of philosophy, at least on this occasion, he clearly saw a conflict between the development of the specialized disciplines and the continued centrality of philosophical synthesis.[4] The trend that concerned him is perhaps best exemplified by Seignobos' reflections upon the future of the faculty of letters.[5] For Seignobos in fact equated much of philosophy with the *history* of philosophy and the rest with psychology. He then further identified "the psychological and social sciences" with "the sciences of man." The faculty of letters, he thought, was poorly named; for its task was in no sense "literary." Its true domain encompassed the sciences of man, and its future lay in empirical research and "positive" knowledge. There was an obvious tension between this imperialist vision of the human sciences and Boutroux's insistence upon the limits of specialization and the primacy of philosophy.

Much more strident than Boutroux in his defense of philosophy was the social theorist Alfred Fouillée, whom we know as an opponent of the modern curriculum and of democratization in secondary education. In a 1901 tract, Fouillée argued that only a revitalized course in philosophy could restore intellectual and moral coherence to French secondary education.[6] He wrote at a time when the Ribot Commission had completed its work, but the settlement of 1902 had not yet been agreed upon. During this interval, a parliamentary report suggested that the last or "philosophy" grade of the classical secondary program might be abolished, so as to reduce that program to the six-year length of the modern branch, which would achieve parity with the classical stream. Violently opposed to this possible outcome, Fouillée countered with the usual scheme of reconverting the modern option into a short, "practical" and non-baccalaureate preparation for positions in commerce, industry, and agriculture. Within the fully secondary or "classical" track, Fouillée envisaged a tripartite articulation into a Latin–Greek, a Latin–Sciences and a Latin–(Modern) Languages option. His point about the philosophy course was that it should be the main focus of the seventh year not only in the purely classical option, as heretofore, but in Latin–Sciences and in Latin–(Modern) Languages as well. Beyond that, he saw philosophy, particularly ethics and social theory, as a continuous emphasis throughout all secondary grades and courses. This further implied an enlarged place for philosophy on the baccalaureate examination, along with training in philosophy, *not pedagogy*, for all future secondary teachers.

By way of defending his proposal, which was ultimately unsuccessful, Fouillée wrote a polemic against the main disciplinary alternatives to philosophy within the secondary curriculum: the natural sciences, literary studies, and especially history. All of these, he charged, had proven inadequate as vehicles of humanistic edu-

cation. In the natural sciences, there was too much emphasis upon
facts and memorization, rather than upon philosophical and methodological principles. An unacknowledged utilitarianism also tended
to undercut the theoretical emphasis most appropriate to secondary
schooling. The situation was even worse in the languages and in
literature. There was an obsession with philology and "Germanic"
erudition. Equally damaging was the substitution of literary history
for literature itself. Pupils were asked to memorize pointless details
and classificatory schemes, instead of being taught to appreciate the
beauty of the great works and the moral sentiments they conveyed.
There was an obvious need for a perspective that only philosophy
could provide. For even the sciences could adequately address
neither the ultimate questions of metaphysics, nor the burning moral
and social issues of the day.

Fouillée was particularly harsh about the pretensions of the
historians, whose challenge to the primacy of philosophy probably
seemed all the more threatening for being relatively recent. He felt
that history too was taught with an inappropriate emphasis upon
erudition and factual detail. Much of what students learned about
the course of the events in the world, moreover, was far from
edifying. Supplementing these charges, Fouillée offered a critical
reaction to a standard work on historical method by Charles Victor
Langlois and Charles Seignobos that we will shortly consider.
History, he argued, is simply not the reliable "science" it claims to
be. It depends for its evidence upon the testimony of biased
witnesses. Forced to select among huge numbers of facts to construct
a coherent account, historians inevitably intrude their own personal
perspectives as well. To make sense of their material at all, they have
to move from the objective to the subjective realm, trying to imagine
the motives of various agents. They might occasionally identify the
cause of a particular event, but they cannot hope to discover genuine
historical laws. The writing of history is therefore bound to remain
an imaginative art, rather than an objective science. The best that
can be expected from the historians is that they might supply the
evidence for the generalizations of the sociologists.

In a conscious appeal to the politicians, Fouillée stressed the
proven loyalty of the leading academic philosophers to the republic
and to laic morality. He also claimed to detect a fruitful convergence
between positivism and philosophical idealism. The strength of the
emerging synthesis was that it combined a firm commitment to

science with an awareness of its limitations, a sense of the need for philosophical analysis in the realm of metaphysics and, more particularly, of ethics. The central issues of contemporary philosophy, according to Fouillée, had to do with social questions. A philosophy of moral and social action had begun to develop that was ideally suited to the goals of secondary education. Of course specialized work in philosophy should be kept out of the schools. There was no room in the secondary program for the detailed findings of empirical psychology or the technicalities of logic, not to mention the erudition associated with the history of philosophical doctrines. Central to the mission of secondary schooling, on the other hand, was a thorough introduction to the new social philosophy, which Fouillée also called "sociology" or "social science." Given the decline of religion, he argued, "moral and social philosophy" alone could provide the basis for a "civic and democratic education."[7]

Fouillée's position somewhat resembled certain German comments upon disciplinary specialization. We know that negative responses to specialization were less common in France than in Germany, and that some of the leaders of the "new Sorbonne" held views diametrically opposed to those of Fouillée. Perhaps no relevant concepts in France could match the impact of the German distinction between the growth of objective culture and the paralysis of subjective culture. Besides, Fouillée's tract was more unabashedly political than typical German treatments of the topic. Yet Fouillée clearly shared some of the views current among orthodox German academics. Thus he saw specialization as a threat not only to the cognitive coherence of science and scholarship, but to their moral and social influence as well. He hoped that a synthesis of positivism with philosophical idealism would revivify the established educational traditions. He was plainly in pursuit of a *Weltanschauung*, not to say an ideology, that could avert the threat of social conflict, preferably without the need for educational democratization.

The other point to be made about Fouillée concerns his view of "sociology" or of "social science." For he was actually one of the more persistent opponents of Durkheimian sociology. In a lengthy study published in 1905, he briefly restated his contributions to solidarist theory, including the model of the "quasi-contract."[8] He also repeatedly referred to his conception of "idea-forces," ideas that play a causal role in the social process, partly through an inherent tendency to achieve their own realization. Fouillée saw societies as systems of idea-forces. His main purpose in the 1905 book, however, was to prepare the ground for an "ethics of idea-forces" by reviewing the biological and sociological foundations of ethical theory. In his discussion of what he called positivist sociology, he directed his critical attention primarily to the works of Emile Durkheim and of Lucien Lévy-Bruhl. He complained that both of these men treated individuals as mere products, and ideas as mere reflections, of social forces. But even more fundamentally misguided, in his view, was their belief that they could dispense with philosophy. They offered descriptive, historical and causal analyses of moral ideas and practices, while ignoring the need for a discipline that could sustain ethical prescriptions and identify ultimate ends.

Fouillée further objected to Durkheim's social "realism," his alleged tendency to treat society as ontologically independent of its members. Consistent with this displacement of the individual, he thought, was Durkheim's erroneous belief that sociology could be established without a foundation in psychology. In this part of his argument, Fouillée echoed the views of other prominent spokesmen for the psychological approach to social analysis. Thus Gabriel Tarde saw the "psychological" phenomena of "imitation" and "contagion" as the true fundaments of social cohesion and of collective social action.[9] Like Fouillée, Tarde criticized Durkheim's methodological wholism or sociologism, as well as his claim that social facts could exercise a coercive influence upon the individual. Gustave LeBon, the leading theorist of "crowd psychology," also regarded social phenomena as the effects of psychological processes within the individual, or of interactions among such processes. In fact, he anticipated Fouillée in the use of such concepts as "imitation" and "mental contagion." Robert Nye has suggested that "this reliance on an individual model illustrates the lag which the conceptual apparatus of science has frequently suffered in integrating new data into existing knowledge."[10] The observation is apt; for nineteenth-century social analysis was deeply committed to methodological individualism, and to such traditional links between individual and social analysis as social contract theory, utilitarianism, and the assumption of rational choice in classical economics. Yet there is more to the "psychologism" of Fouillée, Tarde and LeBon than this kind of conceptual lag. As we have seen, Fouillée showed little interest in experimental psychology. At the same time, the interpretive "psychology" envisaged by Wilhelm Dilthey within the German hermeneutical tradition had no parallels in France. At least in the cases of Fouillée and of Tarde, therefore, the recommendation of "psychology" was purely abstract. It merely served to underscore the supposed need for such speculative linkages between individual and social analysis as "idea-forces" and "imitation." For Fouillée, these devices were thoroughly integrated into a cluster of ethical and social theories that in turn occupied a vital subject area within *philosophy*. Fouillée's "psychological" critique of "positivist socio-logy" was therefore an incident in the wider conflict between traditional philosophy and the new empirical sciences of man.

Terry Clark has counted teaching positions in French faculties of letters and similar institutions in 1878 and in 1898.[11] His results indicate very little growth during the interval in the classical languages and literatures, and not much more in philosophy. The number of places increased substantially, on the other hand, in modern languages and literatures and, even more markedly, in history and related subjects. The expansion in modern languages and literatures was due, of course, to the growth of the modern secondary program, which also made French the main focus of literary studies. Even while these developments were taking place, according to Antoine Compagnon, literary *criticism* was virtually replaced by literary *history*, and this partly accounts for the reputation of Gustave Lanson.[12] After beginning his career as a provincial secondary teacher and a disciple of the conservative literary critic Ferdinand Brunetière, Lanson published his *History of French Literature* in 1895, and emerged as a prominent Dreyfusard, educational reformist and spokeman for the New Sorbonne by the turn of the century.[13] The evolution of his views on the application of rigorous historical methods to the study of literature can be followed in four essays written between 1895 and 1910.

In the Introduction to his 1895 *History of French Literature*, Lanson took his historian's role rather lightly.[14] He warned against reducing the study of literature to facts and formulas; he did not want manuals to obstruct direct access to the great works. He did urge the pursuit of "positive" historical knowledge; but he also argued that neither the objects nor the methods of literary history were rigor-ously scientific. In the opening pages of a review essay published in 1900, he took a somewhat firmer stand.[15] He noted that there was less new work in literary criticism than in the history of literature and in the auxiliary disciplines of bibliography and textual criticism.

He also clearly associated the history of literature with social history or "the history of civilization." Some of his formulations strongly suggest that, like Fouillée, he had read Langlois and Seignobos' 1898 treatise on historical analysis. Yet he also saw a difference between general history and the history of literature. While historians can only indirectly approach the facts and circumstances that interest them, he observed, historians of literature have direct access to "states of consciousness" represented in texts.

In 1904, at the suggestion of Emile Durkheim, Lanson published an article on the relationship of literary history to sociology.[16] Here he began by drawing a sharp line between "subjective" literary *criticism* and the objective study of literary *history*. He further noted that historians pursue a certain level of generality in their accounts; they are less interested in "battles and great men" than in the "institutions, beliefs and manners" of human groups.[17] At first glance, he wrote, literary history seems to differ from sociology in its emphasis upon individual authors. Further reflection makes clear, however, that the historian of literature typically wants to understand the individual as a representative of a social collectivity. After all, authors write for specific audiences, and they share in the states of consciousness that characterize their group and age. They are influenced by their forerunners and contemporaries, just as they in turn influence others. The literary work is a "social phenomenon"; it evolves as its reception changes.[18] Indeed, Lanson believed that certain limited "laws" or "general facts" could be established about the connections between the individual work and its social context. In that sense, he saw a relationship, at least in principle, between literary history and sociology.[19]

In a 1910 essay on the methodology of his discipline, Lanson began by portraying the difficulties faced by literary historians.[20] To understand a literary work at all, they must "feel" (*ressentir*) its aesthetic force through an "effort of sympathy"; they must engage their "heart, imagination" and "taste." Yet their "personal" reactions must be controlled; the element of subjectivity must not be allowed to invalidate their analysis. Further, they are more interested than most historians in individuals and in their originality. Yet the great authors are unique precisely in their capacity to express the collective life of an epoch or a group.[21] Lanson's main purpose, however, was to answer Agathon's criticism of the New Sorbonne and of his own work in particular.[22] He urged concentration on methods that could yield "exact, impersonal, verifiable" results.[23] He particularly stressed the close study of the "influences" that link particular works to other contemporary writings, as well as to those of earlier and later times. While he warned against directly imitating the procedures of the natural sciences, he praised the caution associated with the scientific spirit. The critics of "sterile erudition" call for "ideas," he observed. They are apparently afraid that "method might stifle genius," and they write "as if they had a personal interest" in the issue.[24] But of course ideas must be well-founded, and no one claims that "erudition" is anything but a means to an end. The "criticism of genius" (*critique de génie*) might be dazzling in its inventiveness; but the contributions of exact research are more permanent. Indeed, the scientific spirit can narrow the divergences among interpretations and thus contribute to the intellectual unification of the nation.

Even more prominent among the "sciences of man" than Lanson's literary history, of course, was history itself. The professionalization of history, its emergence as a rigorous scholarly discipline with commonly accepted methodological standards, was a major element in the reform of the French academic system during the late nineteenth century.[25] When the Ecole Pratique des Hautes Etudes was founded in 1868, its fourth section for philology and history began offering instruction in specialized research methods. Every subsequent step in the reform of French higher education provided similar opportunities. This was true of the institution of "closed courses," of the establishment of scholarships for regular students, and of the introduction of more specialized requirements for the higher degrees.[26] Of course it was true also of the reforms in secondary education, which undermined the primacy of the classical languages.

Throughout, the influence of German scholarly models was probably greater in history than in other disciplines, particularly since the Ministry of Education treated promising graduates to a fellowship year in Germany. Gabriel Monod was one of the early practitioners of the new history and a cofounder of the *Revue historique*, which began publication in 1876. Monod had studied with Georg Waitz in Göttingen. Gaston Paris, an almost equally important medieval philologist, had learned from Friedrich Dietz in Bonn. Among the later representatives of the new erudition, Seignobos too had spent a year in Germany. Yet the critical methods that were a hallmark of the new scholarship also had institutional antecedents in France. The Ecole des Chartes continued a Benedictine tradition of medieval textual studies that influenced Charles Victor Langlois, who helped to write a standard treatise on historical analysis. The *Revue critique d'histoire et de littérature* began to insist upon the new critical methods in history as early as 1866, ten years before the *Revue historique* was launched. Moreover, a number of French historians explicitly qualified their praise of German scholarship. Both Seignobos and Lavisse observed that the Germans neglected the need for synthesis and for the clear presentation of research results.

It has become customary to describe the new French scholarly history of the late nineteenth century as "positivist," and this is not altogether wrong. Yet the term should not be taken to imply a direct relationship to Comte's scientific phenomenalism, or to his view that all "positive" sciences must search for lawlike generalizations. Instead, as we shall see, Seignobos and his colleagues adhered to a much broader and less determinate form of scientism. Though they liked to characterize their discipline as a "science," they did so primarily in order to emphasize the need for scholarly rigour in the criticism and reconstruction of the historical sources. They did not, like many of their German colleagues, see a sharp divide between the natural and the human sciences; but they also avoided overly specific parallels between the methods of historical analysis and the explanatory procedures of the physicist. They sometimes wrote as if the historical "facts" could be established and "added up" without reference to hypotheses of any kind. But while this naive approach has sometimes been labeled "positivist," it should probably be called hyper-empiricism instead.[27] Beyond that, several of the leading French historians of that time drew upon the rhetoric of educational reformism to contrast "positive" knowledge with merely "literary" work. Thus they saw their predecessors, the French historians of the early nineteenth century as essentially "literary" talents. They might admire Jules Michelet's romantic vision of the Revolution, his evocative power, or his interest in the common life of the people; but their appreciation was tempered by the sense that his work was not "scientific."

Christian Simon has argued with some cogency that the French and German historians of the late nineteenth century had a good deal in common.[28] Both groups were about equally committed to the critical methods that had been earliest and most fully developed in

Germany. Both *practiced* a reconstruction of the historical record that was often monographic, and that more or less deliberately assigned a predominant weight to political and diplomatic affairs. Thus social history was not much more fully developed in France than in Germany. Above all, the French and German historians rather resembled each other in their relationship to the state. They not only drew government salaries; they also expected the state to guarantee their freedom of expression as scholars and teachers. They actually looked to their governments for protection against ideological pressures exerted by political or religious factions and pressure groups. Indeed, the competent Ministers and Directors of Higher Education in France and Germany were generally – and about equally – respectful of faculty rights and professional standards in filling vacant faculty positions in history. In return, both French and German historians *voluntarily* supported the political systems that sustained them. They wrote as educators of the nation, and often enough as patriots and nationalists as well. Few among them seriously challenged the existing regimes; most reinforced their legitimacy, so that the states ultimately profited from their financial and moral investment in the academy.

While I consider this argument sound as far as it goes, I am more impressed with the *differences* between French and German historiography during my period. Simon seems fully aware of at least some of these divergences; but he underestimates their significance, because he is preoccupied by the formal parallels that have been suggested. He knows, for example, that the French system of higher education was less homogeneous, both institutionally and ideologically, than its German counterpart. There was a small private system of Catholic higher education (chiefly the Institut Catholique) and a distinctive Catholic historiography. Catholics made up a strong contingent at the Ecole des Chartes, as well as among the early collaborators on the *Revue historique*, which also had a more exclusively Catholic rival in the *Revue des questions historiques*. The Ecole Libre des Sciences Politiques, which schooled many future civil servants and diplomats, developed a distinctive national orientation in the history of international relations that resembled certain German scholarly preferences. The "monarchist" historians of the Action française led the attack upon the "official doctrine" of the republican Sorbonne in ways that might have pleased at least a few orthodox German university professors. Thus there were overt and occasionally heated political conflicts among French historians.[29] And these were significant, surely, in that they politicized scholarly disagreements and brought methodological assumptions too into the realm of the debatable and the explicit. I have consistently focused upon the reformist historians of the New Sorbonne; but I do not mean to imply that their ascendancy was never contested.

Even more important were the *political* differences between French and German historians; quite simply, the two groups supported dissimilar regimes. In France, despite a considerable diversity of opinion, the leaders of the New Sorbonne were firm to militant republicans. Even moderate socialist sympathies were not unknown among French academics, especially in the younger generations. In Germany, the orthodox majority of German academics was firmly committed to the bureaucratic monarchy and generally hostile not only to socialism, but in many cases to parliamentary democracy as well. The outlook of German historians was decisively affected by the early nineteenth-century need to create an adequate political form for the cultural unity that had emerged. In the "mandarin" political tradition, moreover, the "cultural state" was assigned a mission that tended to elevate it above the mundane concerns of civil society. Its purpose was not just to keep the peace, and certainly not to pursue the worldly interests of its citizens, but to foster and protect the nation's moral and cultural development. Thus its legitimacy derived less from the consent of the governed than from the vitality of the cultural life it sustained. Even its right to assert itself abroad was bound in principle to its role as the earthly representative of German culture. But this tendency to elevate the state above the ordinary concerns of constituent social groups, as Simon explicitly recognizes, was bound to affect the assumptions and aims of historical scholarship.[30] For example, it was not likely to encourage a profound interest in social history.

The historians of the new Sorbonne must certainly not be pictured as ideologically detached scientists.[31] On the contrary, they saw themselves as political educators of the nation, and they were deeply interested in the "lessons" of the past. Lavisse's primers for the elementary grades were known for their nationalism. Alphonse Aulard came to history via an enthusiasm for the political rhetoric of the Jacobins. Seignobos and other educational reformists wrote as champions of the Radical Republic. These men certainly intended to strengthen the republican regime, by fostering shared commitments to the "principles of 1789," by encouraging patriotism and a sense of civic "solidarity," and/or by demonstrating the interdependence of order and progress. In the conceptual world of French republicans, as Simon points out, the nation was constituted by common experiences and interests; it was not grounded in biology or in blind fate. It also reflected active citizenship, and it therefore became fully meaningful only in 1789. Since the people consciously formed the nation, which in turn created and sustained the state, there could be no permanent conflict between state and society. This not only suggested parliamentary representation; it also located the motor of political change in society or in "the people." Even without recourse to Marxist or sociological theories, French republican historians could thus treat constitutions and political arrangements as outgrowths of social needs and processes. The worldly concerns of social groups could be taken seriously. Indeed, the emphasis upon the constitutive role of "the people" could encourage an interest in the lives of ordinary peasants and artisans. Again, all this seems clear in Simon's own analysis, and yet he seems unwilling to draw the obvious conclusions, with respect to social history, for example.[32]

The issue of social history is of particular interest because Georg Iggers has argued, convincingly I believe, that during the decades around 1900, French historians were generally more receptive to social history than their German colleagues. Iggers traces this circumstance partly to the differences between the two political systems and cultures. But he also assigns great weight to the divergent *methodological* preferences of French and German historians, which Simon rather neglects – and again I agree with Iggers.[33] We have already discussed the philological and interpretive tradition in German scholarship and its roots in the ideology of *Bildung*. The principles of empathy and individuality shaped the works of German historians, whether or not they were expressed in fully developed doctrines. The principle of empathy could foster a legitimate past-mindedness; but it could also engender subjectivist theories of interpretation. The principle of individuality probably helped to focus attention upon the role of "great men" in history; it also encouraged teleological images of change, rather than causal ones. Whole cultures could be conceived as unique individualities, which made cross-cultural concepts problematic or actually illegitimate. Thus the "problem of *Historismus*" arose partly because *verstehen* as identification tended to undermine the independent standpoint of the interpreter, and partly because the idea of trans-cultural norms was difficult to reconcile with cultural systems imagined as strictly unique constellations. The ideal of the "cultural state," finally, suggested that diplomatic and military conflicts among states were also world-historical competitions among divergent cultural possibilities.

Leopold von Ranke himself described his conception of history in the language of empathy and individuality. He thought the forces at work in world history could not be "defined" or "subsumed under abstractions"; but they could be "felt" or grasped in "intuition" (*Mitgefühl, Anschauung, lebendige Ansicht*). Moreover, he was interested in the "originality" of the "particular," not in the general.[34] Explicitly rejecting social contract models, he regarded states as "individualities" with their own distinctive "principles" or "ideas." He believed that they represented cultural and moral energies, and that this gave a higher meaning to the struggles among them.[35] One could almost regard him as an intellectual historian; but of course his real emphasis was upon international relations. Indeed, he originated a thesis that came to be termed "the primacy of foreign policy." States, he wrote, are forced "to arrange all domestic affairs as a means to the end of asserting themselves." He saw "the realm of power and of international affairs" as the true domain of politics and therefore also of history.[36]

From the late 1880s on, Wilhelm Dilthey, Heinrich Rickert and others reexamined the methodological fundaments of the German tradition in the humanistic disciplines. Yet this philosophical analysis did not lead to notable innovations in the writing of history. If anything, it codified the notion that the historian's task is not generalization or causal explanation, but the interpretive understanding of the uniquely individual. Probably more significant for the future of German historiography was the work of the younger German historical economists led by Gustav Schmoller, who drew upon the cameralist heritage of the German *Staatswissenschaften*, studying economic institutions in their relationship to public policy. Among the historians themselves, Otto Hintze was encouraged by Schmoller's influence and support. His pioneering work in Prussian administrative, economic and social history was respected by many of his colleagues, perhaps, as Simon suggests, because he treated socio-economic realities as preconditions and tools of Prussian state-craft.[37] Together with Ernst Troeltsch and a handful of other scholars, typically modernists in politics, Hintze nevertheless opened some avenues toward social history. In the history of ideas, Friedrich Meinecke developed a line of investigation that was not really alien to the Rankean tradition.

That most German historians nevertheless long remained hostile to social and cultural history became very clear during the Lamprecht controversy of the 1890s. In his *German History* of 1891 and elsewhere, Karl Lamprecht projected a "cultural history" of mankind based upon universal socio-psychological "laws." Giving attention to economic and social change as well as to cultural orientations, he conceived a succession of "cultural epochs" (*Kulturzeitalter*) characterized by a stepwise advance of "psychic differentiation." Human beings, he believed, had moved away from a primary identification with their groups toward an ever increasing individualism and "subjectivism." His work was a rather turbulent mixture of anthropological information, imaginative portraiture and gratuitous rhetoric about the workings of the "social psyche." He really had something in common with such psychologizing French social theorists as Fouillée, Tarde, and LeBon. Yet the fierce attacks upon him by so many of his colleagues went far beyond legitimate scholarly criticism. He was not only accused of Western "positivism" and other forms of disloyalty to the German tradition; there were plainly political objections as well. He was repeatedly suspected of "materialism," which clearly meant Marxism. Particularly the orthodox wing of the German historical profession – Georg von Below, for example – suggested that democrats and the masses might be interested in "cultural history"; but that right-thinking scholars would continue to emphasize the state, the nation, and the collective concepts developed by the German Romantics. Some of the criticisms directed against Lamprecht were narrower and more controlled. Yet it is no exaggeration to say that the German historical profession as a whole virtually ostracized him and his pupils. One of the consequences was a turning away from the kind of social history that would have broken with the individualizing method and the political focus of the Rankean school.

There was no such animus against new historical approaches in France. Indeed, Iggers has described a whole cluster of French works published from the 1890s on that can be classified as economic, social or cultural history. Thus Henri Sée specialized in economic history, while Henri Hauser portrayed workers and merchants in early modern France, including their modes of life, their housing and clothing. François Simiand, more a social statistician than a historian, investigated long-term fluctuations in wage levels. The "socialist history" of Jean Jaurès linked political developments to social movements and described the material situation of the lower classes; it also influenced Albert Mathiez and Georges Lefebvre, who transformed the historiography of the French Revolution by giving serious attention to economic conditions and to collective states of mind. Lucien Febvre's 1911 work on "Philip II and the Franche Comté," subtitled "A Study in Political, Religious and Social History," opened the era of the *Annales* school that has extended to the present day.[38] And even if Iggers' list were successfully challenged on some issue of comparability or categorization, he would have to concede only that many influential historians in France as in Germany long continued to emphasize political and diplomatic history *in practice*. For there is no evidence that social history met with the kind of *theoretical* and *ideological* hostility in France that Lamprecht encountered in Germany. One could try to explain this difference by citing the French Enlightenment, particularly Montesquieu and Voltaire, who certainly looked beyond politics to society or to "civilization." Alexis de Tocqueville might be called a social or structural historian of politics, and Hippolyte Taine's environmentalism might be cited as well.

Again, however, I am not really convinced by such references to individual antecedents. That is why I would point once more to certain characteristics of the French debate over the future of secondary and higher education. We have noted that all participants in that debate knew they were engaged in a conflict among politically represented social groups. Certainly the reformists saw themselves as spokesmen for hitherto excluded portions of the middle and lower middle classes. Again and again, they stressed the need to adjust the educational system to an increasingly "complex" and democratic society. As determined advocates of social change, they could hardly overlook the importance of social history. They also liked to portray the traditional "literary" education as historically appropriate for the age of Louis XIV. This committed them to a species of historicism that was easily combined, however, with a firm belief in the rationality of their own standpoint.

We have also observed that the traditionalists in the French education debate did not develop a coherent model of interpretation. Emphasizing the "latinity" of French culture and the timeless significance of the classical texts, they in effect suppressed the distance between these texts and the modern reader. This is exactly where the reformist historians found their opportunity. They promptly identified the absence of history as the fatal flaw in the traditional curriculum. They saw only two ways of reading texts, a "literary" and a historical one, and of course they knew which of the two was sounder. They accordingly converted the classics into historical "documents," which made history the modern heir of classical studies. In principle, they might then have developed something like a historical hermeneutic, but they did not have a strong interpretive tradition to draw upon. On the other hand, the French concept of "civilization" traditionally encompassed institutions and practices, along with ideas and values. The reformist historians therefore in effect recovered the distance that had been suppressed by the classicists *not* as a *hermeneutical* (or psychological) *gap* between a reader and an author, but as a *historical distance* between two integral "civilizations." It followed that the history contained in the classical texts – and in more modern ones as well – could only be the history of "civilizations." Under no circumstances could it have been the history of politics or of international relations alone. If the new French historians were going to replace the "literary men" as educators of the nation, in short, they could do so only as historians of "civilization."

CHARLES SEIGNOBOS AND THE NEW SCIENTIFIC HISTORY

In 1898, Charles-Victor Langlois and Charles Seignobos published their *Introduction to Historical Studies*. Based upon a course of lectures at the Sorbonne, the book quickly became the standard work on the methodology of the new history in France. In a preface, the two authors announced that they would not provide a substantive "philosophy of history." Their purpose, rather, was to offer practical instruction on the critical analysis of historical sources and the construction of historical accounts. In the early portions of the book, Langlois duly outlined the procedures involved in the "external criticism" of manuscripts. He discussed the "auxiliary sciences" of epigraphy, paleography, and diplomatics. He described the methods used in the reconstruction of texts, in the critical analysis and classification of variations, and in the establishment of a manuscript's origins. He even gave advice on the management of notecards and files. His colleague Seignobos then covered the "internal criticism" of texts, and the construction of historical narratives and descriptions. Three years after the appearance of the volume, Seignobos published a further set of lectures delivered at the private Collège Libre des Sciences Sociales. These addressed *The Historical Method Applied to the Social Sciences*.[39] What follows is an account of Seignobos' arguments in both of these works.

Historical documents, according to Seignobos, are traces left by the "facts" of the past, or by the "thoughts and actions" of former times. Only a few among the facts of the past have left traces in this way. The purpose of textual criticism is to recover these facts by retracing the steps that led to their more or less adequate registration by the authors of the surviving documents. History is not a "science of observation"; for its knowledge is "indirect," based upon the typically untrained observations recorded – or distorted – in the sources. If a manuscript meets the tests of external criticism, each of the "affirmations" contained in it is then subjected to a process of "internal criticism" that encompasses two stages. First, the "critique of interpretation" or "hermeneutic" establishes what the author of the document meant to convey. Then the critiques of "sincerity" and of "correctness" (*exactitude*) assess the probabilities, respectively, that the author did not lie, and that he correctly perceived and reported the fact in question. Reasoning by inference, the critic seeks to determine whether the writer of the document was in a situation that either encouraged misrepresentation or impeded direct and undistorted perception. The claims made in the document must not be accepted without truly independent confirmation. Only after enough pertinent facts have been found credible can the historian begin to construct either a static description of historical conditions or a dynamic account of historical evolution.[40]

In further describing the "critique of interpretation," Seignobos focused upon the historians' need to master the languages of their sources. Obviously, medieval historians must know Latin. Indeed, they must know the forms of Latin prevalent in the regions and periods they intend to study. Languages tend to change at least slightly over time and from place to place. This is true particularly of terms that characterize social groups and common practices. Historians must learn these variations in usage. As a matter of fact, they must understand the possibly distinctive idioms of specific documents. The writer of a text might have used certain words in a figurative sense. Historians can only hope to find passages in which even idiosyncratic formulations have unambiguous meanings. In any case, they must locate individual terms in the contexts that help to define them.[41]

Beyond that, Seignobos offered little detailed advice, not to mention a coherent theory of interpretation. He used the term "hermeneutic" without further comment. The aim of the interpretive critique, he wrote at one point, is to arrive at "the conceptions of the author [of a document], the images he had in mind, the general concepts by means of which he represented the world." He included these images and concepts among the "facts" that have left traces in the historical sources. Yet he reasoned almost as if the task of interpretation was essentially descriptive. Thus he apparently regarded the "hermeneutic" as the easier of the two stages of historical criticism. He named a whole cluster of historical specialties that seemed to him further advanced than social and political history, precisely because they could dispense with the critiques of "sincerity" and "correctness." They could draw upon the explicit contents of the sources, without asking whether they adequately reflected reality. This was true of the history of literature and of philosophical and religious doctrines. It was true also of histories that treated laws, moral codes and institutional regulations *as norms*, rather than as reports of actual practices. He made a similar point about the history of legends and popular beliefs, which he assigned to the domain of "folklore" (in English).[42] Clearly, he was not deeply interested either in interpretation or in intellectual history.

He was very much concerned, on the other hand, with the critiques of "sincerity" and of "correctness." These ascertain whether a source offers reliable testimony about "external reality." Interpretive criticism yields a number of "affirmations" that the author of a document meant to put forward. *Each one of these* is now subjected to a series of critical questions. Did the writer intentionally misrepresent a state of affairs? Or if "sincere," was he well placed to observe what he recorded? Or did he unintentionally distort the facts through bias or error? In putting these queries, the critic must try to envisage the situation in which the document was written. Were there reasons to lie, opportunities for careful observation, emotions conducive to biased reporting? Seignobos warned against relying on oral traditions and legends. He particulary mentioned the distortions typical of "literary sources," which tend to invent "noble" sentiments and intense feelings. At the same time, he stipulated that reliable reporting was likely where the facts ran counter to the author's expectations or preferences, or could have been easily checked by contemporaries, or were so "gross" that they could scarcely be missed. While he carefully distinguished the "critique of correctness" from the "critique of sincerity," he thought the two could be combined in practice. Unless the historian hopes to write a biography, he argued explicitly, the writer of a document is of interest *only* as an intermediary, a means of access to the facts. The two related critiques are purely "negative"; their point is to identify any and all grounds to distrust a documentary "affirmation." In any case, a fact should not be considered established unless it is reliably reported by two absolutely independent sources. And no claim should be accepted, of course, if it conflicts with our scientific knowledge of the world.[43]

Once established, the facts must be combined in the construction of a historical account, which may be either static or dynamic. In developing this portion of his treatise, Seignobos pointed to the formative role of what historians know about the present. We must have an "image" of how human beings behave, how a society is constituted, and how the different elements of the social process interact. But we can only derive this image from the present. Indeed, according to Seignobos, we could not understand the past if human beings and social situations did not to some degree resemble each other across the ages. Immediately upon reading a document, we find ourselves "imagining" the persons and circumstances mentioned in it. In fact, we tend unconsciously to add details not actually mentioned in our source. As we learn more, we progressively correct our initial impressions, of course, but we never quite abandon the initial assumption of a similarity between the past and the present. It follows that our historical perceptions will progress along with our knowledge of the present. Like other reformist historians, Seignobos had a firm and confident relationship to his environment and to its rational norms. He was utterly unconcerned with the "problem of historicism" that was shortly to trouble some of his German colleagues.

On the other hand, he detected a "subjective" element in the historical methods he described. Unlike the "sciences of observation," history must establish its facts indirectly, reconstructing the "psychological" or "subjective" processes that intervened between the original facts and the possibly distorted "affirmations" in the documents. The syntheses constructed by historians, too, are "subjective" in some sense. They lack the "real" integration that unites the various aspects of a material object. The elements and relationships historians attribute to the societies of the past are established by analogical reasoning, patterned upon those of their own societies; they are "imagined," not observed. Somehow, Seignobos saw the inferences involved as "subjective."[44]

This did not prevent him from promptly suggesting a universal framework for the study of past societies. Confronted with an unsorted mass of more or less general facts, he thought, the historian needs a model of the social world as a guide for the work of synthesis. Here are the categories of the table he constructed for this purpose.

I. *Material conditions*

1. Population: (physical) anthropology, demography;
2. General material environment: natural environment (geography), artificial environment (agriculture, buildings, means of transport, etc.).

II. *Intellectual customs*

1. Written language;
2. Fine arts, in several branches;
3. Technical arts;
4. Religion;
5. Ethics and metaphysics;
6. The sciences.

III. *Voluntary material customs*

1. Practices of material life (food, clothing, finery, hygiene);
2. Practices of private life (daily schedules, ceremonies, entertainments, travel);
3. Economic practices, production (agriculture, mining, industry), transportation, exchange, appropriation, transfers and contracts.

IV. *Social institutions*

1. Property arrangement and inheritance;
2. The family;
3. Education;
4. Social classes.

V. *Public institutions*

1. Recruitment and organization of government personnel (central government and special services), official regulations of government, actual procedure of government operations (central and special);
2. Organization, recruitment, regulations and practices of church government;
3. Organization, recruitment, regulations and practices of local authorities.

VI. *Relations among sovereign social groups*

1. Organization of the personnel in charge of international relations;
2. Conventions, regulations, and common customs making up international law, officially and in reality.[45]

Obviously, the table does not aim at narrative political history. Instead, it suggests a strong interest in social history, broadly defined. Indeed, it strongly anticipates the approach that was later championed by the *Annales* school of French historians. Anthropology in France at that time was predominantly physical anthropology. Under the heading of geography, Seignobos also included the climate and soil conditions; geography had a long tradition in France, a firm place in the secondary curriculum, and a new paradigm in the "human geography" of Vidal de la Blanche. Beyond that, Seignobos came back again and again to "typical" or repeated patterns of behavior, to customs, common practices, and "habits" (*habitudes*), including "intellectual habits." "Voluntary" practices, in his terminology, are practices not regulated by explicit rules and sanctions; he noted that established patterns of behavior often engender "obligatory" conventions. In describing common practices, he cautioned, the historian must carefully specify the groups or subgroups in which they occur; political groupings are not necessarily appropriate units of analysis in economic history. He urged his students not to overestimate the internal homogeneity of groups or the sharpness of the boundaries between them.[46]

In his lectures at the Collège Libre des Sciences Sociales, Seignobos tried to specify the relationship between history and the social sciences. Partly in response to critical attacks upon history by Durkheim and his school, he defended the autonomy, and even the primacy, of his own discipline. He defined the "social sciences" to encompass social statistics, economic practices, and the history of economic doctrines. Given conflicts among the definitions offered by various sociologists, he reported, the *ad hoc* definition he used had simply emerged in practice, probably in connection with the German concept of the *Staatswissenschaften* (roughly "political economy"). Explaining why he lectured at the Collège, Seignobos argued that the social sciences are inevitably to some degree retrospective. Most of their evidence is drawn from historical documents, so that social scientists have to learn the critical methods of the new history. Much of the knowledge of the social sciences, he further specified, must be quantitative; it must deal with "distributions" and "structures," not only with singular facts. He accordingly discussed the difficulties involved in measuring, counting, estimating, and sampling social phenomena. Although his tone was consistently cautious, even skeptical, he conceived the possibility of arriving at chronological curves of certain frequencies. He even suggested that such curves might be compared, so as to identify possible relationships among different types of social facts.[47]

Throughout, Seignobos was preoccupied with the dangers inherent in generalization or abstraction. His strongest suspicions were directed against biological theories of society. He pointed out that most social phenomena have no physiological basis, and he flatly rejected theories of "race." Talk about "functional" relationships among the parts of a socio-political system struck him as metaphorical and potentially misleading. We ought not to discuss "industry" or "the Church" as if they were agents, he wrote, although we may treat "the clergy" as a real group. Then there is the difficult issue of what the Germans call *Zusammenhang*: the apparent unity, or interconnectedness, or "solidarity" among the different elements in the life of a society. Montesquieu first pointed to this phenomenon, which certainly cannot be ignored. But we must not try to explain it by developing "semi-mystical" theories about the "genius" or "spirit" of a people, in the manner of Gottfried von Herder or of Karl Lamprecht. Assumptions about the "collective consciousness" of a people, too, are premature.[48]

One way to avoid misleading generalizations, according to Seignobos, is to keep in mind that societies are made up of real human beings. These may have certain characteristics in common, if they live in the same environment. Still, the real agents in history are individuals. Collective actions are sums of individual acts, and the "social fact" posited by "some sociologists" is a philosophical construction, not a reality. Historians may choose to emphasize phenomena that are "collective, general and durable"; or they may attend primarily to the "individual, particular and passing." In Germany, disagreements about these alternatives have provoked the controversy surrounding (Lamprecht's) "cultural history." In France, some scholars have championed the history of "institutions, manners and ideas"; others have practiced political history, which has been deprecated as "battle history" by its critics. Seignobos urged his students not to exclude either of the two dimensions of history, but he particularly stressed the importance of the individual. He was committed, in short, to methodological individualism.[49]

His other defense against dangerous abstraction was an insistence upon the "psychological" character of social life. Especially in his lectures at the Collège, he gave much space to this part of his position. Historians cannot limit their field to material objects and external human behaviors, he said; they have to address "internal processes" and "representations." They must uncover the "motives" that are the causes of human actions, or at least their points of departure. The spread of beliefs and of material practices is based upon the psychological mechanisms of education and "imitation," which help to account for the *Zusammenhang* that has been mentioned. Political relationships are governed by conventions that have psychological origins. Even economic transactions cannot be understood apart from the "subjective" judgments that determine the value of goods. To explain changes in the frequency of suicides, one has to imagine the individual motivations involved. This imagining is "subjective"; but the hypotheses it suggests may be sustained by comparative statistical analysis. Comte believed that the scientific study of society should focus upon external conditions and behaviors; but he simply overlooked the psychological roots of social phenomena. Here and elsewhere, in his remarks about "social facts" and the "collective unconscious," Seignobos was clearly reacting to Durkheimian sociology. Yet he never challenged Durkheim directly, and he never actually named him.[50]

He was more forthcoming, if a little simplistic, about Karl Marx. Again primarily in his lectures at the Collège, he developed a sympathetic but ultimately negative position on "the economic interpretation of history." He saw this interpretation as a partly legitimate reaction against the excesses of idealist history. The role of literature and of the arts, he wrote, has been much exaggerated by our "literary" tradition. Conversely, economic issues are more significant than they appear in most historical documents. Incomes and living conditions certainly affect political and intellectual orientations. Thus one "cannot study the history of manners, of legal institutions or of politics without taking account at least of the general conditions and great transformations of economic life." On the other hand, non-economic matters play a role as well, even in the material environment; the facts of geography and of demography must not be neglected. More important, material circumstances in general are preconditions, rather than unilateral causes, of historical change. There is no evidence that economic circumstances consistently shape all other elements in the social process, or that human beings are universally motivated by economic concerns. On the contrary, non-economic factors strongly influence the economy. Science and technology help to define methods of production. The customs of private life create patterns of consumption that dictate what is produced. Beliefs, especially if they are effective, rather than nominal only, shape economic orientations as well. Then there are the political institutions that set the frameworks for economic activity. The great political and intellectual leaders, finally, can change the course of institutional development and invent the beliefs that come to be perpetuated through "imitation."[51]

As he developed these arguments, Seignobos gradually moved away not only from economic history, but also from social history and from his table of the social system. That table itself aimed at something like a total description, rather than an explanation of selected social relationships. It was also essentially static, though Seignobos had a lively interest in social dynamics. But the more he focused upon change, the more he moved economic and social history into the role of "background." He also distinguished such "special histories" as those of language and of law from "general history." The special histories seemed to him "abstract," in that they artificially isolate aspects of human life. The history of politics, however, had never become a specialty; it remained a part of general history. In the light of these definitions, Seignobos began to urge the need to understand the historical process in its "concrete" totality. Defending general history, he in effect recommended political history as well. After all, wars and revolutions, though political in character, may become great turning points in general history. They can mark out whole epochs by altering the direction of change. When Seignobos concluded his lectures at the Collège with a plea for the "total history of societies," he may not have meant to exclude economic and social history. In a way, he was still referring to his synoptic table of the social system. On the other hand, he had begun to assign much of the foreground of history to political events.[52]

In much of what he said about these issues, a partly tacit view of historical causation played a role. At one point, he defined a cause as a "necessary condition," which joins with other conditions to affect the course of events, such that without it, the outcome would not be what it is. The other conditions involved he described a little vaguely as "not sufficient." At the same time, he argued that in the language of history, which is ordinary language, a cause is what immediately precedes the effect. Thus the cause of a rock ledge being blown up, for the historian and the ordinary person, is the lighting of the powder, though a philosopher might cite the explosive force of the chemical. The study of society, Seignobos suggested, focuses upon conditions that are "passive, negative, permanent" and "necessary but not sufficient." Narrative history, by contrast, deals with causes that are "positive, active, momentary," and that immediately precede the effect. We have already encountered his contrast between a background of long-term "preconditions" and a fore-ground of short-term causes that "actively" bring about particular events. (It may be endemic to historical reasoning.) Seignobos was apparently somewhat more confortable with "active" than with "passive" causes. He commented that the historian finds it easier to locate "the causes of particular accidents" than those of "general transformations."[53]

Elsewhere, Seignobos argued that history does not provide "abstract knowledge of general relations among facts"; rather, it is the "explicative study" of a real evolution that has occurred only once. The explication he had in mind was clearly causal. One cannot adequately select among the mass of facts, he observed, unless one identifies those that have brought about important effects. Histor-ians are interested in the persons and events that have "modified the state of society." Historical change is not produced by "abstract laws," but by the "chance" concurrence of "facts of different kinds." These "unique" concurrences are "accidents"; but they can determine the direction of historical evolution. Obviously pleased with the idea of "accidents" that shape history, Seignobos even enlarged upon the importance of such "small facts" as the shape of Cleopatra's nose.[54]

Altogether, Seignobos was not much of a "positivist," even

broadly defined. One could call him a "hyper-empiricist," for he sometimes wrote as if "the facts" would add up of their own accord. He habitually conceived these facts as "external"; but he also insisted upon the "psychological" character of social life. That insistence had something in common with Fouillée's theorizing, in that it engendered neither practical applications nor further specifications, apart from an occasional reference to "imitation." In particular, there was no developed theory of interpretation; neither the "critique of interpretation" nor the muddle about the "subjectivity" of historical inference provided an adequate substitute. The commitment to methodological individualism and to the "uniqueness" of historical "accidents" did not become as systematic as certain German theories of individuality and uniqueness, partly because it was anchored in a strong causalism. At least at the level of theory, this supports Iggers' claim that the historical profession was *relatively* more receptive to social history in France than in Germany around 1900. Certainly one cannot imagine Seignobos joining the orthodox German historians in their passionate attack upon Lamprecht's "cultural history."

The real point to be made, however, is that Seignobos stood in an intellectual field that had little in common with the German context. He was primarily a French educational reformist. Though threatened by Durkheimian sociology from a more genuinely "positivist" direction, he still championed "science" as the obvious alternative to "literature." The question whether history is an art or a science occasionally struck him as "puerile." At other times, he pointed to the differences between history and the "sciences of observation." Nevertheless, his predominant emphasis was upon the "scientific" status of the new history and the rigor of its critical standards. Like every science, he wrote, history starts from a position of "methodical doubt." The force of this identification with "science" was drawn almost entirely from the confrontation with "literature." Thus his colleague Langlois castigated the "pompous and empty literary mode" of the old history. Seignobos warned students to distrust any "picturesque" effects and "dramatic" incidents mentioned in the sources. Commenting upon the marginal place of history in the unreformed secondary system, he described the classical curriculum as "founded upon the study of [esthetic] forms and indifferent to social facts." It is this contrast, more than anything else, which nourished his interest in social history.[55]

If Seignobos gave his lectures at the Collège Libre des Sciences Sociales during the year preceding their publication, then they coincided with the foundation of Henri Berr's *Revue de synthèse historique* in 1900. Berr launched this journal to oppose what he considered the narrow factualism of the French historical profession at that time. Contemporary historians have generally accepted his view of the situation. They have also stressed his influence upon Lucien Febvre, cofounder of what has become the dominant *Annales* tradition in twentieth-century French historiography. Thus Martin Siegel describes Berr as a principled critic of French historical "empiricism" and "positivism." He traces Berr's interest in "synthesis" to the influence of the philosopher Emile Boutroux. In his 1899 doctoral dissertation, Berr expressed the hope that a scientifically grounded philosophy of history could bridge the divide between philosophy and the empirical disciplines. Febvre was a student at the Ecole Normale when the *Revue de synthèse* began to appear. Twenty-five years later, he credited the new scholarly journal with rekindling his interest in history.[56]

Even before Siegel provided these particulars, H. Stuart Hughes identified Berr as an important precursor of the *Annales* school, though he qualified this claim in several respects. He pointed out that Febvre was also much affected by the example of Jules Michelet, whose vivid recreation of the past extended well beyond the actions of politicians and diplomats. He further called attention to Durkheim and his school, who certainly anticipated some of the concerns of contemporary French social historians. Turning to Berr himself, Hughes detected an "idealist" element in his thought, which Siegel also noted. According to Hughes, Berr "held that the historical past existed 'only to the extent' that it was 're-created by the mind'." On the other hand, Berr was "science-oriented," and "much of his language carries the ring of nineteenth-century positivism." The important qualification conveyed in the last sentence gains additional significance from Hughes' characterization of French historiography around the turn of the century. Langlois, Lavisse, Seignobos, and other French academic historians, Hughes argues, were primarily interested in political and institutional history. They might "in a loose sense be called 'positivists' "; for they believed "that 'the facts' of history could speak for themselves without the intrusion of hypothesis or theory." Nevertheless, "their particular brand of positivism" was "comparatively benign." They wrote with grace, and they were "far from being pedants or antiquaries."

Such are some of the reasons why a revolt against positivism in historical studies came later in France than in Germany and Italy and in rather different form. The professional landscape in France gave less cause for radical dissatisfaction, Hence the neo-idealist movement associated with such names as Croce and Meinecke largely passed the French by.[57]

I share Hughes' views of particular works and individuals; they are carefully balanced, as one would expect. I should also note that he has surveyed the *practices* of French historians around the turn of the century, whereas I know only how Langlois and Seignobos rationalized their methods. Nevertheless, I would be even more cautious than Hughes in applying the terms "positivism" and "idealism." I have trouble seeing Meinecke and other German historians of his time reacting against positivism; I see them codifying and extending an established idealist tradition. In France, I see Seignobos trying to articulate a position that was only loosely positivist, that actually anticipated much of the subsequent development of French social history, and that was hardly altered by Berr in particular.

In the opening pages of the *Revue de synthèse*, Berr briefly outlined his hopes for the new journal. He expressed his respect for the rigorous critical methods of the new history. He promised that there would be no attempt to revive the speculative philosophy of history; the *Revue* was committed to "science, true science." Even so, he urged scholars engaged exclusively in "detailed research" to accept the potential benefits of "general ideas." Analysis and synthesis, he wrote, are logically inseparable. The outstanding success of sociology was due, he thought, to its ability to reunite history with philosophy. While some sociologists lost their way in fantastic formulations, Durkheim's "positive sociology" combined historical evidence with comparative methods to develop precise empirical hypotheses. The Durkheimian school had discovered the importance of "the social in history"; Berr proposed to assign a permanent place to it in his journal.[58] At the same time, Berr called attention to the role of the individual in history. Once established by textual criticism, he argued, the "raw facts" of history could be combined either to seek general patterns or to focus upon "individual particularities" that could explain even great transformations. Like Seignobos, he was especially interested in the role of ideas, which he associated with individual creativity. Indeed, this concern for the individual guided him in his most significant methodological commitment. From the beginning, he assigned the task of historical synthesis primarily to a "historical psychology," which would be partly social and partly individual. Wilhelm Wundt's "psychology of peoples" (*Völkerpsychologie*) struck him as too "vague"; he hoped that investigations of provincial life would prove more fruitful. Beyond that, however, he really had little to say about psychology, except that it could give more attention than sociology to the role of great individuals in history. In sum, he largely shared Seignobos' views.[59]

In 1903, François Simiand, an affiliate of the Durkheimian school, wrote a lengthy review article for the *Revue de synthèse historique* on "Historical Method and Social Science." While he briefly touched upon other works as well, his essay was primarily a severe critique of Seignobos' lectures at the Collège Libre des Sciences Sociales.[60] He began by objecting to the notion that historical knowledge is "subjective." He agreed that it is often indirect, based upon the testimony of documents. He also fully accepted Seignbos' assertion that social phenomena are "psychological"; they certainly entail mental representations. But he accused Seignobos of confounding the psychological with the "subjective," and of other confusions as well. All empirical knowledge, of course, is based upon "subjective" sensations; but we soon learn to distinguish those among them that are independent of our inner states. They are combined to constitute objective phenomena, and the regularities of coexistence and succession among these phenomena are "objective" in the same way. To say this is not to claim that we have direct access to the metaphysical reality of "things." "In our empirical knowledge as in our positive science, 'objective' signifies nothing but: independent of our individual spontaneity." But precisely this independence characterizes social phenomena. Legal rules, customs and forms of social organization are objectively given, not individually chosen. Nor can they be resolved into sums of individual phenomena. They have no existence apart from human consciousness, of course; but they are autonomous phenomena in their own right. To deny that is to exclude the possibility of a science of society.[61]

Simiand was equally categorical about Seignobos' conviction that "social facts" are "abstract," while only the individual is real. He traced this notion to the metaphysics of common sense, which assumes that knowledge reproduces the substance of the world. In fact, of course, cognition always abstracts a particular aspect of reality, depending upon its analytical purposes. In some sense, therefore, the "individual" too is an abstraction. In any case, social phenomena are no more abstract than chemical phenomena. This makes it inappropriate, Simiand grumbled, to engage in "nominalist trifling" exclusively with respect to the social world. Of course sociologists do not regard such complexes as "mechanization" or "the Church" as physical entities. But like any other science, sociology must move beyond the language of common sense to posit strategically selected concepts. Besides, there is no reason to suppose that "the clergy" is somehow more "real" than "the Church." In choosing its "abstractions," a positive science looks to the possibility of discovering regularities and laws in the phenomenal world.[62]

Simiand further suspected Seignobos of the misconceptions often associated with the idea of the "social contract." One can ignore the autonomy of the social by imagining that society is constituted by the rational decisions of individuals. It was this penchant, Simiand believed, that led Seignobos to dwell upon the role of "social conventions." As empirical studies have shown, however, the independent individual is a relatively recent phenomenon. The further back one moves in time, the stricter one finds the rules that bind the person to the group. Much of what Seignobos wrote about psychology, too, grew out of his methodological commitment to the individual. Yet as Simiand pointed out, he virtually admitted the uncritical character of this "psychology"; for he knew that the motives of historical agents must be "imagined" on the assumption that they resemble our own. Even if motives were conclusively established for all past actions, moreover, we could not be satisfied. For we know that very often, the real causes of social phenomena have little to do with what the agents intend.[63]

Simiand next turned to the issue of causation. A little unfairly, he dismissed Seignobos' tentative distinction between necessary and sufficient conditions as simply confused. Following John Stuart Mill, he defined the cause of a phenomenon as an "invariable and unconditioned antecedent condition." The causal relation, he continued, is neither between an agent and an action, nor between a force and a result; it obtains between two phenomena of exactly the same order. Thus the cause of the rock ledge being blown up is neither the lighting of the powder nor its explosive force, but the expansion of the gas released by the combustion. Indeed, a causal relation implies the existence of a regularity or law that links the two phenomena involved. Where there is no law, at least conceivably, there is no cause, so that a strictly unique phenomenon cannot be causally explained. Seignobos' "causes" are really selected at random among an indefinite number of anterior conditions.[64] "An accident," Simiand continued, is the convergence of two known processes that are considered independent of each other; here he did not disagree with Seignobos. He believed that accidents occur, and he further acknowledged that social phenomena may have individual aspects or unique features. His main point was just that students of society must seek to discover relationships that are social and recurrent. They must concentrate upon relatively stable patterns and long-term causes, upon social structures and institutions, rather than upon individuals and events. They must not be mesmerized by incidents that may precipitate particular developments. To name an "accident" or to cite the importance of Cleopatra's nose is really not to explain anything at all. A physician may be unable to establish exactly how a particular individual caught a certain disease; but he may nonetheless attain – and apply – the scientific knowledge that will cure the patient.[65]

In his lectures at the Collège Libre des Sciences Sociales, as Simiand pointed out, Seignobos envisaged a division of labor between the historians and the sociologists. While the historians establish the facts and evolve an ever more complete representation of the past, the sociologists build their theories upon the empirical foundations thus provided. But Simiand felt unable to accept this convenient arrangement. Written history, he repeated, is not a photographic reproduction of the past. It is a selection, and it is organized according to certain categories. The difficulty is that historians of Seignobos' orientation are interested primarily in chronology and in political events. The classifications that structure their accounts are therefore largely irrational. The idea of "total history" is simply an illusion. Seignobos points to the interconnections (*Zusammenhang*) among the elements of a society. But of course he cannot begin to demostrate this "solidarity" without developing adequate techniques of analysis and, more particularly, of cross-cultural comparison. His schematic table of the social system reflects popular notions, rather than scientific principles. Having insisted that social phenomena are psychological, he here separates "material" from "intellectual" facts. He draws a line between "public" and "private" life, as if that divide were characteristic of all societies, and he assigns an equally universal role to the triadic scheme of "agriculture, industry and commerce."[66]

The basic error in all this, Simiand pointed out again, is the notion of a theory-free representation of the past. In reality, every fact listed already implies a theoretical choice. In the study of society as in other fields, "analytical investigation" must interact with "the constructive synthesis of science." There can be no division of labor that would separate the history from the science of social phenomena. Historians must focus from the beginning upon aspects of the past that may yield viable hypotheses. They cannot postpone the formulation of such hypotheses until more facts have been accumulated. On the contrary, many now available facts will have to be ignored until a stronger science has been developed. Above all, one must abandon the "idols of the tribe" of historians: the idol of politics, the idol of chronology, and the idol of the individual. A merely "empiric practice" must give way to a "well-considered and truly critical method."[67]

One cannot help feeling that Simiand was more categorical in his criticisms than he had to be. He might have given a more sympathetic hearing to some of Seignobos' concerns, even if they were not well formulated. Simply uninterested in interpretation, he provided no alternative to Seignobos' marginal efforts in this area. He also failed to recognize the role of singular causal explanation in historical reasoning, which Seignobos vaguely sensed, though he was unable to state his case.[68] Simiand might have learned much from Max Weber, who was just then writing to clarify the German historical tradition. On the other hand, Simiand came very close to anticipating the "covering law" model of historical explanation, and that is remarkable. What mainly concerns us as historians, however, is where he stood in the French intellectual field of his day. Obviously, he was greatly influenced by Durkheim's sociology, and he can be called a "positivist" in a precise sense of that term.

This is not true of Seignobos. His tacit commitment to the theory-free accumulation of "facts" may strike some observers as "positivist"; but it was precisely this "empiric practice" that came under attack from a genuinely positivist direction. Simiand too called for "synthesis," and he did more than Berr to explain what he meant. I have tried to suggest that twentieth-century French historiography was launched in a certain direction by the reformist position in the French education debate. Lacking an interpretive tradition, it was relatively receptive to the project of social history, at least in theory. But there was another major force in the conceptual field, even before the turn of the century, and that force was Durkheimian sociology. At the institutional level, as we shall see, Durkheim's school was by no means well established within the French academic system of that time. Simiand in particular was almost a marginal figure, as Philippe Besnard has shown.[69] Yet the *intellectual* presence of Durkheimian sociology can be detected in Gustave Lanson's essays, as well as in Seignobos' methodological writings, where it initially provoked defensive reactions. Its relevance to the project of social history is perfectly exemplified in Simiand's critical review. Fully to understand Seignobos, along with the subsequent development of French social history, I would conclude, one could ignore Berr; but one certainly has to read Simiand.

EMILE DURKHEIM ON EDUCATION

The institutionalization of Durkheimian sociology was part of a broader trend in which the social sciences gradually penetrated the French academic system. From the middle of the nineteenth century on, a whole series of new teaching positions was created *within the law faculties* for such subjects as comparative law, political economy, public finance, and statistics. While some of the new specialties were juridical in character, others represented a new emphasis upon economics and public administration in the tradition of the German "cameral" sciences or *Staatswissenschaften*. The definition of the "social sciences" offered by Seignobos in his lectures at the Collège Libre des Sciences Sociales was consistent with this tradition. The new courses in the law faculties were clearly designed to broaden the professional preparation of future civil servants. The number of law faculty positions in the social sciences and related disciplines advanced from 85 in 1865 to 198 in 1919, to which one must add a few personal appointments in the Collège de France.[70]

Within the faculties of letters, of course, history was the great success of that period. From 1871 on, there was modest growth also in geography; the human geography of Vidal de la Blanche became highly influential late in the century. By 1892, chairs in geography existed in 13 of 15 faculties of letters. For sociology and for immediately adjacent specialties, however, progress was much slower. This was due in large measure to the fact that the new discipline could offer no accreditation for spcific professions. For a time, Durkheim and other early French sociologists functioned as university lecturers on the "science of education"; but the enthusiasm for pedagogy, which had arisen in the debates on educational reform after 1880, did not long survive the context of its origins. There were seven chairs of education at the Sorbonne and in provincial faculties of letters by 1892; but the number never rose as high as ten even during the interwar period, and it ultimately declined to one by 1952. Durkheim's whole academic strategy, moreover, was in some ways more ambitious than practical. The sociology he developed was a subfield within philosophy, more comparable to psychology than to history or geography in that respect. Durkheim and his collaborators aimed at the apex of the academic hierarchy. They held the highest credentials within the system; they were usually *Normaliens* and *agrégés* in philosophy. But as specialized competitors within a slowly growing discipline, they acquired little secure territory of their own. In any case, sociology and the specialties taught by would-be sociologists reached only ten university-level positions in France by 1910, four of them in faculties of letters. As late as 1952, while student enrollments had doubled, there were still only eleven positions, six of them in faculties of letters.

Durkheim's own career reflected some of these difficulties. In 1886, after four years as a philosophy teacher in provincial *lycées*, he had a decisive interview with Louis Liard, the powerful Director of Higher Education. After a fellowship year in Germany, Durkheim obtained a new teaching appointment (*chargé de cours*) for Social Science and Pedagogy in the faculty of letters at Bordeaux in 1887, which in 1896 became the first full professorship of Social Science (no longer "and Pedagogy") within the French university system. While at Bordeaux, Durkheim published three major works in five years: *The Division of Labor in Society* (1893), *The Rules of Sociological Method* (1895), and *Suicide* (1897). He also became Secretary of the local branch of the Dreyfusard Ligue des Droits de l'Homme. The year 1898 saw the first appearance of the journal *L'Année sociologique*, around which Durkheim ultimately gathered about a dozen close collaborators, the Durkheimian school of sociology.[71] In 1902, Durkheim was called to the Sorbonne as *chargé de cours* in the Science of Education. He was promoted to full professor in 1906, but his position was not renamed "for Science of Education *and Sociology*" until 1913, four years before his death. At the Sorbonne in 1902–03, he began to offer a regular course of lectures in the science of education, with the emphasis upon "moral education" in the primary schools. Two years later, he launched a course on the history of French secondary schooling that was made a requirement for the secondary teaching *agrégation*, to Agathon's distress, in 1906. His last major work, *The Elementary Forms of the Religious Life*, appeared in 1912.

Victor Karady has rightly described the institutional history of Durkheimian sociology within the French academic system as a "near-failure"; but there can be no question of its success as a scholarly and intellectual enterprise.[72] While Durkheim's early works met with a good deal of skepticism, his scientific reputation was largely secure by the time he arrived at the Sorbonne. While establishing the theoretical primacy of sociology among the social sciences, he also managed thoroughly to identify sociology with his own work, at least in France.[73] His influence and that of his school extended well beyond his own discipline, to affect such neighboring fields as history and anthropology. As Agathon realized, he was also a major political force, a leader of the New Sorbonne, a particularly effective Dreyfusard, and one of the foremost academic defenders of the Radical Republic. A prominent champion of educational reform, he also provided a scientific foundation for the solidarist consensus. His telling critique of *laisser faire* economic doctrines and of their theoretical foundations in methodological individualism helped to legitimate progressive middle-class social policies. While he did not believe in class war or in revolution, he was in sympathy with the reformist socialism of Jaurès; several of his younger collaborators contributed to *L'Humanite* and actively supported socialist causes.[74]

There can be no question here of surveying all of Durkheim's work.[75] Instead, I want to discuss his views on the issues raised by the reforms in French secondary and higher education, including his vision of science and of its role in society. By way of an introduction to these topics, however, I must briefly consider his proposals for secular "moral education" in the primary schools, which also reflected his general theory of education.[76] In this as in other realms, Durkheim opposed individualist doctrines. He particularly disliked utilitarian arguments; but he also rejected Kant's conception of education as the full and harmonious development of the individual, the point of departure for the German theory of *Bildung*. According to Durkheim, Kant's conception cannot be fully realized; for it conflicts with another important rule of human conduct, which enjoins individuals to devote themselves to specialized and limited tasks. Modern society simply cannot survive without the division of labor, and it therefore imposes a degree of specialization upon its members. More generally, the goals of education must be adjusted to the needs of society. We know that educational arrangements have changed over time and from place to place; we can observe how closely they have been connected with other salient characteristics of the societies in which they have functioned. This tells us that we cannot simply postulate a single, timeless, and individual objective of education, without regard for the social circumstances. Nor can we arrive at an understanding of education on the basis of introspection, abstract reflection, or a priori principle. Rather, we must study education as we must study all other aspects of social life; objectively, in its actual historical evolution. Moreover, we must recognize the autonomous (*sui generis*) character of social facts. Resisting the temptation of methodological individualism, we must realize that statements about society are not simply summative propositions about individuals.[77]

In the spirit of social realism that characterized the French educational reformists, Durkheim himself defined education as the socialization of the immature generations by the mature ones. The process entails the transmission of the knowledge and of the entire "civilization" accumulated by a society. The group's future members must be able to continue the work of their predecessors. In a sense, they must begin by *reproducing* the social world into which they were born, including its means of subsistence. Thus the training of the young must anticipate the actually existing occupational differentiation. At the same time, the coming generations must share a number of sentiments and practices. A degree of commonality, especially in the realm of morality, must accompany the diversity in the roles to be filled. In primitive societies, the shaping of the young may proceed informally and almost unconsciously, because the heritage itself is simple and homogeneous. Modern society, however, must transmit a large body of knowledge and a civilization that is both rich and diverse. That is why much of the task of socialization has gradually been assigned to specialized educational institutions. The complexity of modern society, *not only* its degree of economic development, demands complexity in the educational system as well.

The work of transmission has become ever more laborious and differentiated, and it ought to be done more consciously and rationally as well.[78]

Durkheim knew that society's shaping of individuals to suit its needs might be perceived as a species of "tyranny." But he argued that in the unsocialized young, society confronts an "almost blank slate." In fashioning these raw beings to its own specifications, it confers a great boon upon them. It passes on to them the accumulated experience of their ancestors. It gives them not only their language, their science, and their forms of thought, their skilled practices and techniques, but also their moral traditions and ethical ideals. In making these gifts their own, the young also internalize an image of society. But this social part of themselves encompasses what is best within them and makes them truly human.[79] In Durkheim's model of socialization, children, like savages, have virtually no distinctive traits of their own. There are hereditary differences among the young, of course; but "fortunately," they are "vague and general." Children are emotionally inconstant; but they are also traditionalists, creatures of custom and habit. Their attention wanders, and they have no stable will of their own; they are therefore highly suggestible. Durkheim detected a certain capacity for empathy in their tendency to imitate adult gestures, and he also noted a traditionalist attachment to familiar objects, persons, and environments. These propensities suggested a potential for "altruism," for attachments outside the self. Yet Durkheim's emphasis was mainly and sometimes exclusively upon the inborn "egoism" of infants, which is rooted in their preoccupation with their own organic states. Durkheim concluded that society cannot simply develop what is naturally given within the child; it must create a "new" social and moral being.[80]

Here, in his account of the child as a savage, Durkheim left room not only for the contributions of experimental psychologists, but also for a type of speculative psychology that fit poorly into his overall theory. He portrayed school classes as potential "crowds" or "mobs," subject to irrational suggestion, imitation and "contagion." In his work on *Suicide*, he challenged the indiscriminate use of "imitation" as an explanation for divergent forms of social interaction. But he also painted a lurid portrait of the asocial individual as a creature of "infinite appetite," always ready to break through the bounds of discipline and civilized restraint. Where society imposes no limits upon this striving beyond all attainable goals, he argued, the "malady of infinite aspiration" will lead to pessimism and to "anomic" suicide. This theory of "infinite appetite" reappeared in his lectures on "moral education." Though he never specified exactly where these appetites came from, he apparently ascribed them to the child as a pre-social individual.[81]

In any case, Durkheim stressed the need for restraints not only upon the natural egoism of children, but also upon their appetites, which will otherwise lead them to exhaustion and despair. Like human beings generally, the young need limiting rules that are imperative, in that they must be followed from a pure sense of duty, not in the light of their possibly imponderable consequences, whether for the individual or for others. Such rules must issue from an authority that is outside and above the child, from a sacred realm that can only be society itself. This circumstance alone shows that society cannot be conceived as a sum of individuals; for obligations to other individuals could never take on the absolute authority of social imperatives. Thus one of the two aspects of morality that the primary teacher must pass on to pupils is simply *discipline*, the capacity to observe social rules from a non-expedient sense of duty. Discipline introduces an element of regularity into personal lives, without which modern social organization could not function. It entails the ability to predict one's future actions; it thus also means self-mastery, which is a precondition of "freedom" in the Kantian sense of autonomy.[82]

In developing these arguments, Durkheim did not mean to advocate recourse to rigorous sanctions in the schools, not to mention physical punishment. The "orgy of violence" that accompanied the schooling of the young at least from the Middle Ages on, he observed, was not characteristic of primitive societies. It can be historically traced to the strain initially occasioned by the need to transmit a complex civilization, to the differences of education that long separated teachers from their charges, and to the fact that the early schools were hidden from public view. In modern times, corporal punishment would itself be immoral, since it would offend the collective commitment to the dignity of the human person. Moreover, while punishment is not designed simply to discourage future offenses, as the utilitarians claimed, it should not be conceived as pure retribution either. Its real purpose is to reconfirm the sanctity of the rule that has been violated. Teachers will most easily achieve this reconfirmation by a quiet but unmistakable demonstration of their disapproval. This must of course be grounded in their own conviction that the school's regulations are just, not excessively detailed, and legitimate as vital aspects of socialization, rather than only as means of control in the classroom. Indeed, Durkheim's whole purpose in the lectures on "moral education" was to restore the good conscience of teachers in the state primary schools. He wanted them to "radiate" a benevolent and impersonal authority as secular missionaries of society.[83]

If discipline is one of the two main elements in morality, according to Durkheim, the other is *altruism*, or attachment to social groups and collectivities. Teachers must foster it partly by encouraging their classes to develop a group life of their own, a sense of tradition and of collective responsibility. Pupils can begin to appreciate the joys of sociability only by experiencing them. This is particularly urgent in France, where a rampant individualism has virtually extinguished the potential for mutuality. According to Durkheim, the history of modern France has been characterized by the gradual elimination of all "intermediate" forms of association, and by the emergence of a direct confrontation between the centralized state and the family unit. In reality, there is a whole hierarchy of increasingly general groupings to which the individual can feel attached. Loyalty to subordinate groups does not preclude commitment to more comprehensive collectivities, all the way up to the level of humanity. Nevertheless, the most important attachment for the modern individual is to the nation, and it is mainly this commitment the schools must encourage. Local and regional identifications are fading, and humanity is not, or not yet, an organized society. On the other hand, the modern nation has increasingly been identified with the broadest impersonal ideals, with justice and a universalist respect for the dignity of the individual. Especially in France, the religion of the fatherland is a religion of humanity as well. Other nations, of course, have their own distinctive visions of humanity.[84]

Durkheim repeatedly suggested that sociology could solve major problems in systematic philosophy. In *The Elementary Forms of the Religious Life*, he rounded out this part of his argument by pointing to the ancient and collective origins of the logical forms of thought, including the category of causality. While the radical empiricists have to suppress the transcendental character of the categories, he argued, the Kantians cannot empirically account for it. Thus only sociology can escape a classic dilemma. In his lectures on "moral education," he noted a perennial conflict in ethics between theories based upon the concept of duty and philosophies committed to the pursuit of the good. Sociology can solve this riddle by showing that morality has to encompass both discipline and altruism. In the same way, Durkheim detected a difficulty in Kant's view of rational autonomy. The problem is that Kantian autonomy can be attained only when the imperfections of human nature have been so thoroughly conquered that the restraints of positive law can be discarded. In contrast to this counsel of perfection, Durkheim argued, sociology can show that inherited social rules are gradually transformed by their rational comprehension, even while they retain their imperative character as curbs upon human nature. The vision of an advance toward a collective rational autonomy was crucial to his whole project. Thus he insisted that rationalism really adds a new dimension to our moral traditions. As we become more sensitive to the universalist principles of reason, we begin to see injustice as "unreasonable and absurd," and we acquire a new respect for the sanctity of the individual. The morality of the future is therefore not just the old morality without its religious foundations; it is the incipient rule of reason and a step toward human autonomy.[85]

Durkheim considered the French especially receptive to ethical universalism, and of course he approved of a commitment that ultimately asserted itself in the Dreyfus Affair. On the other hand, he saw French weaknesses not only in an exaggerated individualism, but also in an oversimplified Cartesian rationalism. Always ready to dissolve complex ideas into simple ones, he believed, the French were fatally inclined toward such atomistic theories as methodological individualism. The only way to correct this fault was to confront French youth with the complexities of empirical reality, including social reality. Thus, while Durkheim really said little about the subjects taught in the primary schools, he strongly recommended the natural sciences, as against literature on the one hand, and mathematics on the other. He also assigned an important role to history as a surrogate for sociology. And of course he urged that history be conceived, not as a narrative of great individuals and their deeds, but as a field in which "collective and anonymous" forces set the long-term trends in the evolution of societies.[86]

Though relatively neglected in Durkheim's discussion of primary schooling, curricular issues moved to center stage in his analysis of the secondary system. His whole approach changed as he shifted his attention from socialization to the transmission of knowledge and the schooling of the intellect. His systematic restatement of the reformist position on the secondary curriculum can be found primarily in the course of lectures he gave at the Sorbonne beginning in 1904-5 on the history of (secondary) education in France. We shall consider his methodological introduction and his concluding chapters, which trace the development of "pedagogy" from the early modern period to his own day.[87] He opened his argument by stipulating that he would approach the issues in contemporary secondary schooling from a historical perspective, using the "scientific" method of the "historical and social sciences." He saw the advantage of this method, as compared with direct reflection upon contemporary alternatives, in the analytical distance it provides. It allows us to survey the field of education like an "unknown territory." We can treat educational reform projects and pedagogical doctrines as objective "social facts," as symptoms of the occasionally conflicting social needs and aspirations that gave rise to them. Some of the underlying forces we can thus identify are still acting upon us, Durkheim continued; but they would elude introspection, since their presence within us is largely "unconscious." On the other hand, we are not interested in historical "erudition" for its own sake; we need to know the past to understand the present and, above all, to choose among our options for the future. For the educational system is traversing a "crisis" in the classic Durkheimian sense of that term. While much of the heritage has been discredited, the guiding principles of a new era have not yet been clearly defined.[88]

Durkheim in fact worked with a more developed version of the historicist tactic that was typical of the reformist argument. He distinguished between institutions or practices that are "normal" for a given epoch, including the present, and others that are abnormal or even pathological. The "normal," in his scheme, is functionally and/or causally integrated into its social environment; it answers "objective needs," which also means that it is sustained by a "long chain of causes and effects." Educational practices that are not thoroughly linked to their context in this way may be accidents or outright errors; for there are "illegitimate successes" in history. Conversely, pedagogical experiments that were once rejected may today be recognized as early symptoms of a new dynamic; for history also knows "unjustified and regrettable defeats." We must not assume that everything old is outdated, or that everything new will prove fruitful; the rational presumption is in favor of what has endured. Yet there are institutions that have clearly outlived the conditions that gave rise to them, and the classical curriculum is one such institution.[89]

In tracing the history of classical humanism, Durkheim assigned an important role to Christianity, particularly to the Jesuits of the seventeenth century. The thought of the Greeks, he said, had aimed at an understanding of the world. For Christianity, however, a profound divide separated the potentially sacred realm of the human spirit from the profane world of matter. Throughout the Christian era, therefore, students were taught to see nature only through the medium of the human mind; *texts* were in effect interposed between them and the real world. Durkheim believed that this contrast between the spiritual and the temporal was still alive in the mentality of his contemporaries, causing them to despise the natural sciences. The Jesuits, he conceded, could not entirely avoid the education of secular man; their turn to classical antiquity was an unavoidable concession to their worldly clients. Yet they had no interest in Greece or Rome as living civilizations; their aim was merely to imitate the writings of the ancient authors. They accordingly extracted the classical texts from the historical world in which they originated, relocating them in a timeless realm of pure abstraction. They thus also continued a "formalist" direction in pedagogy, a neglect of "positive" knowledge, that dated back as far as the eighth century of the Christian era.[90]

The Jesuits' teaching of Latin and of grammar, according to Durkheim, greatly stimulated the development of the French language. Thus it was precisely during the seventeenth century, when the vernacular was virtually excluded from the secondary schools, that French matured as a classical language in its own right. This suggested that the study of a foreign language and the experience of translation can foster vital analytical skills and thus indirectly enhance the cogency of our own formulations. Durkheim in fact gave credit to the Jesuits for the proverbial clarity and precision of the French language. He also traced certain traits of French classical literature and of French intellectual life more generally to the way in which the classics were taught in the *collèges* of the early modern period. In French classical literature, the characters are general human types, rather than real individuals. The sentiments they express are simple, universal, and almost impersonal. Events unfold in an "ideal, abstract environment that is outside space and time," since it represents all places and times. Thus the Jesuit approach to the classics accounts for the deep-seated cosmopolitanism of the French. Unfortunately, it also engendered a certain "simplism," a tendency to deny the complexity of the real world, or to reduce it to simple components. The universal mathematics of the Cartesians is a product of French "simplism." So is the "abstract individualism" of the French *philosophes* of the eighteenth century, their "atomistic conception of society and their disregard for history." More generally, the "superb rationalism" of the French reflects a penchant for "the abstract, the general and the simple," which is too often coupled with the "illusion" that complexity is a mere appearance, rather than an irreducible attribute of reality.[91]

Durkheim thought it no accident that the rise of a new pedgogy began in the Protestant countries, particularly in the German *Realschulen* of the eighteenth century. It soon spread to all European societies, however, since economic and political change everywhere created a need for useful knowledge and for pre-professional schooling. Basic to the new educational philosophy was the direct study of *things*; the texts that had been interposed between the student and the world were now removed. The new educational ideal was encyclopedic, not only because pupils had to learn a little about all aspects of reality, but also because the encyclopedia stood for the ideal unity of science. Durkheim called the new pedagogy "realistic" (as in *Realschulen*), rather than "scientific," because it aimed less at mathematics and Cartesian rationalism than at "positive" knowledge and the empirical study of nature. In France, the encyclopedic educational program of the *philosophes* was continued in the reform projects of the Convention and in the establishment of the revolutionary "central schools." These endured for only six years. Their organization was based upon separate course sequences for each subject. They thus answered a genuine need for diversity in education, but they also eliminated the traditional age class as a focus for group loyalties. The empirical natural sciences dominated the curriculum of the central schools, but the study of man was not excluded. During the last two years of the six-year program, history was offered along with "general grammar," the then current form of logic. On the other hand, Latin was taught only in a single first-year course, just enough to provide an analytical perspective upon

French. Latin thus visibly took on the character of a "survival" (*survivance*); it was sustained only by inertia, or by an automatic respect for tradition.[92]

Turning to the practical lessons to be drawn from his history of French education, Durkheim insisted that secondary schooling had never been vocational or professional, but always theoretical and general. While specialization was necessary in higher education, the secondary curriculum had always been designed to prepare students for the universities by awakening their capacity for reflection. Durkheim considered this objective appropriate not only for future members of the liberal professions, but for the leading positions in industry and commerce as well. He thus simply shrugged off the alleged incongruity between academic secondary schooling and the "practical" needs of the economy. From his perspective, if a modern curricular emphasis was sound at all, then it suited everyone who reached the secondary level. Like other prominent reformists, he resisted the temptations of economic functionalism to make a broader case for educational modernization. He still saw an important difference between the practical emphasis of the vocational schools and the theoretical direction of the secondary curriculum; but he also remarked that the institutional barriers between the primary and secondary systems were based on little more than "prejudice."

If secondary education is a schooling of the mind, an awakening of the capacity for reflection, then are the "formalists" right after all? By no means, said Durkheim; for we can still reject their assumption that the intelligence can be schooled in a vacuum, apart from any engagement with a specific subject matter. We know that on the contrary, the forms of thought vary with the nature of their objects. This brings us back, in fact, to the underlying conflict about *what* to study: texts or "things," the human spirit or the material world? The literary education of the *honnête homme* may strike us as incomplete; but it could appear truly general as long as natural realities were excluded from consideration. Since the French Revolution, Durkheim observed, an alliance has developed in France between Catholicism and the classical curriculum. Whereas in earlier times, Christian divines occasionally warned against the pagan contents of the ancient literatures, they have now thoroughly identified the Church with classical humanism. In part, they may be reacting against the preference of the French revolutionaries for the natural sciences; for curricular questions have become political issues. At a deeper level, however, we are still dealing with the Christian divide between the spiritual realm of human consciousness and the profane world of matter. We are still trying to decide whether nature or only man is a legitimate object of investigation. Until that problem is resolved, the crisis of secondary education will continue.[93]

Durkheim's next step was both tactically sound and characteristic of him. Beneath the supernatural assumptions that we cannot accept, he argued, Christian dualism harbors a great "positive truth." An education that merely enables us to "act more effectively upon things" may enhance our prosperity; but it does not touch our inner life. Yet "human consciousness" is our primary concern, the "incomparable value to which all the rest must be related." The "proper function of education" is to "cultivate man, to develop the seeds of humanity in us." As long as the natural sciences are valued only for their utility, therefore, as long as they are conceived as "turned entirely toward the outside" and away from ourselves, they will be relegated to the "subaltern role" they actually play in the French educational system. But of course this one-sided conception of the natural sciences is itself a mere "survival." In reality, the sciences of nature and of man "imply each other" and "strive toward the same goal." We must begin to recognize the human relevance of an education in the natural sciences. After all, man is a part of the natural world; there is no religion without a cosmology, and science has deeply affected our world view. More important, "science is human reason in action"; its history is certainly far richer than any individual mind. Its procedures and ways of thought make up a real logic, including a logic of induction, that no account of human consciousness can any longer ignore. Our philosophies must do justice to the complexity of our scientific methods, which we are just beginning to apply to human affairs as well. Thus the natural sciences may *seem* at first to direct our attention outward; but they will ultimately bring us back, enriched, to the study of man.[94]

Durkheim offered a similar perspective upon the natural sciences in an 1895 article on the *agrégation* in philosophy. Here too he began by repudiating the merely "formal" training of the mind. With the collapse of Cousin's eclecticism, he argued, formalism developed as a way to evade the confrontation of contradictory doctrines in the philosophy class. Thus the discussion of the great philosophical problems and systems became a mere pretense for intellectual "gymnastics." To habituate youth to use ideas without regard for their substantive value, however, is to breed a "literary talent" of a truly "degenerate" type. Students learn that philosophical terms and propositions may be combined at will to charm almost any "taste." Candidates in the examination for the *agrégation*, Durkheim reported, display what is considered philosophical "talent" by shunning "positive knowledge" as useless baggage. The result is an "anarchic dilettantism" and a contempt for science that tends to engender "mysticism" as well.[95]

One way to find a new substantive direction in philosophy, Durkheim continued, is to give some attention to contemporary social questions, not by preaching solutions in the classroom, but by teaching students to see human institutions as objects of rigorous scientific investigation, complex objects that cannot be changed at will. Though sociology is still in its infancy, it can provide at least a few examples. At the same time, philosophers must seriously study the methods of the natural and human sciences. The best way to do this is to focus upon the real procedures of scientific experimentation and induction, not upon philosophies preoccupied with meta-scientific problems. Thus philosophy teachers are needed who actually know something about the work of the natural sciences. Candidates for philosophy degrees must be given incentives to develop a minimal competence in this area. Prior to the *agrégation*, they might be provided with a list of specific topics to pursue for a year. The questions could be taken from the fields of psychology or sociology; but they must be genuinely scientific problems; they must call for positive knowledge, and not just for dialectical tactics. In short, philosophy must be fortified by the "spirit of science." The teachers of our youth need more than "talent"; that "talent must be applied to a subject matter and shaped by a severe discipline."[96] In making these recommendations, Durkheim also rejected a certain kind of pedagory. His tone throughout suggested a *moral* objection to the display of "talent" in the examinations for the *agrégation*. One is reminded of Agathon's claim that the leaders of the New Sorbonne despised "talent" and favored mediocrity. Perhaps they felt something like Durkheim's contempt for the vacuous "gymnastics" encouraged by the formalist approach to philosophical issues. A pedagogy that utterly ignores "positive" knowledge may merely confirm the differences in language skills that students bring with them from their home environments. Worse yet, it may convey the impression that nothing new can be *taught or learned*. That, after all, is the underlying conviction of the "dilettante." Under its impact, a purely "literary talent" may indeed become "degenerate," and a kind of intellectual corruption may spread. A man of Durkheim's convictions may then be moved to call for "severe discipline" not only as a champion of science, but also as a moralist.

As we know, Durkheim's enthusiasm for the natural sciences did not prevent him from assigning a preeminent role to the study of man. Indeed, some of the most interesting conclusions he drew from his account of French secondary schooling had to do with history and with literature. The basic weakness of classical humanism, as he pointed out again, was its assumption that human nature is "always and everywhere the same." The modern "historical and social sciences" have totally undermined this view. We now know that "even the fundaments of human mentality and morality" are perpetually being transformed, and that there are as many ethical systems as there are societies. We have learned to appreciate the variety and wealth of human nature. Contemporary psychology, moreover, has taught us that there is an unconscious psychic life. Thus we have come to recognize the limits of introspection, and to understand that we must study man as an "unknown reality," objectively, as we study nature. Of course neither psychology nor sociology are advanced enough to be taught in the secondary schools. Since it is the historical diversity of humanity that must be grasped, moreover, history is the ideal teaching subject. The historical and the social sciences are very closely related to each other and will ultimately merge in any case.[97]

The way to bring history into the classroom, however, is not to offer expert lectures, and certainly not to survey the history of the world. Durkheim insisted that students must focus upon particular civilizations, and they must have access to the "documents" in which the past is most truly alive. He was thinking essentially of *literary* sources. He briefly suggested that the study of a less-advanced civilization might prove fruitful; but he particularly recommended the literatures of Greece and of Rome. These seemed to him educational mainly because they *differed* from those of modern times. Students must be taken out of their own environment (*dépayser*), he argued again; they must learn that there are "other ideas, other customs, other political constitutions . . . and other logics." He was not surprised to find himself back in the neighborhood of the old classical curriculum. Our aim, after all, is still to "awaken and develop the understanding of humanity that the humanist, to his honor, has always been concerned to cultivate." He also urged the study of French history, and he briefly referred to the perspective that the modern foreign literatures could provide. Yet he stressed the primacy of the Greek and Roman classics, even while conceding that they might be read in translation. Above all, he urged a new *approach* to the literary sources. We must discard the shallow notion of schooling the "taste" he said, along with the misguided conception of "formal gymnastics." Students must engage with the *substance* of the ideas they encounter, even while learning to understand them as elements in a *civilization* that differs from their own.[98]

In the concluding passages of his history of French secondary education, Durkheim turned to a discussion of language learning. He observed that a language subdivides and structures the texture of thought. It literally articulates what is inherently continuous, and it does so in a particular way. A language or a grammar is therefore a kind of logic. The learning of a foreign language is a fruitful schooling in the analysis and recomposition of ideas, particularly (again) if the language involved is very different from our own. The classical languages offer significant educational advantages in this respect, since they in fact diverge more sharply from the modern European languages than the latter diverge from each other. The shift away from the ancient languages in the modern curricular stream, Durkheim warned, may create a pedagogical deficit. The loss will be especially great if the modern foreign languages are taught by the "direct method," without the "transposition" of ideas in translation. Durkheim concluded by recommending a renewed emphasis upon the study of grammar and the writing of essays. While he clearly did not mean to attack the institution of the modern curriculum, his remarks can be interpreted as a qualified defense of Latin (or of Chinese). Nevertheless, in his critique of the formalist fallacy, in the clarity of his position on the natural sciences, and in his thoroughgoing historicism, he was the most cogent and systematic spokesman for French educational reformism around the turn of the century.[99]

The place of educational reform in his broader social theory is briefly indicated in his works on the division of labor and on suicide. In the "caste" regime of simpler societies, he argued, occupations were transmitted by heredity; but the "progressive decline of castes . . . is an historical law." Modern societies "normally" require a more meritocratic distribution of social functions. If "organic solidarity" is to be achieved, and if "pathological" conflicts are to be avoided, then individuals must generally reach the positions that suit their abilities; for "all external inequality compromises organic solidarity." At least in principle, therefore, the contemporary division of labor must be "spontaneous," rather than "forced."

Labor is divided spontaneously only if . . . social inequalities express natural inequalities. But for that it is necessary and sufficient that the latter be neither enhanced nor lowered by some external cause.[100]

This is the meritorcratic argument that proved so attractive to French educational reformists. Taken to its logical conclusion, as it was by Goblot and others during the interwar period, it stipulates that all social differences must be reduced to "merited" ones. At the same time, of course, it implies that the problems of social inequality can be entirely resolved by the institution of meritocracy, or that social hierarchy is acceptable *if only* it can be made to reflect "natural inequalities." Durkheim has repeatedly and rightly been accused of ignoring or trivializing the realities of class by redescribing them as functional correlates of a rational division of labor. All I want to suggest here is that his blindness to the class issue grew out of an unquestioning commitment to meritocracy that he shared with some of the leading French educational reformists of his day.

As a matter of fact, Durkheim extended meritocratic arguments to justify inequalities that were *not* or *not yet* fully "spontaneous." He noted that caste "prejudices" still ascribed "distinction" to favored individuals independently of their "merit," and that the transmission of wealth continued to be hereditary. Nevertheless, he wrote, society has begun to assist the disadvantaged, showing that it "regards as unjust any inferiority which is not personally merited." There is a mounting sentiment in favor of equality, but what it *aims at* can only be "equality in the external conditions of conflict." This faintly recalls those educational reformers who frankly acknowledged that the removal of curricular barriers in secondary schooling would not eliminate the deeper causes of social inequality, including the economic ones. As long as a society is committed *in principle* to equalizing "external conditions of conflict," Durkheim seems to hint, it may legitimately expect all its members to accept the *de facto* inequalities that remain.

In *Suicide*, while arguing the need for limits upon individual "appetities," Durkheim claimed that society must regulate access to favored occupations. He noted that contemporary society "recognizes no *other* inherent inequality than hereditary fortune and merit." He conceded that the need for restraint would be reduced if "inheritance were abolished," since the results of the competitive struggle among individuals would then appear just.

But it is only a matter of degree. One sort of heredity will always exist, that of natural talent. Intelligence, taste, scientific, artistic, literary or industrial ability, courage and manual dexterity are gifts received by each of us at birth, as the heir to wealth receives his capital or as the nobleman formerly received his title and function. A moral discipline will therefore still be required to make those less favored by nature accept the lesser advantages which they owe to the chance of birth.[101]

The passage plainly conflicts with Durkheim's claim elsewhere that children inherit only "very general faculties."[102] For he here assigns considerable weight to *biologically grounded* differences of talent. More important, he comes very close to legitimating "hereditary fortune" by associating it with other, presumably unavoidable sources of inequality in the distribution of life chances.[103] One's impression that the existing hierarchies are thus largely confirmed is heightened by Durkheim's recurrent emphasis upon the need to limit human "appetites." For the whole passage on opportunity and "merit" in *Suicide* is preceded by a vision of a society in which "each in his sphere . . . realizes the . . . limit set to his ambitions and aspires to nothing beyond. At least if he respects regulations and is docile to collective authority, that is, has a wholesome moral constitution, he feels that it is not well to ask more."[104] The best one can say about these sentences is that they are remarkably frank.

SCIENCE AS A VOCATION

In the remainder of this chapter, I want to look a little more generally at Durkheim's conception of science, especially of social science, and I want to consider a few German comparisons as well. Particularly distinctive about Durkheim, as compared with the German tradition of the *Geisteswissenschaften*, was his indifference or hostility to interpretation. He really said almost nothing about how one arrives at the meaning of a text or at an agent's reasons for performing certain actions. His silence on this subject was clearly connected with his explicit claim that the "motives" and "ideas" of individuals are often not the true causes of social phenomena.[105] Indeed, he may have held the more problematic view that conscious reasons *never* cause social actions or processes, whether at the individual or at the aggregate level. A genuine positivist and a careful reader of Comte, he presumably identified causation with regular succession, much as Simiand did. This may have deepened his distrust of social explanations based upon individual beliefs. In any case, he never rested from his lifelong battle against methodological individualism. The rational explanations of aggregate behavior offered by the classical economists not only struck him as hypothetical, precarious, or in need of correction; he saw no point in them at all.[106] He was constantly and almost obsessively on guard, of course, against attempts to reduce sociology to psychology; indeed, his tactical insistence upon the *sui generis* character of "social facts" was largely justified in the light of the nominally "psychological" counter-models proposed by Fouillée, Tarde, LeBon, and others. Even so, I do not believe that his bias against interpretation follows *necessarily* from his legitimate case against methodological individualism. I am struck, too, by the almost evasive character of his responses to the interpretive issues he actually faced. In his remarks about the educational character of foreign language study, for example, he actually referred to the "transposition" of ideas in translation. He stressed the structural differences among languages, suggesting that a certain kind of intellectual work is required to bridge them. Yet he described that work only as an analysis and recomposition of thought. He thus virtually suppressed the obvious questions about the procedures involved in producing and evaluating a translation.

In the same way, Durkheim continually emphasized the divergences among the "mentalities" and even the "logics" of different societies. He recommended the ancient literatures, even in translation, because they were distant from the students' own habits of thought. Yet in his history of secondary education, he treated the pedagogical doctrines of the past much as Seignobos treated the intellectual "facts" transmitted in documents: as if they were immediately and unproblematically intelligible, even to an observer from another civilization. In describing the rise of "realistic" pedagogy, he really gave little attention to the expressed beliefs of the authors involved. He moved very quickly to the *causes* that presumably engendered the German *Realschulen* along with French encyclopedism. Political and economic change, he claimed, gave rise to a new interest in useful knowledge and vocational preparation. This explanation seems sparse indeed, especially since Durkheim himself *rejected* the proposition that the natural sciences ought to be studied for their usefulness. Indeed, he *knew* that his arguments might appear contradictory; for he explicitly remarked that our grounds for continuing a pedagogical direction need not be identical with the causes that originally launched it.[107] But that leaves us with an awkward break between two adjacent historical epochs: one in which the new education is sustained by circumstantial causes, and one in which a sudden irruption of good reasons takes over the causal role. Here again, Durkheim's approach seems forced, to say the least.

In his study of *Suicide*, of course, Durkheim deliberately excluded the consideration of individual motives. In a way, he had no other choice. He could not trust official records on the subject, even where they were available. Indeed, he might have been more cautious than he was. As Seignobos could have told him, suicide may not always be reported *as suicide*. The propensity to lie about this matter – and the opportunity to misinform the authorities – may vary with the religious and social environment. In any case, Durkheim chose to trust the numbers, but not the reasons, that found their way into the public documents. At the same time, he turned his exclusion of motives into a methodological principle. He insisted that it was possible to classify suicides exclusively in terms of their social *causes*, and nothing in his subsequent analysis suggests that he *consciously* broke with this theoretical restriction. Yet in practice, his explanations continually ascribe motives to individual agents. Indeed, the whole treatise could be read as an example of Max Weber's interpretive sociology. Such literary figures as Lamartine's Raphael, Goethe's Werther, and Chateaubriand's René do not overtly take up their role as ideal types until Durkheim introduces the individualized forms of socially caused suicide. Still, one is left with a somewhat hazy sense of how individual and social experiences come together.[108]

Even before he turns to individualization, moreover, Durkheim enlivens his statistical analyses with vivid portraits of feeling states. Here are two passages on the causes of *anomie*.

To pursue a goal which is by definition unattainable is to condemn oneself to a state of perpetual unhappiness. Of course, many may hope contrary to all reason, and hope has its pleasures even when unreasonable ... but it cannot survive the repeated disappointments of experience indefinitely.

The man who has always pinned all his hopes on the future and lived with his eyes fixed upon it, has nothing in the past as a comfort against present afflictions, for the past was nothing to him but a series of hastily experienced stages. What blinded him to himself was his expectation always to find further on the happiness he had so far missed.[109]

While this is not truly an analysis of actions in terms of reasons, it surely ascribes sentiments and even beliefs. The passages are vivid and not implausible. They support the claim that the disorientation of expectations in commercial crises, for example, may drive some individuals to suicide. Yet Durkheim never acknowledges how much his causal classification of suicides owes to such psychological suppositions, and he never provides empirical examples other than statistics. Like his claims about the "infinite appetite" of the asocial individual, these loosely interpretive passages remain incompletely assimilated elements in his work.

Durkheim's last major book, *The Elementary Forms of the Religious Life*, is a study of the religious beliefs and rites of certain primitive tribes. Early in the first chapter, he insists that the beliefs must be described before the rites can be addressed.[110] He offers a number of causal and functional explanations, including the general argument that religious practices serve to maintain the cohesion of social groups. Yet his primary emphasis is upon "collective represen-tations," and his approach to these might be called *quasi-interpretive*. He claims that the true object of worship in the early religions is society itself. Religious artifacts and ceremonies symbolically repre-sent aspects of the social system, and this fully accounts for the attitudes displayed toward them. But of course the tribesmen do not know what they are doing. Their own accounts of their religion merely maintain a veneer of surface rationality. The analyst must penetrate to the *unconscious thoughts* that really govern practice. Once the true objects of workship are resubstituted for their symbolic surrogates, the system as a whole can be interpreted as essentially rational. The parallels to Freudian psychoanalysis are striking. In any case, Durkheim continues to hold that the *conscious* reasons of agents are rarely or never the causes of their actions.

We know that a certain bias against interpretation was character-istic not only of Durkheim, but of several reformist historians as well. One way to explain this is to say that they were all more or less consistent positivists. Along with the search for socio-historical laws in Simiand's sense, the neglect or suppression of interpretation may legitimately be identified as a hallmark of "positivism," especially if it is linked, as in Durkheim's work, with a functional or causal analysis of human affairs that *fails to include good reasons* among the possible causes of actions and beliefs. On the other hand, this would understate the differences between Seignobos and Durkheim, for example; it would also fail to explain why some opponents of Durkheimian sociology and of the New Sorbonne were not deeply affected by the positivist current. I therefore come back to the suggestion that the methodological preferences of the leading reformists were shaped directly by the education debate. The only form of interpretation that figured in that confrontation at all was the traditionalists' ahistorical reading of the classical texts. In repudiating it, the reformists moved immediately to the counter-argument that texts are symptoms of a "civilization" encompassing institutions and practices as well as beliefs. In the heat of the argument, as it were, they tended to suppress the text as an intermediary between themselves and another belief system. They forgot to ask how a text – or a practice – becomes intelligible to an outsider in the first place. They insisted in seeing *through* the text to the underlying facts and causes. They did this even if, like Seignobos, they acknowledged the role of "psychology" in history, or if, like Durkheim, they stressed the divergences between historical "mentalities" or "logics." In any case, this was one of the most striking differences between the academic cultures of France and of Germany during the decades around 1900.

A second distinctive characteristic of Durkheim's scientific perspective, as compared with the German tradition, was his consistently positive view of disciplinary specialization. The specialization of research repeatedly served him as it served his German colleague Georg Simmel, for example: as a model of the broader social division of labor. While Simmel saw both intellectual specialization and the division of labor as threats to "subjective culture," however, Durkheim took a strenuously positive view of both phenomena.[111] The main point of his first book, of course, was that the division of labor inevitably accompanies the long-term transformation of society from "mechanical" to "organic solidarity." It is an inescapable necessity; for modern societies could not survive without it. Moreover, it is desirable, or at least not simply regrettable; for it "normally" leads to new forms of social cooperation, to human diversity, and to something like rational autonomy. In any case, Durkheim believed that the modern individual has a moral obligation to contribute to the welfare of his society, and that he can do so only in a specialized capacity.

To illustrate this point, Durkheim repeatedly portrayed the pursuit of *culture générale* in a negative light. In one of his lectures on "moral education," the tone is relatively mild.

> The man who devotes himself to the cultivation of his intellect or to the refinement of his aesthetic faculties with the single aim of success or, even more simply, for the satisfaction of feeling more complete, richer in knowledge and feelings, for the solitary enjoyment of the picture he presents to himself – such a man does not invoke in us any feeling of morality.[112]

The passage allows Durkheim to distinguish between egoism and altruism. Self-cultivation for its own sake is his main example of egoism; indeed, it is the only one he develops in any detail. The context of the education debate thus helps to shape a major element in his sociology. The man who merely enriches himself in knowledge and feeling is of no use to his fellows; he is "solitary," and there is something unattractive about his narcissism. The paragraph could have been provoked by the occasional reduction of *Bildung* to a higher selfishness; but of course it was a response to the even more shadowy "survival" of *culture générale*. It thus also evoked the contrast between aesthetic "formalism" and "positive knowledge."

In Durkheim's *Division of Labor* too, disciplinary specialization serves as the defining instance of the division of labor. It is introduced, very near the beginning of the book, as an established trend.

> Not only has the scholar ceased to take up different sciences simultaneously, but he does not even cover a single science completely any more ... At the same time, the scientific function, formerly always allied with something more lucrative, like that of physician, priest, magistrate, soldier, has become more and more sufficient unto itself.[113]

Interestingly enough, Durkheim here confirms Charle's claim that the French elites became more separated from each other during the late nineteenth century, and that the academics lost the broader role they had formerly played as social and political notables.[114] Describing the division of labor as "a law of nature," Durkheim then asks whether it is "a moral rule of human conduct" as well. Consistent with his empirical approach to questions of morality, his essentially affirmative answer rests upon a description of public opinion.

Opinion is steadily inclining towards making the division of labor an imperative rule of conduct, to present it as a duty ... The time has passed when the perfect man was he who appeared interested in everything without attaching himself exclusively to anything ... finding means to unite and condense in himself all that was most exquisite in civilization. This *culture générale*, formerly lavishly praised, now appears to us as a loose and flabby discipline ... We disapprove of those men whose unique care is to organize and develop all their faculties ... as if each man were sufficient unto himself, and constituted an independent world. It seems to us that this state of detachment and indetermination has something anti-social about it. The praiseworthy man of former times is only a dilettante to us ... Briefly, in one of its aspects, the categorical imperative of the moral conscience is assuming the following form: *Make yourself usefully fulfill a determinate function.*[115]

Durkheim goes on to concede that there are some who view the division of labor with "a sort of uneasiness and hesitation"; but the concession remains nominal. In fact, the typically historicist argument against self-cultivation has been thoroughly transformed into a "categorical imperative." The opposition to *culture générale*, which negatively and almost single-handedly defines the division of labor as a whole, has become sharply critical in tone. The "exquisite" self-enhancement of the former generalist has become "flabby" and undisciplined, and his "detachment" can be dismissed as "anti-social." One is reminded of Durkheim's angry portait of the miseducated philosophy candidate, who has "talent" but is fundamentally indifferent to substantive issues, so that he evades the "severe discipline" of "positive knowledge."

In the conclusion of his *Division of Labor*, Durkheim comes back once more to our "duty" to "concentrate and specialize" our activity, rather than "trying to make ourselves a sort of creative masterpiece ... Public sentiment," he claims again, "reproves an ever more pronounced tendency on the part of dilettantes ... to be taken up with an exclusively general culture." Commenting upon the fear that the division of labor may "bring on a diminution of individual personality," he wonders "why it would be more in keeping with the logic of human nature to develop superficially rather than profoundly." He insists that specialization actually "develops" the individual. It makes him "something more than a simple incarnation of the generic type of his race and his group," so that he becomes an "autonomous source of action."[116]

So certain was Durkheim of his position on disciplinary specialization that he resolutely criticized Comte's divergent view of the matter. As Durkheim explained, Comte saw a need for experts in intellectual "synthesis." A few widely learned scholars and scientists, Comte thought, should combine the findings of the specialists into a "small number of common principles." Durkheim disagreed; for he suspected that such "grand syntheses" would be "premature generalizations." Out of touch with the actual practice of research, he argued, the unifiers would miss the real "spirit" of science, which lies in the conflict among competing hypotheses, not in a few established conclusions.

It is not, then, by this means that we shall ever be able to take the positive sciences out of their isolation. There is too great a chasm between detailed researches which are their backbone and such syntheses... [Thus] if particular sciences can take cognizance of their mutual dependence only through a philosophy which embraces all of them, the sentiment of unity [among them] will always be too vague to be efficacious.

Durkheim even believed that the role of philosophy as the "collective conscience of science" would shrink with the advance of specialization.[117]

The natural sciences, Durkheim continued, are not really strangers to each other. It is the moral and social sciences that subsist in a truly anarchic state, because they have only recently become positive sciences. Within these younger disciplines, investigations do indeed proceed as if they dealt with different worlds, and yet "they penetrate one another from all sides." For the moment, the scholars working on these subjects are scattered over a wide area, which is why they have not yet been able to formulate the terms of their interaction.

But solely because they will push their researches farther from their points of departure, they will necessarily end by reaching and... becoming conscious of their solidarity. The unity of science will thus form of itself, not through the abstract unity of a formula... but through the living unity of an organic whole. For science to be unitary, it is not necessary for it to be contained within... one and the same consciousness – an impossible feat anyhow – but it is sufficient that those who cultivate it feel that they are collaborating in the same work.

Thus it is with disciplinary specialization as it is with the division of labor more generally: given a dense enough network of interactions, the terms of cooperation and "organic solidarity" will "normally" emerge of their own accord. True, Durkheim was always ready to help nature along by regrouping the work of the other human sciences under the broad banner of sociology. Working with the remarkable "team" of *L'année sociologique*, which reviewed new work across the whole spectrum of the moral and social sciences, he actually practiced some of the synthesis he did not preach.[118]

In Germany, as we have noted, disciplinary specialization had few defenders, most of them modernists. During the 1920s, in fact, the general revulsion against the subdivision of intellectual work gave rise to a widespread demand for "synthesis" that ultimately encouraged subjectivist perspectives in the *Geisteswissenschaften* as well. Even before 1920, in his famous lecture on *"Wissenschaft* as a Vocation," Max Weber warned against a mounting enthusiasm for intuition and "vital experience" (*Erleben*). He insisted not only upon rigorous methods and scholarly objectivity, but also upon the inescapable advance of specialization.[119] In important respects, therefore, he took a position very close to that of Durkheim. Yet there was a great difference between the two men. Weber saw specialization as a tragic necessity; he vividly described the tensions between the emotional needs of the individual and the requirements of scientific progress. His fundamental pessimism contrasts sharply with Durkheim's confidence that the unity of science will assert itself in the long run, and that scholars will be able to "*feel* that they are collaborating in the same work." We are really talking about contrasting experiences of alienation in scientific research: one in which the impoverishment of the individual is heroically accepted, and one in which the participant in a common enterprise is compensated by an awareness of the collective purpose. In any case, we are surely dealing with experiences and expectations, rather than only with theories and predictions. How scholars and scientists feel about their work, it seems to me, will depend in part upon how they imagine its impact upon the wider society. But if this is true, we cannot avoid looking into the experiential *grounds* of Weber's pessimism and, more particularly, of Durkheim's optimism.

I have suggested that German academic culture during the decades around 1900 was characterized by an experience of decline. From the hopeful alliance between the universities and the reforming state around 1800, the trajectory led downward to a widespread sense of impotence in the face of "mass civilization." A particularly ambitious vision of *Wissenschaft* as a spiritual agent proved hard to transform into a more realistic sense of the connection between learning and social practice, especially since the orthodox majority of German academics could find no positive relationship to a vastly enlarged field of public opinion. Max Weber tried to lead the way toward a modest but viable view of the scholar as a technical adviser to the responsible party politician. His project required a distinction between socio-political means and ultimate ends. It also called for a certain resignation; for it left the selection of ends to the interest politics of the political parties. But most German academics, especially under the Weimar Republic, felt unable to accept the implied demotion from sage to technician. While the modernists actually proposed moderate *institutional* reforms, the academic opponents of the Republic preached an "intellectual and spiritual revolution" against the democratic status quo. They seemed to believe (1) that the critical thrust of such *intellectual* forces as "positivism" and "materialism" had helped to undermine the nation's *social unity*, along with its cultural traditions, and (2) that a "revival of idealism" or a similar *intellectual* change could yet restore the world they had lost. The leading modernists earnestly tried to explain that these assumptions were fallacious, and that a partial accommodation to modernity could not be avoided. Yet they were unable to assert themselves against the "merciless moralizing" that tempted so many of their colleagues.[120]

The contrast with the French educational reformists, and particularly with Durkheim, could not be more complete. The leading representatives of the New Sorbonne knew that they stood at the opening of a new era in French intellectual life. They were well aware of their contribution to an educational reform program that had profound social and political implications as well. Valued political allies of the Radical Republic, they also saw themselves, and rightly, as effective leaders of public opinion. Durkheim in particular had great faith in the practical significance of sociological knowledge. He occasionally asserted that the scholar must "know for the sake of knowing, without concerning himself with the practical consequences." But more often, he took the opposite position. Like every "positive science," he wrote, sociology seeks to explain present realities and thus to guide our "ideas and acts."[121]

In *The Rules of Sociological Method*, Durkheim responds to a challenge that has a distinctly neo-Kantian ring to it, and that Max Weber certainly would have understood.

According to a theory whose partisans belong to the most diverse schools, science can teach us nothing about what we ought to desire. It is concerned, they say, only with facts...; it observes and explains but does not judge them... It can indeed tell us how given causes produce their effects, but not what ends should be pursued... To this we can reply that by revealing the causes of phenomena, science furnishes the means of producing them. Every means is from another point of view an end... There are always several routes that lead to a given goal; a choice must therefore be made between them. If science cannot indicate the best goal to us, how can it inform us about the best means to reach it?... If science cannot guide us in the determination of ultimate ends, it is equally powerless in the case of those secondary and subordinate ends called "means."

To supplement this begging of the question, Durkheim accuses his critics of "mysticism"; but he does have another answer as well.

Briefly, for societies as for individuals, health is good and desirable; disease, on the contrary, is bad and to be avoided. If, then, we can find an objective criterion, inherent in the facts themselves, which enables us to distinguish scientifically between health and morbidity in the various orders of social phenomena, science will be in a position to throw light on practical problems and still remain faithful to its own method.[122]

The reference is to the distinction between the "normal" and the "pathological," which Durkheim first introduced in *The Division of Labor*. In *The Rules of Sociological Method*, he developed his historicist case more fully. He identified the normal with the widespread and frequent; but he also continued to stress its causal and functional relationships to other, more basic social conditions and processes. The pathological, as he defined it, is typically a consequence of incomplete adjustment to a changing environment. The sociologist, he liked to say, is fundamentally "conservative"; for he knows that social arrangements cannot be altered at will. There is at least an initial presumption in favor of any institution that has endured, since it is probably sustained by long-term causes and social needs. In any case, social scientists will not be tempted to resort to mere "verbal influence" and "exhortation"; for they have outgrown the primitive faith in the magical power of words. They will not preach a new religion. On the other hand, as Durkheim explained most fully in *The Elementary Forms of the Religious Life*, collective *representations and ideals* are integral parts of the social system. The sociologist is therefore in a position to identify the normative commitments that correspond to a given state of society, even if his contemporaries are not yet fully aware of them. That is why, in Durkheim's analytical framework, social scientists need not confine themselves to giving technical advice to politicians. They can tell their audiences, for example, that *culture générale* is now discredited – and why, or what the mounting belief in "equality" truly signifies. They can locate, articulate, and clarify appropriate social ideals and thus in effect contribute very broadly to the enlightenment and orientation of public opinion.[123]

In a 1904 essay on "The Intellectual Elite and Democracy," Durkheim again anticipated Charle's view that there was a change in the role of French academics during the late nineteenth century.[124] In the past, Durkheim observed, the intellectual could "become a deputy or senator without ceasing . . . to be a writer or scholar"; but this is no longer the case. "The lecturer of today must not be suspected of being the candidate of tomorrow."

What I mean is that above all our action must be exerted through books, seminars and popular education. Above all, we must be *advisers, educators*. It is our function to help our contemporaries know themselves in their ideas and in their feelings, far more than to govern them . . . It has . . . been said that the mob was not made to understand the intellectuals, and . . . democracy and its so-called dull-witted spirit have been blamed for the sort of political indifference scholars and artists have evinced during the first twenty years of our Third Republic. But this indifference was ended as soon as a great moral and social problem was posed before the country.[125]

We have thus come back to the Dreyfus Affair, and to a particular view of it. Julien Benda and others saw the Dreyfusard intellectuals as "clerics" asserting eternal verities.[126] In Durkheim's carefully considered tactical scheme, however, the intellectuals neither preached nor "governed"; they were neither paternal sages nor technical advisers to politicians. They simply "helped [their] contemporaries to know themselves in their ideas and in their feelings." It was in the name of this tactic – and of its success – that Durkheim repudiated an arrogant and ultimately debilitating vision of "the mob."

Another important element in what should really be called Durkheim's historicists strategy was a highly specific view of the relationship between tradition and reason. He claimed essentially that (1) once eroded, tradition cannot be artificially restored, (2) reason is not responsible for the decline of tradition, and (3) reason can largely replace lost traditions. In Germany, to simplify a little, the modernists consistently asserted the first of these propositions; the orthodox sometimes flatly contradicted the second, and almost no one really believed the third. Nonetheless, all three of these theses can easily be found in Durkheim's major works. In *The Division of Labor*, for example, Durkheim observes that "our faith has been troubled; tradition has lost its sway." But "the remedy for the evil is not to seek to resuscitate traditions and practices which, no longer responding to present conditions of society, can only live an artificial, false existence." This is the first of the three theses, and the second shortly follows.

Our illness is not ... of an intellectual sort ... Our anxiety does not arise because the criticism of scholars has broken down the traditional explanation we use to give to our duties; consequently, it is not a new philosophical system which will relieve the situation.[127]

The implication is not only that the roots of our difficulties lie very deep, but also that ideas and doctrines are too weak to dislodge traditions, unless the latter have already been weakened at a more practical level.

In *Suicide*, these issues become particularly pressing, because Durkheim detects a triple covariation between high suicide rates, the presence of Protestantism, and high levels of popular education. Now covariations of this sort are notoriously mute about the direction of the causal connections they may reflect. Though Durkheim generally ignored this difficulty, he was clearly anxious to forestall unsound conclusions in this instance. He therefore intervened vigorously, *as an educator*, and with the emphasis of repetition. Protestant or not, he lectured, men do not need or seek freedom of inquiry until their inherited beliefs have partly or wholly lost their authority. Reflection only then "intervenes to fill the gap that has appeared, but which it has not created." Free inquiry "multiplies schisms," but it already "presupposes them." Enlightenment is sought only when customary practices "no longer correspond to new necessities," and philosophy appears only when "religion has lost its sway."

Knowledge is not sought as a means to destroy accepted opinions but because their destruction has commenced ... Faith is not uprooted by dialectic proof; it must already be deeply shaken by other causes to be unable to withstand the shock of argument. Far from knowledge being the source of the evil, it is its remedy, the only remedy we have. Once established beliefs have been carried away by the current of affairs, they cannot be artificially reestablished; only reflection can guide us in life after this. Once the social instinct is blunted, intelligence is the only guide left us and we have to reconstruct a conscience by its means ... Let those who view anxiously and sadly the ruins of ancient beliefs, who feel all the difficulty of these critical times, not ascribe to science an evil it has not caused but rather which it tries to cure![128]

In the later portions of this passage, Durkheim in fact moves on to his third thesis, to the effect that science can cure an "evil it has not caused ... "Reflection [can] guide us, he believes, not by "artificially reestablishing" lost beliefs, but by helping us to adjust our institutions and practices to new "necessities." Thus sociology may make us recognize that we must reinstitute modern versions of the ancient occupational "corporations" to resolve the anarchy of production and of class conflict. Or it may teach us that we must move toward more meritocratic arrangements in our educational system. We may learn that we must give more attention to "the spirit of discipline" in our lower schools, and that we must provide our youth with classroom experiences of cooperation as well. While sociology or "the science of opinion" cannot simply "make opinions," moreover, it can "observe them and make them more conscious of themselves."[129] It may encourage us to recognize and to act upon ideals that we have only just begun to be aware of. Perhaps that is how we can "reconstruct our conscience" by means of "intelligence."

Yet Durkheim also meant something else. Especially in his lectures on "moral education," he projected a gradual and collective movement toward "autonomy." In the natural sciences, he suggested, we internalize the laws of nature in such a way that we can reproduce the universe in thought.

We liberate ourselves through understanding; there is no other means of liberation. Science is the wellspring of our autonomy.

Extending this image to the social sciences, Durkheim did *not* evoke the manipulation of "the masses" that appealed to certain "crowd psychologists." Instead, he wrote about "our" insight into social needs.

Now we are able to check on the extent to which the moral order is founded in the nature ... of society – which is to say to what extent it is what it ought to be. In the degree that we see it as such, we can freely conform to it.

The word "conform" is rather obtrusive, as is the implied permanence of "the social order." One misses the transformative potential contained in the concept of *Bildung*. But my object here is only to show that Durkheim really believed in the replacement of tradition by reason. As students move upward from the primary schools, he thought, they will examine the moral rules and commitments they have been taught. And unless we are mistaken, they will freely give their assent, at least to begin with. In all likelihood, they will then continue the reinterpretation of their heritage. Rationality may further enhance their sense that "injustice is absurd." At least in principle, therefore, Durkheim's third thesis does not forbid new social definitions of humanity. It merely asserts that as we learn to understand our moral rules, these *"do not on that account lose their imperative character"* (my emphasis).[130] If they did, we might have grounds to fear the advance of reason. Since they do not, we can safely commit ourselves to the clarification of tradition.

Conclusion: education as interpretation

Instead of trying to summarize the various causal arguments that have been developed, or to outline the further evolution of the French intellectual field since the days of the New Sorbonne, I propose to review the theories we have encountered in which advanced education is linked to the interpretation of texts. In the European tradition, this vision of learning originated in classical humanism, but it ultimately broke through the classical framework. The originally narrow and well-defined canon of great texts has been progressively enlarged, and of course the natural sciences have been added to the curriculum. We now know that our students must learn a great deal more about the natural sciences than they do at present, and this not primarily because the sciences are "practical," or because the economic functionalists have finally made their case. Rather, following Durkheim and Jaurès, we have come to recognize the natural sciences as important exemplars of our cognitive capacity and as vital elements in our culture. We know that we could not understand either our world or ourselves without them.

Nevertheless, much of our advanced education continues to rotate around the interpretation of texts, and this is as it should be. For the reading of texts is a paradigm both for our understanding of other human beings and for the self-knowledge that typically results from our interpretive efforts. In commenting upon the several models of textual interpretation we have been examining, I do not expect to arrive at a fully articulated theory of my own. But I may be able to suggest at least some of what an adequate model would have to encompass, along with some of what it should probably avoid.

The German concept of *Bildung* in its most coherent form points to an interpretive *interaction* between a reader and a text in the process of self-cultivation. The learner is depicted imagining *possible* readings, which are then tested against the text to see whether they "make sense" of what would otherwise seem obscure. In any case, the interpreter brings something of his own to the act of reading; his standpoint is clearly distinguished from that of the author or text. This separation between the reader and the text is a prerequisite for any viable conception of interpretation. As we have seen, the most thoroughly fallacious approaches to the reading of texts tend simply to ignore one of the two basic elements in the interpretive interaction, suppressing the distance between them. The French classicists did this partly by assuming that human nature remains essentially unchanged over time, and partly by equating modern France with classical Rome. The French reformist historians reacted by emphasizing the historical difference between the civilization of the modern reader and that of classical antiquity. This was the whole thrust of their historicism, and it was certainly sound as far as it went. On the other hand, Lavisse and Seignobos really ignored the difficulties involved in the reading of particular documents. For Seignobos, the beliefs expressed in texts, as distinct from the "facts" they alleged, were immediately accessible, so that the problem of interpretation seemed not to arise. Durkheim was aware of the "transposition" of ideas in translation; but his approach to the pedagogical treatises of the past implied that their manifest contents were unproblematically available, and that they were interesting primarily as symptoms of functional disequilibria. At some level, therefore, French reformist social science bracketed the hermeneutic distance between particular readers and particular texts. One could say that it suppressed the distinctiveness of the *text*, partly by submerging it in its "civilization," and partly by implicitly attributing to it the standpoint of the present-day reader. This approach, as I have suggested, may legitimately be called "positivist."

The most damaging way to eliminate the hermeneutic distance, however, is to suppress the independent standpoint of the *interpreter*. This tended to happen in the subjectivist variant of the German humanistic and historical tradition, in which readers were pictured as empathetically identifying with the authors and/or reproducing the experiences expressed in the texts. The model had its ideological uses, which may explain why it survived so long. For the readers' self-abandonment helped them to absorb the spiritual values embodied in the great literary sources. On the other hand, the identificationist fallacy almost literally made a mystery of the historians' "genius" for "putting themselves in the place of" the persons they studied. Reinforced by an obsession with the "uniqueness" of the objects investigated in the human sciences, the fallacy also gave rise to the bewilderments of *Historismus*.

Against the "positivism" of Seignobos as well as against the identificationist strand in the German tradition, we must insist that interpretation is a complex *empirical and rational* enterprise analogous to translation, and that the distinctiveness of the elements involved in it must not be obscured. Along with the text and the standpoint of the reader, these elements encompass at least the emerging interpretation or "translation", and the topic or subject matter addressed. As I suggested in the Introduction, the interpretation aimed at should, as far as possible, be internally consistent and rational in the light of the evidence available about the subject at issue. Proposed equivalents for particular sub-units within the original text should be selected so as to maximize the coherence of the whole translation in relation to the topic. The standpoint of the interpreter is crucial; for it supplies the standards of evidence and of rationality involved. Of course the original may be guided by assumptions not shared by the reader; or it may be partly incoherent, or express beliefs that are irrational, false, or neither true nor false. But the interpreter should not attribute more such imperfections to the text than necessary, and the imperfections should be as mild and explicable as possible. The issue of explicability arises where the reader is forced to account for more or less gratuitous assumptions or habits of thought, empirical misinformation or logical inconsistencies, that apparently cannot be purged from the text by more adequate readings. At that point and no sooner, the interpreter should explain such deviations from rationality by tracing them to causally relevant aspects of the environment in which the text originated.

Of course this brief sketch of interpretation upon the rationality model is ideal typical only; it does not adequately represent the full complexity of the reasoning that leads to a particular reading. Indeed, the idea of a simple optimal interpretation is misleading; for there are surely several good readings of a given text. On the other hand, some interpretations are just as surely better than others, and the rationality model helps to identify the grounds upon which we discriminate among them. In the same way, we should expect texts to be occasionally but not infinitely self-contradictory. I write this in response to a critical objection by Martin Jay. For, citing deconstructionist doctrines, Jay has emphasized "the multiple, elusive, sometimes contradictory ways in which texts both signify and confound signification, solicit paraphrastic synopsis, and thwart it, 'say' one thing and 'mean' possibly many others."[1] He rightly suspects that my conception of interpretation conflicts with his vision of multiple readings. But I am not at all sure that the fault lies with the rationality model, or with my account of it. Instead, I wonder how the notion of "many other meanings" can be reconciled with *any* systematic account of interpretation as an empirical and rational enterprise. If no limits at all can be placed upon the inventiveness of the interpreter, then there is no way to evaluate particular readings. Interpretation then becomes a form of free play that need not and cannot be taught. But if that outcome is unacceptable to Jay, as it is to me, then he must offer an alternate account of how we discriminate among a theoretically infinite number of possible readings.

In my view, our freedom to interpret is limited not only by the methodological constraints of the rationality model, but also by the need to locate texts in their intellectual fields. As I have tried to show in the Introduction, following Bourdieu, the intellectual field in turn is grounded in the cultural preconscious, in the doxa perpetuated by the established institutions, practices, and social relations. The historian, I have argued, must move outward by steps from interpretation on the rationality model to the traditional and ideological explication of beliefs. I have recommended Max Weber's crucial claim that the rational interpretation of actions and beliefs is a form of singular causal explanation, in which good reasons function as causes. I have sought to convince my readers, finally, that the methodologically and morally significant divide between good reasons and other causes of actions and beliefs is by no means absolute in our analytical practice. Reasons are often combined with other causes of belief. More important, there are cases in which we must ask whether a sequence of actions can be more consistently explained in terms of reasons or of other causes, and we cannot do this without treating reasons as *possible* causes.

I recall these considerations because they help to identify the strengths and weaknesses of the French reformist approach to textual analysis. The great strength of the French reformists was their determination to integrate the texts they confronted into their respective "civilizations." Repudiating the blatantly unhistorical readings of their classicist colleagues, they insisted that the written sources of the past are elements in socio-historical totalities that encompass institutions and practices as well as beliefs. They in effect recovered the distance between the inherited sources and the contemporary audience; but they constructed this distance, *not* as a *hermeneutical* gap between a reader and a text, but as a *historical* difference between two "civilizations." Thus texts, in their scheme, may be "documents" in the sense that they report "facts"; or they may be "monuments" that represent whole ways of life. In either case, they cannot be understood in isolation from their environments. So firm was this conviction that the divide between interpretation and explanation, so prominent in the German tradition, received virtually no attention in France. The meanings expressed in the sources of the past were taken to be immediately accessible, except in so far as they formed parts of larger wholes, which in turn were conceived primarily as functional and causal structures. I find much to admire in this form of historicism, including its robust causalism. I frankly believe that intellectual history would lose its vitality and coherence if it were totally separated from the causal analysis of real socio-cultural worlds. The main weakness of French reformist social science, apart from its naive neglect of interpretation, was that it ignored the *indirections* involved in the complex relationship between a text and its civilization. But here Bourdieu's work can serve as a corrective; for it posits the intellectual field as an irreducible intermediary between the individual work and the larger society.

A more problematic aspect of the reformists' approach to the sources has less to do with their methodological commitments than with their cognitive interests. One cannot help but notice that their attention was never directed at any text for its own sake, but always beyond it, to the historical process or the social system. Consistent with this focus, they saw no need to evaluate texts as more or less excellent or educative. The obvious contrast is with Arnold's emphasis upon "the best that has been thought," which was linked to the Utopian "pursuit of perfection." In the German conception of *Bildung*, too, the reading of the great works took its significance from the Utopian aim of self-fulfillment. At their best, and especially during the decades around 1800, German theories of education as interpretation sought to transcend the inherited social and cultural horizons. This aspiration was of great historical significance; for it encouraged critical perspectives upon present-day obstacles to human self-realization. But the Utopian thrust it embodied had no real counterpart in France after 1870. Though a powerful presence in

Rousseau's radical pedagogy, of course, it was plainly absent from the functionalist reform program of the interwar Compagnons, for example. This should not really surprise us; for a narrowing of middle-class ideologies was generally characteristic of the nineteenth century. In Germany, the Utopian implications of *Bildung* receded or became purely theoretical. In France, the realistic pursuit of "democracy" and meritocracy probably helped to displace more far-reaching ambitions, at least within the academic spectrum we have examined.

In any case, I believe that the reading of texts can and should have a transforming impact upon our whole frame of reference; to that extent I share the Utopian view of education. It seems infinitely preferable to the rising tide of functionalism that threatens to engulf us. There is some irony in the fact that we are beset precisely by the narrowest economic functionalism, which has so largely failed as a research program. We are asked to believe, at least implicitly, that there are no human possibilities beyond the existing pattern of socio-occupational roles. As we know, even Durkheim occasionally used the meritocratic ideology mainly to preach acceptance of the established social hierarchy. In the face of such limited horizons, we can only insist that education can radically transform both our understanding and our way of life. It still seems to me that Arnold has best expressed this Utopian perspective. Above all, his sturdy formulations avoid some of the problems inherent in the German ideology of *Bildung*, and a few further remarks on that subject are in order.

It seems significant, for example, that Arnold defined "culture" as the "*pursuit* of our total perfections," not as an attained state of spiritual excellence. We may not even be able to conceive perfection itself, but only to aspire beyond our present limitations. We are not to imagine ourselves elevated by our contact with the values embodied in the great texts. Arnold firmly repudiated the reduction of culture to a socially distinguishing characteristic of the highly educated. Indeed, he deliberately excluded the possibility of a purely individual self-fulfillment. What we must aim at, he wrote, is "*general* perfection, developing all parts of our society." Strictly speaking, the isolated individual is incapable of perfection. One is reminded of Durkheim's sense that social ideals, like ordinary institutions, are *collective* achievements. Durkheim in fact had little respect for *culture générale* as an individual trait, and he could only scoff at the spectacle of the self-cultivating "dilettante" as a "work of art." I find myself sharing this attitude.

The other aspect of Arnold's work that should be mentioned is his emphasis upon cognition and upon critical reflection. He recommended "getting to *know* the best that has been *thought*," which suggests that our relationship to what we read should be primarily intellectual. The great works are not icons to be worshipped, but sources of ideas and of arguments that we can learn to restate in our own terms. Our stance as readers is actively rational, not passively reverent, and our own thoughts play a role in our interaction with the texts. The practice of interpretation certainly has an effect upon us; but what Arnold has in mind is an exercise in critical analysis, not a mysterious enhancement of the self. He writes of "turning a stream of fresh and free thought upon our stock notions and habits." He thus comes close to what I have described as the clarification of tradition; but there are parallels also with Durkheim's account of the movement toward rational autonomy. For in Durkheim's view, the socialization of the younger generation only *begins* as a molding of essentially passive pupils in the light of the society's norms. At the secondary and university levels, the emphasis shifts to the active mastery of an intellectual inheritance. Examining the rational grounds for social arrangements and beliefs that were initially accepted without question, the maturing students gradually transfer their allegiance to the authority of reason and of evidence. They thus eventually become equal participants in the collective enterprise of science. Durkheim did not specifically address the role of texts in the learning process. He also understated the contradictions, dialectical tensions and heterodox reversals that are surely present in every intellectual inheritance. But this bias reflects his personal preoccupation with order, rather than the inherent logic of his theory. Even the conflict between that theory and Arnold's Utopian perspective is not as irreconcilable *in principle*, as it appears at first glance.

Much more difficult to bridge is the contrast between learning conceived as rational clarification and certain dimensions of the German tradition. I refer to the non-cognitive and purely personal objectives of education through interpretation. The interwar dictionary definition of *Bildung* I cited earlier pictures a "forming" of "the soul," the fostering of a "value-saturated personality," "richness of mind and person," "inner unity" and "firmness of character."[2] Obviously, these very high expectations cannot be fulfilled through an engagement of the intellect alone, even if that engagement is with "the best that has been thought." As we have repeatedly observed, the process of *Bildung* was thought to involve the whole person; the "inner unity" aimed at was more cognitive, and the relationship to the text entailed a "re-experiencing" that engendered the "value-saturated personality." The practice of *Wissenschaft* was widely associated with the attainment of a unified *Weltanschauung*, of personal wholeness and wisdom. Though eminently desirable in themselves, these goals placed a great burden upon teachers and students, precisely because they reached far beyond the capacity to reason, even about great texts. A recurrent theme in the German pedagogical reform literature of the decades around 1900 was the repudiation of "merely" intellectual training, which was considered lamentably insufficient almost by definition. If one adds that the self-realization intended was unique for each individual, one has certainly left the framework of rational analysis behind. The work of reason, after all, is never a purely individual enterprise. Like Max Weber, however, I believe that educators of young adults cannot and should not teach anything more than how to do that work.[3]

Throughout this book, I have expressed my conviction that the interpretation of written works is an exercise in rational analysis. I have done this mainly by insisting upon the hermeneutical and historical distance between the reader and the text. As teachers, I hold, we should encourage our students not to suppress any of the steps involved in the development of a full, rational and historical interpretation, but to be as self-conscious as possible about their inferences, as well as about the partly self-referential character of their suppositions. We should firmly oppose the temptation to attempt some sort of immediate identification with the author, which tends to express itself in an ostensibly "reproductive" paraphrasing of key passages. Young people apparently find it difficult to perceive what they read as anything but inevitable. They tend unthinkingly to assimilate the text to their own frames of reference, to cover it with what Shelley has called the "veil of the familiar."[4] Only an awareness of their own contribution to the interpretive process, developed through practice, can help them to break this veil, and thus actually to *see* the turn of an argument or the structure of an experience. That is why I am so emphatic about the need for "distance" from the text.

To appreciate this need is to contribute at least marginally to a debate that has been neglected in these pages. None of the works we have considered tell us how to locate the "great texts" we should read. Arnold's ability to identify "the best that has been thought" was largely doxic, since the canon of the classical texts was still firmly established in his time. Given our much more difficult relationship to tradition, we can help ourselves only by reflecting upon the objectives we must pursue in our reading. We clearly want works that are perceptive, penetrating and articulate about the human condition, and not only descriptive or "representative" of their socio-historical contexts. We are certainly interested in the self-knowledge and autonomy that comes from a critical understanding of our own culture. In some sense, therefore, our reading should "begin at home." Yet the range of what falls within *our* cultural home has been much enlarged in recent times, and we do not want to ignore this inescapable and potentially creative widening of our awareness. Moreover, we have a methodological and *pedagogical* interest in the distant and unfamiliar, because it will enable our readings closer to "home." This is not a direct answer to the curricular questions we face; but it may help to clarify some of the issues involved in our debates about these matters.

Another persistent concern of mine, finally, has been to ensure that interpretation be recognized as a *teachable* skill *in principle*. This determination has reinforced my distrust of the identificationist fallacy, of "re-experiencing" conceived as a subjective miracle, or as the achievement of an empathetic genius. For related reasons, I have come to dislike the unacknowledged tendency to regard the masterpieces of our literature as "elevated" and "elevating," and to ascribe to them a charismatic quality than can transfer itself to their acolytes. We do not need *that* kind of distance between the reader and the text. As it is, some of our students seem paradoxically disposed to locate the great texts in a "higher" world that is plainly closed to them, and that inspires a mixture of truculence and awe. Historians who draw an absolute line between "elite" and "popular" culture, as if there were no interactions between the two, will tend to reinforce that predisposition.

In the face of these obstacles to reading, we must convey our sense that the great authors are not spiritually removed beyond our horizons, but merely more thoughtful than most of us about our common dilemmas. We may never totally eliminate the socially classificatory effect of advanced education; but we must do what we can to reduce its symbolic force, if only to increase the likelihood of effective communication in the classroom. We must let our students know, somehow, that the realm of "culture" is neither closed nor esoteric, but accessible to anyone *in principle*. As educators, we cannot convey wisdom or "elevation"; but we can try to transmit a rational competence that is a necessary, if not a sufficient, condition of wisdom. And at a minimum, we can cure the moral idiocy that comes from never having supposed that other people too have a rational standpoint, that it may differ from ours, that it probably reflects aspects of their situation, and that it is not utterly impenetrable.

Notes

INTRODUCTION

Publishers are indicated only for books published since 1980, and places of publication are not listed separately if they occur in the publisher's name.

1. Fritz K. Ringer, *The Decline of the German Mandarins: The German Academic Community, 1890–1933* (Cambridge, Mass., 1969) is translated (with quotations in the original German) as *Die Gelehrten: Der Niedergang der deutschen Mandarine, 1890–1933* (Stuttgart: Klett-Cotta, 1983). The book has recently been reissued (with a new Introduction) by University Press of New England, but page references in these notes apply to both editions. See also Fritz K. Ringer, "Differences and Cross-National Similarities among Mandarins," *Comparative Studies in Society and History*, vol. 28 (January 1986), pp. 145–164.

2. Ringer, *Decline of the German Mandarins*, pp. 1–3, 15, 84.

3. Fritz K. Ringer, *Education and Society in Modern Europe* (Bloomington and London, 1979). See also Detlef K. Müller, Fritz Ringer and Brian Simon, eds., *The Rise of the Modern Educational System: Structural Change and Social Reproduction, 1870–1920*, (Cambridge University Press, 1987), especially pp. 1–12.

4. For what follows, see Pierre Bourdieu, "Intellectual Field and Creative Project," *Social Science Information*, vol. 8 (1969) pp. 89–119; Pierre Bourdieu, "The Genesis of the Concepts of *Habitus* and of *Field*," *Sociocriticism*, no. 2 (1985), pp. 11–24.

5. Quentin Skinner, "Social Meaning and the Explanation of Social Action," in Patrick Gardiner, ed., *The Philosophy of History* (Oxford, 1974), p. 114.

6. Ringer, *Decline of the German Mandarins*, pp. 295–301.

7. *Ibid.*, pp. 128–143, 269–295.

8. *Ibid.*, pp. 427–428; Karl Mannheim, "On the Interpretation of *Weltanschauung*," in Mannheim, *Essays on the Sociology of Knowledge*, ed. P. Kecskemeti (London, 1952), pp. 33–83.

9. Erwin Panofsky, *Gothic Architecture and Scholasticism* (New York, 1967).

10. Bourdieu, "Intellectual Field," p. 91.

11. *Ibid.*, p. 116. See also Pierre Bourdieu, "Systems of Education and Systems of Thought," *International Social Sciences Journal*, vol. 19 (1967), pp. 338–358.

12. Pierre Bourdieu, *Outline of a Theory of Practice*, trans. R. Nice (Cambridge, 1977), especially pp. 164, 168–169.

13. Bourdieu, "Intellectual Field," pp. 116–118, for this and what follows.

14. W. Paul Vogt, "Identifying Scholarly and Intellectual Communities: A Note on French Philosophy, 1900–1939," *History and Theory*, vol. 21 (1982), pp. 267–278.

15. A perfect example of this viewpoint can be found in Wolfgang J. Mommsen, *Max Weber and German Politics, 1890–1920*, trans. Michael S. Steinberg (The University of Chicago Press, 1984), p. 418.

16. A good example of an intellectual biography in which this is clear is John McCole, *Walter Benjamin and the Antinomies of Tradition*, forthcoming at Cornell University Press.

17. For what follows, see Pierre Bourdieu, "Cultural Reproduction and Social Reproduction," in Jerome Karabel and A. H. Halsey, eds., *Power and Ideology in Education* (New York, 1977), pp. 487–511; Pierre Bourdieu and Jean-Claude Passeron, *Reproduction in Education, Society and Culture*, trans. Richard Nice (London, 1977); Pierre Bourdieu, "Les Trois états du capital culturel," *Actes de la recherche en sciences sociales*, no. 30 (Nov. 1979), pp. 3–6. See also Pierre Bourdieu, *La distinction: Critique sociale du jugement* (Paris, 1979).

18. "Status" adequately translates Weber's distinctive use of *Stand*. See the discussion and annotation in Ringer, *Education and Society*, pp. 14–16.

19. Edward Shils, *The Intellectuals and the Powers, and Other Essays* (Chicago, 1972), pp. 3, 7.

20. J. P. Nettl, "Ideas, Intellectuals and Structures of Dissent," in Philip Rieff, ed., *On Intellectuals: Theoretical Studies; Case Studies* (Garden City, N. J., 1970), pp. 57–134.

21. Florian Znaniecki, *The Social Role of the Man of Knowledge* (New York, 1965).

22. Shils, *The Intellectuals*, p. 154.

23. Pierre Bourdieu, "The Social Space and the Genesis of Groups," (Paris: Collège de France, 1985), especially p. 727.

24. Hans-Georg Gadamer, *Wahrheit und Methode: Grundzüge einer philosophischen Hermeneutik* (Tübingen, 1975), especially pp. 162–290; H. G. Gadamer, "The Problem of Historical Consciousness," and Paul Ricoeur, "The Model of the Text: Meaningful Action Considered as a Text," in Paul Rabinow and William M. Sullivan, eds., *Interpretive Social Science: A Reader* (Berkeley, 1979), pp. 103–160, and 73–101, respectively.

25. Bryan Wilson, ed., *Rationality: Key Concepts in the Social Sciences* (Oxford,

1970), especially the essays by Alasdair MacIntyre and Steven Lukes, pp. 112–130, 194–213.
26. Imre Lakatos, "Falsification and the Methodology of Scientific Research Programmes," in Lakatos and Alan Musgrave, eds., *Criticism and the Growth of Knowledge* (Cambridge, 1970), pp. 91–195; Imre Lakatos, "History of Science and Its Rational Reconstructions," in *Boston Studies in the Philosophy of Science*, vol. 8 (1971), pp. 91–136; Thomas S. Kuhn, "Notes on Lakatos," in *Ibid.*, pp. 137–146.
27. Donald Davidson, "Actions, Reasons and Causes," in Davidson, *Essays on Actions and Events* (Oxford: Clarendon, 1980), pp. 4–19. For this paragraph and what follows, see also Fritz Ringer, "Causal Analysis in Historical Reasoning," *History and Theory*, vol. 28 (1989), pp. 154–172.
28. See Ringer, "Differences and Cross-National Similarities," pp. 148–149.
29. Karl Mannheim, *Ideology and Utopia: An Introduction to the Sociology of Knowledge*, trans. L. Wirth and E. Shils (New York, 1955); Ringer, *Decline of the German Mandarins*, pp. 425–433.
30. *Ibid.*, pp. 433–434.
31. For a contemporary discussion of relativism, see Martin Hollis and Steven Lukes, *Rationality and Relativism* (Cambridge, Mass., MIT Press, 1982), especially the essays by Barry Barnes and David Bloor, and by Steven Lukes, pp. 21–47, 261–305.

1. EDUCATION, THE MIDDLE CLASSES, AND THE INTELLECTUALS

1. For what follows, see Fritz K. Ringer, *Education and Society in Modern Europe* (Bloomington and London, 1979), especially the Introduction; Detlef K. Müller, Fritz Ringer, and Brian Simon, eds., *The Rise of the Modern Educational System: Structural Change and Social Reproduction 1870-1920* (Cambridge University Press, 1987), especially the Introduction (Ringer), and chapters 1 (Müller), 2 (Ringer), and 3 (Simon).
2. Detlef K. Müller, *Sozialstruktur und Schulsystem: Aspekte zur Theorie und Praxis der Schulorganisation im 19. Jahrhundert* (Göttingen, 1977).
3. See Anthony J. LaVopa, *Grace, Talent and Merit: Poor Students, Clerical Careers and Professional Ideology in Eighteenth-Century Germany* (Cambridge University Press, 1988), especially pp. 19–133.
4. While important English educational data are reported as *access percentages* for whole age groups and as *relative access chances* or ratios for socio-occupational categories within age groups, French and German data are typically *distribution percentages*, i.e. percentages of all students in a given set of institutions who come from a certain social background or category. If such a distribution percentage were divided by the percentage of the whole age group who come from the same social background or category, the resulting *relative distribution ratio* would be

mathematically identical with the relative access chance for that social category. This makes it possible to compare English to Continental data on students' social origins, though the lack of relevant Continental data for specific age groups usually forces us to have recourse instead to the occupational census for the adult working population, and thus to arrive at *opportunity ratios* that are only roughly comparable to relative access chances. In the measurement of segmentation, on the other hand, social distributions for particular sets of institutions can be directly related to comparable distributions for most or all institutions serving that age group, and relative distribution ratios can thus be exactly calculated that *are* mathematically identical with the corresponding relative access chances. See the illustration and exposition in the opening pages of my chapter 2 in Müller, Ringer, and Simon, *Rise of the Modern Educational System.*

5. Hans-Ulrich Wehler, "Vorüberlegungen zur historischen Analyse sozialer Ungleichheit," in Wehler, ed., *Klassen in der europäischen Sozialgeschichte* (Göttingen, 1979), pp. 9–32.

6. R. Steven Turner, "The Growth of Professorial Research in Prussia, 1818-1948: Causes and Context," *Historical Studies in the Physical Sciences* (1971), pp. 137–182; R. Steven Turner, "University Reformers and Professorial Scholarship in Germany, 1760–1806," in Lawrence Stone, ed., *The University in Society: Studies in the History of Higher Education* (Princeton, 1974), vol. 2, pp. 495–531.

7. See Charles E. McClelland, *State, Society and University in Germany 1700–1914* (Cambridge University Press, 1980), especially on Göttingen.

8. See Werner Conze and Jürgen Kocks, eds., *Bildungsbürgertum im 19. Jahrhundert,* part I: *Bildungssystem und Professionalisierung in internationalen Vergleichen* (Stuttgart: Klett-Cotta, 1985), especially the introduction. Also Ulrich Engelhardt, *"Bildungsbürgertum": Begriffs und Dogmengeschichte eines Etiketts* (Stuttgart: Klett-Cotta, 1986).

9. La Vopa, *Grace, Talent, and Merit,* especially pp. 137–245.

10. For the *propriétaires* as a social category in nineteenth-century France, see Terry Shinn, *Savoir scientifique & pouvoir social: L'Ecole Polytechnique, 1794–1914* (Paris: Presses de la Fondation Nationale des Sciences Politiques, 1980), p. 66; Ringer, *Education and Society,* p. 162; John H. Weiss, *The Making of Technological Man: The Social Origins of French Engineering Education* (Cambridge, Mass.: MIT Press, 1982), p. 71, and further annotation and bibliography there.

11. Examples in Ringer, *Education and Society,* pp. 283–284, 303–304, 309, including such related terms as *Verwaltungsfach* and *Bureaudienst.* See Jürgen Kocka, *Die Angestellten in der deutschen Geschichte, 1850–1980* (Göttingen: Vandenhoeck & Ruprecht, 1981), pp. 70–77.

12. Luc Boltanski, "Taxinomies sociales et luttes de classes: la mobilisation de 'la classe moyenne' et l'invention des 'cadres' ", *Actes de la recherche en sciences sociales,* no. 29, (September 1979), pp. 75–104.

13. Examples in Ringer, *Education and Society*, pp. 92–93, 282, 284, 304, 308–309, including for what follows.
14. Fritz K. Ringer, *The Decline of the German Mandarins: The German Academic Community, 1890–1933* (Cambridge, Mass., 1969) is translated (with quotations in the original German) as *Die Gelehrten: Der Niedergang der deutschen Mandarine, 1890–1933* (Stuttgart: Klett-Cotta, 1983). The book has recently been reissued (with a new introduction) by University Press of New England, but page references in these notes apply to both editions. The original source for the Weber quote is his 1917 'Wahlrecht und Demokratie in Deutschland', in *Gesammelte politische Schriften*, 2nd edn., J. Winckelmann (Tübingen, 1958), pp. 235–236.
15. A key work on this whole subject is still Theodor Geiger, *Aufgaben und Stellung der Intelligenz in der Gesellschaft* (Stuttgart, 1949).
16. What follows is essentially a summary of Ringer, *Education and Society*, pp. 113–156. Along with the bibilography there, see Antoine Prost *Histoire de l'enseignement en France 1800–1967* (Paris, 1968), and two excellent anthologies in the field: Donald N. Baker and Patrick J. Harrigan, eds., *The Making of Frenchmen: Current Directions in the History of Education in France, 1679–1979* (*Historical Reflections* 7, 1980), and Robert Fox and George Weisz, *The Organization of Science and Technology in France 1808–1914* (Cambridge University Press, 1980).
17. Shinn, *Savoir scientifique*, pp. 22–23.
18. Robert J. Smith, *The Ecole Normale Supérieure and the Third Republic* (Albany: State University of New York Press, 1982).
19. R. R. Palmer, "Free Secondary Education in France before and after the Revolution," *History of Education Quarterly* (1974), pp. 437–452.
20. John W. Bush, "Education and Social Status: The Jesuit Collège in the Early Third Republic," *French Historical Studies*, vol. 9 (1975), pp. 125–140.
21. C. R. Day, "Technical and Professional Education in France: The Rise and Fall of *l'enseignement secondaire spécial*, 1865–1902," *Journal of Social History*, vol. 6 (1972–73), pp. 177–201.
22. A regulation of 1907 still required Latin for the *licence* in letters. Classical graduates were long given advantages even in the entrance examination for the Ecole Polytechnique.
23. The faculties of sciences were somewhat less rigorously tied to the secondary curriculum than the faculties of letters. See Victor Karady, "Recherches sur la morphologie du corps universitaire littéraire sous la Troisième République," *Le mouvement social*, vol. 69 (1976), pp. 47–49; Victor Karady, "L'accès aux grades et leurs fonctions universitaires dans les facultés des sciences au 19e siècle: examen d'une mutation," in Baker and Harrigan, *Making of Frenchmen*, pp. 397–414, for this and what follows.
24. This was true of the Ecole Polytechnique and of the Ecole Centrale, for example. Between 1860 and 1880, about three-fourths of entrants to

the Ecole Polytechnique had the baccalaureate, according to Shinn, *Savoir scientifique*, p.51.

25. Weiss, *Making of Technological man.*
26. C. R. Day, "The Making of Mechanical Engineers in France: The Ecoles d'Arts et Métiers, 1803–1914," *French Historical Studies*, vol. 10 (1978), pp. 439–460.
27. For what follows, see George Weisz. *The Emergence of Modern Universities in France, 1863–1914* (Princeton University Press, 1983); Terry Shinn, "The French Science Faculty System, 1803–1914: Institutional Change and Research Potential in Mathematics and the Physical Sciences," *Historical Studies in the Physical Sciences*, vol. 10 (1979), pp. 271–332.
28. John E. Talbott, *The Politics of Educational Reform in France, 1918–1940* (Princeton, 1969).
29. Ringer, *Education and Society*, pp. 131–134, and the following pages for what follows.
30. In 1912–13, for example, French science faculties awarded some 1,250 basic science certificates for medical students, and almost 500 university diplomas in applied science and engineering, as compared to less than 400 *licences* in science. See Weisz, *Emergence of Modern Universities in France*, p. 184.
31. In 1910–11 and 1930–31, university enrollments per age group appear to have been somewhat higher than the number of secondary graduates per age group. Foreign students at French universities and French candidates for university diplomas in technology, who did not need the baccalaureate, probably account for much of this anomaly.
32. For a systematic Franco-German comparison of social mobility and equality of chances, including access to higher education, see Hartmut Kaelble, *Soziale Mobilität und Chancengleichheit im 19. und 20. Jahrhundert* (Göttingen: Vandenhoeck, 1983), especially pp. 170–195, 245–259.
33. Ringer, *Education and Society*, pp. 45–50.
34. Lenore O'Boyle, "The Problem of an Excess of Educated Men in Western Europe, 1800–1850," *Journal of Modern History*, vol. 42 (1970), pp. 471–495. See also George Weisz, "The Politics of Medical Professionalization in France 1845–1848," *Journal of Social History*, vol. 12 (1978-79), pp. 3–30, especially pp. 17–20.
35. Ringer, *Education and Society*, pp. 52–54, and the following pages for what follows.
36. The slogan about an "academic proletariat," coined in Germany during this period, was quickly taken up in France. See Müller, *Sozialstruktur und Schulsystem*, pp. 274–280. See also James C. Albisetti, "The Debate on Secondary School Reform in France and Germany," in Müller, Ringer, Simon, *Rise of the Modern Educational System*.
37. Weisz, "Politics of Medical Professionalization," p. 28 notes that only 2,052 out of 4,895 law students in 1867 intended to pursue legal

careers. See also Weisz, *Emergence of Modern Universities*, pp. 188–189, for what follows.

38. Ringer, *Education and Society*, pp. 149–156; Ringer, "Introduction," in Müller, Ringer, Simon, *Rise of the Modern Educational System*.

39. The following are approximate sizes of each of three classes at some notable *grandes écoles* at various times: Ecole Normale: 20–30 during the early nineteenth century, and 35–45 from the late nineteenth century on; Ecole Polytechnique: 125–175 during the early nineteenth century, and 225–275 from the late nineteenth century on; Ecole Centrale: around 100 soon after its foundation in 1829, 225–275 during the late nineteenth century, and 250–325 by the mid-twentieth century. The *écoles d'arts et métiers* were also three-year schools, with approximate class sizes, collectively, of around 200 during the early nineteenth century, around 400 during the late nineteenth century, and some 600–700 by the early twentieth century. Enrollments at the Ecole Centrale and at the *écoles d'arts et métiers* together amounted to around 0.1 percent of the age group during the late nineteenth century. If enrollments at the *grandes écoles* and related institutions were added to university enrollments, the latter would be increased by some 10–15 percent from the 1880s on, and another 5–6 percent could be added for religious higher education as well. See Ringer, *Education and Society*, pp. 338–340.

40. Like R. Anderson before him, Harrigan has been impressed by the number of students in the survey who came from lower middle-class homes. While recognizing that the lower classes were essentially excluded, he has stressed the relatively "democratic" character of the French system; but he has not fully specified his standards of comparison. He *has* insisted that secondary students were no less progressively recruited in France than in Germany during the nineteenth century; but he has not in fact considered the comparative data discussed here and in Ringer, *Education and Society*, pp. 160–170. See Patrick J. Harrigan, *Mobility, Elites, and Education in French Society of the Second Empire* (Waterloo, Ontario: Wilfrid Laurier University Press, 1980), especially pp. 14, 17–19, 26–27.

41. Statistique de la France, *Resultats généraux du dénombrement de 1872* (Nancy, 1874), and Ringer, *Education and Society*, pp. 177–178 for annotation.

42. *Ibid.*, pp. 231–232, which draws on T. W. Bamford, "Public Schools and Social Class, 1801–1850," *British Journal of Sociology*, vol. 12 (1961), pp. 224–235.

43. K. E. Jeismann, *Das Preussische Gymnasium in Staat und Gesellschaft . . . 1787–1817* (Stuttgart, 1974), p. 165. The chronological gap between Jeismann's sample and the French survey is unfortunate, of

course. But the intervening enrollment changes were not great in either system, and Prussian data for 1875–99 (discussed below) confirm much of what Jeismann observed for 1800.

44. Wilhelm Ruppel, *Über die Berufswahl der Abiturienten Preussens in den Jahren 1875–1899* (Fulda, 1904), and Ringer, *Education and Society*, pp. 70–78, 280–284 for what follows.

45. The most pertinent ratios (relation of *Oberrealschule* graduates to all graduates in the Prussian survey) are: learned professions 0.26, primary teachers 0.33, technical professions 1.8, "industrialists" 2.2, commerce 4.3, artisans 2.1. It should be recalled that the corresponding ratios for the "special" program in the French survey of 1864 were: *propriétaires*, large merchants, intermediate white-collar employees, and industrialists and engineers all 0.8–1.1, and primary teachers 1.8.

46. Patrick Harrigan with Victor Negila, *Lycéens et collégiens sons le Second Empire: Etude statistique sur les fonctions sociales de l'enseignment secondaire publique d'après l'enquête de Victor Duruy* (1864–1865) (Paris, 1979), table 15.

47. Shinn, *Savoir scientifique*, p. 185; Ringer, *Education and Society*, pp. 170–173.

48. Weiss, *Making of Technological Man*, pp. 72, 74.

49. Smith, *Ecole Normale*, p. 42. For a somewhat different grouping of Smith's data, see Ringer, *Education and Society*, pp. 175–176.

50. *Ibid.* pp. 191–201, 344–348 for this and following paragraphs.

51. Natalie Rogoff, "Social Stratification in France and in the United States," in Reinhard Bendix and S. M. Lipset, eds., *Class, Status and Power: Social Stratification in Comparative Perspective* (New York, 1966), pp. 580–582.

52. On the relationship between the Instituts d'Etudes Politiques and the crucial Ecole Nationale d'Administration, see Ringer, *Education and Society*, pp. 125–126.

53. From Gerhard Kath, ed., *Das soziale Bild der Studentenschaft in Westdeutschland und Berlin, Sommersemester 1963* (Deutsches Studentenwerk, Berlin, 1964) as annotated and discussed in Ringer, *Education and Society*, pp. 104–110, 201–205, 312–315. Less than 2 percentage points for the liberal professions pertain to men without university education; "big businessmen" are manufacturers, wholesale merchants, and a few others in business with university education; "executive employees" include employed engineers and architects; "workers" must include domestics, as in the French data in table 1.3, since they are not otherwise mentioned.

54. See Ringer, *Education and Society*, pp. 85–97, 107–112 for this and what follows.

55. On the high standing of the writer in French society, see Priscilla P. Clark, *Literary France: The Making of a Culture* (Berkeley: University of California Press, 1987).
56. Régine Pernoud, *Histoire de la bourgeoisie en France: les temps modernes* (Paris, 1962), especially pp. 32–81, 390–393.
57. *Ibid.*, pp. 77–78.
58. On the *collèges* of the seventeenth and eighteenth centuries, see Willem Frijhoff and Dominique Julia, *Ecole et société dans la France d'ancien régime* (Paris, 1975), and the discussion in Ringer, *Education and Society*, pp. 157–160.
59. Norbert Elias, *Über den Prozess der Zivilisation: Soziogenetische und psychogenetische Untersuchungen*, vol. 1: *Wandlungen des Verhaltens in den weltlichen Oberschichten des Abendlandes* (Frankfurt, 1978), especially pp. 1–64. See also Ringer, *Decline of the German Mandarins*, pp. 87–90, 95–102 and later passages, including further annotation, on the origins and subsequent development of the concepts *Kultur* and *Zivilisation*.
60. Weiss, *Making of Technological Man*, especially pp. 27–56.
61. Dumas cited in *Ibid.*, p. 49.
62. Cesar Graña, *Modernity and its Discontents: French Society and the French Man of Letters in the Nineteenth Century* (New York, 1967).
63. *Ibid.*, p. 32.
64. *Ibid.*, p. 25.
65. *Ibid.*, pp. 61, 63.
66. *Ibid.*, p. 93.
67. *Ibid.*, p. 97.
68. Though consistent with Graña's analysis, this is my own brief interpretation of Stendhal, *The Red and the Black*, trans. L. C. Parks (New York, 1970), with citations, in order, from pp. 483, 103, 46, 461, 149.
69. Graña, *Modernity and Its Discontents*, p. 117.
70. *Ibid.*, p. 108.
71. Gustave Flaubert, *Sentimental Education*, trans. R. Baldwick (New York, 1964).
72. Jerrold Seigel, *Bohemian Paris: Culture, Politics, and the Boundaries of Bourgeois Life, 1830–1930* (New York: Viking, 1986).
73. Christophe Charle, *Les Elites de la République (1880–1900)* (Paris: Fayard, 1987), pp. 7–120.
74. *Ibid.*, pp. 74, 461–462.
75. For the Ecole Normale in the nineteenth century, see above at note 49. See also Victor Karady, "L'expansion universitaire et l'évolution des inégalités devant la carrière d'enseignant au début de la IIIe République," in *Revue française de sociologie*, vol. 14 (1973), pp. 443–470; Victor Karady, "Normaliens et autres enseignants à la Belle Epoque," *Revue française de sociologie*, vol. 13 (1972), pp. 35–58. Unfortunately, differences and imprecisions of categorization have so far prevented a detailed comparison of data available on French Normaliens and

Parisian academics with data on German university faculty that is currently being reanalyzed by my doctoral student, David Vampola.

76. See Christophe Charle, *Naissance des 'intellectuels', 1880–1900* (Paris: Les Editions du minuit, 1990), especially pp. 38–44, 82–116 for this and what follows.

77. Edmond Goblot, *La barrière et la niveau: Etude sociologique sur la bourgeoisie française moderne* (Paris, 1967).

78. Rogoff, "Social Stratification," pp. 580–582.

79. Goblot, *La barrière et le niveau*, p. 31.

80. *Ibid.*, p. 35.

2. THE MEANINGS OF EDUCATION, I

1. From *Der grosse Brockhaus*, fifteenth edn., (1928–35) as cited in Fritz K. Ringer, *The Decline of the German Mandarins: The German Academic Community 1890–1933* (Cambridge, Mass., 1969), p. 86; for German originals of texts cited, see the German translation: *Die Gelehrten: Der Niedergang der deutschen Mandarine 1890–1933* (Stuttgart: Klett-Cotta, 1983). The English version has recently been reissued (with a new introduction) by University Press of New England, but page references in these notes apply to both editions.

2. What follows is not intended as an analysis of a few individual texts, but as a summary description of a "random sample" of writings, and of *average* or *majority* opinions expressed in these writings. The sample covers men holding full appointments in "philosophical" faculties of selected German universities between 1890 and 1933, except for those in the natural sciences. See also Fritz Ringer, "Differences and Cross-National Similarities among Mandarins," *Comparative Studies in Society and History*, vol. 28 (January 1986), pp. 145–164.

3. Georg Simmel, "Der Begriff und die Tragödie der Kultur," in G. Simmel, *Philosophische Kultur: Gesammelte Essais* (Leipzig, 1911), p. 248.

4. *Ibid.*, p. 179.

5. *Ibid.*, pp. 90–99, 102–103.

6. *Ibid.*, pp. 315–334; Hans-Georg Gadamer, *Wahrheit und Methode* (Tübingen, 1975).

7. Ringer, *Decline of the German Mandarins*, pp. 99–102, 108, 117–118.

8. *Ibid.*, pp. 324–325. Wilhelm Windelband, "Geschichte und Naturwissenschaft," his 1894 Rectoral Address, was reprinted in his *Präludien: Aufsätze und Reden zur Einleitung in die Philosophie*, third edn (Tübingen, 1907), pp. 355–379.

9. Ringer, *Decline of the German Mandarins*, pp. 100–101 and pp. 160, 185–187, 195–196 for the context that follows. The quotation is from Ernst Troeltsch, *Naturrecht und Humanität in der Weltpolitik: Vortrag bei der zweiten Jahresfeier der Deutschen Hochschule für Politik* (Berlin, 1923), pp. 13–14. Steven Lukes also draws on this essay, as well as on Simmel, in a

clear comparative account of the German concept of individuality; see Steven Lukes, *Individualism: Key Concepts in the Social Sciences* (Oxford, 1973), especially pp. 17–32.

10. Ringer, *Decline of the German Mandarins*, pp. 103–107.
11. *Ibid.*, pp. 109–113.
12. *Ibid.*, pp. 141–143, 218–219.
13. See especially Rudolf Vierhaus, "Bildung," in Otto Brunner, Werner Conze, Reinhart Kosellek, eds., *Geschichtliche Grundbegriffe*, vol. 1. (Stuttgart, 1972), pp. 508–551. New and very helpful is Anthony J. La Vopa, *Grace, Talent and Merit: Poor Students, Clerical Careers, and Professional Ideology in Eighteenth-Century Germany* (Cambridge University Press, 1988). See also Ulrich Engelhardt, '*Bildungsbürgertum': Begriffs und Dogmengeschichte eines Etiketts* (Stuttgart: Klett-Cotts 1986).
14. Pierre Bourdieu, *La distinction* (Paris, 1979), p. 23. Bourdieu's work has had much influence on mine.
15. Humboldt's sense of "*reine Wissenschaft*" was probably less formal than some of his later German interpreters have suggested; he thought the universities and research should not aim at usefulness, but might then prove practically beneficial in fact. See Wilhelm von Humboldt, "Über die innere und äussere Organisation der höheren wissenschaftlichen Anstalten in Berlin," in *Die Idee der deutschen Universität: Die fünf Grundschriften* (Darmstadt, 1956), pp. 377–386; David Sorkin, "Wilhelm von Humboldt: The Theory and Practice of Self-Formation (*Bildung*), 1791-1810," *Journal of the History of Ideas* (1983), pp. 55–73; Ringer, *Decline of the German Mandarins*, pp. 23–25, 110–111, 115–117, 126–127.
16. See W. H. Bruford, *The German Tradition of Self-Cultivation: 'Bildung' from Humboldt to Thomas Mann* (Cambridge, 1975), and my review of this book in *Central European History*, vol. 11 (March 1978), pp. 107–113.
17. Ringer, *Decline of the German Mandarins*, pp. 26–32, 48–51, 292–293. For a good account of changes in the accreditation of German secondary programs during the late nineteenth century, as well as of the public discussion on these issues, see James C. Albisetti, *Secondary School Reform in Imperial Germany* (Princeton University Press, 1983).
18. Ringer, *Decline of the German Mandarins*, pp. 67–74, 274–279.
19. *Ibid.*, pp. 282–289, especially pp. 287–288.
20. *Ibid.*, p. 109.
21. *Ibid.*, p. 288.
22. *Ibid.*, pp. 77–79 especially p. 79.
23. Matthew Arnold, *Culture and Anarchy*, ed. J. D. Wilson (Cambridge University Press, 1966), p. 6.
24. *Ibid.*, p. 43.
25. *Ibid.*, p. 52.
26. *Ibid.*, p. 65.
27. *Ibid.*, pp. 11, 48.
28. *Ibid.*, p. 70.

29. *Ibid.*, p. 108.

30. *Ibid.*, p. 96.

31. *Ibid.*, p. 97.

32. Raymond Williams, *Culture and Society, 1780–1950* (New York, 1958).

33. Arnold, *Culture and Anarchy*, p. 49.

34. Martin Wiener, *English Culture and the Decline of the Industrial Spirit, 1850–1980* (Cambridge University Press, 1981).

35. Fritz K. Ringer, *Education and Society in Modern Europe* (Bloomington and London, 1979), pp. 106–247; Detlef K. Müller, Fritz Ringer, and Brian Simon, eds., *The Rise of the Modern Educational System: Structural Change and Social Reproduction 1870–1920* (Cambridge University Press, 1987), especially the chapter by Brian Simon.

36. *Ibid.*, especially the chapters by Steedman, Reeder, Honey, and Lowe; see also Fritz K. Ringer, "The Education of Elites in Modern Europe," *History of Education Quarterly*, vol. 18 (1978), pp. 159–172, especially pp. 168–169.

37. Sheldon Rothblatt, *The Revolution of the Dons: Cambridge and Society in Victorian England* (New York, 1968).

38. David Blackbourn and Geoff Eley, *The Peculiarities of German History: Bourgeois Society and Politics in Nineteenth-Century Germany* (Oxford University Press, 1984), pp. 206–221.

39. Along with the social and institutional summary in chapter 1, see especially C. R. Day, "Technical and Professional Education in France: The Rise and Fall of *l'enseignement secondaire spécial*, 1865–1902," *Journal of Social History*, vol. 6 (1972-73), pp. 177–201. More general on the French secondary education debate of the late nineteenth and early twentieth centuries are Georges Weill, *Histoire de l'enseignement secondaire en France, 1802–1920* (Paris, 1921), especially pp. 154–200, and Clement Falcucci, *L'humanisme dans l'enseignement secondaire en France au XIXe siècle* (Toulouse and Paris, 1939), pp. 257–523, which reproduces substantial portions of key texts. A suggestive account of similarities between the French and German education debates is James Albisetti's chapter 8 in Müller, Ringer, Simon, *Rise of the Modern Educational System*, pp. 181–196.

40. Falcucci, *L'humanisme*, p. 271.

41. On the institution of these Councils, see also George Weisz, *The Emergence of Modern Universities in France, 1863–1914* (Princeton University Press, 1983), especially pp. 121–123.

42. Falcucci, *L'humanisme*, p. 285.

43. *Ibid.*, p. 288.

44. *Ibid.*, p. 291

45. *Ibid.*, pp. 297–298.

46. *Ibid.*, p. 333.

47. *Ibid.*, pp. 295, 362, 382, 386, 388–389, including for what follows.

48. *Ibid.*, pp. 382–385.

49. *Ibid.*, p. 463.

50. *Ibid.*, pp. 412–435 for the instructions of 1890, and p. 413 for the quotation.

51. Greek could be begun as an elective within the first-cycle classical stream. *Lycées* and *collèges* were given the option of introducing two-year practically oriented programs as a fifth alternative, but this happened rarely if at all. Graduates of the purely modern option (Sciences–Languages) faced minor diadvantages at the university level for some years after 1902. See above at chapter 1, note 22, along with Falcucci, *L'humanisme*, pp. 505–523, and especially Isambert-Jamati, "Une réforme" (note to table 2.1), pp. 24–33, 46–52.

52. *Ibid.*, pp. 181–184.

53. See above at chapter 1, note 28, and John E. Talbott, *The Politics of Educational Reform in France, 1918–1940* (Princeton, 1969).

54. Bérard's "questionnaire," which in effect asked for comments on a developed proposal, was reprinted in the journal *L'Education*, vol. 13 (October–December 1921), pp. 1–3, with published responses following. For this and what follows, see especially Viviane Isambert-Jamati, *Crises de la société, crises de l'enseignement* (Paris, 1970), pp. 185–191.

55. Paul Bourget, *Le disciple* (Paris, 1889).

56. *Ibid.*, especially pp. 29–30, 33–37, 63–66. Taine in particular is suggested by the focus on psychological determinism, by certain parallels between Taine's career and those of Sixte and Greslou, and by Bourget's remark (p. 75) that Sixte was a political oddity as an atheistic monarchist, which applied to Taine by the 1880s.

57. *Ibid.*, pp. 8–14.

58. Bourget, *Le disciple*, especially pp. 28–33, 38–39, 42–44. The responsibility of the "*honnête homme de lettres*" is invoked in the opening paragraph of the preface (p. 7).

59. Maurice Barrès, *Les déracinés* (Paris, 1898), identified as part of the trilogy entitled *Le Roman de l'énergie nationale*; publication date is for the ten thousandth printing. On p. 20, a real philosophy *professeur* named Burdeau is quoted as sharing Bouteiller's views. The reference is to Auguste-Laurent Burdeau, who earned the *agrégation* in philosophy in 1874, taught at various *lycées*, including Nancy (where Barrès was one of his pupils) and Paris (Louis-le-Grand). In 1881, he took a position in the Ministry of Education, and in 1885, he was elected deputy on the "Opportunist" ticket. Thereafter, he pursued a successful political career until his death in 1894. Another possible model for the character of Bouteiller was Jules Lagneau (1851–94), who entered the Ecole Normale in 1872, earned the *agrégation* in philosophy in 1875, taught at the *lycées* of Sens, Saint-Quentin, Nancy (1879–83, with Barrès among his pupils) and Vanves/Michelet (Paris 1884–3). He is said to have exerted a great intellectual and moral influence upon his students, though he did not write much, and he apparently distrusted politics.

See the editor's notes in Jules Lagneau, *Célèbres Leçons et fragments* (Paris, 1950), pp. 1–7.
60. Barrès, *Les déracinés*, pp. 14–15, including for what follows.
61. *Ibid.*, pp. 22–23; see also pp. 192–194.
62. *Ibid.*, pp. 18–20, 32.
63. *Ibid.*, especially pp. 237–243; also pp. 482–484, 256–262.
64. *Ibid.*, pp. 199–200, and especially pp. 194, 196–197, 241 for what preceded.
65. *Ibid.*, pp. 196–197.
66. *Ibid.*, pp. 2–3.
67. *Ibid.*
68. *Ibid.*, especially pp. 52–55, 128.
69. *Ibid.*, pp. 30, 145–146, 191, 240.
70. *Ibid.*, pp. 132–133, 144, 146, 367, 464.
71. *Ibid.*, especially pp. 19–21, 302.
72. Henry Bérenger, "Les prolétaires intellectuels," in Henry Bérenger *et al.*, *Les Prolétaires intellectuels en France* (Paris, 1901), pp. 1–51, pp. 5–6 for quoted passage, and pp. 1–2 for what preceded.
73. *Ibid.*, pp. 21–22.
74. *Ibid.*, pp. 25, 28, and pp. 32–33 for what follows.
75. *Ibid.*, pp. 33–39.
76. *Ibid.*, pp. 44–47, especially pp. 45–46.
77. Cambre des Députés, session de 1899, Commission de l'Enseignement (pres. Ribot), *Enquête sur l'enseignement secondaire: Procès-verbaux des dépositions*, vol. 1 (Paris, 1899), pp. 488–494.
78. *Ibid.*, pp. 494–499.

3. THE MEANINGS OF EDUCATION, 2

1. I began by reading all individual depositions before the Ribot Commission by university-level faculty, scholars, and academicians. There were about fifty of these, depending on how certain double affiliations are counted. From among these, I chose *not* to cite (a) relatively short statements, (b) statements dealing primarily with subjects not fully treated in what follows, i.e. the baccalaureate, boarding arrangements (*internat*), and the role of supervisory tutorial personnel (*répétiteurs*), (c) statements that merely outlined positions more fully stated elsewhere, and (d) where the remaining statements were still overly repetitive of each other, those by less prominent individuals. In addition, I chose to cite (1) a response to Bérard's project of 1923 by Henri Bergson, (2) Gustave Lanson's highly influential commentary on the settlement of 1902, and (3) articles and books on education (1890–1925) by a few of the authors I had retained.
2. For what follows, see especially Chambre des Députés, Session de 1899, Commission de l'Enseignement (pres. Ribot), *Enquête sur l'enseignement*

secondaire: Procès-verbaux des dépositions, vols. I–II (Paris, 1899). Only these two (out of six) volumes contain depositions by individuals; they will henceforth be cited as Ribot I and Ribot II. The ten individuals to be cited in this section of the chapter, with their affiliations (and the location of their statements), are as follows: Henri Bergson, Collège de France 1900–1914 and Académie Française as of his 1923 response to Bérard, cited below; Charles Bouchard, Paris faculty of medicine and Institut (Ribot I, pp. 521–533); Emile Boutroux, Paris faculty of letters and Institut (Ribot I, pp. 328–342); Paul Brouardel, Paris faculty of medicine (dean) and Académie des Sciences (Ribot I, pp. 207–216); Ferdinand Brunetière, Académie Française (Ribot I, pp. 176–186); Alfred Croiset, Paris faculty of letters (dean) and Institut (Ribot I, pp. 91–106); Alfred Fouillée, Institut (Ribot I, pp. 270–276); Paul Leroy-Beaulieu, Collège de France and Institut (Ribot I, pp. 144–150); Pierre Emile Levasseur, Collège de France and Institut (Ribot I, pp. 159–169); Georges Perrot, Ecole Normale Supérieure (director) and Institut (Ribot I, pp. 133–144). See also Alexandre Ribot, *La réforme de l'enseignement secondaire* (Paris, 1900).

3. Ribot I, pp. 337–338. See also *L'Education*, vol. 13 (1921), pp. 3–4.
4. Ribot I, pp. 134–135.
5. Henri Bergson, "Les études gréco-latines et l'enseignement secondaire." *Revue de Paris* (May 1923), pp. 5–8, 9–10: reprint of an address before the Académie des sciences morales.
6. Ribot I, pp. 145–146.
7. Alfred Croiset, 'Les études gréco-latines et la démocratie', in Ernest Lavisse *et al.*, *L'Education de la démocratie* (Paris, 1903), pp. 195, 196–197, 203, 205–206, 208–211, 211–213. See also Ribot I, pp. 98–99. Croiset presided over the Society for the Study of Questions of Secondary Education, which was educationally conservative; see above at note 50.
8. Emile Littré, *Dictionnaire de la langue française*, in which I consulted an early volume of the second edition of 1875–89. See also Pierre Larousse, *Grand dictionnaire universel du XIXe siècle* (1869); *Larousse du vingtieme siècle* (1929); *Le Grand Larousse encyclopédique* (1960).
9. See above at chapter 1, note 59.
10. Ribot I, pp. 331–332, 335, and pp. 337, 339–340 for what follows.
11. Ferdinand Brunetière, "Education et instruction," *Revue des deux mondes*, vol. 127 (February 1895), pp. 914–920, especially pp. 917–919.
12. *Ibid.*, p. 926.
13. Steven Lukes, *Individualism: Key Concepts in the Social Sciences* (Oxford, 1973), especially pp. 3–22, 67–72.
14. Ribot I, pp. 181, 186.
15. Ribot I, pp. 207–211, 214.
16. Ribot I, pp. 136–139.
17. Ribot I, pp. 94–95, 97–98; Croiset, "Les études gréco-latines," pp. 215–219.

18. Ribot I, pp. 149.
19. Ribot I, pp. 166–168.
20. Bergson, "Les études gréco-latines," pp. 11, 18.
21. Ribot I, pp. 521–523.
22. Ribot I, pp. 526–529.
23. Ribot I, pp. 270–276, especially p. 271.
24. Alfred Fouillée, *Les Etudes classiques et la démocratie* (Paris, 1898), pp. 2–4.
25. *Ibid.*, pp. 5, 187–189.
26. *Ibid.*, pp. 21–22, and pp. 6–7 for what preceded.
27. *Ibid.*, pp. 75, 225.
28. *Ibid.*, pp. 32–33, 60–62.
29. *Ibid.*, pp. 228, 230–232.
30. See above at notes 1–2. The twelve individuals to be cited in this section of the chapter, with their affiliations (and the location of their depositions), are as follows: Charles Andler, Ecole Normale (Ribot II, pp. 62–67), Alphonse Aulard, Paris faculty of letters (Ribot I, pp. 455–464); Marcelin Berthelot, Collège de France, Académie des Sciences (*secrétaire perpétuel*), and former Minister of Education (Ribot I, pp. 15–30); Alexis Bertrand, Lyon faculty of letters (Ribot II, pp. 535–543); Léon Bourgeois, former Minister of Education (Ribot II, pp. 682–705); Ferdinand Buisson, Paris faculty of letters and former Director of Primary Education (Ribot I, pp. 435–444); Gaston Darboux, Paris faculty of sciences and Académie des Sciences (Ribot I, pp. 303–313); Jean Jaures, politician, formerly Toulouse faculty of letters (Ribot II, pp. 38–43); Gustave Lanson, Paris faculty of letters as of his commentary, cited below; Ernert Lavisse, Paris faculty of letters and Académie Française (Ribot I, pp. 35–46); Jules Lemaître, Académie Française (Ribot I, pp. 186–191); Charles Seignobos, Paris faculty of letters (Ribot I, pp. 224–235).
31. Ribot I, pp. 36–37, including for what follows.
32. *Ibid.*, pp. 37–38, 40–41. See also Clement Falcucci, *L'humanisme dans l'enseignement secondaire en France au XIXe siècle* (Toulouse and Paris, 1939), pp. 453–455. In addition to *certificats d'études*, so-called *livrets scolaires* were repeatedly mentioned by reformers; they would have resembled cumulative transcripts. The *juries d'examination* were also a popular concept. In Lavisse's scheme, they would have met in each *département*, with a university professor as chairman. Students with good records from schools known to maintain adequate standards (including some private schools) would have been awarded diplomas automatically, so that the oral examinations would have served as residual controls. Among the critics of the baccalaureate, many also recommended examinations at the point of entry into university-level institutions and/or the educated professions. The supervision of the Catholic private schools was obviously a major factor in the ultimate survival of the baccalaureate. Among the benefits of curricular flexibility and

institutional "autonomy" (a much-used term), Lavisse also conceived a liberalization of school disciplinary regimes, especially for the older students. He further suggested that the rigid age-grade system might be modified to permit students occasionally to take classes above or below their grade level. I have chosen not to pursue these interesting specifics through all the texts under consideration, and essentially to ignore the lively and socially significant debates over boarding arrangements (the *internat*) and over the role of supervisory lower-ranking teachers (the *répétiteurs*). My focus is on structural conceptions and underlying assumptions.

33. Ribot I, pp. 41–42.
34. *Ibid.*, pp. 303–305, 307–309. See also Falcucci, *L'humanisme*, p. 465.
35. Ribot II, pp. 686–687, 693–694, 697–698, 701–702, 704.
36. *Ibid.*, pp. 683, 696.
37. *Ibid.*, pp. 696, 699–700.
38. *Ibid.*, pp. 697–709, 700–701.
39. Ribot I, pp. 186–191, especially p. 187, for this and what follows. See also Falcucci, *L'humanisme*, pp. 448–449.
40. Ribot I, pp. 22–25, and pp. 28–29 for what follows. See also Falcucci, *L'humanisme*, pp. 458–460.
41. Ribot I, pp. 435–436, and pp. 437–439 for what follows.
42. *Ibid.*, pp. 438–441, especially pp. 438, 441.
43. Ribot II, pp. 40–41.
44. *Ibid.*, pp. 38, 41–42, especially p. 41.
45. Ribot II, pp. 536–539.
46. *Ibid.*, p. 541.
47. *Ibid.*, pp. 537–538, 542.
48. Ribot I, pp. 458, 461.
49. *Ibid.*, pp. 457–459.
50. Ribot II, pp. 63–64, 67.
51. *Ibid.*, pp. 63–65, including for what follows.
52. Ernest Lavisse, "Souvenirs d'une éducation manquée," in E. Lavisse *et al.*, *L'Education de la démocratie* (Paris, 1903), pp. 5–8 for main quotation, and pp. 3–4, 10 for what preceded and follows.
53. *Ibid.*, pp. 11, 15, 18, 21–22.
54. *Ibid.*, pp. 23–28. The argument about the subjects of Louis XIV occurs also in Lavisse's testimony at Ribot I, p. 39.
55. Lavisse, "Souvenirs." pp. 31–32, 34; Ribot I, p. 43.
56. Ribot I, pp. 227, 230, 233–235.
57. Charles Seignobos, "L'Organisation des divers types d'enseignement," in Lavisse, *L'Education de la démocratie*, pp. 99–119, especially 100–102, 105.
58. *Ibid.*, pp. 106–109, especially pp. 107–108.
59. *Ibid.*, pp. 110–114.
60. *Ibid.*, pp. 114–116, 118–119, including for what follows.

61. Gustave Lanson, *L'Université et la société moderne*, (Paris, 1902), pp. v–vi; Falcucci, *L'humanisme*, pp. 520–523.
62. Lanson, *L'Université*, pp. 7–9, 23–25, 81, 84–86.
63. *Ibid.*, pp. vii, 6, 8, 20–23, 41, especially p. 20.
64. *Ibid.*, pp. 41, 58, 90–91, 94–95, 98.
65. *Ibid.*, pp. 58–59.
66. *Ibid.*, pp. vii–xi.
67. *Ibid.*, pp. 102–105, and especially pp. 106–107.
68. *Ibid.*, pp. 110–111, 114–115, especially p. 114.
69. *Ibid.*, pp. 114–116, especially p. 115.
70. *Ibid.*, pp. 116–117.
71. *Ibid.*, pp. 118–120.
72. For the following, see Les Compagnons, *L'Université nouvelle* (*Les cahiers de Probus*, 1), third edn. (Paris, 1919); Jean-Marie Carré, "L'histoire des 'Compagnons'," in J.-M. Carré, A. Girard *et al.*, *Les Compagnons de l'université nouvelle* (Paris, 1920), pp. 3–15; Albert Girard, "La Doctrine des 'Compagnons'," in *Ibid.*, pp. 16–35. See also John Talbott, *The Politics of Educational Reform in France, 1918–1940* (Princeton, 1969) especially pp. 34–64.
73. Les Compagnons, *L'Université nouvelle*, pp. 24–26, 67–79; Girard, "La doctrine," pp. 21–26.
74. Les Compagnons, *L'Université nouvelle*, pp. 32–33.
75. *Ibid.*, pp. 34–40.
76. *Ibid.*, pp. 17–18, 53–67, 80–88.
77. *Ibid.*, pp. 13–17, 40–47; Girard, "La Doctrine," pp. 16–27. The Compagnons did not think the *agrégation* should be sought by future secondary teachers.
78. Les Compagnons, *L'Université nouvelle*, pp. 19–21, 34–35.
79. *Ibid.*, pp. 21–22, 25–56; Girard, "La Doctrine," pp. 19–20.
80. See above at chapter 1, note 28.
81. See above at chapter 1, note 77.

4 THE NEW FRENCH UNIVERSITY

1. Fritz K. Ringer, *The Decline of the German Mandarins: The German Academic Community, 1890–1933* (Cambridge, Mass., 1969), pp. 253–258, 295–304, including for what follows. The book has recently been reissued (with a new introduction) by University Press of New England, but page references in these notes are to the 1969 edition.
2. *Ibid.*, p. 307. The quote is from Wilhelm Windelband, *Die Philosophie im deutschen Geistesleben des 19. Jahrhunderts*, 3rd edn (Tübingen, 1927), pp. 83–84.
3. *Ibid.*, pp. 308–309.
4. Carl Becker once compared the German universities to "fortresses of the grail," with a spiritual rather than a utilitarian influence upon the

world around them. See *Ibid.*, p. 104. The politics of German academics before 1918 are well described in Rüdinger vom Bruch, *Wissenschaft, Politik und öffentliche Meinung: Gelehrtenpolitik im Wilhelminischen Deutschland (1890–1914)* (Husum: Matthiesen, 1980).

5. See Golo Mann, "The German Intellectuals," and Roberto Michels, "Intellectual Socialists," in George B. de Huszar, ed., *The Intellectuals: A Controversial Portrait* (Glencoe, Ill.,1960), pp. 459–469, 316–321. The term *Zivilisationsliterat* is from Thomas Mann, *Betrachtungen eines Unpolitischen* (Berlin, 1925). For a good example, see Istvan Déak, *Weimar Germany's Left Wing Intellectuals: A Political History of the Weltbühne and its Circle* (Berkeley, 1968). Michels and Déak note the high proportion of young Jewish intellectuals among intellectual socialists and writers for *Die Weltbühne*, which originated as an Expressionist journal.

6. Ringer, *Decline of the German Mandarins*, pp. 263–265, and note 22. The key essays are "Persönliche und sachliche Kultur," *Neue deutsche Rundschau*, vol. 11 (1900), pp. 700–712; "Der Begriff und die Tragödie der Kultur," *Philosophische Kultur: Gesammelte Essais* (Leipzig, 1911), pp. 245–277; and *Der Konflikt der modernen Kultur: Ein Vortrag*, 2nd edn (Munich, 1921); but see also "Die Arbeitsteilung als Ursache für das Auseinandertreten der subjektiven und der objektiven Kultur" (1900), in Georg Simmel, *Schriften zur Soziologie: Eine Auswahl*, ed. H. J. Dahme and O. Rammstedt (Frankfurt: Suhrkamp, 1983).

7. Ringer, *Decline of the German Mandarins*, pp. 261–269.

8. *Ibid.*, pp. 144–148, 234, 241–250.

9. *Ibid.*, pp. 128–130, 213–227, 237.

10. *Ibid.*, pp. 130–134, 203–213, 236, 239, 269–282, including for what follows.

11. *Ibid.*, pp. 236–241 for the situation of the radical modernists; the Brecht is from the *Dreigroschenoper* (*Threepenny Opera*), near the end of Act II.

12. The members of the Frankfurt School had little impact in Germany before Hitler's accession to power and their own subsequent emigration, which is why I did not discuss their work in the *Decline of the German Mandarins*. I mention them here because I want at least to indicate what a more complete sketch of the German intellectual field (not only of the universities before 1933) would have to include. See Martin Jay, *The Dialectical Imagination* (Boston, 1973), especially pp. 293–296. The basic texts in English are Max Horkheimer, *Critical Theory: Selected Essays* (New York, 1972); Max Horkheimer, *Eclipse of Reason* (New York, 1974); and especially (in the present context) Max Horkheimer and Theodor W. Adorno, *Dialectic of Enlightenment* (New York, 1972). See also Theodor W. Adorno, "Scientific Experiences of a European Scholar in America," in Donald Fleming and Bernard

Bailyn, eds., *The Intellectual Migration: Europe and America, 1930–1960* (Cambridge, Mass., 1969), pp. 338–370.

13. Ringer, *Decline of the German Mandarins*, pp. 334–373, 380–403.
14. *Ibid.*, pp. 340–345.
15. D. G. Charlton, *Positivist Thought in France during the Second Empire, 1852–1870* (Oxford, 1959), especially pp. 51–71.
16. Gertrud Lenzer, ed., *Auguste Comte and Positivism: The Essential Writings* (New York, 1975), especially p. 72. See also Auguste Comte, *Introduction to Positive Philosophy*, ed., Frederick Ferré (Indianapolis: Hackett, 1988).
17. *Ibid.*, p. 56.
18. Charlton, *Positivist Thought in France during the Second Empire, 1852-1870* (Oxford, 1959), pp. 86–157.
19. John A. Scott, *Republican Ideas and the Liberal Tradition in France, 1870-1914* (New York, 1951), pp. 87–106. See also Claude Nicolet, *L'idée républicaine en France (1789–1924); Essai d'histoire critique* (Paris: Gallimard, 1982).
20. See also Phyllis Stock-Morton, *Moral Education for a Secular Society: The Development of Morale Laique in Nineteenth Century France* (Albany: State University of New York Press, 1988), especially pp. 97–122.
21. Scott, *Republican Ideas*, pp. 52–86.
22. At the Ecoles des Hautes Etudes Sociales, a private institute founded in 1900, public lectures on solidarism were held in the winters of 1901–2 and 1902–3. Along with Bourgeois and Buisson, the philosopher Emile Boutroux contributed to the lecture series that was subsequently published. In addition to *Ibid.*, pp. 152–186, see J. E. S. Hayward, "The Official Social Philosophy of the Third Republic: Léon Bourgeois and Solidarism," *International Review of Social History*, vol. 6 (1961), pp. 19–48.
23. Claude Digeon, *La crise allemande de la pensée française (1870-1914)* (Paris, 1959), especially pp. 102–103, 178–254, 302–314, 364–383, 403–448, including for what follows.
24. This is the thesis of Pierre Lasserre, *Le Romantisme français* (Paris, 1928); the first edition appeared in 1907.
25. See above at chapter 2, notes 64–65.
26. See above at chapter 2, notes 55–58.
27. See above at chapter 1, note 27.
28. For this and what follows, see George Weisz, *The Emergence of Modern Universities in France, 1863–1914* (Princeton University Press, 1983), especially pp. 55–89; this is now the standard work on its subject. The Société pour l'Etude des Questions d'Enseignement Supérieur was founded in 1878 and renamed Société de l'Enseignement Supérieur in 1881. It published the *Revue internationale de l'enseignement*. As of 1880, members of the Society were proportionately more numerous in the

provinces than in Paris, and in faculties of letters and of medicine and pharmacy than in faculties of sciences and of law: *Ibid.*, p. 67.

29. Robert J. Smith, *The Ecole Normale Supérieure and the Third Republic* (Albany: State University of New York Press, 1982), pp. 70–75. Gustave Lanson succeeded Lavisse as Director of the Ecole in 1919.

30. See Christophe Charle, "L'élite universitaire française et le système universitaire allemand (1880–1900)," *Transferts* (Paris, 1988), pp. 345–358.

31. Weisz, *Emergence of Modern Universities*, p. 63; George Weisz, "Le corps professoral de l'enseignement supérieur et l'idéologie de la réforme universitaire en France, 1860–1885," *Revue française de sociologie*, vol. 18 (1977), pp. 201–232.

32. Weisz, *Emergence of Modern Universities*, pp. 79–80.

33. For much of what follows, see *ibid.*, pp. 76–86; also Weisz, "Le corps professoral," and Harry W. Paul, *From Knowledge to Power: The Rise of the Science Empire in France, 1860–1939* (Cambridge University Press, 1985), pp. 38–40.

34. Weisz, *Emergence of Modern Universities*, p. 76 somewhat exaggerates the similarity between *science* and *Wissenschaft*.

35. Ernest Lavisse, "Souvenirs d'une éducation manquée," in Lavisse *et al.*, *L'Education de la démocratie: Lecons professées a l'Ecole des Hautes Etudes Sociales* (Paris, 1903), p. 11.

36. See above at chapter 3 notes 45–46, the testimony of Alexis Bertrand.

37. Paul, *From Knowledge to Power*, pp. 60–92 suggests that this was true of Claude Bernard. I am not a competent judge in the matter, but I know that French humanists and social scientists were actively affected by positivism, and I wonder whether ideology can be as totally ruled out even in the natural sciences as Paul seems to suggest.

38. Weisz, *Emergence of Modern Universities*, p. 86.

39. Christophe Charle, "Le Champ universitaire Parisien à la fin du 19e siècle," *Actes de la recherche en sciences sociales*, no. 47–48 (June 1983), pp. 77–89, especially p. 78. See also Christophe Charle, *Les Elites de la République (1880-1900)* (Paris: Fayard, 1987), pp. 7–120, especially p. 74.

40. Pierre Bourdieu, *Homo academicus* (Paris: Editions du minuit, 1984), especially pp. 55–72, 132–133, 149, 155, for this and what follows.

41. Christophe Charle, "La Faculté des lettres de Paris et le pouvoir (1809–1906)," in C. Charle and Régine Ferre, eds., *Le Personnel de l'enseignement supérieur en France aux XIXe et XXe siècles* (Paris: Editions du CNRS, 1985), pp. 151-165. See also Charle, *Elites de la Republique*, pp. 410–423.

42. Smith, *The Ecole Normale*, especially pp. 104–131. Fourteen graduates of the Ecole Normale entered parliamentary politics between 1880 and 1914, not as many as some contemporary critics of the school

implied. Charle's and Bourdieu's point has to do with faculty, rather than with alumni.

43. On the Affair as a whole, see Jean Denis Bredin, '*L'affaire*' (Paris: Julliard, 1983). I am chiefly following Christophe Charle, *Naissance des "intellectuels," 1880–1900* (Paris: Les Editions de minuit, 1990) especially pp. 139–169. See also Pascal Ory and Jean-François Sirinelli, *Les intellectuels en France de l'Affaire Dreyfus à nos jours* (Paris: Colin, 1986), pp. 5–8, 13–40.

44. Lewis A. Coser, *Men of Ideas: A Sociologist's View* (New York, 1965), pp. 215–225; Louis Pinto, "La Vocation de l'universel: La formation de la représentation de l'intellectuel vers 1900," *Actes de la recherche en sciences sociales*, no. 55 (November 1984), pp. 23–32; Charle, *Naissance des 'intellectuels'*, pp. 38–44, 54–137. (The word *intellectuel* appears on p. 92, not on p. 90 of the 1930 edition of *Le disciple*.)

45. See above at chapter 2, note 59; also the excellent readings in Pinto, "Vocation de l'universel."

46. Christophe Charle, "Champ littéraire et champ du pouvoir: Les écrivains et l'Affaire Dreyfus," *Annales*, no. 2 (March–April 1977), pp. 240–264; also Charle, *Naissance des intellectuels*, pp. 200–222.

47. *Ibid.*, pp. 170–200.

48. Ferdinand Brunetière, "Apres le procès," *Revue des deux mondes*, vol. 148 (March 1898), pp. 428–446, especially pp. 428, 442–443.

49. *Ibid.*, pp. 444–445.

50. *Ibid.*, p. 446.

51. See above at chapter 2, note 58.

52. Emile Durkheim, "Individualism and the Intellectuals," in Durkheim, *On Morality and Society*, ed. R. N. Bellah (Chicago, 1973), pp. 43–57, especially p. 44. "L'Individualisme et les intellectuels" was initially published in the *Revue Bleue*, 4e série, 10 (2 July 1898), pp. 7–13.

53. Durkheim, "Individualism," pp. 48–49.

54. *Ibid.*, pp. 51, 54.

55. *Ibid.*, pp. 49–50.

56. *Ibid.*, p. 57.

57. Weisz, *Emergence of Modern Universities*, pp. 309–314; Lucien Mercier, *Les Universités populaires, 1899–1914: Education populaire et mouvement ouvrier au début du siècle* (Paris: Editions ouvrières, 1986).

58. I am not quite certain when the term was first used. Smith, *Ecole Normale*, p. 72 seems to suggest about 1903. We shall encounter the polemical use of the term later in this chapter.

59. Lavisse, *L'Education de la démocratie* includes lectures given in the winter of 1902–3 by Lavisse, Croiset, Seignobos, and Lanson, along with additional lectures on secondary schooling by Paulin Malapert and Jacques Hadamard, which I will not consider, since I want to

stay with the cast of characters that has been defined. Alfred Croiset *et al.*, *Enseignement et démocratie: Lecons professées a l'Ecole des Hautes Etudes Sociales* (Paris, 1905) includes lectures given in the winter of 1903–4 by Croiset, Lanson, and Seignobos, along with additional lectures by E. Devinat, J. Boitel, and A. Millerand on primary, higher primary and vocational schooling, P. Appell on higher education in the sciences, and Ch.-V. Langlois on education in the United States. Some of the above lectures have already been considered in a previous chapter. The Ecole des Hautes Etudes Sociales was privately founded in 1901.

60. Gustave Lanson, "L'Enseignement secondaire," in Croiset, *Enseignement et démocratie*, pp. 185, 204.

61. *Ibid.*, pp. 192–194, 196; Gustave Lanson, *L'Université et la société moderne* (Paris, 1902), pp. 10–11. On Lanson, see also Antoine Compagnon, *La Troisième République des lettres, de Flaubert à Proust* (Paris: Eds. du Seuil, 1983), pp. 21–212.

62. Gustave Lanson, "Les Etudes modernes dans l'enseignement secondaire," in Lavisee, *L'Education de la démocratie*, pp. 163, 173; Lanson, "L'Enseignement secondaire," pp. 184, 187–188.

63. *Ibid.*, pp. 190–195, 200, and Lanson, "Etudes modernes," pp. 168, 161–162 for concluding quotations.

64. *Ibid.*, pp. 169, 171, 175–176, 179–180.

65. *Ibid.*, pp. 183, 185.

66. *Ibid.*, p. 181.

67. *Ibid.*, p. 187.

68. Alfred Croiset, "Les diverses types d'enseignement et leurs rapports," and "Conclusion," in Croiset, *Enseignement et démocratie*, pp. 1-27, 319-343, especially pp. 20–21, 331–337. For a discussion of Alfred Croiset, "Les études gréco-latines et la démocratie," in Lavisse, *L'Education de la démocratie*, pp. 189–221, see above at chapter 2, note 64.

69. Alfred Croiset, "Les besoins de la démocratie en matière d'éducation," in Lavisse, *L'Education de la démocratie*, pp. 40–43.

70. *Ibid.*, pp. 54–55.

71. *Ibid.*, p. 48.

72. *Ibid.*, p. 50, and pp. 51–53 for what follows.

73. *Ibid.*, pp. 57–64, especially p. 64.

74. *Ibid.*, p. 75, and pp. 76–78 for what follows.

75. *Ibid.*, p. 83.

76. *Ibid.*, pp. 87–89.

77. *Ibid.*, pp. 91, 93.

78. *Ibid.*, pp. 94–97.

79. For what follows: discussion of Ernest Lavisse, "Souvenirs d'une éducation manquée," in Lavisse, *L'Education de la démocratie*, especially pp. 11, 18–21, 31–32; see also above at chapter 3, notes 52–55.

80. For discussion of Charles Seignobos, "L'Organisation des divers types d'enseignement," in Lavisse, *L'Education de la démocratie*, pp. 99–119, see above at chapter 3, notes 57–60.
81. Charles Seignobos, "L'Enseignement supérieur," in Croiset, *Enseignement et démocratie*, pp. 259–288.
82. *Ibid.*, pp. 267–268.
83. *Ibid.*, pp. 269–270, 279–288.
84. *Ibid.*, p. 270 and especially p. 271.
85. *Ibid.*, pp. 272–275.
86. *Ibid.*, pp. 276–288, especially pp. 283, 279.
87. Emile Durkheim, "The Role of Universities in the Social Education of the Country," ed. George Weisz, *Minerva*, vol. 14 (1976), pp. 377–388, especially pp. 381–382.
88. *Ibid.*, pp. 383–387, especially p. 387.
89. *Ibid.*, pp. 380, 388.
90. Agathon, *L'Esprit de la Nouvelle Sorbonne: La crise de la culture classique, la crise du français* (Paris, 1911). For what follows, see also Wolf Lepenies, *Die drei Kulturen: Soziologie zwischen Literatur und Wissenschaft* (Munich: Hanser, 1985), pp. 49–102.
91. Agathon, *L'Esprit de la Nouvelle Sorbonne*, p. 17, including for what follows.
92. *Ibid.*, pp. 127–132, 192.
93. *Ibid.*, pp. 22, 50, 77, 153.
94. *Ibid.*, pp. 24, 26, 54, 57–58, 79.
95. *Ibid.*, pp. 26–28, 40–41, 57, 64, 94.
96. *Ibid.*, pp. 58–59.
97. *Ibid.*, pp. 27, 99, 101–102, 104, 108.
98. *Ibid.*, pp. 71–72, 74, 105–106, 109–112.
99. *Ibid.*, pp. 35, 39, 70, 74, 81, 142, 165–167.
100. *Ibid.*, pp 35, 70, 78 (including inset quote), 144, 167–168.
101. See above at chapter 2, notes 55–58.
102. See above at note 48.
103. Agathon, *L'Esprit de la Nouvelle Sorbonne*, p. 84.
104. *Ibid.*, pp. 355–356, 207–211.
105. *Ibid.*, pp. 287–302; text of address in "Séance de réouverture des conférences" initially published in the *Revue internationale de l'enseignement* of November 15, 1910.
106. Agathon, *L'Esprit de la Nouvelle Sorbonne*, pp. 269–274.
107. Pierre Lasserre, *La Doctrine officielle de l'Université* (Paris, 1912).
108. Along with Weisz, *Emergence of Modern Universities*, pp. 341–356, and Phyllis H. Stock, "Students versus the University in Pre-World War Paris," *French Historical Studies*, vol. 7 (1971), pp. 93–110, see Terry N. Clark, *Prophets and Patrons: The French University and the Emergence of the Social Sciences* (Cambridge, Mass: 1973); Ory and Sirinelli, *Les*

intellectuels, pp. 47–60, and more broadly Eugen Weber, *The Nationalist Revival in France, 1905–1914* (Berkeley, 1959).

5. PERSPECTIVES UPON SELECTED DISCIPLINES

1. Jean-Louis Fabiani, "Les programmes, les hommes et les œuvres: professeurs de philosophie en classe et en ville au tournant du siècle," *Actes de la recherche en sciences sociales*, no. 47–48 (June 1983), pp. 3–20, and "Enjeux et usages de la 'crise' dans la philosophie universitaire en France au tournant du siècle," *Annales: Economies, Sociétés, Civilisations* (March–April 1985), pp. 377–409.
2. See above at chapter 3, note 44.
3. See above at chapter 4, notes 95–98, 106, including for what follows.
4. Fabiani cites Boutroux in a more pessimistic mood on the same general issues; see Fabiani, "Enjeux et usages," p. 380.
5. See above at chapter 4, notes 82–83.
6. Alfred Fouillée, *La Réforme de l'enseignement par la philosophie* (Paris, 1901).
7. *Ibid.*, p. 207.
8. Alfred Fouillée, *Les Eléments sociologiques de la morale* (Paris, 1905).
9. Gabriel Tarde, *On Communication and Social Influence*, ed. Terry N. Clark (Chicago, 1969), especially pp. 1–69 (Clark's introduction), 73–105, 112–135. Gabriel Tarde was the father of Alfred de Tarde, co-author of the "Agathon" tract.
10. Robert A. Nye, *The Origins of Crowd Psychology: Gustave LeBon and the Crisis of Mass Democracy in the Third Republic* (London, 1975), especially p. 64.
11. Terry N. Clark, *Prophets and Patrons: The French University and the Emergence of the Social Sciences* (Cambridge, Mass: 1973), pp. 31, 60–64; the Ecole Normale Supérieure and the Collège de France are counted along with the faculties of letters.
12. Antoine Compagnon, "Gustave Lanson, l'homme et l'œuvre," in his *La Troisième République des lettres, de Flaubert à Proust* (Paris: Editions du Seuil, 1983), pp. 21–212.
13. Following Péguy, Compagnon suggests that Lanson's support for Dreyfus was designed to aid his career; but I am not sure this can be demonstrated, and I find the issue of marginal interest in any case. Compagnon may not give enough attention to Lanson's involvement in educational reform, and he somewhat neglects Lanson's methodological essays as well. He does point out that the four pure *littéraires* at the Sorbonne were anti-Dreyfusards.
14. Gustave Lanson, *Histoire de la littérature française* (Paris, n.d. [1955]), pp. v–xvi; this is the original introduction dated July 1984.
15. Gustave Lanson, "Histoire littéraire, littérature française (époque

moderne)," in *Revue de synthése historique*, vol. 1, no. 1 (1900), pp. 52–83, especially pp. 52–55.

16. Gustave Lanson, "L'histoire littéraire et la sociologie," *Revue de métaphysique et de morale*, vol. 12, no. 4 (January 1904), pp. 621–642.
17. *Ibid.*, p. 623.
18. *Ibid.*, pp. 626–631.
19. *Ibid.*, pp. 634–640.
20. Gustave Lanson, "La Méthode de l'histoire littéraire," *La Revue du mois*, vol. 10 (July–December 1910), pp. 385–413.
21. *Ibid.*, pp. 389–391.
22. Agathon's views began to appear in article form in July 1910.
23. Lanson, "La Méthode," p. 393.
24. *Ibid.*, p. 409.
25. For what follows, see William R. Keylor, *Academy and Community: The Foundation of the French Historical Profession* (Cambridge, Mass., 1975).
26. See above at chapter 1, note 27.
27. Keylor, *Academy and Community*, pp. 8–10.
28. For what follows, see Christian Simon, *Staat und Geschichtswissenschaft in Deutschland und Frankreich 1871–1914: Situation und Werk von Geschichtsprofessoren an den Universitäten Berlin, München, Paris* (Bern: Peter Lang, 1988), vol. I, especially pp. ix–xxvi, 81–501, 643–652, and my review of the book in *History and Theory*, vol. xx (1990), pp. 95–106.
29. Simon, *Staat und Geschichtswissenschaft*, pp. 583–640; Keylor, *Academy and Community*, pp. 202–207; also William R. Keylor, "Clio on Trial: Charles Péguy as Historical Critic," in Dora B. Weiner and William R. Keylor, eds., *From Parnassus: Essays in Honor of Jacques Barzun* (New York, 1976), pp. 195–208.
30. In addition to the opening section of chapter 4, see Simon, *Staat und Geschichtswissenschaft*, pp. 1–79.
31. Ursula Becher has argued that the change from the history written in France during the early nineteenth century to the "scientific" history of the late nineteenth century may be traced to a shift in the society's "need for orientation." She has tried to substantiate this claim by investigating the preferences reflected in subscriptions officially awarded to selected works of history during the Second Empire. I have two problems with the thesis. First, I would want to be *shown* that changes in the society's "need for orientation" *actually affected* the way historians thought about their work. Secondly, I cannot share Becher's partly implicit view that the French historians of the late nineteenth century withdrew into scientist models in a kind of flight from ideological engagement, and/or in order to avoid challenges to a particularly precarious social consensus. This is a conventional view of the relationship between "positivism" and engagement; but I do not believe it applies to French "positivist" intellectuals in the age of the

Dreyfus Affair. See Ursula A. J. Becher, *Geschichtsinteresse und historischer Diskurs: Ein Beitrag zur Geschichte der französischen Geschichtswissenschaft im 19. Jahrhundert* (Wiesbaden: Franz Steiner, 1986); key terms can be found in the summary on p. 65.

32. Simon, *Staat und Geschichtswissenschaft*, especially pp. 503–581, and evidence of his indecision about comparative conclusions on pp. xvii–xix, 415, 519, 533, 536–537, 555–556, 573, 647.

33. For what follows, see Georg G. Iggers, "Geschichtswissenschaft in Deutschland und Frankreich 1830 bis 1918 und die Rolle der Sozialgeschichte: Ein Vergleich zwischen zwei Traditionen bürgerlicher Geschichtsschreibung," in Jürgen Kocka with Ute Frevert, eds., *Bürgertum im 19. Jahrhundert: Deutschland im europäischen Vergleich*, vol. 3 (Munich: Deutscher Taschenbuch Verlag, 1988), pp. 175–199, especially pp. 185-195; Fritz K. Ringer, *The Decline of the German Mandarins: The German Academic Community 1890–1933* (Cambridge, Mass., 1969), pp. 142–151, 302–304, 316–334. This book is translated (with quotations in the original German) as *Die Gelehrten: Der Niedergang der deutschen Mandarine, 1890–1933,* and has recently been reissued in English, with a new introdution, by University Press of New England, but page references in these notes apply to both editions. See also Georg G. Iggers, *The German Conception of History: The National Tradition of Historical Thought from Herder to the Present* (Middletown, Conn., 1968).

34. Leopold von Ranke, *Die grossen Mächte*, ed. F. Meinecke (Leipzig, 1916), pp. 60–61; Leopold von Ranke, *Das politische Gespräch und andere Schriften zur Wissenschaftslehre* (Halle, Saale, 1925), pp. 8, 22.

35. *Ibid.*, pp. 19, 23–25, 33, and good examples in *Die grossen Mächte*, pp. 42–45.

36. Ranke, *Das politische Gespräch*, pp. 23–24, 29.

37. Simon, *Staat und Geschichtswissenschaft*, pp. 22–41.

38. Iggers, "Geschichtswissenschaft," pp. 192–194.

39. Charles-Victor Langlois and Charles Seignobos, *Introduction aux études historiques* (Paris, 1898); Langlois contributed pp. 1–116. See also Charles Seignobos, *La Méthode historique appliquée aux sciences sociales* (Paris, 1901).

40. Langlois and Seignobos, *Introduction*, pp. 1–2, 43–50, 117–119; Seignobos, *Méthode*, pp. 1–6, 17–25.

41. *Ibid.*, pp. 50–60; Langlois and Seignobos, *Introduction*, pp. 120–126.

42. *Ibid.*, pp. 127–129.

43. *Ibid.*, pp. 130–179; Seignobos, *Méthode*, pp. 61–93.

44. Langlois and Seignobos, *Introduction*, pp. 181–192; Seignobos, *Méthode*, pp. 115–121.

45. *Ibid.*, pp. 138–140; see also the somewhat expanded but very similar version in Langlois and Seignobos, *Introduction*, pp. 202–203.

46. *Ibid.*, pp. 206–208; Seignobos, *Méthode*, pp. 217–223, 231–235.
47. *Ibid.*, pp. 7–15, 199–212, 227–228; see also Langlois and Seignobos, *Introduction*, pp. 237–245.
48. *Ibid.*, pp. 208–210, 245–246; Seignobos, *Méthode*, pp. 136–138, 149–150, 224, 247–254.
49. Langlois and Seignobos, *Introduction*, pp. 188, 204–205, 253–254; Seignobos, *Méthode*, pp. 107–108.
50. *Ibid.*, pp. 108–115, 150–152, 173–176, 230–231, 251.
51. *Ibid.*, pp. 260–268, 277–300, especially p. 284.
52. Langlois and Seignobos, *Introduction*, pp. 213–214, for example; Seignobos, *Méthode*, pp. 313–315.
53. *Ibid.*, pp. 237–238, 270–271; Langlois and Seignobos, *Introduction*, pp. 252–253.
54. *Ibid.*, pp. 212–215, 234.
55. *Ibid.*, pp. 92, 131, 144–145, 206, 282.
56. Martin Siegel, "Henri Berr's *Revue de synthèse historique*," *History and Theory*, vol. 9 (1970), pp. 321–334, especially pp. 321–325, 328.
57. H. Stuart Hughes, *The Obstructed Path: French Social Thought in the Years of Desperation, 1930–1960* (New York, 1966), pp. 21–27; all quotations are from pp. 23–24.
58. Henri Berr, "Sur notre programme," *Revue de synthèse historique*, vol. 1 (1900), pp. 1–8, especially pp. 3–4, 7–8.
59. *Ibid.*, especially pp. 2, 5–6.
60. François Simiand, "Méthode historique et science sociale," *Revue de synthèse historique*, vol. 6 (1903), pp. 1–22, 129–157. The other books very briefly considered were Paul Lacombe, *De l'histoire considérée comme science* (Paris, 1894), and Henri Hauser, *L'Enseignement des sciences sociales* (Paris, 1903).
61. *Ibid.*, pp. 1–7, especially p. 6.
62. *Ibid.*, pp. 8–12.
63. *Ibid.*, pp. 12–16.
64. *Ibid.*, pp. 14, 17. Simiand's "*phénomène antécédent invariable et inconditionné*" seems imperfectly formulated.
65. *Ibid.*, pp. 17–20.
66. *Ibid.*, pp. 130–147.
67. *Ibid.*, pp. 148–151, 153–155, 157.
68. See also Fritz Ringer, "Causal Analysis in Historical Reasoning," *History and Theory*, vol. 28 (1989), pp. 154–172.
69. Philippe Besnard, "The Epistemological Polemic: François Simiand," in P. Besnard, ed., *The Sociological Domain: The Durkheimians and the Founding of French Sociology* (Cambridge University Press, 1983), pp. 248–262.
70. For this and the following, see Victor Karady, "Durkheim, les sciences sociales et l'université: bilan d'un semi-échec," *Revue française*

de sociologie, vol. 17 (1976), pp. 267–311; George Weisz, "L'idéologie républicaine et les sciences sociales: Les Durkheimiens et la chaire d'histoire d'économie sociale à la Sorbonne," *Revue française de sociologie*, vol. 20 (1979), pp. 83–112. The faculties of law tried to prevent the establishment of social sciences positions at the Ecole Libre des Sciences Politiques and at the faculties of letters. See also Clark, *Prophets and Patrons*, especially pp. 162–195.

71. Philippe Besnard, "La formation de l'équipe de *l'Année sociologique*," *Revue française de sociologie*, vol. 20, (1979), pp. 7–31.

72. Karady, "Durkheim, les sciences sociales."

73. Clark, *Prophets and Patrons*, pp. 104–116, 147–161 briefly discusses the Le Playists, as well as René Worms and the *Revue internationale de sociologie*. For complete accounts of responses to Durkheim, of his debates with such critics and rivals as Gabriel Tarde, as well as of Durkheim's own works, see Steven Lukes, *Emile Durkheim, His Life and Work: A Historical and Critical Study*, (New York, 1972).

74. For the relationship of Durkheim and of his collaborators to the wider political and ideological context, see W. Paul Vogt, *The Politics of Academic Sociological Theory in France, 1890–1914*, Ph.D. dissertation (Ann Arbor, Mich.: University Microfilms, 1976). See also Phyllis Stock-Morton, *Moral Education for a Secular Society: The Development of Morale Laique in Nineteenth Century France* (Albany: State University of New York Press, 1988), pp. 97–137. Weisz, "L'idéologie républicaine" shows that the Republic's need for ideological defenses against socialism occasionally became quite explicit in the negotiations that preceded the establishment of new social sciences positions in the faculties of law and of letters. Perhaps it helped Durkheim's cause that in the report he wrote upon his return from the fellowship year in Germany, he remarked that revolutions were as impossible as miracles. See Emile Durkheim, "La Philosophie dans les universités allemandes," *Revue internationale de l'enseignment*, vol. 13 (1887), pp. 313–338, 423–440, especially pp. 437, 439–440. But while Durkheim continued to emphasize that social facts cannot be changed at will, there is no doubt about his sympathy for reformist socialism.

75. The job has been well done in any case. Basic on Durkheim is Lukes, *Emile Durkheim*. See also Dominick LaCapra, *Emile Durkheim: Sociologist and Philosopher* (Ithaca, 1972).

76. Emile Durkheim, *Education et sociologie*, ed. P. Fauconnet (Paris, 1968); this was originally published in 1922; pp. 31–58 reproduce Durkheim's entry on "Education" in a 1911 pedagogical encyclopedia; pp. 81–102 reproduce the opening lecture in his 1902–3 course on the "Science of Education" at the Sorbonne. The rest of the lectures in that course were originally published in 1925 (also edited by P. Fauconnet), and are now available in English translation as Emile

Durkheim, *Moral Education: A Study in the Theory and Application of the Sociology of Education* (New York, 1961).

77. Durkheim, *Education et sociologie*, pp. 31–37, 83–91; see also Durkheim, *Moral Education*, pp. 21–22, 86–88.
78. Durkheim, *Education et sociologie*, pp. 37–45, 91–93.
79. *Ibid.*, pp. 45–48; Durkheim, *Moral Education*, pp. 69, 88–89.
80. Durkheim, *Education et sociologie*, pp. 51–55, 97–100; Durkheim, *Moral Education*, pp. 129–143, 207–222.
81. *Ibid.*, pp. 36, 40–43, 150–151. See also Emile Durkheim, *Suicide: A Study in Sociology*, ed. G. Simpson (Glencoe, Ill., 1951), pp. 124, 214, 247–257, 360.
82. Durkheim, *Education et sociologie*, pp. 56–58; Durkheim, *Moral Education*, pp. 27–46.
83. *Ibid.*, pp. 144–190.
84. *Ibid.*, pp. 74–79, 230–249.
85. *Ibid.*, pp. 8–14, 96–125. See also Emile Durkheim, *The Elementary Forms of the Religious Life*, trans. J. W. Swain (New York, 1965).
86. *Ibid.*, pp. 249–266, 275–281.
87. Emile Durkheim, *L'Evolution pédagogique en France* (Paris, 1969), pp. 1–21, 304–399; this 1904–5 course was first published by M. Halbwachs in 1938. See also Durkheim, *Education et sociologie*, pp. 103–120; this is a 1905 opening lecture for a course similar to the above. Finally, see Emile Durkheim, "L'Enseignement philosophique et l'agrégation de philosphie," *Revue philosophique de la France et de l'étranger*, vol. 39, (1895), pp. 121–147.
88. Durkheim, *Education et sociologie*, pp. 115–117; Durkheim, *L'Evolution pédagogique*, pp. 15–20.
89. Durkheim, *Education et sociologie*, pp. 117–120; Durkheim, *L'Evolution pédagogique*, pp. 20–21.
90. *Ibid.*, pp. 304–310, 318–324.
91. *Ibid.*, pp. 310–317, especially pp. 312, 315–317.
92. *Ibid.*, pp. 324–350.
93. *Ibid.*, pp. 355–366.
94. *Ibid.*, pp. 385–393, especially pp. 386, 389.
95. Durkheim, "L'Enseignement philosophique," pp. 126–134, especially pp. 128–129.
96. *Ibid.*, pp. 134–147, especially p. 147. Part of Durkheim's proposal was to require candidates for the *agrégation* in philosophy to earn the PCN, a certificate awarded by the faculties of sciences to future medical students for a year of introductory study in the basic sciences.
97. Durkheim, *L'Evolution pédagogique*, pp. 367–380, especially pp. 368, 370, 372.
98. *Ibid.*, pp. 380–385, especially pp. 381, 383–384.
99. *Ibid.*, pp. 393–399, especially p. 396.

100. Emile Durkheim, *The Division of Labor in Society*, trans. G. Simpson, (New York, 1964), pp. 375–381, especially pp. 377–379, including for what follows.
101. Durkheim, *Suicide*, p. 251.
102. Durkheim, *Division of Labor*, p. 315, for example.
103. Christophe Charle points out that Durkheim was well integrated by marriage into the wealthy Jewish bourgeoisie, so that he combined economic with cultural capital. See Christophe Charle, "Le beau mariage d'Emile Durkheim," *Actes de la recherche en sciences sociales*, no. 55 (November 1984), pp. 45–49.
104. Durkheim, *Suicide*, p. 250.
105. *Ibid.*, p. 151, for example.
106. Emile Durkheim, *The Rules of Sociological Method*, ed. G. E. G. Catlin (New York, 1964), pp. 23–25.
107. Durkheim, *Evolution pédagogique*, pp. 385–386.
108. Durkheim, *Suicide*, pp. 278–279, 286–287.
109. *Ibid.*, pp. 248, 256.
110. Durkheim, *Elementary Forms*, p. 51.
111. Simmel's view is discussed above at chapter 4, note 6.
112. Durkheim, *Moral Education*, p. 57.
113. Durkheim, *Division of Labor*, p. 40, and p. 41 for what follows.
114. See above at chapter 1, notes 73–74, and chapter 4, note 41.
115. Durkheim, *Division of Labor*, pp. 42–43, including for what follows; the last sentence is italicized in the original.
116. *Ibid.*, pp. 401–403.
117. *Ibid.*, pp. 359, 361–364, especially p. 364.
118. *Ibid.*, pp. 367–368, 370–371, especially pp. 370–371.
119. For the German response to specialization, including the "synthesis" movement, see above at chapter 4, note 13. See also Ringer, *Decline of the German Mandarins*, pp. 228–230, 384–403 for the synthesis movement and the involvement of sociology, and pp. 352–356 on Max Weber, *Wissenschaft als Beruf*, second edn. (Munich, 1921).
120. See above at chapter 4, notes 8–11, 13; also Ringer, *Decline of the German Mandarins*, pp. 241–252 on the crisis of mandarin politics. See also Max Weber, "Politik als Beruf," in Max Weber, *Gesammelte politische Schriften*, third edn. J. Winckelmann (Tübingen, 1971), pp. 505–560.
121. Durkheim, *Moral Education*, p. 210; Durkheim, *Elementary Forms*, p. 13.
122. Durkheim, *Rules of Sociological Method*, pp. 47–49, especially p. 49.
123. Durkheim, *Division of Labor*, pp. 33–35, 339; Durkheim, *Rules of Sociological Method*, pp. xxxix, 55–75; Durkheim, *Suicide*, p. 387 on "verbal influence"; Durkheim, *Elementary Forms*, pp. 470–471.
124. See above at chapter 4, note 41.
125. Emile Durkheim, "The Intellectual Elite and Democracy," in Emile

Durkheim, *On Morality and Society*, ed. R. N. Bellah (Chicago, 1973), pp. 58–60, especially p. 59.

126. The view is implied, mostly by contrast, in Julien Benda, *The Treason of the Intellectuals*, trans. R. Aldington (New York, 1969); see also Lewis A. Coser, "Julien Benda on 'Intellectual Treason'," *Encounter*, vol. 40 (1973), pp. 32–36, which somewhat overstates the parallels between Benda and Max Weber.

127. Durkheim, *Division of Labor*, pp. 408–409.

128. Durkheim, *Suicide*, pp. 158–159, 162, 169, especially p. 169.

129. Durkheim, *Elementary Forms*, p. 487.

130. Durkheim, *Moral Education*, pp. 114–119, especially pp. 116–118; my emphasis.

CONCLUSION: EDUCATION AS INTERPRETATION

1. Martin Jay, "Fieldwork and Theorizing in Intellectual History: A Reply to Fritz Ringer," in *Theory and Society*, vol. 19 (June 1990), p. 315.

2. See above at chapter 2, note 1.

3. The reference is to Max Weber, *Wissenschaft als Beruf*, second edn., (Munich, 1921).

4. Percy Bysshe Shelley, "A Defense of Poetry," in John B. Halsted, ed., *Romanticism* (New York, 1969), p. 97.

Bibliography

Official statistics are listed under France, Germany, and Prussia. Where several articles of interest are taken from the same volume, only the volume is listed here.

PRIMARY WORKS IN INTELLECTUAL HISTORY

Adorno, Theodor W., "Scientific Experiences of a European Scholar in America," in Donald Fleming and Bernard Bailyn, eds., *The Intellectual Migration: Europe and America, 1930–1960* (Cambridge, Mass., 1969)

Agathon, *L'Esprit de la Nouvelle Sorbonne: La crise de la culture classique, la crise du français* (Paris, 1911)

Arnold, Matthew, *Culture and Anarchy*, ed., J. D. Wilson (Cambridge, 1966)

Barrès, Maurice, *Les déracinés* (Paris, 1898)

Benda, Julien, *The Treason of the Intellectuals*, trans. R. Aldington (New York, 1969)

Bérenger, Henry *et al.*, *Les Prolétaires intellectuels en France* (Paris, 1901)

Bergson, Henri, "Les études gréco-latines et l'enseignement secondaire," *Revue de Paris* (May 1923), pp. 5–8

Berr, Henri, "Sur notre programme," *Revue de synthèse historique*, vol. 1 (1900), pp. 1–8

Bourget, Paul, *Le disciple* (Paris, 1889)

Brockhaus, der grosse, fifteenth edn (1928–35)

Brunetière, Ferdinand, "Après le procès," *Revue des deux mondes*, vol. 148 (March, 1898), pp. 428–446

"Education et instruction," *Revue des deux mondes*, vol. 127 (February 1895), pp. 914–920

Carré, J.-M., A. Girard, *et al.*, *Les Compagnons de l'université nouvelle* (Paris, 1920)

Compagnons, Les, *L'Université nouvelle* (*Les cahiers de Probus*, I) third edn (Paris, 1919)

Comte, Auguste, *Auguste Comte and Positivism: The Essential Writings*, Gertrud Lenzer, ed., (New York, 1975)

Introduction to Positive Philosophy, Frederick Ferré, ed. (Indianapolis: Hackett, 1988)

Croiset, Alfred, *et al.*, *Enseignement et démocratie: Lecons professées a l'Ecole des Hautes Etudes Sociales* (Paris, 1905)

Durkheim, Emile, *The Division of Labor in Society*, trans. G. Simpson, (New York, 1964)

Education et sociologie, ed. P. Fauconnet (Paris 1968)

The Elementary Forms of the Religious Life, trans. J. W. Swain (New York, 1965)

L'Evolution pédagogique en France (Paris, 1969)

Moral Education: A Study in the Theory and Application of the Sociology of Education (New York, 1961)

On Morality and Society, ed. R. N. Bellah (Chicago, 1973)

The Rules of Sociological Method, ed. G. E. G. Catlin (New York, 1964), pp. 23–25

Suicide: A Study in Sociology, ed. G. Simpson (Glencoe, Ill., 1951)

"L'Enseignement philosophique et l'agrégation de philosophie," *Revue philosophique de la France et de l'étranger*, vol. 39. (1895), pp. 121–147

"La Philosophie dans les universités allemandes," *Revue internationale de l'enseignement*, vol. 13 (1887), pp. 313–338

"The Role of Universities in the Social Education of the Country," ed. George Weisz, *Minerva*, vol. 14 (1976)

Flaubert, Gustave, *Sentimental Education*, trans. R. Baldwick (New York, 1964)

Fouillée, Alfred, *La Réforme de l'enseignement par la philosophie* (Paris, 1901)

Les Eléments sociologiques de la morale (Paris, 1905)

Les Etudes classiques et la démocratie (Paris, 1898)

France, Chambre des Députés, Session de 1899, Commission de l'Enseignement (pres. Ribot), *Enquéte sur l'enseignement secondaire: Procès-verbaux des dépositions*, vols. I–II (Paris, 1899)

Goblot, Edmond, *La barrière et le niveau: Etude sociologique sur la bourgeoisie française moderne* (Paris, 1967)

Horkheimer, Max, *Critical Theory: Selected Essays* (New York, 1972)

Eclipse of Reason (New York, 1974)

Horkheimer, Max, and Theodor W. Adorno, *Dialectic of Enlightenment* (New York, 1972)

Humboldt, Wilhelm von, "Über die innere und äussere Organisation der höheren wissenschaftlichen Anstalten in Berlin," in *Die Idee der deutschen Universität: Die fünf Grundschriften* (Darmstadt, 1956)

Langlois, Charles-Victor and Charles Seignobos, *Introduction aux études historiques* (Paris, 1898)

Lanson, Gustave, *Histoire de la littérature française* (Paris, n.d. [1955])

L'Université et la société moderne (Paris, 1902)

"Histoire littéraire, littérature française (époque moderne)," in *Revue de synthése historique*, vol. 1, no. 1 (1900), pp. 52–83
"L'histoire littéraire et la sociologie," *Revue de métaphysique et de morale*, vol. 12, no. 4 (January, 1904), pp. 621–642
"La Méthode de l'histoire littéraire," *La Revue du mois*, vol. 10 (July–December 1910), pp. 385–413
Larousse, Pierre, *Grand dictionnaire universel du XIXe siècle* (1869)
Larousse du vingtieme siècle (1929)
Larousse encyclopédique, Le Grand (1960)
Lasserre, Pierre, *La Doctrine officielle de l'Université* (Paris, 1912)
Le Romantisme français (Paris, 1928)
Lavisse, Ernest *et al.*, *L'Education de la démocratie: Leçons professées à l'Ecole des Hautes Etudes Sociales* (Paris, 1903)
Lenzer, Gertrud, ed., *Auguste Comte and Positivism: The Essential Writings* (New York, 1975)
Littré, Emile, *Dictionnaire de la langue française* (Paris, 1875)
Mann, Thomas, *Betrachtungen eines Unpolitischen* (Berlin, 1925)
Mannheim, Karl, *Ideology and Utopia: An Introduction to the Sociology of Knowledge*, trans. L. Wirth and E. Shils (New York, 1955)
"On the Interpretation of *Weltanschauung*," in Mannheim, *Essays on the Sociology of Knowledge*, ed., P. Kecskemeti (London, 1952), pp. 33–83
Ranke, Leopold von, *Das politische Gespräch und andere Schriften zur Wissenschaftslehre* (Halle, Saale, 1925)
Die grossen Mächte, ed. F. Meinecke (Leipzig, 1916)
Rothblatt, Sheldon, *The Revolution of the Dons: Cambridge and Society in Victorian England* (New York, 1968)
Seignobos, Charles, *La Méthode historique appliquée aux sciences sociales* (Paris, 1901)
"L'Organisation des divers types d'enseignement," in Lavisse, *L'Education de la démocratie*, pp. 99–119
Shelly, Percy Bysshe, "A Defence of Poetry," in John B. Halsted, ed., *Romanticism* (New York, 1969), pp. 81–97
Simiand, François, "Méthode historique et science sociale," *Revue de synthèse historique*, vol. 6 (1903), pp. 1–22
Simmel, Georg, "Persönliche und sachliche Kultur," *Neue deutsche Rundschau*, vol. 11 (1900), pp. 700–712
"Der Begriff und die Tragödie der Kultur," *Philosophische Kultur: Gesammelte Essais* (Leipzig, 1911), pp. 245–277
Der Konflikt der modernen Kultur: Ein Vortrag, second edn., (Munich, 1921)
Schriften zur Soziologie: Eine Auswahl, ed. H. J. Dahme and O. Rammstedt (Frankfurt: Suhrkamp, 1983)
Stendhal (Henri Beyle), *The Red and the Black*, trans. L. C. Parks (New York, 1970)
Tarde, Gabriel, *On Communication and Social Influence*, ed. Terry N. Clark (Chicago, 1969)

Troeltsch, Ernst, *Naturrecht und Humanität in der Weltpolitik: Vortrag bei der zweiten Jahresfeier der Deutschen Hochschule für Politik* (Berlin, 1923)

Weber, Max, *Gesammelte politische Schriften*, third edn., J. Winckelmann (Tübingen, 1971)

Wissenschaft als Beruf, second edn., (Munich, 1921)

Windelband, Wilhelm, *Die Philosophie im deutschen Geistesleben des 19. Jahrhunderts*, third edn., (Tübingen, 1927), pp. 83–84

"Geschichte und Naturwissenschaft," reprinted in his *Präludien: Aufsätze und Reden zur Einleitung in die Philosophie*, third edn., (Tübingen, 1907), pp. 355–379

SECONDARY WORKS IN INTELLECTUAL HISTORY

Becher, Ursula A. J., *Geschichtsinteresse und historischer Diskurs: Ein Beitrag zur Geschichte der französischen Geschichtswissenschaft im 19. Jahrhundert* (Wiesbaden: Franz Steiner, 1986)

Besnard, Philippe, "La formation de l'équipe de *l'Année Sociologique*," *Revue française de sociologie*, vol. 20 (1979), pp. 7–31

"The Epistemological Polemic: François Simiand," in P. Besnard, ed., *The Sociological Domain: The Durkheimians and the Founding of French Sociology* (Cambridge University Press, 1983), pp. 248–262

Bourdieu, Pierre, *La distinction: Critique sociale du jugement* (Paris, 1979)

Outline of a Theory of Practice, trans. R. Nice (Cambridge, 1977)

"Cultural Reproduction and Social Reproduction," in Jerome Karabel and A. H. Halsey, eds., *Power and Ideology in Education* (New York, 1977), pp. 487–511

"The Genesis of the Concepts of *Habitus* and of *Field*," *Sociocriticism*, no. 2 (1985), pp. 11–24

"Intellectual Field and Creative Project," *Social Science Information*, vol. 8 (1969), pp. 89–119

"Systems of Education and Systems of Thought," *International Social Sciences Journal*, vol. 19 (1967), pp. 338–358

Bruch, Rüdinger vom, *Wissenschaft, Politik und öffentliche Meinung: Gelehrtenpolitik im Wilhelminischen Deutschland (1890–1914)* (Husum, Germany: Matthiesen, 1980)

Bruford, W. H., *The German Tradition of Self-Cultivation: "Bildung" from Humboldt to Thomas Mann* (Cambridge, 1975)

Charle, Christophe, "Champ littéraire et champ du pouvoir: Les écrivains et l'Affaire Dreyfus," *Annales*, no. 2 (March–April 1977), pp. 240–264

Naissance des "intellectuels", 1880–1900 (Paris: Les Editions de minuit, 1990)

Charlton, D. G., *Positivist Thought in France during the Second Empire, 1852–1870* (Oxford, 1959)

Clark, Priscilla P., *Literary France: The Making of a Culture* (Berkeley: University of California Press, 1987)

Clark, Terry N., *Prophets and Patrons: The French University and the Emergence of the Social Sciences* (Cambridge, Mass., 1973)

Compagnon, Antoine, *La Troisième République des lettres, de Flaubert à Proust* (Paris: Editions du Seuil, 1983)

Coser, Lewis A., "Julien Benda on 'Intellectual Treason'," *Encounter.*, vol. 40 (1973), pp. 32–36

Davidson, Donald, "Actions, Reasons, and Causes," in Davidson, *Essays on Actions and Events* (Oxford: Clarendon, 1980), pp. 4–19

Déak, Istvan, *Weimar Germany's Left Wing Intellectuals: A Political History of the Weltbühne and its Circle* (Berkeley, 1968)

Digeon, Claude, *La crise allemande de la pensée française (1870–1914)* (Paris, 1959)

Elias, Norbert, *Über den Prozess der Zivilisation: Soziogenetische und psychogenetische Untersuchungen*, vol. 1: *Wandlungen des Verhaltens in den Weltlichen Oberschichten des Abendlandes* (Frankfurt, 1978)

Engelhardt, Ulrich, *"Bildungsbürgertum": Begriffs- und Dogmengeschichte eines Etiketts* (Stuttgart: Klett-Cotta, 1986)

Fabiani, Jean-Louis, "Enjeux et usages de la 'crise' dans la philosophie universitaire en France au tournant du siècle," *Annales: Economies, Sociétés, Civilisations* (March–April 1985), pp. 377–409

"Les programmes, les hommes et les œuvres: professeurs de philosophie en classe et en ville au tournant du siècle," *Actes de la recherche en sciences sociales*, no. 47–48, (June 1983), pp. 3–20

Gadamer, Hans-Georg, *Wahrheit und Methode: Grundzüge einer philosophischen Hermeneutik* (Tübingen, 1975)

Graña, Cesar, *Modernity and Its Discontents: French Society and the French Man of Letters in the Nineteenth Century* (New York, 1967)

Hayward, J. E. S., "The Official Social Philosophy of the Third Republic: Léon Bourgeois and Solidarism," *International Review of Social History*, vol. 6 (1961), pp. 19–48

Hollis, Martin and Steven Lukes, *Rationality and Relativism* (Cambridge, Mass.: MIT Press, 1982)

Hughes, H. Stuart, *The Obstructed Path: French Social Thought in The Years of Desperation, 1930–1960* (New York, 1966)

Iggers, Georg G., *The German Conception of History: The National Tradition of Historical Thought from Herder to the Present* (Middletown, Conn., 1968)

"Geschichtswissenschaft in Deutschland und Frankreich 1830 bis 1918 und die Rolle der Sozialgeschichte: Ein Vergleich zwischen zwei Traditionen bürgerlicher Geschichtsschreibung," in Jürgen Kocka with Ute Frevert, eds., *Bürgertum im 19. Jahrhundert: Deutschland im europäischen Vergleich*, vol. III (Munich: Deutscher Taschenbuch Verlag, 1988), pp. 175–199

Jay, Martin, *The Dialectical Imagination* (Boston, 1973)

"Fieldwork and Theorizing in Intellectual History: A Reply to Fritz Ringer," in *Theory and Society*, vol. 14 (June, 1990), p. 315

Keylor, William R., *Academy and Community: The Foundation of the French Historical Profession* (Cambridge, Mass,. 1975)

"Clio on Trial: Charles Péguy as Historical Critic," in Dora B. Weiner and William R. Keylor, eds., *From Parnassus: Essays in Honor of Jacques Barzun* (New York, 1976), pp. 195–208

Kuhn, Thomas S., "Notes on Lakatos," in *Boston Studies in the Philosophy of Science*, vol. 8 (1971), pp. 137–146

LaCapra, Dominick, *Emile Durkheim: Sociologist and Philosopher* (Ithaca, N.Y. 1972)

Lakatos, Imre, "Falsification and the Methodology of Scientific Research Programmes," in Lakatos and Alan Musgrave, eds., *Criticism and the Growth of Knowledge* (Cambridge, 1970), pp. 91–195

"History of Science and Its Rational Reconstructions," in *Boston Studies in the Philosophy of Science*, vol. 8 (1971), pp. 91–136

LaVopa, Anthony J., *Grace, Talent, and Merit: Poor Students, Clerical Careers and Professional Ideology in Eighteenth-Century Germany* (Cambridge University Press, 1988)

Lepenies, Wolf, *Die drei Kulturen: Soziologie zwischen Literatur und Wissenschaft* (Munich: Hanser, 1985)

Lukes, Steven, *Emile Durkheim, His Life and Work: A Historical and Critical Study* (New York, 1972)

Individualism: Key Concepts in the Social Sciences (Oxford, 1973)

McCole, John, *Walter Benjamin and the Antinomies of Tradition* (forthcoming at Cornell University Press)

Mommsen, Wolfgang J., *Max Weber and German Politics, 1890–1920*, trans. Michael S. Steinberg (The University of Chicago Press, 1984)

Nicolet, Claude, *L'idée républicaine en France (1789–1924): Essai d'histoire critique* (Paris: Gallimard, 1982)

Nye, Robert A., *The Origins of Crowd Psychology: Gustave LeBon and the Crisis of Mass Democracy in the Third Republic* (London, 1975)

Ory, Pascal, and Jean-François Sirinelli, *Les intellectuels en France de l'Affaire Dreyfus à nos jours* (Paris: Colin, 1986)

Panofsky, Erwin, *Gothic Architecture and Scholasticism* (New York, 1967)

Paul, Harry W., *From Knowledge to Power: The Rise of the Science Empire in France, 1860–1939* (Cambridge University Press, 1985)

Pinto, Louis, "La Vocation de l'universel: La formation de la représentation de l'intellectuel vers 1900," *Actes de la recherche en sciences sociales*, no. 55 (November 1984), pp. 23–32

Rabinow, Paul and William M. Sullivan, eds., *Interpretive Social Science: A Reader* (Berkeley, 1979)

Ringer, Fritz K., *The Decline of the German Mandarins: The German Academic Community, 1890–1933* (Cambridge, Mass., 1969) is translated (with quotations in the original German) as *Die Gelehrten: Der Niedergang der deutschen Mandarine, 1890–1933* (Stuttgart: Klett-Cotta,

362 *Bibliography*

1983). The book has recently been reissued (with a new introduction) by the University Press of New England, 1990

"Causal Analysis in Historical Reasoning," *History and Theory*, vol. 28 (1989), pp. 154–172

"Differences and Cross-National Similarities among Mandarins," *Comparative Studies in Society and History*, vol. 28 (January 1986), pp. 145–164

Scott, John A., *Republican Ideas and the Liberal Tradition in France, 1870–1914* (New York, 1951), pp. 87–106

Seigel, Jerrold, *Bohemian Paris: Culture, Politics, and the Boundaries of Bourgeois Life, 1830–1930* (New York: Viking, 1986)

Seigel, Martin, "Henri Berr's *Revue de synthèse historique*," *History and Theory*, vol. 9 (1970), pp. 322–334

Simon, Christian, *Staat und Geschichtswissenschaft in Deutschland und Frankreich 1871–1914: Situation und Werk von Geschichtsprofessoren an den Universitäten Berlin, München, Paris* (Bern: Peter Lang, 1988)

Skinner, Quentin, "Social Meaning and the Explanation of Social Action," in Patrick Gardiner, ed., *The Philosophy of History* (Oxford, 1974), pp. 106–126

Sorkin, David, "Wilhelm von Humboldt: The Theory and Practice of Self-Formation (*Bildung*), 1791–1810," *Journal of the History of Ideas* (1983), pp. 55–73

Stock, Phyllis H., "Students versus the University in Pre-World War Paris," *French Historical Studies*, vol. 7, (1971), pp. 93–110

Stock-Morton, Phyllis, *Moral Education for a Secular Society: The Development of Morale Laique in Nineteenth Century France* (Albany: State University of New York Press, 1988)

Vierhaus, Rudolf, "Bildung", in Otto Brunner, Werner Conze, Reinhart Kosellek, eds., *Geschichtliche Grundbegriffe*, vol. I (Stuttgart, 1972), pp. 508–551

Vogt, W. Paul., *The Politics of Academic Sociological Theory in France, 1890–1914*, Ph.D dissertation (Ann Arbor, Mich.: University Microfilms, 1976)

"Identifying Scholarly and Intellectual Communities: A Note on French Philosophy, 1900–1939," *History and Theory*, vol. 21 (1982), pp. 267–278

Weber, Eugen, *The Nationalist Revival in France, 1905–1914* (Berkeley, 1959)

Weisz, George, "Le corps professoral de l'enseignement supérieur et l'idéologie de la reforme universitaire en France, 1860–1885," *Revue française de sociologie*, vol. 18 (1977), pp. 201–232

"L'idéologie républicaine et les sciences sociales: Les Durkheimiens et la chaire d'histoire d'économie sociale à la Sorbonne," *Revue française de sociologie*, vol. 20 (1979), pp. 83–112

Wiener, Martin, *English Culture and the Decline of the Industrial Spirit, 1850–1980* (Cambridge University Press, 1981)

Williams, Raymond, *Culture and Society, 1780–1950* (New York, 1958)

Wilson, Bryan, ed., *Rationality: Key Concepts in the Social Sciences* (Oxford, 1970)

SOCIAL AND INSTITUTIONAL HISTORY

Albisetti, James C., *Secondary School Reform in Imperial Germany* (Princeton University Press, 1983)
"The Debate on Secondary School Reform in France and Germany," in Müller, Ringer, Simon, *Rise of the Modern Educational System*
Baker, Donald N. and Patrick J. Harrigan, eds., *The Making of Frenchmen: Current Directions in the History of Education in France, 1679–1979* (Historical Reflections VII, 1980)
Bamford, T. W., "Public Schools and Social Class, 1801–1850," *British Journal of Sociology*, vol. 12 (1961), pp. 224–235
Blackbourne, David and Geoff Eley, *The Peculiarities of German History: Bourgeois Society and Politics in Nineteenth-Century Germany* (Oxford University Press, 1984), pp. 206–221
Boltanski, Luc, "Taxinomies sociales et luttes de classes: la mobilisation de 'la classe moyenne' et l'invention des 'cadres'," *Actes de la recherche en sciences sociales*, no. 29, (September 1979), pp. 75–104
Bourdieu, Pierre, *Homo academicus* (Paris: Editions du minuit, 1984)
"Les Trois états du capital culturel," *Actes de la recherche en sciences sociales*, no. 30 (November 1979), pp. 3–6
"The Social Space and the Genesis of Groups," (Paris: Collège de France, 1985)
Bourdieu, Pierre and Jean-Claude Passeron, *Reproduction in Education, Society and Culture*, trans. Richard Nice (London, 1977)
Bredin, Jean Denis, *"L'affaire"* (Paris: Julliard, 1983)
Bush, John W., "Education and Social Status: The Jesuit Collège in the Early Third Republic," *French Historical Studies*, vol. 9 (1975), pp. 125–140
Charle, Christophe, "Le beau mariage d'Emile Durkheim," *Actes de la recherche en sciences sociales*, no. 55 (November 1984), pp. 45–49
"L'élite universitaire française et le système universitaire allemand (1880–1900)," *Transferts* (Paris, 1988), pp. 345–358
Les Elites de la République (1880–1900) (Paris: Fayard, 1987)
"La Faculté des lettres de Paris et le pouvoir (1809–1906)," in C. Charle and Régine Ferre, eds., *Le Personnel de l'enseignement supérieur en France aux XIXe et XXe siècles* (Paris: Editions du CNRS, 1985), pp. 151–165
"Le Champ universitaire Parisien à la fin du 19e siècle," *Actes de la recherche en sciences sociales*, no. 47–48, (June 1983), pp. 77–89
Conze, Werner, and Jürgen Kocka, eds., *Bildungsbürgertum im 19. Jahrhundert*, part I: *Bildungssystem und Professionalisierung in internationalen Vergleichen* (Stuttgart: Klett-Cotta, 1985), especially the Introduction

Coser, Lewis A., *Man of Ideas: A Sociologist's View* (New York, 1965)

Day, C. R., "The Making of Mechanical Engineers in France: The Ecoles d'Arts et Métiers, 1803–1914," *French Historical Studies*, vol. 10 (1978), pp. 439–460

"Technical and Professional Education in France: The Rise and Fall of *l'enseignement secondaire spécial*, 1865–1902," *Journal of Social History*, vol. 6 (1972–73), pp. 177–201

de Huszar, George B., ed., *The Intellectuals: A Controversial Portrait* (Glencoe, Ill., 1960)

Dictionnaire de biographic française, vols. 1–10 (Paris, 1933–61)

Falcucci, Clément, *L'humanisme dans l'enseignement secondaire en France au XIXe siècle* (Toulouse and Paris, 1939)

France, *Annuaire statistique de la France*, vols. 42 (1926), 72 (1966)

Chambre des Députés, *Enquête sur l'enseignement secondaire* (1899)

INSEE, *Population par sexe, age et état matrimonial de 1851 à 1962* (Etudes et Documents, 10) (Paris, 1968)

INSEE, *Recensement général de la population de may 1954: Résultats du sondage au 1/20ème, Population active, I: Structure professionnelle*

Les Conditions de développement, de recrutement, de fonctionnement et de localisation des grandes écoles en France (La Documentation Française, 1964)

Ministère de l'Education Nationale, *Informations statistiques*, vol. 69 (1965)

Ministère de l'Instruction Publique, *Bulletin Administratif de l'Instruction Publique*, 52 (April, 1854)

Ministère de l'Instruction Publique, *Rapport au Roi par . . . (Villemain) . . . sur l'instruction secondaire* (1843)

Ministère de l'Instruction Publique, *Statistique de l'enseignement secondaire en 1865* (1866)

Ministère de l'Instruction Publique, *Statistique de l'enseignement secondaire en 1876* (1878)

Ministère de l'Instruction Publique, *Statistique de l'enseignement secondaire en 1887* (1889)

Ministère de l'Instruction Publique, *Statistique de l'enseignement supérieur*, 4 vols. (1868–1900)

Statistique de la France, *Resultats généraux du dénombrement de 1872* (Nancy, 1874)

Fox, Robert and George Weisz, *The Organization of Science and Technology in France 1808–1914* (Cambridge University Press, 1980)

Frijhoff, Willem, and Dominique Julia, *Ecole et société dans la France d'ancien régime* (Paris, 1975)

Geiger, Theodor, *Aufgaben und Stellung der Intelligenz in der Gesellschaft* (Stuttgart, 1949)

Germany, *Deutsche Hochschulstatistik*, vol. 7

Jahrbuch für das höhere Schulwesen im Deutschen Reich, vol. 1 (1933)

Statistisches Jahrbuch, vols. 9, 34, 52, 54, and vol. for 1952

Statistik der Bundesrepublik, vol. 199

Harrigan, Patrick J., *Mobility, Elites, and Education in French Society of the Second Empire* (Waterloo, Ontario: Wilfrid Laurier University Press, 1980)

Harrigan, Patrick with Victor Negila, *Lycéens et collègiens sous le Second Empire: Etude statistique sur les fonctions sociales de l'enseignement secondaire publique d'après l'enquête de Victor Duruy (1864–1865)* (Paris, 1979)

Isambert-Jamati, Viviane, *Crises de la société, crises de l'enseignement* (Paris, 1970)

"Une réforme des lycées et collèges," *L'Année sociologique*, 3e série, vol. 20 (1969), pp. 9–60

Jeismann, K. E., *Das Preussische Gymnasium in Staat und Gesellschaft . . . 1787–1817* (Stuttgart, 1974)

Kaelble, Hartmut, *Soziale Mobilität und Chancengleichheit im 19. und 20. Jahrhundert* (Göttingen: Vandenhoeck, 1983)

Karady, Victor, "Durkheim, les sciences sociales et l'université: bilan d'un semi-échec," *Revue française de sociologie*, vol. 17 (1976) pp. 267–311

"L'accès aux grades et leurs fonctions universitaires dans les facultés des sciences au 19e siècle: examen d'une mutation," in Baker and Harrigan, *Making of Frenchmen*, pp. 397–414

"L'expansion universitaire et l'évolution des inégalités devant la carrière d'enseignant au début de la IIIe République," in *Revue française de sociologie*, vol. 14 (1973), pp. 443–470

"Normaliens et autres enseignants à la Belle Epoque," *Revue française de sociologie*, vol. 13 (1972) pp. 35–58

"Recherches sur la morphologie du corps universitaire littéraire sous la Troisième République," *Le mouvement social*, vol. 69 (1976) pp. 47–79

Kath, Gerhard, ed., *Das soziale Bild der Studentenschaft in Westdeutschland und Berlin, Sommersemester 1963* (Deutsches Studentenwerk, Berlin, 1964)

Kocka, Jürgen, *Die Angestellten in der deutschen Geschichte, 1850–1980* (Göttingen: Vandenhoeck & Ruprecht, 1981)

Lexis, Wilhelm, ed., *Das Unterrichtswesen im Deutschen Reich*, vol. II (Berlin, 1904)

McClelland, Charles E., *State, Society and University in Germany 1700–1914* (Cambridge University Press, 1980)

Mercier, Lucien, *Les Universités populaires, 1899–1914: Education populaire et mouvement ouvrier au début du siècle* (Paris. Editions ouvrières, 1986)

Müller, Detlef K., *Sozialstruktur und Schulsystem: Aspekte zur Theorie und Praxis der Schulorganisation im 19. Jahruhundert* (Göttingen, 1977)

Müller, Detlef K., Fritz Ringer and Brian Simon, eds., *The Rise of the Modern Educational System: Structural Change and Social Reproduction, 1870–1920*, (Cambridge University Press, 1987)

Nettl, J. P., "Ideas, Intellectuals and Structures of Dissent," in Philip Rieff, ed., *On Intellectuals: Theoretical Studies: Case Studies* (Garden City, N.J. 1970), pp. 57–134

Neue Deutsche Biographie, vols. 1–4 (Berlin, 1953–1964)

O'Boyle, Lenore, "The Problem of an Excess of Educated Men in Wetern Europe, 1800–1850," *Journal of Modern History*, vol. 42 (1970), pp. 471–495

Palmer, R. R., "Free Secondary Education in France before and after the Revolution," *History of Education Quarterly* (1974), pp. 437–452

Pernoud, Régine, *Histoire de la bourgeoisie en France: les temps modernes* (Paris, 1962)

Piobetta, J. B., *Le baccalauréat* (Paris, 1937)

Prost, Antoine, *Histoire de l'enseignement en France 1800–1967* (Paris, 1968)

Prussia, *Preussische Statistik*, vols. 204, 236

    Statistische Mitteilungen über das höhere Unterrichtswesen im Königreich Preussen, vol. 28 (1911)

    Statistisches Handbuch/Jahrbuch für den Preussischen Staat, vols. 2 (1893), 11 (1913)

Ribot, Alexandre *La réforme de l'enseignement secondaire* (Paris, 1900)

Ringer, Fritz K., *Education and Society in Modern Europe* (Bloomington and London, 1979)

    "The Education of Elites in Modern Europe," *History of Education Quarterly*, vol. 18 (1978), pp. 159–172

Rogoff, Natalie, "Social Stratification in France and in the United States," in Reinhard Bendix and S. M. Lipset, eds., *Class, Status and Power: Social Stratification in Comparative Perspective* (New York, 1966)

Ruppel, Wilhelm, *Über die Berufswahl der Abiturienten Preussens in den Jahren 1875–1899* (Fulda, Germany, 1904)

Shils, Edward, *The Intellectuals and the Powers, and Other Essays* (Chicago, 1972)

Shinn, Terry, "The French Science Faculty System, 1803–1914: Institutional Change and Research Potential in Mathematics and the Physical Sciences," *Historical Studies in the Physical Sciences*, vol. 10 (1979), pp. 271–332

    Savoir scientifique et pouvoir social: L'Ecole Polytechnique, 1794–1914 (Paris, 1980)

Smith, Robert J., *The Ecole Normale Supérieure and the Third Republic* (Albany: State University of New York Press, 1982)

Talbott, John E., *The Politics of Educational Reform in France, 1918–1940* (Princeton, 1969)

Turner, R. Steven, "The Growth of Professorial Research in Prussia, 1818–1948: Causes and Context," *Historical Studies in the Physical Sciences* (1971), pp. 137–182

    "University Reformers and Professorial Scholarship in Germany, 1760–1806," in Lawrence Stone, ed., *The University in Society: Studies in the History of Higher Education* (Princeton, 1974), vol. II, pp. 495–531

Wehler, Hans-Ulrich, "Vorüberlegungen zur historischen Analyse sozialer Ungleichheit," in Wehler, ed., *Klassen in der europäischen Sozialgeschichte* (Göttingen, 1979), pp. 9–32

Weill, Georges, *Histoire de l'enseignement secondaire en France, 1802–1920* (Paris, 1921)

Weiss, John H., *The Making of Technological Man: The Social Origins of French Engineering Education* (Cambridge, Mass: MIT Press, 1982)

Weisz, George, *The Emergence of Modern Universities in France, 1863–1914* (Princeton University Press, 1983)

"The Politics of Medical Professionalization in France 1845–1848," *Journal of Social History*, vol. 12 (1978–79), pp. 3–30

Znaniecki, Florian, *The Social Role of the Man of Knowledge* (New York, 1965)

INDEX

Abitur (German secondary leaving
certificate), 37, 41, 43, 48, 52, 55, 106
academic culture, definition of, 13–14
"academic (intellectual) proletariat":
anxieties over, 30–1, 32; in France, 87,
127–40, 156, 159, 220, 329 n. 36; in
Germany, 52; Seignobos' approval of,
235
academics, 22–3, 26
  French (*see also* classicists; reformists),
  249; relationship to state, 161, 218–19,
  259, 260–1; social origins and
  education, 67–75, 86–7, 218
  French and German compared, 67–75,
  87, 158, 159, 217, 220, 223, 303, 307–8
  German orthodox (*see also* modernists),
  1–4, 39–40, 110, 111, 192, 253; and
  concept of *Bildung*, 2, 95–108; reaction
  to modernization and
  "democratization," 3, 105–7, 196–207,
  249, 307–8, 354 n. 120; relationship to
  state, 104–5, 202–3, 259, 260; social
  origins and education, 67–75, 87
Académie des Sciences, 160
Académie Française, 141, 160, 219, 221
Action Française, 246, 259
Adorno, Theodor W., 205
Agathon's criticism of New Sorbonne, 237–
  47, 250, 256, 284, 295
agrégation, 43–4, 45–6, 54, 87, 238, 240, 284,
  294; *agrégés*, 248
agricultural metaphor of schooling, 145–6
altruism, Durkheim on, 286, 288, 289, 304
"anarchist" sentiments, 88, 220
Andler, Charles, 175–6, 177, 339 n. 30
Annales school, 264, 276
L'Année sociologique, 283, 307
anthropology, 269, 270
"aristocratic essentialism," 104, 109
Arnold, Matthew, 108–12, 113, 114, 145,
  318–20, 322
Aster, Ernst von, 204

Aulard, Alphonse, 174–5, 177, 238, 240,
  260, 339 n. 30

baccalauréat (French secondary leaving
certificate), 40, 41–2, 43–4, 55, 120,
123; admission of "modern" secondary
students to (1891), 33, 116; awards
(1840–1950), 48–51, 53; as basis of
bourgeois status, 43, 91, 139, 194;
proposals for abolition of, 162, 163,
167, 168, 171; proposals for reform,
191, 235, 251
Baden neo-Kantians, 198
Barrès, Maurice, 138, 140, 161, 219, 221,
  222, 244–5; *Les déracinés*, 127–8, 129,
  130–7, 212, 219–20, 250
Baudelaire, Charles Pierre, 80, 81, 82
belief systems, 11–12, 20–2, 23–4, 317; and
  social environment, 22–3
Below, Georg von, 263
Benda, Julien, 310
Bérard, Léon, 126–7, 142, 337 nn. 1 and 2
Bérenger, Henry, 127, 137–40
Bergson, Henri, 142–3, 145, 152–3, 211,
  246, 337 nn. 1 and 2
Berr, Henri, 276, 277–8, 281, 282
Berthelot, Marcelin, 160, 167–8, 172, 173,
  339 n. 30
Bertrand, Alexis, 172–4, 216, 339 n. 30
Besitzbürgertum (German propertied and
entrepreneurial middle class), 68
Besnard, Philippe, 282
Bildung, concept of, 2–3, 38, 40, 95–108,
  133, 200–7, 313; compared with
  Arnold's definition of "culture," 108–
  14, 319; compared with French *culture*,
  146–9, 158, 304; and interpretation of
  texts, 96–8, 261, 314–15, 318, 320–1;
  and principle of "individuality," 96–7,
  98–9, 100, 106–7, 109, 146–7, 149,
  201, 284–5, 319
Bildungsbürgertum (German educated middle

368